AF622546

This World *in a* Teacup

Studies in Pacific Worlds

Series Editors

Rainer F. Buschmann

Katrina Gulliver

Editorial Board

Gregory Cushman

John Gascoigne

Andrea Geiger

Noriko Kawamura

Judith Schachter

This World *in a* Teacup

Credit, Taste, and Power in the U.S.-China Tea Trade, 1784–1911

Dan Du

UNIVERSITY OF NEBRASKA PRESS · LINCOLN

© 2026 by the Board of Regents of the University of Nebraska

Chapter 1 was previously published as "Green Gold and Paper Gold: Seeking Independence through the Chinese-American Tea Trade, 1784–1815," *Early American Studies: An Interdisciplinary Journal* 16, no. 1 (2018): 151–91. Reprinted in Chinese in *Nankai shixue* 27, no. 1 (2019): 265–303.

All rights reserved

The University of Nebraska Press is part of a land-grant institution with campuses and programs on the past, present, and future homelands of the Pawnee, Ponca, Otoe-Missouria, Omaha, Dakota, Lakota, Kaw, Cheyenne, and Arapaho Peoples, as well as those of the relocated Ho-Chunk, Sac and Fox, and Iowa Peoples.

♾

For customers in the EU with safety/GPSR concerns, contact:
gpsr@mare-nostrum.co.uk
Mare Nostrum Group BV
Doelen 72
4831 GR Breda
The Netherlands

Library of Congress Cataloging-in-Publication Data
Names: Du, Dan (Associate professor of history) author
Title: This world in a teacup: credit, taste, and power in the U.S.-China tea trade, 1784–1911 / Dan Du.
Description: Lincoln: University of Nebraska Press, [2026] | Series: Studies in Pacific worlds | Includes bibliographical references and index.
Identifiers: LCCN 2025042590
ISBN 9781496244338 hardback
ISBN 9781496247650 epub
ISBN 9781496247667 pdf
Subjects: LCSH: Tea trade—United States—History—19th century | Tea trade—China—History—19th century | Credit—History—19th century | United States—Commerce—China | China—Commerce—United States | United States—Foreign economic relations—China | China—Foreign economic relations—United States | BISAC: HISTORY / United States / 19th Century | HISTORY / United States / General
Classification: LCC HD9198.A2 D83 2026
LC record available at https://lccn.loc.gov/2025042590

Designed and set in Adobe Garamond Pro by K. Andresen.

Contents

Illustrations

FIGURES

TABLES

This World *in a* Teacup

Introduction

Thomas Jefferson, writing in 1781, acknowledged that habits had placed tea, along with sugar and coffee, "among the necessaries of life with the wealthy part of our citizens." "As long as these habits remain," Jefferson noted, "we must go for them to those countries which are able to furnish them."[1] Samuel Shaw, the first U.S. consul in China, was even more direct about the importance of tea. "The inhabitants of America must have tea," declared Shaw in 1787.[2] Shaw had sailed with the ship *Empress of China* to Canton in 1784, thus initiating U.S.-China trade even before the ratification of the U.S. Constitution. The *Empress* left China on December 28, 1784, with a mixed cargo.[3] Black and green teas, valued at 66,100 taels (a unit of weight and, by extension, currency), accounted for 92 percent of its estimated value.[4] In the next decade, the United States grew to be the second-largest importer of Chinese tea, a status that Americans maintained through most years of the nineteenth century.

However, the pivotal U.S.-China tea trade has been largely forgotten. Despite the flourishing literature on the British and Dutch tea trade with China and the global history of tea, historians have completed only a few article- or chapter-length analyses of U.S. tea trade and consumption after the American Revolution.[5] Works on U.S.-China relations, China's global tea trade, and tea production in Asia also briefly mention Americans' engagement with China's tea business.[6] The scholarship on American tea consumption is equally thin. Rodris Roth, Jane T. Merritt, and James R. Fichter analyzed American tea culture and its political life before the country's independence.[7] Susan Boslego Carter, John Rogers Haddad, Robert Hellyer, and Erika Diane Rappaport extended the focus to postrevolutionary America, examining British and American companies' tea advertisements, the transatlantic tea culture, and the postbellum U.S.-Japan tea trade.[8] Therefore the complete history of the Sino-American exchanges in tea commerce and the transpacific trade's influence on U.S. tea consumption patterns remains understudied. Drawing on bilingual historical sources and transpacific perspectives, *This World in a Teacup* offers the first comprehensive examination of the U.S.-China tea trade in the long nineteenth century.

This book foregrounds the credit system of the transpacific tea trade to trace Americans' tea ventures and consumption. Highlighting credit reconsiders the image of a silverized Chinese economy. The rigorous and vigorous research on silver has established China as the center of the world's silver flow since the sixteenth century, after it adopted this precious metal as the major currency.[9] While some of the silver scholarship challenges the image of China trade as a primitive barter economy, the preoccupation with China's silver influx led others to slight the importance of credit in China. Some publications assert that China's credit economy has been "underdeveloped" throughout its long history, that commercial credit was "unproductive," "speculative," or only euphemistic for debts, and that Chinese merchants loathed to adopt the credit system when trading with Americans.[10] In truth, a robust and sophisticated credit system sustained the commercial transactions of U.S. and Chinese tea merchants as early as the late eighteenth century. Yet despite the system's importance, with relevant information scattered across studies of disparate topics, the existing scholarship presents only a fragmented, Eurocentric, and obscure picture of the credit system of U.S.-China trade. The incomplete understanding helps perpetuate the stereotype of China trade as inherently cumbersome. *This World in a Teacup* reconstructs the dynamic transpacific credit system jointly developed by Chinese and American merchants through their credit transactions and instruments from the late eighteenth to the early twentieth century. By doing so, this research reconsiders Eurocentric perceptions of Chinese credit and silver's role in China's foreign trade finance. Focusing on credit in the global tea trade also illuminates the interconnectedness of global financial networks and shifts in U.S. tea consumption patterns. These findings position this book in the new historiography of U.S.-China trading relations.

To further demonstrate the significance of this research on tea in America and credit in China, the first section of this introduction overviews the importance of tea in the U.S. context. Shifting focus to China's credit system, the second part defines credit transactions and credit instruments, revisits the existing literature that examines the transpacific credit economy, clarifies how credit functioned in the U.S.-China tea trade, and explains the contribution of this research to the field of U.S.-China relations. The last section outlines the structure of this book.

Tea

The stark contrast between the abundant archival resources and the scant scholarship on the U.S.-China tea trade leads one to wonder whether the presumption that "the United States did not become a nation of tea drinkers" diverted scholars' attention away from the topic.[11] Popular histories often claim that the patriotic act of boycotting tea during the American Revolution transformed the young republic into a coffee-drinking nation, although historians have disputed the narrative.[12] Indeed, the public never ceased their desire for tea during the Revolution, and tea imports continued to grow after American independence, yet Americans' per capita consumption of coffee, in pounds, dwarfed that of tea (see figure 1).[13] Therefore it appears plausible that the United States emerged out of the American Revolution as a coffee country and thus Americans' engagement in the global tea trade was insignificant.[14]

However, using the absolute weight to gauge tea and coffee consumption misunderstands and underestimates the importance of tea. After all, rather than directly eating tea leaves and coffee beans, consumers used them to brew hot beverages. Tea was lighter and more economical than coffee in this regard. Francis Beatty Thurber clarified in his 1884 book that a pound of tea supplied a family as many cups of hot drinks as four pounds of coffee. Thus historian of coffee Steven Topik argued that Americans still drank 80 percent as many cups of tea as cups of coffee in 1880.[15] Nineteenth-century tea merchants and experts were more optimistic about the economical nature of tea. They asserted that a pound of tea yielded two to three hundred cups of hot beverage, while a pound of coffee made only forty cups.[16] As Oscar W. Riggs concluded in 1883, tea was "popular with persons in moderate circumstances, since one pound will go as far as five pounds of coffee."[17] Adopting the lower ratio, 1:4, to estimate the relative importance of tea and coffee in Americans' lives, we see that coffee did not obtain an absolute advantage over tea until the late 1820s (see figure 1).

Moreover, tea drinkers usually reused their leaves multiple times. An 1818 pamphlet asserted that green teas commonly seen in England and America—hyson and gunpowder—bore four to five waters, while the strength of other common greens could endure three to four waters or less. As for black tea, bohea lost its strength with three waters and congou could bear twice drawing.[18] Indeed, the leaves' capacity of retaining flavor through repeated steepings marked tea's quality. As the *Chinese Repository* introduced to its readers in 1839, the strength of the tea water, along with the color, clearness, and taste, was "the most important criteri[on]" when assessing green tea, and "as many as fifteen 'drawings' are obtained from the richest flavored teas."[19] Returning to Washington DC in 1890, an American merchant complained that, even in the most fashionable circle, the hosts repeatedly brewed the same pot of tea and added new leaves over the stale ones, even though the price of tea was unprecedentedly low in the 1890s (see chapter 5).[20] Therefore it is highly likely that tea drinkers in all walks of life reused their leaves. By making a second cup of tea out of the same leaves, Americans still drank more tea than coffee during most of the nineteenth century (see figure 1).

It is unsurprising that nineteenth-century documents consistently identified Americans as the top tea drinkers in the West. "In the consumption of tea, the United States rank next to Great Britain," French and Russian sources analyzing China's global tea trade during 1821–40 concluded.[21] Annually ingesting 13–20 million pounds, Americans remained the second-largest tea consumer outside Asia in the mid-nineteenth century.[22] Americans' per capita tea consumption rivaled or surpassed the Dutch during the 1870s–90s, lagging behind only British consumption levels. Even when the U.S. per capita consumption fell behind such countries as Australia, New Zealand, and Canada in the last decade of the nineteenth century, the aggregate amount consumed by Americans still exceeded that of most nations, except the United Kingdom and Russia.[23]

Corresponding with the quantitative data, nineteenth-century Americans also described the prevalence of tea among not only the upper tier of society but also ordinary folk. While Chinese goods became the necessities of life early in the nineteenth century, "the consumption of Tea alone has obtained, in actual use, an importance almost equivalent to that of bread" even for humble households, Robert Waln Jr., of Philadelphia, observed around 1819.[24] Extant documents also record the popularity of the drink

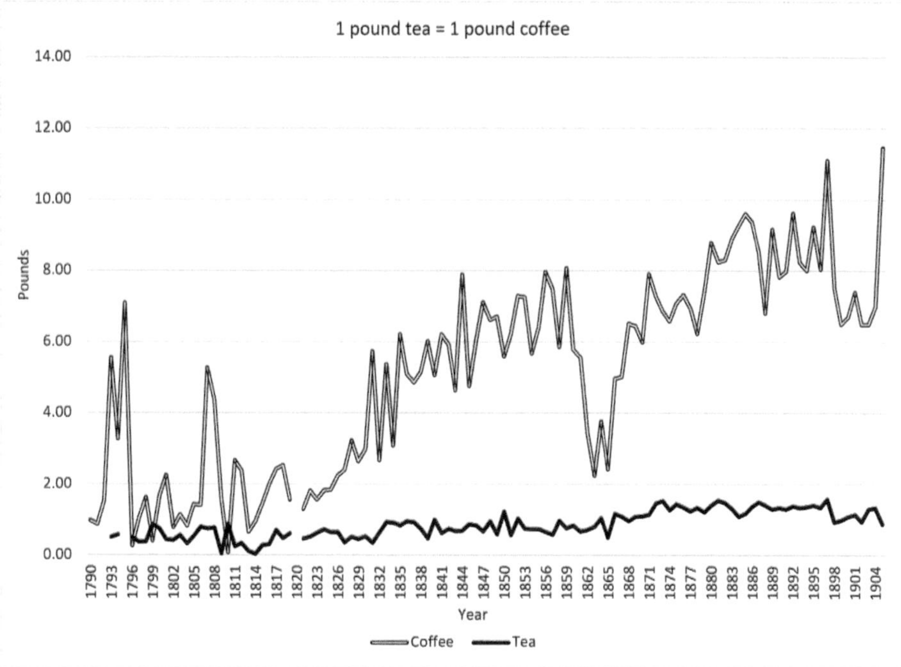

Fig. 1. Annual tea and coffee consumption per capita, 1790–1910. Per capita consumption of tea and coffee for 1790 to 1819 was derived by dividing annual net tea imports by the corresponding U.S. population figures. Sources: Net imports of tea and coffee, 1790–1819: U.S. Department of Commerce and Labor (USDCL), "World's Production," 90–91, 138. Population, 1790–1819: "National Population and the Demographic Components of Change: 1790–2000 [Annual Estimates]," in Carter et al., *Historical Statistics of the United States*, Aa9. 1821–1904 per capita tea and coffee consumption: USDCL, "World's Production," 97, 141. 1900–1910 per capita tea and coffee consumption: Grigg, "Worlds of Tea and Coffee," 290. I converted the data from kilograms to pounds.

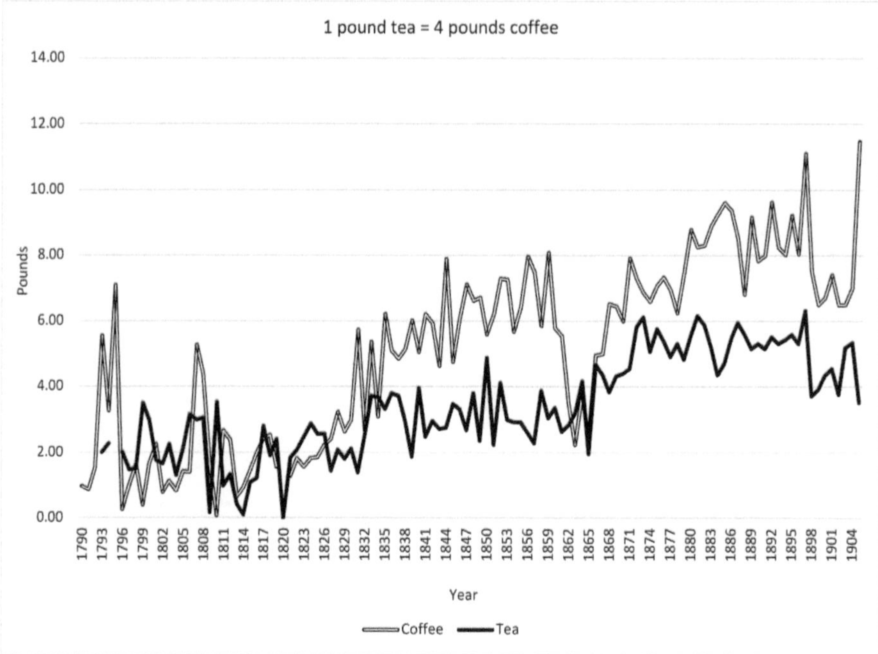
1 pound tea = 4 pounds coffee
Pounds
Year
Coffee
Tea

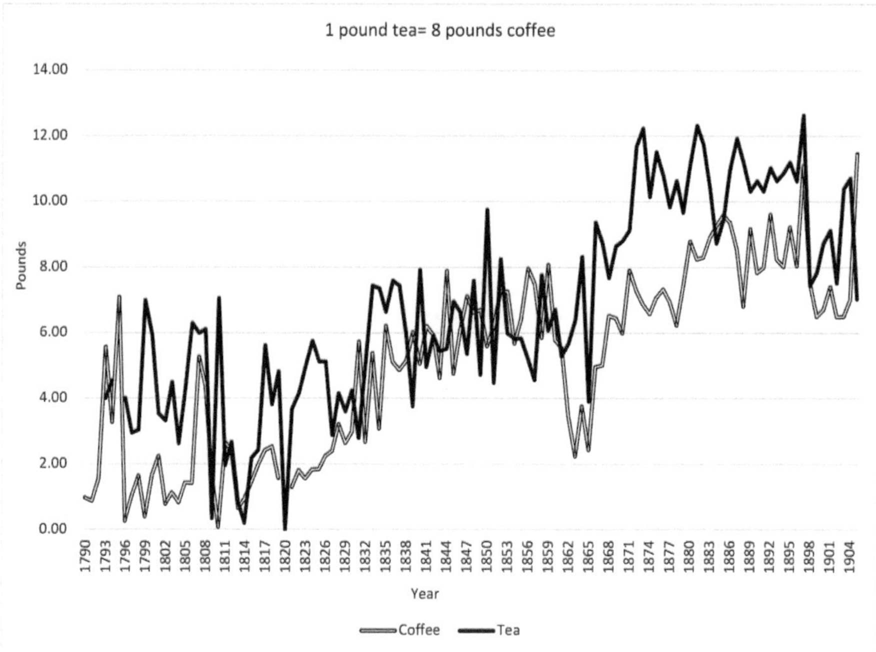
1 pound tea= 8 pounds coffee
Pounds
Year
Coffee
Tea

in some parts of the American South. An author named J. B. W. from Charleston remarked in 1836 that "tea forms an important part, nay, from habit, almost an essential part, of the luxuries of the humble peasant," which "constitutes the common beverage of all classes of society."[25] An American magazine thus declared in 1857 that "the price of tea is almost the only piece of commercial news, or part of the 'list of prices current,' in which our amiable countrywomen seem to take any very lively-interest."[26]

Therefore it is unsurprising that tea gained pivotal importance in U.S.-China trading relations. China monopolized the global tea trade before the mid-nineteenth century. This single commodity accounted for over half of China's entire exports to the world before 1876. Although the percentage later dropped to approximately 40 percent, tea remained the most important Chinese export to the world until 1888, when silk took precedence in China's foreign trade.[27] Tea thus carried considerable weight in Americans' investments in China, often accounting for 40 to 80 percent of the aggregate U.S. imports from China in most decades of the nineteenth century (see figure 2). Even during the last decade of the nineteenth century, when the U.S.-China tea trade declined, Great Britain dramatically reduced its Chinese tea imports, and Russia replaced America to become the world's second-largest tea importer, the English newspaper *Saturday Review* still insisted that the United States "ranks as the second largest consumer" of Chinese tea.[28]

Credit

Weaving through the fluctuations of the U.S.-China tea trade is a simple question: how did Americans purchase tea from China? The most convenient answer is silver. It is a well-known story that to procure expensive Chinese tea without exhausting their stock of silver, British traders smuggled opium into China, thus leading to the Opium War. As the tea buyer second only to Britons, Americans took measures to finance their tea trade that were of equal economic and political significance, not to mention that Americans supplied over 90 percent of the silver imported into China during most decades of the nineteenth century.[29] However, silver was not necessarily the means of payment for each transaction. The credit economy, including credit transactions and credit instruments, often buttressed de facto transactions in tea between Chinese and American merchants.

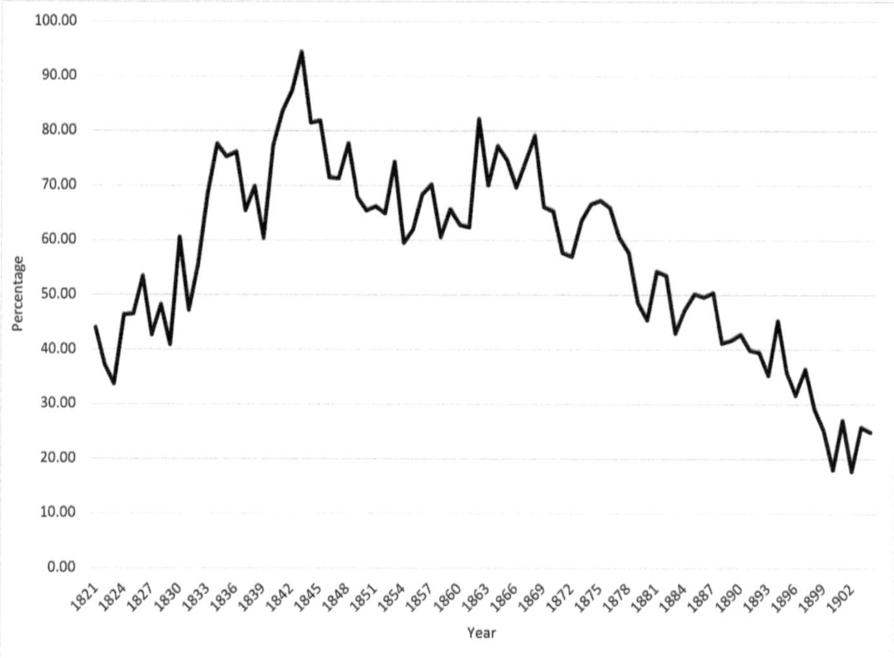

Fig. 2. Percentage of tea in the aggregate value of U.S.-China trade, 1821–1904. For the years 1821–42, annual data were calculated from October 1 to September 30; for the years 1843–1915, annual data were calculated from July 1 to June 30. Sources: Value of Chinese tea imported into the United States: U.S. Department of Commerce and Labor, "World's Production," 140. Value of imports from China to the United States: U.S. Bureau of the Census, *Historical Statistics of the United States*, 552–53, Series U134-151.

To understand the significance of the transpacific credit economy, it is imperative to define the key concepts—credit, credit transactions, and credit instruments. Scholars have defined credit as a transfer of a commodity without an actual transfer of an equivalent on the spot.[30] The nature of credit, defined by the gap of time, even led some medieval Europeans, such as William of Auxerre, a French theologian and official in the Roman Catholic Church, to attack usury. The evil of usury arose from not only the high interest but also the fact that a usurer "sells time, which," the French theologian asserted, "is common to all creatures."[31] The temporal gap in transactions generates either commercial credit (the sale of commodities without an immediate transfer of monetary objects) or financial credit (the lending or remittance of money).[32] China's global tea trade exemplified these commercial and financial credit transactions through advance payments, account sales, consignments, respondentia, and loans extended by merchants and banks.

While scholars' publications on China's global trade have explored some of the credit transactions, the information on such practices in the transpacific tea commerce remains incomplete. Weng Eang Cheong, Kuo-tung Ch'en, and Paul Van Dyke analyzed how European companies made advance payments to contract tea from Chinese merchants in the eighteenth century, but Americans' engagement with the advance system was obscure.[33] In the research of CHEN Ciyu, Robert Gardella, and Yen-p'ing Hao on China's global tea trade after 1853, American commission houses, along with British companies as well as foreign and native banks, had offered advance payments to Chinese tea dealers.[34] Therefore a temporary gap exists in the existing research relating to Sino-American credit transactions. In contrast, Americans' gradual but active engagement with credit transactions is a major thread of this book. Moreover, as Man-houng Lin contended in a case study of Taiwan's tea economy, previous scholars usually emphasize foreign credit, supplied primarily by British and sometimes American capital to the Chinese, and provided limited information on the agency of Chinese traders in credit transactions.[35] While Ch'en, Chen, Gardella, Lin, Andrew Liu, William Rowe, and Van Dyke have mentioned the credit relations between Chinese brokers and interior tea producers in the late eighteenth century or the last three decades of the nineteenth, this book details the credit extended by Chinese tea merchants to their American counterparts and interior native dealers through various credit transactions during the entire nineteenth century.

Undergirding credit transactions were credit instruments. Regardless of how unfamiliar the term may sound, credit instruments are prevalent in current daily lives. Checks are vital to Americans' everyday finance. Paper money, the device that is critical to the modern economy, originated in China as a bill of exchange and developed in Europe from the promissory note issued by goldsmiths.[36] Indeed, modern credit instruments refer to promissory notes, bills of exchange, and checks.[37] Rather than buying and selling time, credit instruments bridge the gap of time, and often distance, in credit transactions. A promissory note is a promise to pay on a future date. A bill of exchange or a check represents an order to pay at a different location.[38] While most bills of exchange save the cost and risk of shipping cash in international trade, inland bills and checks usually circulate between different locations, and sometimes in the same place, within the issuing country.[39] A promissory note links the past with the future through a documented promise. A bill of exchange and a check add a spatial dimension to the credit relationship by mitigating the cost and risk of transporting cash between different locations. Employing these credit instruments enables transactions to transcend time, space, and the physical confines of cash, thus expanding trade exponentially, especially when transportation was underdeveloped.

Scholars have placed credit instruments primarily in European and American contexts.[40] Some even define them as the technique of European capitalism or an invention of industrialism.[41] However, the use of credit instruments was more a common characteristic of world trade than an advantage of the West during modern times. The techniques began in antiquity, evidenced by the clay tablets in Mesopotamia that served as credit instruments during the Old Babylonian (1830–1531 BCE) and Neo-Babylonian (ca. 620–539 BCE) periods.[42] Other civilizations that developed their practices and terminology of credit instruments before the rise of capitalism and industrialism in Europe are exemplified by the *hundi* in India and the *ruq'a*, *saftaji*, and *sakk* in the Islamic Empire.[43] Beginning in the ninth century, the Chinese employed various credit instruments, such as the *feiqian*, *jiaozi*, *huipiao*, and *hangpiao*, which had close-knit but sometimes inverse correlation with paper money in China.[44] Despite diverse global practices, European and American commercial codes that define and standardize modern credit instruments encompassed world finance through colonization and international laws, such as the Uniform Law of the Hague Convention in 1910 and 1912, Uniform Laws for Bills of Exchange passed by the League of Nations in 1930 and 1931, as well as the United Nations Convention on International Bills of Exchange and International Promissory Notes from 1968.[45] China adopted the European legal framework to rename and recategorize their native credit instruments at the beginning of the twentieth century.[46]

Before that period, credit instruments had commonly facilitated the U.S.-China tea trade. Yet the existing historiography pertaining to this subject remains marked by temporal and spatial gaps. Research with a transnational focus has shown the critical role of credit instruments in U.S.-China trading relations. The largest body of the scholarship mentions bills of exchange brought by Americans to China.[47] In particular, the publications of Cheong, Hao, and especially Takeshi Hamashita explore bills of exchange in China's foreign trade finance, respectively during 1812–15 and the 1820s–60s.[48] However, their broad strokes and fragmented timeframes hardly depict a nuanced picture of this instrument's history in the U.S.-China trade or emphasize the critical role of Chinese traders in handling it. Scholars who elaborate on other credit instruments offer more details about Chinese players. Frederic D. Grant and John D. Wong revealed the large amount of promissory notes that Chinese merchants issued to their U.S. counterparts during the late eighteenth and early nineteenth centuries, but their analyses prioritize the lawsuits between these traders over the credit system.[49] Studies of compradors and native banks also mention the credit instruments handled by the Chinese after 1842 but fail to provide detailed interpretations of the financial techniques.[50] Transnational scholarship also rarely illuminates the Chinese financial context, even though information on domestic credit instruments abounds in research on Chinese banking and monetary history. In contrast, scholarly works focusing on the Chinese context typically place native credit instruments within the Chinese domestic economy or the history of Chinese paper money, so they rarely provide clear theoretical frameworks to explain how credit instruments financed China's foreign commerce, including the U.S.-China tea trade.[51] *This World in a Teacup* thus bridges the gap between the studies of China's international credit economy and those of its domestic one.

This book further challenges the Orientalist narratives that perpetuate the stereotype of China's cumbersome hard-money system. The existing literature on transnational and domestic credit economy—while rigorous and nuanced in interpretations—has yet to effectively dispel the three Eurocentric frameworks: the linear monetary theory, the "dual economy" model, and the "financial divergence" hypothesis. The linear monetary theory chronologizes a progression from primitive commodity money and hard money to nominal currencies, such as paper money, and ultimately credit money.[52] Societies associated with silver such as China appear to be at the bottom of the pyramid, whereas the more advanced capitalist nations in Europe and America employed credit instruments to nurture their active economic activities. Likewise, the "dual economy" model presents a precapitalist East, which features isolated peddlers, fragmented monetary standards, and noneconomic communal networks, to contrast with the capitalist West supported by large-scale commerce, corporations, industrialization, and economic rationalism.[53] Some scholars even posit a "financial divergence" theory to depict a robust West against a stagnant East in terms of financial innovations or credit institution development.[54] Accordingly, scholarship focusing on China's international payments reinforces notions of economic duality and financial divergence. These works emphasize Western merchants' agency in bringing credit instruments to China while highlighting the Chinese reliance on silver and barter economies. Furthermore, they portray silver and credit as separate, rather than complementary, mechanisms in financing the China trade.[55] Consequently, some of the transnational research characterizes China's credit system as "primitive (if sometimes ingenious)," highlights the U.S.-China trade as "a cash business," or slights China's financial internationalization before the advent of European banks.[56] Even the scholars exploring Chinese credit instruments downplay the importance of credit in settling China's foreign trade balance, underestimate the vitality of the credit economy in China compared with that of Europe, or deny the significance of Chinese paper devices before the 1920s.[57] In the past three decades, a large number of scholarly publications have sought to refute the gap between Chinese and Western economic practices, such as accounting, business management, banking, or commercialization.[58] *This World in a Teacup* follows this trend to reconstruct an equally advanced and complicated credit economy in China's arguably largest export business. Rather than placing a single player at the center, this book highlights both Chinese and U.S. merchants in developing transpacific credit networks, thus restoring the complex power dynamics of the international trade and finance.

The transpacific credit economy had functioned continuously since the inception of the U.S.-China tea trade. From as late as the 1790s, Chinese tea merchants employed such credit transactions as account sales, consignments, and respondentia as well as a large number of promissory notes to facilitate their business with Americans. When some of their U.S. counterparts were unable or unwilling to redeem the promissory notes and repay their debts, particularly during the Embargo of 1807–9 and the War of 1812, Chinese creditors brought lawsuits in U.S. courts or petitioned President

James Madison to protect their property in America, revealing the large size of credit generated by the tea trade (chapter 1). Bills of exchange became Americans' chief medium of tea purchase in the late 1820s, enabling Americans to reduce their silver shipments to China to a tenth of what it had been within a decade. Chinese merchants also traded foreign bills of exchange. An exchange market thus developed in Canton and fluctuated with the tea business (chapter 2). Although Chinese and U.S. merchants resorted to barter and silver payments in the immediate years after the Opium War, adapting to the new trading environment, Chinese merchant-bankers issued a new form of promissory notes (*zhuangpiao*, or bankers' orders) and native bills of exchange (money orders) to streamline their commercial transactions. American companies also introduced checks, known as "comprador's orders," to pay tea sellers in southern Chinese ports. Moreover, despite the Atlantic-centric perception that Americans relied primarily on English sterling bills to make international payments before World War I, Americans had issued U.S. dollar bills in Chinese treaty ports during the latter part of the nineteenth century. These notes, bills, and checks reconstructed the credit system of the tea trade and formed coastal exchange markets across the growing number of Chinese trading ports, further interlinking the transpacific credit economy with global financial systems (chapter 3).

Highlighting the broader financial and political influences of the transpacific credit economy situates *This World in a Teacup* in the new trend of scholarship on U.S.-China trading relations. By the 1970s historians in the United States espoused at least two schools of thought to interpret the long years of business interactions between the United States and China. The "realist school" denied the importance of the commercial relationship and instead emphasized the obstacles that the Chinese placed in the way of U.S. trade. On the other hand, the "Wisconsin school" recognized the significance of transnational commerce but portrayed China as merely an outlet for U.S. capitalist surplus.[59] Research after the 1990s, however, started to restore Chinese agency in the relations. Flipping the narrative, scholars have depicted China as a mine of wealth for capital-scarce but ambitious American traders, and the China trade as having shaped U.S. industry, banking, foreign policy, immigration, and even national identity.[60] *This World in a Teacup* continues with the inquiry, but the trading relations in this book develop from new perspectives: the financial techniques dominated by Eurocentric theories and the global commodity that possessed considerable significance to both countries. Their interplay elucidates the significance of the U.S.-China trade to not only the two nations but also the global economy.

This World in a Teacup reveals how tea and credit integrated U.S. and Chinese economies with nineteenth-century world finance. During the early years of the transpacific tea trade, Chinese traders loaned millions of dollars to their U.S. counterparts through credit transactions and promissory notes. The new lines of credit and profit lubricated the money-scarce early U.S. economy and facilitated economic development in New England and the mid-Atlantic region. The interconnected commercial and financial networks also transmitted the adverse effects of the Depression of 1807 and the Embargo of 1807–9 to the other side of the Pacific Ocean, thus crippling Chinese merchants' finance and the China trade (chapter I). After the season of 1826–27, Americans adopted bills of exchange as the primary instrument for tea purchase and dramatically reduced their silver shipments to China. While the increased monetary stock fueled inflation in the U.S. economy during the mid-1830s, the diminished silver influx aggravated China's silver drain, ultimately contributing to both the Panic of 1837 in the United States and the Anglo-Chinese Opium War in 1839 (chapter 2). Credit grew essential to the U.S.-China tea trade in the second half of the nineteenth century. Americans brought another credit instrument—checks—to China. Credit markets proliferated in Chinese treaty ports. Chinese and Western banks also began to financialize the U.S.-China tea trade formerly dominated by commercial credit (chapters 3 and 4). Despite the efficiency of the credit system, the reliance on credit transactions and instruments exacerbated the economic woes of Chinese and American tea merchants after 1873, when the adoption of the gold standard triggered global economic crises and worldwide price deflation (chapter 5). Thus the transpacific credit relationships interlocked U.S. and Chinese tea merchants' fate with cycles of booms and busts in the global economy. World economic depressions and financial crises, such as the Depression of 1807, the Panic of 1837, the commercial and financial crisis of 1865–67, and the global Long Depression of 1873–97, kept interrupting, disrupting, shaping, and remaking the U.S.-China tea trade throughout the nineteenth century.

The tea trade's credit system influenced not only both economies but also American tea consumption after the Revolution. This book argues that the power dynamics between American, British, and Chinese merchants in the credit economy reshaped U.S. tea consumption patterns in the nineteenth century. During the first half-century of the U.S.-China tea trade, the heavily capitalized and well-connected English East India Company (EIC) dominated the advance system, a credit transaction that enabled Britons to contract tea with Chinese merchants months before the market was open to Americans. Lacking sufficient capital to make payments in advance, Americans had to purchase teas insignificant on the EIC's list, thus prompting the shift in U.S. consumers' taste from black tea to green tea early in the nineteenth century. However, after forging strong bonds with Chinese merchants, who were willing to extend credit, issue them promissory notes, and accept their bills of exchange, U.S. merchants enhanced their purchasing power and dominated green and oolong tea markets in China. The growth of the U.S.-China tea trade slowed when the profit margin slimmed and global competition for the American tea market intensified after 1873. British financial capital dominated the credit economy of the U.S.-China tea trade and partially controlled tea's supply chain from Asia to America. Consequently, early in the twentieth century, English breakfast tea, a seller's brand created for the United States, transformed itself from a pure Chinese black tea to a blend of products from English colonies, crystalizing the eventual fall of the U.S.-China tea trade.

The Book

Tea and credit entwine in this book, illustrating the changing power dynamics in transpacific trade. This narrative is based on sources in the repositories of the United States and China, including business letters, financial documents, consular and official reports, customs records, local gazetteers, historical periodicals, and advertising materials, that document the U.S. demand for and China's supply of tea. Americans' business records, in particular, contain extensive details about the credit economy in China. To thread the massive information into a cohesive story, three types of tea constitute the warp, and the credit economy serves as the weft, of the analyses. Each part of this book features one of the most popular teas in America—young hyson, oolong, and English breakfast tea—to establish the historical setting for the trade. The chapters in each part, focusing on the transitional phases, trace the development of the transpacific credit economy and its power dynamics.

Part 1, "Green Tea," portrays the transition in U.S. consumption from black tea to green tea, particularly young hyson, as a consequence of the power dynamics between American, British, and Chinese merchants in the credit economy of the international tea trade. Examining the credit transactions and instruments employed by Chinese and American tea merchants, chapters 1 and 2 explain how credit networks formed and shaped the power structure of tea's supply chain. Chapter 1 discusses the first three decades of the U.S.-China tea trade, when the United States arose as the second-largest importer of Chinese tea during the French Wars (1793–1814), aided by Chinese merchants' credit. From at least the 1790s, American and Chinese merchants employed account books, consignments, respondentia, and promissory notes to develop the transpacific credit system that buttressed their tea trade for the coming century. The new line of credit that was extended through credit transactions and instruments from Chinese merchants also enhanced the development of the early U.S. economy and the independence of the young republic. Chapter 2 explains how the bills of exchange employed in the U.S.-China tea trade contributed to the Panic of 1837 in America and the first Anglo-Chinese Opium War (1839–42). After the season of 1826–27, this credit instrument gained prominence in facilitating the triangular trade of tea, opium, and cotton. Americans brought private bills—generated in their transatlantic cotton trade or issued by the Bank of the United States—to China and offered British-Indian opium smugglers a cheap means to remit their proceeds back to India and England. As these bills became the chief means of Americans' tea purchase, their value fluctuated in rhythm with the tea season for decades thereafter. Americans amassed substantial fortunes in the bill trade and dramatically reduced their silver shipments to China. This structural change in financing the U.S.-China tea trade exacerbated inflation in the U.S. economy and depleted China's stock of silver, thus providing another stepping stone for the Panic of 1837 and the Opium War in 1839.

Oolong tea is the theme of part 2. The post–Opium War years saw the rising popularity of oolongs in the United States and Americans' growing influence in newly opened Chinese ports. Chapters 3 and 4 trace the extension of the credit network beyond Canton and the financialization of the credit system in the new ports, which reflected and facilitated the changing landscape of the U.S.-China tea trade during 1842–73. Chapter 3 examines the restoration and extension of the credit economy after the Opium War. Although American merchants continued to use bills of exchange to finance their tea ventures in Canton, the business in the newly opened ports initially resorted to barter and silver payments. The promissory notes and bills of exchange issued by Chinese native banks, the checks written by compradors, and the inland dollar bills issued by American companies developed trust relations between Chinese and U.S. tea merchants. Centering on Shanghai and Hong Kong, coastal exchange markets also developed across the treaty ports, interlinking more regions in China with global financial centers through the tea trade. In this process, Chinese banks started to financialize the transpacific tea trade in the wider Shanghai area, while Americans' commercial credit facilitated tea transactions on the southeastern coast of China. Chapter 4 traces the financialization of the U.S.-China tea trade during 1865–73, a process in which native and Western banks replaced mercantile capital to control the credit economy. Chinese banks distributed financial resources to Chinese tea dealers through professional brokers known as *chazhan*, or tea warehouses. While financing U.S. commission houses' tea ventures, European banks also competed with American merchants for the bill market in China. The growing influence of financial capital and the easy credit from European banks drove waves of speculation on Chinese tea until the American tea market collapsed in 1873. Competing interests of American, Chinese, and European merchants and banks complicated the financialization process, awaiting the global depression to completely transform the power structure of the transpacific tea trade.

Part 3 investigates how English breakfast tea, originally a type of high-rank black tea from China, developed into a blend of Chinese black with Indian and Ceylon products. The changing identity of English breakfast tea crystalizes the decline of the U.S.-China tea trade, a process accelerated by the financialization of the tea trade's credit system during the global Long Depression of 1873–97. Chapter 5 investigates the declining U.S.-China tea trade during the world economic crisis. After the United States and Europe adopted the gold standard in 1873, which arguably triggered the global long depression, the value of silver and tea depreciated to an unprecedented low. Consequently, the profit of the tea trade became increasingly slim in the following decades. American and Chinese merchants, both operating on borrowed capital and fragile credit networks, faced mounting pressures amid the global depression and gloomy tea economy. With U.S. banks' absence from China, American merchants grew dependent on London bankers, and most withdrew from the tea trade. The thinly capitalized Chinese traders reconfigured their business strategies by manufacturing inferior teas more rapidly and in smaller quantities, seeking to reduce the overall costs of the credit-dependent tea economy. This model, however, weakened Chinese tea merchants' competition with well-capitalized and centrally managed British and Japanese companies, not to mention that the latter weaponized modern advertising and lobbying to market their products against Chinese tea in America. The U.S.-China tea trade ultimately declined. While the United States arose as an economic and political powerhouse, the withered tea trade further impoverished the already destabilized Qing Empire (1644–1912), which eventually collapsed after the Revolution of 1911.

The conclusion reemphasizes the importance of tea to U.S. history and the centrality of credit to China's foreign trade. Moreover, it offers a preliminary comparative analysis of the transpacific credit economy with Americans' credit operations in the Atlantic world, thus providing useful information for future studies of global credit systems.

PART 1 *Green Tea*

In 1835 grocer Mr. Parmelee set up an advertising board outside his store, proclaiming,

> I have just received direct from York,
> My fall supply of Wares,—
> As prime a lot as e're was brought,
> To the Chittenango lair.
> . . .
> My *Groceries* are superior still,
> Selected all to please;
> *Imperial* and Fresh *Hyson Skin*,
> *Old* and *Young Hyson Teas*.
> . . .
> To tell you all the goods I've got
> Would take a month or more,—
> I'll tell you where they can be bought,
> AT PARMELEE'S CHEAP CASH STORE.[1]

While modern readers might be impressed by Parmelee's talent as a rhymester, they may find the teas—imperial, hyson skin, hyson, and young hyson—bewildering. Even nineteenth-century Americans felt the transliterations of the Chinese names "strange sounding," although these teas were household items.[2] Their eighteenth-century ancestors might also have found Mr. Parmelee's selections puzzling, for their favorite black teas—bohea, congou, and souchong—were missing from the cash store. Thus Mr. Parmelee's poetical advertisement in the 1830s crystalized the changing landscape of U.S. tea consumption. Americans shifted from black to green tea during the early part of the nineteenth century and favored young hyson in particular, which was a variety of green tea manufactured primarily for the U.S. market.

The postrevolutionary shifts in U.S. tea consumption reflected not a political decision prompted by American independence but the power dynamics between American, British, and Chinese merchants in U.S.-China trade undergirded by transnational credit networks. With limited financial resources, U.S. tea merchants were initially disadvantaged in the tea trade, while Europeans, and especially the British, dominated the credit transaction—the advance system—in China to monopolize their favorite teas, particularly various black teas. Failing to compete with the British East India Company (EIC) and private merchants, American importers had to shift from black to green tea, thus refashioning domestic tea consumption. However, Americans' tea trade grew when Chinese traders extended long-term, high-value credit to their U.S. counterparts beginning in the late eighteenth century. American merchants' purchasing power continued to improve after they brought new credit instruments—private bills of exchange—into China during and after the War of 1812. Consequently, Americans became the largest importer of green tea from China. Young hyson, a mid-grade green tea, became the most popular tea in the United States. Focusing on tea and taste, part I traces the changes in U.S. tea consumption by the mid-nineteenth century. The following two chapters place the consumption patterns into the financial context and power structure of the U.S.-China tea trade before the Opium War, thus reconstructing the formation and development of the transpacific credit system.

After American independence, citizens of the young republic retained their colonial-era taste for black tea, a preference inherited from England.[3] Therefore, when the ship *Empress of China* left Canton for New York in 1784, black tea, valued at 49,240 taels, was the most expensive commodity that Supercargo Samuel Shaw procured, while the 16,860 taels of green tea was only a third of black tea's value. A 1790 report from Alexander Hamilton, U.S. secretary of the treasury, showed that Americans imported more black tea (bohea, souchong, and others) than green tea, with the former amounting to 1.5 million pounds while the latter totaled merely 100,000 pounds.[4] A decade later, in 1802, Americans still shipped 42,624 piculs of black tea and 10,293 piculs of green tea from China, with green tea constituting less than 20 percent of the aggregate tea imports.[5] Given that less than 10 percent of the imported tea was reshipped out of the United States and more greens were re-exported before 1800, black tea still dominated U.S. tea consumption in the decades following the American Revolution.[6]

Throughout the eighteenth century and early in the nineteenth, Americans continued to favor the varieties of teas that were popular in both England and America during the colonial era. Between 1740 and 1834, the EIC acquired black teas (primarily bohea, congou, and souchong) and green teas (predominantly singlo, twankay, hyson, and hyson skin) for England.[7] These varieties, along with the lesser-known pekoe (black tea) and imperial (green tea), also recurred in American newspaper advertisements and patriotic poems before the Revolution.[8] After the war, U.S. citizens remained committed to these teas (see figure 3). The *Empress of China* carried such greens as gunpowder, hyson, singlo, and blacks—including bohea and souchong—back to New York for sale. Captain John Green also purchased hyson, gunpowder, and bohea for his private investments.[9] Bohea, the cheap black tea, was popular in the United States during the 1790s, although it gradually faded from most American parlors in the early nineteenth century.[10] An 1829 prose work, "Wonders of a Cup of Tea," depicted more traditional teas as the "'hissing urn throws up a steamy column,' fragrant with hyson, powerful with imperial, strong with gunpowder, or black with bohea." Thus the conventional green (hyson, imperial, and gunpowder) and black (bohea) teas still brewed the "wonder-working beverage within" in the republic.[11]

However, U.S. tea consumption changed dramatically in the early nineteenth century. Unlike their British counterparts and colonial forebears who favored black tea, nineteenth-century Americans cultivated a taste for green tea. During the trading season of 1833–34, Americans took "more than *two-thirds* of their investment in *Green* Teas," whereas the EIC "took about *four-fifths* of their investment in *Black* Teas."[12] Americans' distinctive taste changed little when the monopoly of the EIC over the China trade ended in 1833. Green teas had been no less than four-fifths of the entire U.S. tea imports by 1837.[13] By 1845, 60 percent of the tea shipped to America remained green tea, while the composition of British imports was 25 percent green and 75 percent black.[14] A Shanghai newspaper, the *North China Herald*, continued to report in 1870 that the U.S. market "is the main outlet for Green Teas."[15] Some contemporaries even characterized the peculiar tastes for black or green tea as a mark of the old and new civilizations. "It

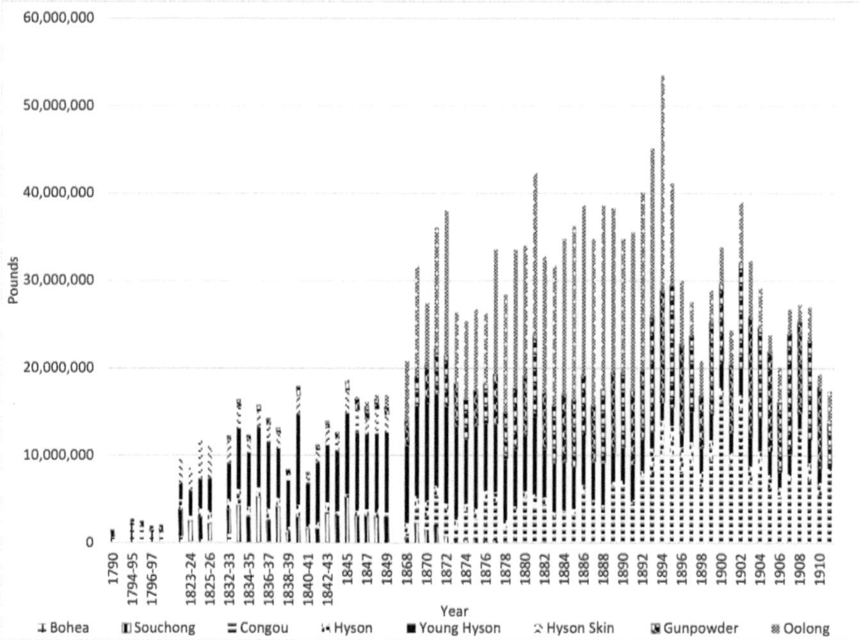

Fig. 3. Varieties of black, green, and oolong tea imported into the United States, 1794–1911. The tea import data for 1794–98 include a minor percentage of teas transshipped from Europe to the United States. Tea quantities for 1822–43 were calculated by converting chests to pounds by using the ratio of 1 chest = 80 pounds. Robert Bennet Forbes's annual records of black and green tea imports, in chests and pounds, indicate that the weight of each chest was about eighty pounds. See Forbes, *Remarks on China*, 25. The data for 1868–1911 were converted from piculs to pounds with the ratio of 1 picul = 133.3 pounds. The category hyson for 1790 refers to all green tea. Young hyson for 1794–98 includes all green teas except hyson. Souchong for 1794–98 comprises congou and a small amount of other black teas. Imperial for 1822–49 incorporates gunpowder. Hyson skin for 1839–40, 1842–43, 1845, and 1846 contains twankay. Sources: 1790–98: Robert Waln Jr., "Commercial Memo," Book of Prices, Canton 1819, 17–19, WFP, Collection of the Historical Society of Pennsylvania. 1822–26: "Exchange Papers," *Niles' Weekly Register*, July 7, 1827, 307, ProQuest American Periodicals. 1832–49: Nye, *Tea: And the Tea Trade*, 23–24. 1868–1911: Zhonguo jiuhaiguan shiliao bianji wenyuanhui, *Zhongguo jiuhaiguan shiliao*, vols. 3–55, 3: 486–87; 4: 14–15, 296–97, 570–71; 5: 14–15, 290–91, 608–9; 6: 14–15, 31, 338–39; 7: 14–15, 406–7; 8: 14–15, 444–45; 9: 14–15, 472–73; 10: 18–19, 442–43; 11: 20–21; 12: 18–19; 13: 18–19; 14: 18–19; 15: 18–19; 16: 18–19; 17: 18–19; 18: 18–19; 20: 18–19; 22: 18–19; 23: 22–23; 24: 22–23; 25: 22–23; 27: 22–23; 29: 22–23; 31: 28–29; 33: 22–23; 35: 22–23; 37: 28–29; 39: 34–35; 41: 94–95; 43: 36–37; 45: 36–37; 47: 36–37; 49: 36–37; 52: 38–39; 55: 40–41.

is noticeable that the use of black teas in various places has succeeded that of green," the *Chinese Commercial Guide* clarified, "the latter being preferred in newly settled countries, as Australia and United States."[16] An 1886 British newspaper article attributed the taste of the "New World" to U.S. commerce with Japan at the time.[17] However, the trend had started during the first decade of the nineteenth century (see figure 4).[18]

Even though green tea had a "disrepute in the Old World,"[19] Americans regarded it as a marker of social status and good taste, reflected or satirized by the literary works in the early nineteenth century. New York writers using the pseudonym Pindar Cockloft, Esq. ranked the social standing of female consumers in accordance with their preferences for teas.

> The wives of our cits, of inferior degree,
> Will soak up repute in little *bohea*;
> . . .
> As our matrons are richer; and rise to *souchong*
> With *hyson*, a beverage that's still more, refined,
> Our ladies of fashion enliven their mind,
> . . .
> While madam, in cambries and laces array'd,
> With her plate and her liveries in splendid parade,
> Will drink, in *imperial*, a friend at a sup,
> OR IN *gunpowder* BLOW THEM BY DOZENS ALL UP![20]
> (author's emphasis)

Women of the humblest households brewed bohea, more refined matrons steeped the premium black tea souchong, whereas ladies of fashion sup green tea—whether hyson, imperial, or gunpowder. An author named Epicurus echoed the perception in 1829. "There are some kinds prepared especially for the benefit of the vulgar," the author warned. "Bohea is at the head of this description, and souchong belongs to the same class." Epicurus reminded "elegant and fashionable" Americans who valued their "gentility" and "refined sensibility," "Green teas are always to have the preference, from which you can select imperial, gunpowder or young hyson."[21]

As suggested by Epicurus's poem, the growing preference for a particular type of green tea, young hyson, further distinguished nineteenth-century U.S. tea consumers from their British counterparts (see figure 3). Green tea

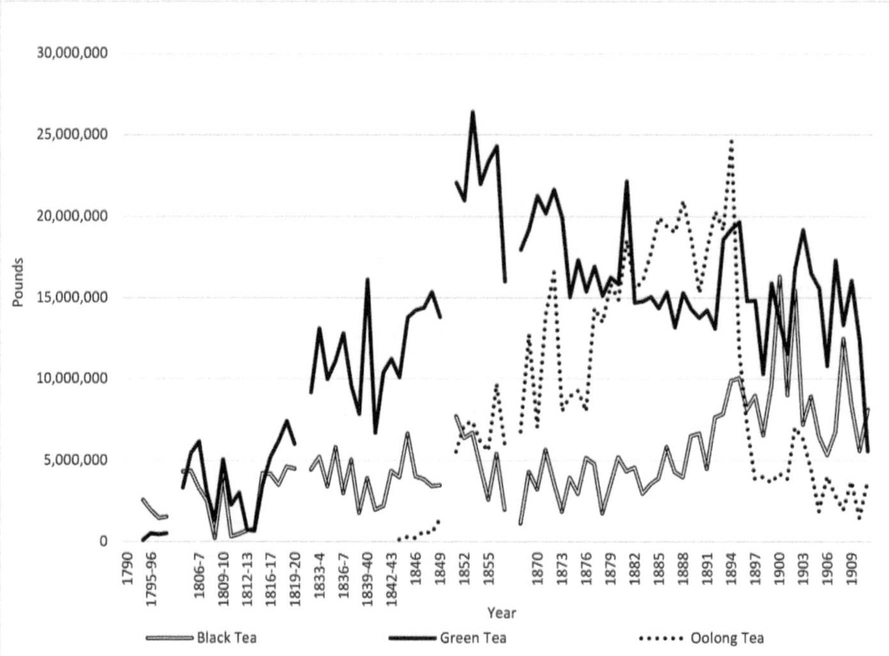

Fig. 4. Quantities of green, black, and oolong tea imported from China to the United States, 1790–1911. Sources: 1790: Robert Waln Jr., "Commercial Memo," Book of Prices, Canton 1819, 17, WFP. 1804–20: Forbes, *Remarks on China*, 25. 1832–49: Nye, *Tea: And the Tea Trade*, 23–25, 26. The quantities of tea, in pounds, during 1822–43 were estimated from the number of chests of tea, with the ratio 1 chest = 80 pounds. See the caption for figure 3 for more details about this ratio. 1851: "Commercial Miscellany," *United States Economist, Dry Goods Reporter, and Bank Railroad and Commercial Chronicle* 1, no. 25 (October 9, 1852): 771. 1852–57: William Appleton & Co. to Captain William Cole, April 19, 1857, box 2, FGDP. 1868–1911: Zhonguo jiuhaiguan shiliao bianji wenyuanhui, *Zhongguo jiuhaiguan shiliao*, vols. 3–55, corresponding page numbers specified in figure 3.

had entered the American market at least by 1710.[22] However, Americans' favorite, young hyson, made its debut during the 1790s, reaching Pennsylvania and Maryland by 1793–94.[23] Nineteenth-century literary works documented young hyson as one of the most commonly used teas in the United States. For instance, a traveler touring along the Mississippi River in 1818–19 found his hostess's rejection of young hyson perplexing: "We had not before imagined that there was any part of the white population of the United States strangers to this plant, so universally in use in our country."[24] Business records confirmed Americans' preference for this green tea. Tea importer J. and T. H. Perkins and Son, in Boston, noted in 1824 that young hyson had "become so great a favorite that people will have it in preference to Hyson at same price."[25] Boston merchant Robert Bennet Forbes ranked young hyson as "one of the staple green teas for the American market" in 1844.[26]

The name of "young" hyson indicates that this American favorite should be a finer and tenderer hyson tea. Hyson is likely a romanization of the Chinese name *Xichun*, which means "flourishing spring."[27] Young hyson, *Yuqian* or *Yucha* in Chinese, means the tea picked in early spring, or, more accurately, before the *Guyu*. *Guyu*, "grain rains," a Chinese solar term that refers to the days in April and early May, is one of the best times to manufacture the finest tea, because tea plants are yielding buds or the tenderest leaves during this early spring period.[28] Accordingly, the leaves to make young hyson were smaller than those of hyson, so U.S. merchant Sullivan Dorr defined this tea as "the inside leaf of Hyson, taken [before] rains."[29] Owing to its tenderness, young hyson should also be more expensive than hyson. In the eighteenth and nineteenth centuries, Europeans had realized that "the fineness and dearness of tea are determined by the tenderness and smallness of the leaf," so "one pound of the best tea is sold for more than a hundred pounds of another sort."[30]

Nevertheless, the tender and finer young hyson preferred by Americans was the least popular tea among British consumers during the same period. The EIC's report to the British parliament tabulates the teas sold for home consumption during 1740–1837. During the entire period, bohea and congou were the most popular black teas, while twankay and hyson were the favorite green teas after 1784. In comparison, throughout the company's ninety-seven-year operation, young hyson appeared only five times in the its report, totaling a mere 62,430 pounds.[31] Private British traders increased their purchases of young hyson after 1834.[32] However, the British were still "eager for Hyson, Gun Powder and Imperial" to satisfy the need for fine teas.[33] The lower-end product, twankay, accounted for "three fourths of the whole importation of green" to meet ordinary consumers' demand.[34] The insignificance of young hyson to Britons was significant enough to reveal the peculiarity of U.S. tea consumption.

The rise of young hyson in the United States does not suggest that Americans consumed better tea than their British counterparts in the early nineteenth century. In truth, most of the young hyson in the U.S. market was fake *Yuqian*, as British diplomat John Francis Davis asserted: "Young Hyson, until it was spoiled by the large demand of the Americans, was a genuine, delicate young leaf."[35] Chinese tea scholars also argued that the genuine green tea produced before *Guyu* was only for sale domestically owing to the limited supply.[36] Americans agreed, explaining that the "very delicacy and tenderness of the leaves render their successful exportation impracticable," "so that, outside of China, we rarely get a taste of real aromatic Young Hyson."[37] Unsurprisingly, the young hyson sold in Canton for foreign markets usually commanded lower prices than hyson, imperial, and gunpowder, indicating its lower grade than the three kinds of green tea popular among British buyers (see table 1). U.S. consumers also acknowledged that the young hyson on their home market was a medium-rank tea. "From humble bohea to exquisite hyson, the quintessence of fragrant delights," an American tea drinker wrote in 1857, "not excepting the intermediate classes," such as hyson skin and young hyson.[38]

Table 1. Average cost of the principal teas from Canton, 1817–28 (cents per lb.)

YEAR	GREEN TEA				BLACK TEA	
	Gunpowder and imperial	*Hyson*	*Young hyson*	*Hyson skin*	*Souchong*	*Bohea*
1817	68	62	46	32	32	N
1818	69	48	40	24	18	14
1819	63	41	34	22	18	15
1820	59	45	35	22	17	12
1821	66	42	30	17	22	12
1822	54	45	32	19	18	11
1823	58	42	34	22	19	11
1824	58	45	41	23	20	N
1825	61	42	50	30	24	13
1828	53 and 51	42	36	20	12–20	N

Note: N = no data.

Source: For data for 1817–25, see Smith and Ilsley, *Trade with China*, 269. For data for 1828, see Archer, *Memorial of the Merchants*, 6.

Indeed, most young hyson in America was a contrived category that the Chinese created to cater to the U.S. market. The British, such as the above-mentioned Davis and EIC's tea inspector Samuel Ball, blamed Americans' demand for young hyson, which was so large "that the manufacturers cannot supply them, except by cutting up the leaves before drying, and making imitations."[39] Since the natural *Yuqian* was made from tender leaves, Chinese factories sliced large leaves or processed small ones into "young hyson" not only in early spring but throughout the tea season. Historical documents detailed the process. After sorting crude leaves gathered from various growers, tea workers sieved the leaves a dozen times to separate small and large ones, a laborious but critical step in manufacturing and refining tea for the overseas market. The bigger leaves retained in the sieves became different ranks of Hyson, while the smaller ones that went through the holes were designated various classes of young hyson. The coarsest large leaves were labeled hyson skin.[40] Today, China's export green tea still adheres to similar processing steps and sieving techniques, suggesting the international tea trade's long-term influence on Chinese tea production.[41] Despite being made with the same process, hyson, young hyson, and hyson skin were marketed outside Chinese factories as different varieties of tea.

Therefore the transition from black to green tea and the rise of the cheaper "young" hyson reflected not only American consumers' changing taste for tea but also the power imbalance between Britons and Americans in China's tea supply chain. After the transpacific tea trade unfolded, the EIC dominated the tea trade with China, the primary supplier of tea to the world, for six decades, partially determining the kinds of teas available to U.S. consumers after the American Revolution. Employing the advance system, the company monopolized all the bohea, "three fifths of the Congo [congou], all the Twankays, and two thirds of the Hysons" annually, even before the market was open to U.S. traders.[42] The EIC imported little of young hyson after the company's inspectors detected the Chinese tactics of cutting up large leaves to make it.[43] In contrast, despite becoming the second-largest importer of Chinese tea, Americans initially lacked the resources and influence to procure premium teas from China (chapter 1). Hence it should not be considered a coincidence that young hyson became increasingly popular from the early nineteenth century, whereas the teas monopolized by the EIC ceased to dominate the U.S. market.

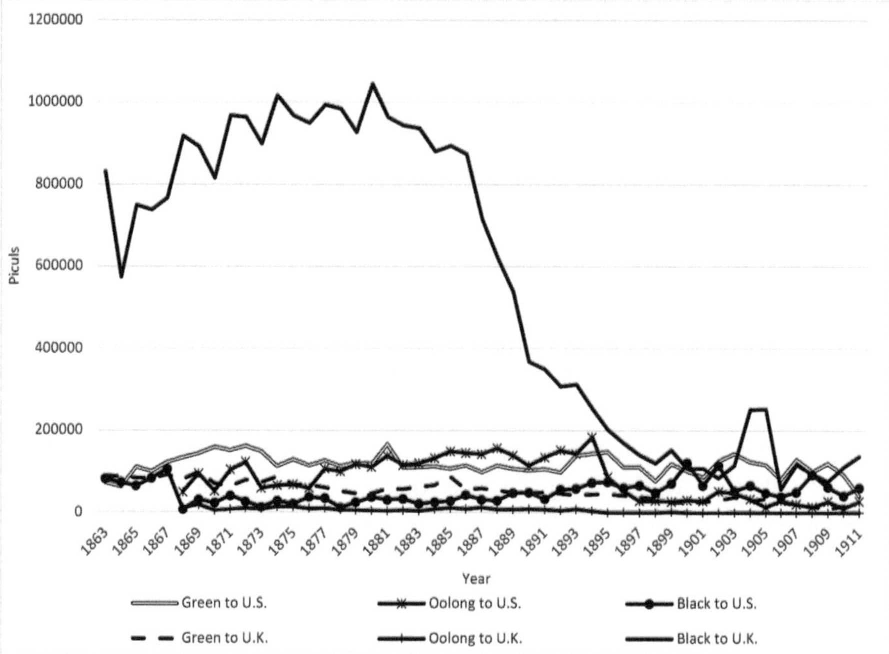

Fig. 5. Quantities of tea exported from China to the United States and Great Britain, 1863–1911. The category of black tea for 1863–67 includes oolong tea. Sources: 1863–67: Inspector General of Chinese Maritime Customs, *Trade Statistics of the Treaty Ports for the Period 1863–1872*, 44. 1868–1911: Zhonguo jiuhaiguan shiliao bianji wenyuanhui, *Zhongguo jiuhaiguan shiliao*, vols. 3–55, corresponding page numbers specified in figure 3.

The peculiar taste for young hyson, however, also reflected Americans' ability to gradually carve out their place in the global tea trade. Amid the transition from black to green tea in the early nineteenth century, Americans initially consumed more hyson skin, the green tea that was even cheaper than young hyson (see figure 3 and table 1). But the popularity of hyson skin waned beginning in the 1830s, when Americans enhanced their purchasing power by selling private bills of exchange in China, India, and Southeast Asia (chapter 2). Thereafter, Americans dominated not only the market for young hyson but also the entire green tea trade with China, although Great Britain was the largest buyer of Chinese black tea. "Prices of greens must depend upon the demand for America," Forbes declared in 1835.[44] The advantage would persist throughout the nineteenth century, except the years during the American Civil War (see figure 5). The rise of young hyson thus demonstrated that Americans not only survived but also thrived in the international tea business. In sum the power dynamics between Americans and Britons in the tea trade with China still influenced U.S. consumers' taste for tea after American independence. Chapters 1 and 2 will examine the driving force of the changing consumption patterns, explaining how the international credit networks buttressed Americans' tea trade with China and reshaped the power structure of American, British, and Chinese merchants in Canton from 1784 to 1842.

I

Paper Gold and Green Gold

BUILDING THE CREDIT ECONOMY, 1784–1815

Even before the *Empress of China* arrived on the American coast in July 1785, Shaw had already drafted a report to the U.S. minister for foreign affairs on this historic expedition. "The first vessel that has been fitted out by inhabitants of the United States of America," wrote Shaw, starting with a celebratory tone, placed "the Americans in a more conspicuous point of view than has commonly attended the introduction of other nations into that ancient and extensive empire."[1] The U.S. Congress shared the sense of pride, informing Shaw of their "peculiar satisfaction in the successful issue of this first effort of the citizens of America to establish a direct trade with China, which does so much honor to its undertakers and conductors."[2] A correspondent for the *New York News* also foresaw a bright future after the ship returned to New York, laden with "such articles as we generally import from Europe." Now that British oppression, in the correspondent's mind, no longer prevented Americans' direct trade with China, the trip would "promote the welfare of the United States in general, by inspiring their citizens with emulation to equal, if not excel, their mercantile rivals."[3]

The tea trade with China, therefore, demonstrated and reinforced Americans' sense of independence after the American Revolution.[4] Even though the tea carried by the *Empress* was mostly a dull sale at home, many Americans took great pride in abandoning a colonial relationship with the EIC.[5] The economic benefits of the trade in the following decades rendered Americans' liberty a reality. When the French Wars wreaked havoc in Europe and disrupted continental Europeans' commerce in China, Americans, trading under a neutral flag, became the primary provider of tea, the "green gold," to Europe.[6] The United States thereby grew to be the second-largest importer of Chinese tea. The direct, legitimate tea trade also enabled Americans to procure new lines of credit from China. Employing promissory notes—generated by such credit transactions as account sales, consignments, and respondentia—to facilitate de facto transactions in the tea trade, Chinese merchants provided millions of dollars of monetary resources to their U.S. counterparts. The promissory note thus represented gold and silver in the early China trade. Furnished with the "green gold" and "paper gold," Americans' reinvestment at home lubricated the money-scarce early republican economy, particularly in New England and the Mid-Atlantic states.

The focus on these credit transactions and instruments highlights the established credit network in the early transpacific commerce. The existing research has elaborated how credit from Europe undergirded Britons' commerce in China or Americans' transatlantic business.[7] Yet much less research exists on the credit system of the early U.S.-China trade. Instead, many looked for silver or barter when examining the international payments made in China. As early as 1843, Thomas H. Benton delivered a speech in the U.S. Senate, claiming that the China trade was conducted on "all ready-money, and hard money, or good products—no credit system, no paper money. For a long time this trade took nothing but silver dollars."[8] Modern researchers reinforced the stereotype by portraying U.S.-China trade, especially during the early years, as a cumbersome hard-money system.[9] This chapter, nonetheless, highlights the credit transactions and instruments that facilitated the early transpacific tea trade, thus illuminating the significance of credit to China's foreign trade and early U.S. economy.

In the late eighteenth century, American and Chinese merchants began to develop a credit economy for their tea trade. Built on trust, healthy credit relationships require time and experience. Thus U.S. tea merchants initially accumulated capital through shipping goods and South American silver to Canton, in contrast with the advance system dominated by European companies. The fluctuations of the commodity and silver markets amplified American newcomers' disadvantage in the tea trade. Hence the importance and convenience of credit is evident. The second section traces the formation of the credit economy between U.S. and Chinese merchants through credit transactions—account sales, consignments, and respondentia—and the first type of credit instruments, the promissory note. The expansive transpacific credit network not only linked the U.S. economy with the China trade but also integrated both regions with financial markets in the Atlantic world.

The third section demonstrates the influence of the credit economy. Chinese tea merchants extended substantial loans to their American trading partners through credit transactions and promissory notes, a new line of financial resources that lubricated the money-scarce early U.S. economy. This era also laid the foundation for future developments in China's credit system, which would shape the rise and fall of the transpacific tea trade for the coming century.

Commodities and Silver

Inspired by the prestige of economic independence and equality, Shaw's account of his second trip to Canton in 1786 portrayed an advantageous adventure, "if not in many respects superior" to Europeans, because ginseng sustained Americans' tea trade. While the nations of Europe purchased tea "with ready money, it must be pleasing to an American to know that his country can have it upon easier terms," Shaw adding, "and that the otherwise useless produce of her mountains and forests will in a considerable degree supply her with this elegant luxury."[10] Ginseng, which grew wild in North America, had great value in China as a medicinal herb. In the early eighteenth century, English and French merchants had begun shipping the plant's roots, gathered by Native Americans, to China.[11] After the American Revolution, U.S. traders established ginseng, one of the few commodities that the Chinese prized, as a major export.[12] Shaw maintained that the abundant American ginseng "has not a little alarmed the Europeans." "They have seen, the first year, a single ship, not one fifth part of whose funds consisted of ready money," Shaw claimed, "procure a cargo of the same articles, and on equally good terms, as those of their own ships," purchased "principally with specie."[13] Assuming that "there will always be a sufficient demand for [ginseng]," Shaw overtly wove the pride of independence into the ethos of an agrarian economy.[14] However, this supercargo failed to mention that the Chinese ginseng market had collapsed by 1786 with the large supply from America.[15]

Prioritizing American ginseng over Europeans' specie, Shaw tacitly acknowledged the problem of money scarcity among early U.S. tea merchants. The long-distance tea trade with China was a costly expedition. The aggregate capital of the *Empress* amounted to around $120,000 in 1784.[16] A mixed cargo during the 1820s, in which tea usually accounted for the greatest value, cost around 120,000 to 180,000 Spanish dollars, or approximately 4.88 to 7.32 billion U.S. dollars in terms of the relative share of GDP in 2024.[17] Therefore, when sending a ship furnished with $50,000–$60,000 to Canton in 1830, Thomas H. Perkins instructed the agent in China to invest only in "low priced Young Hyson Tea" and souchong. "Her funds are small," Perkins emphasized.[18] In contrast, Shaw had only 17,700 Spanish dollars in cash on the *Empress*, and the second American ship to China, Thomas Randall's *Pallas*, possessed $50,000 as working capital.[19] To tackle the problem of cash shortage in the following decades, Americans harvested everything in the world to finance their trade with China, such as furs from the northwest coast of America, sandalwood from Hawai'i, birds' nests from Southeast Asia, and opium from Turkey. However, like ginseng, these commodities' value fluctuated significantly in the market.[20] When Captain Gray and Supercargo Richard Howe failed to sell their furs in Canton in 1789, they purchased only six hundred chests of poor-quality bohea for the returning cargo.[21] The ship *Eliza Cap Rowen* arrived in 1799 with about $98,000, which was an enormous voyage, but only $23,000 was in cash and the remaining in furs and other commodities. The other two ships, *Dispatch* and *Hancock*, carrying furs valued at $54,000, could have sufficient funds to purchase a returning cargo, but only of coarse goods, including tea.[22] Therefore capital scarcity hindered Americans' ability to finance their tea trade. A Chinese tea purser was well aware of early U.S. traders' preference for cheap tea. "American men do not pay as high a price for fashionable Bohea as those Englishmen," the Chinese contended in 1815, not to mention that "the Englishmen all have first-rate Congo tea."[23]

While individual U.S. traders looked for a dependable source of funding for their tea trade, European companies had employed the advance system to secure new teas months before the market was open.[24] Resembling the "forward contract" in modern finance, the advance system "allowed for payment of current market prices ('spot prices') for commodities for future delivery."[25] While the tea season in Canton typically began in September, the EIC usually paid Hong merchants in March at the contract price to secure tea for the new season.[26] Tea reached Canton from the interior in autumn, when the Hongists sent samples to EIC tea tasters, who assessed the quality and finalized the company's purchasing prices.[27] The prices offered by the company usually governed the market rates of tea for that season.[28] The time gap between the delivery of payments and that of goods rendered the advance system a credit transaction. Since the 1720s, the EIC had started to sign secret contracts and make competitive advances to a large number of Chinese merchants, thus enabling the company to avoid monopolistic prices asked by individuals, secure tea from trustworthy suppliers, and outbid European rivals for this scarce commodity. Other Europeans followed suit.[29] Along with the British, the Swedes and the Danes often contracted with the leading Hongist, Phuankhequa, while Dutch and French merchants supported his rival, Yngshaw.[30] The advance system thus crystalized the power dynamics among European powers and Chinese merchants.

Disadvantaged in the established power structure, American newcomers resorted to silver to enhance their competitiveness. While the contracted tea, as the first crop, was usually the finest product, another two or three crops arrived in Canton successively throughout the approximate six-month tea season.[31] Americans could still purchase fresh teas on the open market with silver. Bullion silver, known as sycee, along with copper coins, were the primary currencies in Qing China. The Chinese imported silver primarily from Japan up until the late seventeenth and early eighteenth centuries, when Europeans brought South American specie, or silver coins, into the country.[32] Although various forms of silver coined in South America and the United States had reached China before the 1830s, the Chinese favored the Spanish dollars minted during the reigns of Charles III, Charles IV, and Ferdinand VII (1759–1808), known as Carolus and Ferdinand dollars.[33] Americans had been involved in the South American silver trade since the colonial period. As the monetary unit of the United States, the Spanish dollar was one of America's legal tenders and the overwhelming proportion of the U.S. specie stock.[34] Enjoying a geographical advantage, Americans surpassed Europeans in shipping Spanish dollars to Canton as early as 1793 and controlled the specie trade from South America to China.[35] "Coined and uncoined bullion was formerly a considerable article of import into China," John Phipps, author of *A Practical Treatise on the China and Eastern Trade*, recalled in 1836, "particularly at the commencement of the American trade, when the United States afforded no manufactures marketable at Canton."[36] The Chinese demand for silver and Americans' quests for tea intertwined the commodity and monetary markets. The most favorable season for the disposal of dollars is February and March, "when the Tea merchants & others are going into the interior with their funds for the succeeding year's purchase" and "are generally glad to purchase Carolus & Ferdinands at 3 to 7 per cent" or even 9 to 11 percent premium.[37]

However, the aggregate value of silver carried by Americans to China underestimates the difficulty of gathering and employing specie to finance individual tea transactions. Edward Carrington arrived in Canton as an American consul and mercantile agent at the dawn of the nineteenth century, when Americans had already become the primary supplier of silver to China.[38] However, Carrington's business correspondence in the following decade remained replete with anxieties about acquiring specie, because of the demand for dollars and, consequently, their high price. A Providence merchant, Benjamin Hoppin, wrote to Carrington, in July 1803, "The Dollars cd. [could] not be obtain'd without great trouble, and a high premium."[39] Again, in October 1803, Hoppin reported, "It was our intention to have made you a shipment of 2 or 3,000 Dollars by the *Isis* but the amasing [*sic*] demand for Dollars & high premium given for them renders it rather impracticable."[40] The extreme want of silver dollars paralyzed almost every kind of business in the United States and the trade with China in 1804.[41] On July 31, 1804, King and Talbot, a New York firm, shipped fifteen kegs of specie to Carrington valued at $22,000, the premium of which was 2⅓ percent, or $513.33.[42] In 1806, just before an economic depression hit in 1807, fewer ships entered China because of both the overstock of Chinese goods and the difficulty Philadelphia and Providence merchants had in obtaining specie even "from the remotest parts of the Country" at a 3 to 4 percent premium.[43] Then the U.S. Congress prohibited all exports, including specie, during the Embargo of 1807–9, in response to commercial risks posed by the wars in Europe. Circumstances might have turned more favorable for merchants in 1809, when the premium on dollars dropped to 0.5–2.1 percent.[44] However, everybody was busy collecting, and "very few dollars can be had without paying gold for them."[45] Insurance, transportation, as well as collecting, examining, and storing specie all added extra costs. When John Parker and Sons shipped three casks, containing $6,000, from Salem, Massachusetts, to Carrington in 1810, in addition to the $60 premium, they paid an additional $100 for insurance and handling fees.[46] Thus every silver payment incurred a minimum of 2 percent surcharge for John Parker and Sons. Given the substantial capital invested in the tea trade, the silver economy proved inefficient and expensive in facilitating de facto transactions.

Credit

Nevertheless, the vicissitudes of the silver market did not prevent growth of the tea trade. Despite a slow development in the first ten years, the transpacific tea trade grew steadily from the 1790s and the United States had arisen to be the second-largest tea importer by the beginning of the nineteenth century (see figure 6). Before this direct trade with China, Americans imported tea from either continental Europe or the West Indies.[47] During the late 1780s, the Netherlands still shipped considerable teas to the United States, during a period when European traders were reaping huge profits by smuggling tea to Great Britain and its dependencies.[48] Among the 14 million pounds of tea consumed annually in Britain and its spheres of influence, the EIC's traders sold only 6 million, while Swedish, Danish, and French traders shipped the other 8 million pounds illegally.[49] In 1784, the year the *Empress* sailed to Canton, the British parliament passed the Commutation Act, reducing customs and excise duties on tea from 119 to 12.5 percent ad valorem (according to its value), which curbed tea smuggling.[50] Then the wars in Europe "thoroughly destroyed the tea trade of continental nations" but served Americans well.[51] While the amount of tea shipped from China to Europe by the Dutch, Danes, Swedes, and French dropped by 71.4 percent from the 1770s to the 1790s, American imports surpassed their combined total (also see figure 6).[52] Moreover, the data exclude teas re-exported from the United States, which reached 50 to even 120 percent between 1800 and 1811, implying the massive scale and lucrative profits of the carrying trade with Europe during wartime.[53] Thereafter the United States maintained second place in the global tea trade with China throughout most years of the nineteenth century.[54]

When war-torn Europe opened its tea market to Americans in the late 1790s, Chinese merchants had frequently extended credit to their U.S. counterparts to facilitate de facto tea transactions, thus contributing to the growing U.S.-China tea trade. Hong merchant Pan Kun, from whom Carrington received credit and preferential treatment, was the prime example.[55] When Americans arrived, Qing China's regulated policy, the Canton Trade System, restricted the nation's maritime trade to the single southern port, Canton. Cohong, the quasi-official merchant guild, monopolized Canton's foreign tea trade. Members of the Cohong served as security merchants to pay customs, furnish goods, and provide advice to foreign traders.[56]

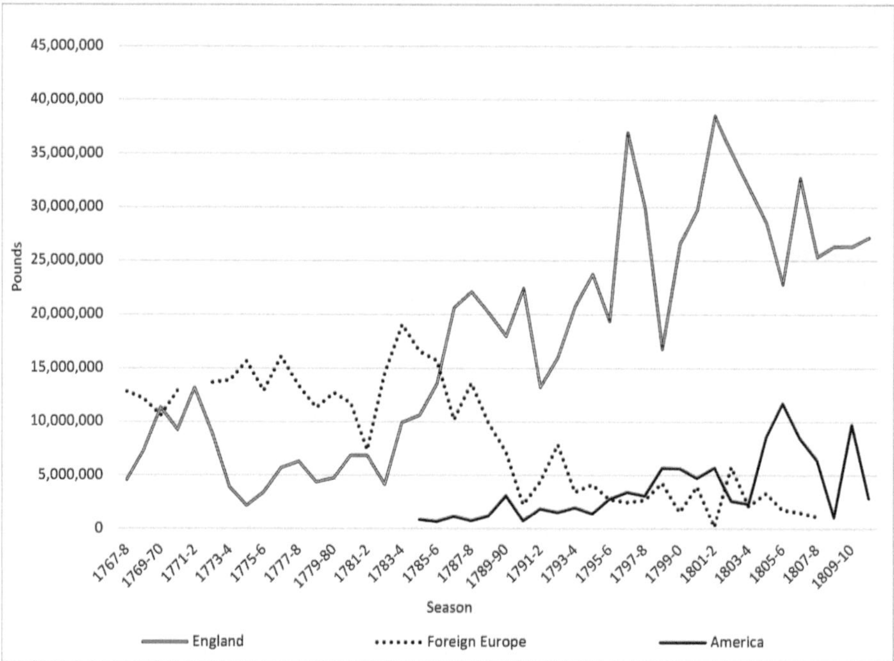

Fig. 6. Exports of tea from China to Europe and America, 1767–1811. Source: Macgregor, *Commercial Statistics*, 5:68.

Pan Kun was the Hong merchant who "dealt more with Americans than any other members of the Co-Hong."[57] Pan had begun to establish close connections with Americans ever since they first landed in Canton. Even though Pan, who had adopted the business name "Conqua," remained a dealer outside the Cohong in 1784, he supplied tea to John Green, captain of the *Empress*.[58] After buying into the Cohong and assuming the trade name Consequa in 1797, Pan patronized U.S. merchants more often than other Hongists.[59] Nonetheless, Dorr, who visited China from 1799 to 1801, ranked Consequa the least-experienced Hong merchant of the eight Cohong members.[60] Consequa rose to fifth in Philadelphian Robert Waln's ratings in 1819 but remained among the worst-standing Hongists.[61] Known as a man "very lavish of promises" who was "not attentive enough to business," and "with whom you cannot talk with safety," Consequa conducted credit relations and reckless operations with U.S. dealers, against the backdrop of a troubled time in American history, that trapped him in long-term debt cycles and dragged him into lengthy but fruitless litigation in the United

States.[62] Yet the disputes left remarkably detailed information, documenting the credit transactions and instruments employed by Chinese and American tea merchants.

ACCOUNT TRANSACTIONS AND CREDIT INSTRUMENT

American merchant John Gibson thought Consequa the "most plausible in his manners, wealthy, easy to make contracts with," yet more importantly, "unbounded in his promises of credit."[63] Therefore an important but less noticed function of Hong merchants was in providing credit to their U.S. trading partners.[64] The business correspondence of the Philadelphia company Willings and Francis details Consequa's credit, which saved them considerable trouble in selling goods or securing specie to finance the tea trade. In May 1805, when the firm sought to secure teas valued at $30,000, William Read, their resident agent at Canton, obtained a credit of $20,000 and "as much more credit from Conseequa as will land the ship [*Bingham*]."[65] Read confirmed in November 1805 that "Consequa has engaged to supply me with whatever I may want on a credit to fill" the *Bingham*.[66] Meanwhile, Read had acquired teas valued at about $15,000 from Consequa, on credit, for another ship, the *New Jersey*.[67] Consequa seldom disappointed Read in extending new loans, even for astonishingly large amounts. On one day, December 12, 1805, Consequa extended at least $31,039.60, equal to $1.6 billion in 2024 in terms of the share of GDP, to Read and other U.S. merchants.[68] When Willings and Francis's supercargo and captain, Mr. Miller, went to Canton for the first time in 1805 to procure a cargo of tea, Consequa secured him a very large credit to acquire the teas, despite "a disagreement between Miller and Conseequa as to the extent of the credit, which Conseequa said he did not expect would be so large."[69] Hence, when Read was trying to convince his principal merchants in Philadelphia that his residence in Canton was mutually beneficial, his reason was Consequa. Read guaranteed that the U.S. firm would not be "disappointed in any arrangement where a credit is required as," he reassured them, he "can obtain whatever may be necessary, say from 100 m. to 150 m. dollars [$100,000–$150,000]," which he had "confirmed from [their] friend Conseequa and mentioned at his request."[70]

Read's confidence in Consequa showcased Chinese merchants' long tradition of extending credit to their commercial partners. Upon the beginning of

U.S.-China trade, Shaw had noticed that the Portuguese, the first European traders reaching China, largely "depended on a credit from the Chinese for their homeward cargoes." According to Shaw, "were it not for this credit" along with other sources of funding, "the commerce of this nation [Portugal] with China would undoubtedly fail."[71] The credit network extended to Americans at least from the 1790s after these newcomers cultivated trade and trust relations with the Chinese. For instance, after Dorr noticed the small funds of the two U.S. ships *Dispatch* and *Hancock* in 1799, he estimated that their supercargoes "most probably shall load them for the Owners a/c [account] procuring credits here [Canton], the Merchants are very ready to credit."[72] Although Dorr never clarified the merchants' nationality, he acquired $5,000 credit, payable in eighteenth months, from a Chinese of good character, named Neuequa or Neuqua, in the same year.[73] Although "the system of barter was very common in the early trade to China," Robert Bennet Forbes recalled in the 1840s, "for many years past it has been carried on sometimes by cash payments, and sometimes it has been done by giving sixty to ninety days credit."[74]

Considering the difficulty of collecting specie in America and the cost of the tea trade, Chinese merchants' credit effectively facilitated tea transactions in China. Financial disruptions highlighted U.S. merchants' dependence on Chinese credit. Three waves of bankruptcy took place among Cohong members in 1779, 1809–15, and 1823–30. In 1812, during the second wave, George W. Talbot of New York reported that "most of the ships are quick of freight, but that the poverty of the Chinese merchts [merchants] will not permit them to ship or to give credits"; therefore "the *Voltaire* brought but two thirds of a cargo."[75] Some Chinese merchant-speculators even took advantage of the credit economy, purchasing inferior teas at low prices and selling them to Americans on long-term credit. Paying silver for top-quality teas was challenging for American buyers with inadequate capital.[76] Thus they were willing to accept higher credit prices and cheap teas offered by the Chinese. Therefore the credit economy proved crucial in sustaining the early transpacific tea trade, although the practice also prompted the supply of low-quality teas to the United States.

Such credit transactions as account keeping documented and buttressed the credit extended from Chinese to U.S. tea traders. Although silver remained the "real" money to liquidate account balances in the China trade, it was not necessarily the means of payment for each transaction. Bookkeeping and bilateral accounts enabled merchants to settle de facto transactions with money on account.[77] Bookkeeping had become ubiquitous in Chinese villages, cities, and market towns by the sixteenth century. The Chinese developed at least three types of single- or double-entry bookkeeping techniques before the introduction of Western accounting into China during the latter part of the nineteenth century.[78] Maintaining bilateral accounts with their foreign trading partners also enabled Chinese merchants to settle international transactions on account books. Although most Hong merchants' account books have gone missing, Americans' business records documented the account transactions with the Chinese. During the *Empress*'s second voyage, Captain Green recounted nine transactions at the value of hundreds of dollars as "Settlement of accounts" with such shopkeepers as Eshing and Woysang in November 1786, although they were not made for tea purchases.[79] Shaw noted in 1787 that Europeans "settled their accounts with the Chinese" before they retired to Macao at the close of the trading season, revealing account transactions as a customary practice in the Canton Trade.[80] Henry Hollingsworth, supercargo of the ship *Lancaster* owned by the Philadelphia merchant Thomas P. Cope, detailed his China trade from January 14 to March 18, 1812, in an account book.[81] The total value of the recorded transactions in such goods as tea, silk, nankeen (textile), and chinaware was $167,405.67, of which payments on account were valued at $114,136.73, approximately 68 percent of his business with such Chinese merchants as Consequa, Kinglun, Achune, Eshing, Chunqua, Mowqua, and Howqua. Dealings in large sums were mostly account transactions. Moreover, Hollingsworth paid $75,045.79 to Howqua, his security merchant, as "Balance on Settlement of Account," clarifying the existence of previous account transactions.[82]

In addition to credit transactions on account, Hollingsworth also clarified the payments of interest on "notes" to such Chinese merchants as Consequa, Eshing, Washing, and Namshing, indicating the existence of a credit instrument: the promissory note. Representing a promise to pay on a future date, the note usually clarifies the maker, payee, amount, duration, and interest rate of the credit.[83] As the earliest form of the three credit instruments, promissory notes were in use in many societies, although some scholars believe that Marco Polo's acclaim for Chinese paper money inspired European goldsmiths to issue promissory notes in exchange for deposits.[84]

Hong merchants had written notes to British and Dutch East India companies or accepted those from the French to sustain their credit relationships in the eighteenth century.[85] As communications and trust grew, Americans also employed promissory notes to trade with the Chinese in Canton. As figure 7 shows, on December 29, 1803, Richard J. Cleveland and William Shaler wrote a note promising to return to Consequa $7,900 in twelve months, and if not, pay interest at a monthly rate of 1 percent. The English and Chinese inscriptions on the back of the note indicate that Carrington paid 8,278.04 Carolus dollars (*fomian yin* [Buddha Head silver]) for them to Consequa's Liquan Hong in 1805.[86] While the note executed by Cleveland and Shaler expired in twelve months, the term of the credit could be longer than a year. For instance, when Willings and Francis purchased tea from Consequa in 1805, Read paid the Hongist $10,967.38 in "notes at fifteen and eighteen months."[87] Consequa extended another $20,072.22 on a single day to finance Read's tea purchases, all in fifteen-month or eighteen-month promissory notes.[88]

Consisting of credit transactions and credit instruments, a credit network thus formed in the late eighteenth century to bolster the U.S.-China tea trade. Even if lacking suitable goods or adequate silver in hand, American supercargoes or agents in Canton settled their tea transactions with the Chinese on account. Chinese merchants usually cleared account balances and outstanding debts on the eve of the Chinese New Year, which is usually around February on the solar calendar.[89] Americans in Canton also wrote promissory notes as proof of debts. Their principals at home then remitted specie to Canton to pay interest and liquidate their obligations to Chinese tea sellers before or after the expiration dates of the notes.[90] After acquiring a full cargo in Canton, U.S. ships took their tea to America or Europe, where, most often, the owners sold them on credit for three, six, and nine months.[91] With the proceeds in cash or on account, these Americans loaded their ships with goods suitable to the China market, such as ginseng, furs, opium, and quicksilver, and started a new voyage bound for Canton. In this way, credit transactions and instruments bridged the time gap between commercial (the transfer of goods) and monetary (the transfer of silver) transactions, setting in motion a commercial and financial cycle in the transnational tea trade. Moreover, the long credit, which was effective

Canton 29th Dec 1803 For value received we promise to pay in twelve months from the date hereof to Mr. Consequa or order the sum of Seven thousand nine hundred dollars, & if not paid in that time, then commences an interest of one per Cent p month to continue till paid.

$7900

Richard J. Cleveland

W. Shaler

Fig. 7. William Shaler and Richard J. Cleveland's promissory note to Consequa, 1803. This note reads "Canton 29th Dec. 1803 For value received we promise to pay in twelve months from the date hereof to Mr. Consequa or order the sum of Seven thousand nine hundred dollars, & if not paid in that time, then commences an interest of one per cent p. month to continue till paid. Richard J. Cleveland & Wm. Shaler." The Chinese characters on the back acknowledged this credit relationship and confirmed Carrington's repayment of the debt. "Miscellaneous Business, 1795–1829," box 3, WSP, Collection of the Historical Society of Pennsylvania.

for a year or even longer, provided Americans with considerable time to sell tea, earn profits, and gather silver to clear their account balances.

Sources from the late nineteenth century remembered the credit system of China's foreign tea trade as an important legacy of the Canton Trade era. Writing often from the English perspective, the *North China Herald* asserted that during the early nineteenth century, "the Hong merchants impoverished themselves by giving long credit to American merchants, who

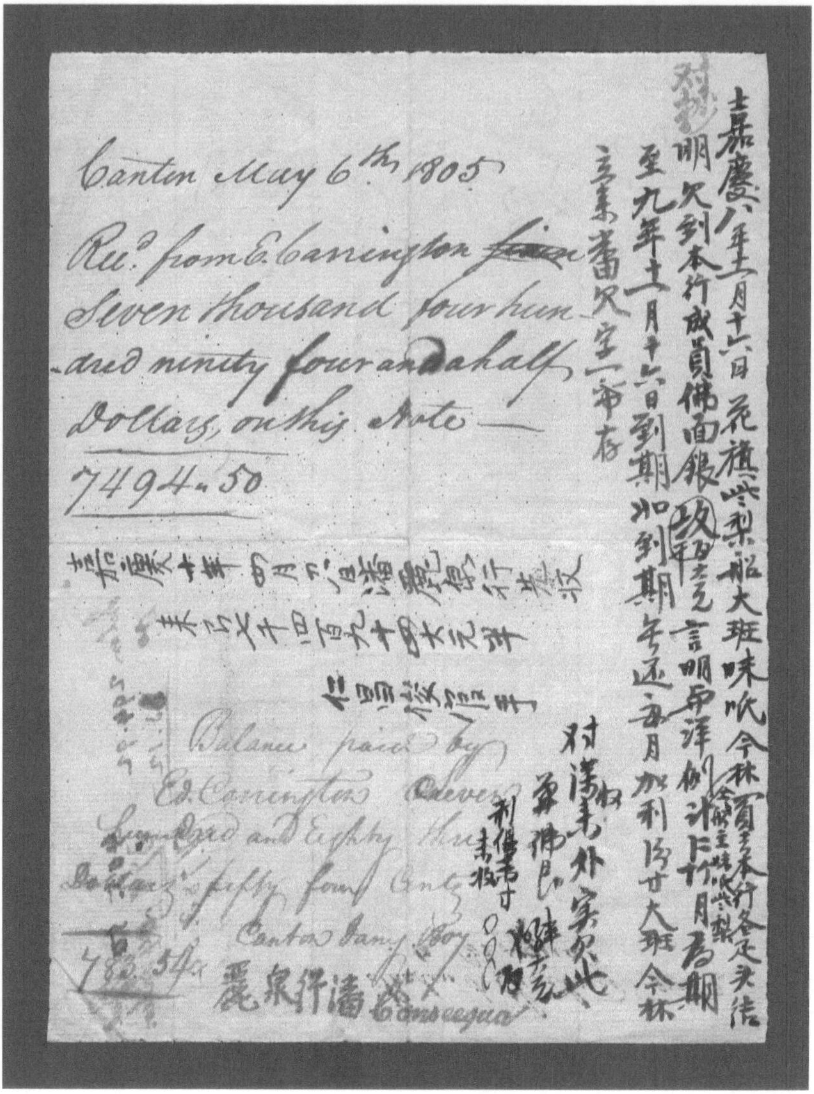
Canton May 6th 1805

Recd. from E. Carrington
Seven thousand four hun-
dred ninety four and a half
Dollars, on this Note —
7494.50

Balance paid by
Ed. Carrington

were thereby induced to overstock the New York market."[92] The long-term credit practiced in Canton piloted the credit system in other trading ports after the Opium War. "Long credit has been more or less a characteristic of the trade since the opening of the port," the *North China Herald* commented on the tea trade in Shanghai, "and was introduced by the first Cantonese teamen who established themselves there."[93] This newspaper article also characterized the long-term, high-value credit offered by the Chinese as the "peculiar principles" in Fuzhou, another major tea port in the latter half of the century. Maintaining running accounts with Chinese teamen, some buyers waited for weeks or even months to deliver payments. The customary practice was to make a nominal settlement once a year. All the practices resembled "the Canton way."[94]

CONSIGNMENT SALES

While expecting American tea buyers in Canton, the Chinese also shipped tea directly to the United States for sale, aided by another two credit transactions: consignments and respondentia. In opposition to the advance system, in which the buyer paid the seller before obtaining goods, consignments and respondentia allowed the delivery of commodities before the receipt of full payment. Consignments dominated the eighteenth- and nineteenth-century international trade in Asia, Europe, and America until the widespread use of electric telegraph communications enabled faster business transactions.[95] American, British, and Chinese merchants often consigned such commodities as tea, cotton goods, opium, and silk to their foreign counterparts and retained the ownership of the goods until their consignees paid them back in full—either with silver or credit instruments.[96] To secure transactions and minimize risks, consignees usually advanced two-thirds or three-quarters of the goods' value, with payments made by writing promissory notes or drawing bills of exchange against the shipment.[97] Consignment arrangements helped consignees without ready cash and benefited consignors expecting financial returns from high rates of compound interest on the undelivered net proceeds. The credit extended through consignments lasted longer than "respondentia," also known as "bottomry," which was a form of mortgage loan that covered the vessel's cost at sea. When their cargoes reached the destination, the prime amounts and interest came due within specific periods. In the case of lost ships, the loans were canceled.[98] Through bottomry contracts, Hong merchants had extended interest-bearing loans to finance Europeans' voyages in the eighteenth century.[99]

During the nineteenth century, through consignment arrangements and respondentia, along with promissory notes generated in the process, the credit network in Canton extended to America. From 1805 to 1818, Consequa consigned Chinese goods, primarily teas, valued at $160,000, to New York merchants Edmund Fanning, Henry Fanning, and Willet

Coles. Consequa never received payments in specie from the United States but rather accepted promissory notes maturing in twelve or fifteen months with compound interest at the rate of 12 percent per annum after the expiration dates. In 1810 these New York merchants were unable to pay the seven-month interest, valued at $2,910.64, on one promissory note, so they wrote another for this amount, promising to pay interest when it came due one year later.[100] In addition to the Hong merchant, Kinglun—a shopman outside the Cohong—consigned tea to King and Talbot in New York. Possibly anticipating the difficulty of making remittance during the Embargo of 1807–9, Kinglun transferred the New York tea proceeds to Carrington's credit. This arrangement likely allowed Kinglun to receive the payment through this American consul in Canton or to settle outstanding debts with Carrington.[101] In addition to consignments, the enormous "system of Respondentia shipments" employed by the Cohong—"the unfettered capitalist"—even alerted Waln Jr. during the 1810s, because "the Capital of the Hong is put in competition with the limited means of private American merchants." "While shipments to an immense amount are annually made by members of the Hong, cover'd [covered] by the names of their friends," respondentia had morphed into "a system that is overflowing the markets East of Philadelphia" and supplied the city with "a Chinese Capital that is undermining our whole commerce with China," Waln warned, suggesting the robustness and expansiveness of the transpacific credit network.[102]

Despite the convenience of the credit economy, the volatile international market easily altered the profitability of an assignment and thus hindered individual merchants' capability of repaying the credit. Failure to remit the proceeds back to consignors incurred interest. The accumulation of compound interest on undelivered proceeds was especially devastating to consignees, Chinese and Americans alike. Consequently, Chinese merchants amassed excessive debts owing to consignments. A 1784 memorial submitted by Chinese officials to Emperor Qianlong blamed the first wave of Hong merchants' bankruptcy in 1779–80 on consignment sales, claiming that some European consignors deliberately delayed their trips to collect the proceeds and charged high compound interest on unremitted amounts held by Hong merchants.[103] Qing officials' understanding should be considered biased, for the first dissolution of the Cohong in 1771 weakened Hong merchants' bargaining power, destabilized the market, and led to the debt crisis of 1779–80.[104] However, their explanation revealed the risk buried in this credit transaction. Likewise the Americans Fannings and Coles were also deeply in debt to Consequa owing to the compound interest incurred by tea consignments. All the original and derivative promissory notes of Fannings and Coles to Consequa remained unpaid when Consequa sued them in New York Chancery Court in 1818, by which time the face value of the notes totaled $82,399.58, but their terminal value amounted to $174,353.94. In other words, the interest generated by these notes, which approximated $91,954.36, exceeded their prime amount.[105]

Fannings and Coles blamed the Embargo of 1807–9 for their failure in remitting the proceeds and the high rate of compound interest for their financial embarrassment. Claiming that the interest rate was supposed to be 10 percent instead of 12 percent, Fannings and Coles protested the rate as "the tyranny and oppression of Consequa, and the other Hong merchants, at Canton."[106] However, they never mentioned that Willings and Francis entrusted their opium to Consequa and charged "the customary interest" of 15 to 20 percent on the proceeds that remained with Consequa in 1805.[107] James Kent, chancellor of the New York Court of Chancery, refuted Fannings and Coles's claims, because the rate was "nothing more than the practice of all those merchants who make annual rests in their accounts" and he trusted Consequa's "frank and manly character."[108] Yet Fannings and Coles's grumbles were unsurprising, given the weight of the mounting debt. Even though Chinese and American merchants had reached an agreement that only "one half interest should be paid on debts detained in America by the Embargo" of 1807–9, the burden generated by the compound interest remained financially damaging to the Philadelphian firm.[109]

Despite the risk, consignment sales generated massive credit for the transpacific tea trade, because Consequa also extended credit through consignments to merchants elsewhere in the United States from as late as 1793, when he was still an outside trader. Grant's investigation of Consequa's litigation showed that the face value of his promissory notes against Philadelphia and Boston merchants, mostly produced by the sale and consignment of tea, amounted to $632,952.58 in 1817, or $23.8 billion in 2024, without taking into account the interest within and after the expiration dates (see table 2).[110] Grant clarified that these numbers were drawn only from disputed debts in the *Records of the Circuit Court for the District of Pennsylvania* and individual merchants' business records. Considering the undisputed and unrecorded credit transactions and instruments between Consequa and his American counterparts, the total amount of the commercial credit extended by this Hongist in the transpacific tea trade should be much larger.

Table 2. An incomplete tabulation of Consequa's loans to Americans, 1793–1817

YEAR	NOTES MADE AND CONSIGNMENT SHIPMENTS	PAYMENTS RECEIVED ON NOTES OTHERWISE NOT KNOWN
1793	$43,821.00	
1798	3,410.50	
1800	33,142.33	
1801	30,827.50	
1803	20,000.00	
1804	12,189.00	
1805	43,680.89	$5,420.18
1806	138,976.56	39,206.00
1807	50,724.63	
1808	1,365.00	
1809	89,690.63	
1810	71,198.86	8,688.00
1811	35,711.50	
1817	4,900.00	
Total	$579,638.40	$53,314.18

Source: Grant, "Failure of the Li-ch'uan Hong," 259.

THE NEGOTIABILITY OF PROMISSORY NOTES

The derivative function of credit instruments also expanded the credit economy between China and the United States. Consequa's promissory notes could be transferred to a third party and employed as a means of remittance and settlement, further enhancing Americans' purchasing power and the tea trade's credit network. Indeed the promissory note is a negotiable instrument. Negotiability refers to the transferability of the instrument from one person to another with or without endorsement. This quality allows credit instruments to circulate like currency until they are cashed.[111] Currency assumes four primary functions: the means of payment, medium of exchange (including the settlement of debt), unit of account, and store of value.[112] While precious metals and commodities, due to their intrinsic value, serve all four purposes, credit instruments usually act as the means of payment and media of exchange. Merchants who used credit instruments as a store of value in the China trade often lost heavily during economic crises (also see chapters 2 and 5). Despite financial risks, through transference to different holders, negotiability allows credit instruments to perform the monetary functions beyond the original credit relationships and, therefore, lubricate cash-scarce economies.

Hence the negotiability of credit instruments enabled Americans to remit Consequa's notes to China as cash or even in preference to dollars. Consequa had written promissory notes in favor of John Innes Clark, a Rhode Island merchant, likely to cover the value of Clark's consignments to him. In 1806, Rhode Island and New York merchants used these notes to liquidate their obligations to Chinese and American traders in Canton. The silver scarcity, the wars in Europe, the difficulty of getting insurance for specie, the economic stagnation in the United States, and Consequa's large tea business all boosted the popularity of this new means of remittance. The New York firm of Minturn and Champlin, for example, purchased Consequa's notes at ten days sight in favor of Clark, valued at $25,000, meaning the notes were payable after ten business days.[113] They then endorsed, or sold, the notes to Mr. Dexter, supercargo of the ship *Projector*, to liquidate part of Dexter's obligation to Consequa. Another New York house, King and Talbot, endorsed such a note to Carrington in Canton as a loan, totaling $5,800 at sixty days' sight. Having approximately two months to arrange a payment, King and Talbot sent the note "in preference to Dollars."[114] In June 1806, with the tea market very dull and dollars scarce, Shaler advised Mr. Arden, one of Carrington's commercial partners in the United States, to take Consequa's notes endorsed by Clark. Shaler deemed them "as good as cash and they greatly facilitate the promptitude of [Carrington's] remittances: dollars could not have been procured to go by me."[115] Remitting these paper devices, instead of specie, gave American and Chinese merchants an easy means to facilitate transactions and more time to arrange payments, thus again manifesting the convenience and importance of the credit economy for the transpacific tea trade.

The adoption of this negotiable instrument in the China trade was not confined to these New Yorkers and Rhode Islanders. It was not uncommon for foreign merchants to purchase Chinese promissory notes in Canton for commercial or financial uses, hinting at the existence of a credit market. In 1809, when Willings and Francis found that Consequa had erroneously drawn on them over $20,000 notes against their agent, Read, they asked George W. Biddle, a supercargo in Canton, to "appear as purchasers of these notes," thus expecting to settle the debt without revealing their identity.[116] During the War of 1812, Waln received from George Blight, his agent in Canton, a set of Chinese notes against several Americans (see table 3). These Chinese merchants—Consequa, Cheonqua, Exchin, and Kingqua—had probably either been settling their transactions with Blight or, without any hope of receiving remittance from their U.S. counterparts during the war, sold him the notes at discount. Waln insisted that it would be advantageous for these indebted Americans to liquidate the notes in the United States rather than Canton after the war, given the amount of interest and the expense of remittance.[117] For example, Waln charged $19,375.72, at sixty days, on Carrington's $14,977 notes to Kingqua (dated March 20, 1810, a fifteen-month loan) and Exchin (dated July 24, 1810, a fourteen-month loan), a sum that was lower than the terminal value if settled at Canton in the future.[118] Thus the credit between Chinese and American merchants was transformed into a type of domestic debt relation that enriched monetary assets in the United States. Such credit relations could be even more transnational. On March 19, 1812, for example, Waln used four English bills of exchange to repay his £3,200 note to Consequa.[119] These transactions reveal an established credit network linking Philadelphia, New York, England, and Canton, where Chinese notes, English bills, and the U.S.-China trade connected the Atlantic and Pacific financial markets in the early nineteenth century.

Chinese Commercial Credits in the United States

The U.S.-China tea trade continued to expand during the first decade of the nineteenth century, but Consequa grew reluctant to extend credit to his U.S. counterparts. Some Americans' delay in liquidating account balances forced Consequa to seek "more speedy recovery of" his massive credit

Table 3. Chinese notes and English bills passed from George Blight to Robert Waln, 1813

DATE OF THE NOTE	PAYER	ORIGIN	CREDITOR	AMOUNT	TERM OF THE CREDIT
1/12/1810	John Field Jr.	Philadelphia	Cheonqua	$5,389.60 with interest ($6,400 paid)	12 mos.
1/12/1810	John Field Jr.	Philadelphia	Cheonqua	$2,400 with interest	18 mos.
1/29/1810	Stephen Dexter	Providence	Consequa	$19,166.05/100 with interest ($5,559 paid)	2 mos.
3/20/1810	Edward Carrington	Providence	Kingqua	$6,977	15 mos.
7/24/1810	Edward Carrington	Providence	Exchin	$8,000	14 mos.
1/2/1811	Samuel Moore	Philadelphia	Kingqua	$580 with interest	Unmentioned
1/7/1811	William H. Smith	Philadelphia	Kingqua	$6,006.33/100 with interest	Unmentioned
2/12/1812	Thomas Bryant	Philadelphia	Kingqua	$1,185	Unmentioned
10/8/1812	Minturn & Champlin	New York	Consequa	£3,875 (payable in London)	6 mos.

Source: Robert Waln to John Field Jr., Robert Waln to Stephen Dexter, Robert Waln to Edward Carrington, Robert Waln to William H. Smith, Robert Waln to Samuel Moore, Robert Waln to Thomas Bryant, Robert Waln to Minturn & Champlin, March 8, 1813, Robert Waln Letterbooks 1808–1814, vol. 19, WFP, Collection of the Historical Society of Pennsylvania.

in America. With Carrington and John Wharton as witnesses, the Hong merchant appointed his "Friend Edward Hallowell of the City of Philadelphia" as his lawful attorney.[120] In April 1804, Hallowell started suing in U.S. courts to redeem Consequa's notes, usually without success, particularly during the Depression of 1807 and the Embargo of 1807–9, when U.S. merchants had either gone bankrupt or countersued Consequa for poor-quality teas.[121] The Philadelphia firm Edward Dunant and Joshua and Thomas Gilpin, for example, had received a cargo of tea in August 1806 and stored an unsold portion until March 1807, when they shipped it to Amsterdam for auction in August 1807. Since this tea failed to command prices in Amsterdam as high as others of the same kind, and in response to Consequa's debt collection, Dunant and the Gilpins countersued in 1808, attributing their economic losses in the Netherlands to the poor quality of Consequa's tea, notwithstanding that their supercargo had been satisfied with the teas when he purchased them in Canton three years previously. The quality of the portion sold in Philadelphia was uncontested, so the court focused on whether an auction sale furnished a just criterion of value, and on whether storage in Philadelphia and sea transit to the Netherlands had deteriorated the tea before it reached Amsterdam. The jury, however, found for Dunant and the Gilpins and awarded them $5,556.[122] Willings and Francis also started a suit regarding the poor quality of Consequa's teas, even though their agent, Read, had assessed the teas himself in 1805.[123] Read thought himself "a tolerable judge of teas" when buying the disputed cargo, but he admitted to his reluctance to continue assessing tea after engaging more in this business.[124] The jury verdict, nevertheless, awarded $60,134 in compensation to Willings and Francis, although by 1816 they still owed Consequa $71,183.57.[125]

Consequa was likely to be responsible for some teas' quality, since Dorr described him as a person "adept at mixing teas," who had $60,000 worth of tea returned by the EIC in 1798.[126] Nonetheless, against the backdrop of a sluggish economy, some U.S. merchants exploited Hong merchants' guarantee of tea quality, which remained valid even after overseas sales, to escape their debts. As Consequa observed, when trade was flourishing, his U.S. trading partners followed the rules. "Of late years, however," Consequa noted in 1814, he had "been able to obtain returns in a very trifling proportion to the extent of the Capital" confided to American traders. "Some resi[s]t payment of their Debt(s) contending inferior quality of the Goods," but Consequa insisted that he "always admitted and desired inspection of his Goods before purchase, and his Debtors being professed Merchants in the articles, ought to have possessed, and exercised due skill, and knowledge respecting them."[127] Similar claims by U.S. merchants against other Chinese tea merchants also emerged during the period. In May 1809, for example, Nixon and Walker, a Philadelphia firm, instructed Biddle, the supercargo in Canton, to liquidate a note to Youqua, but they refused to pay the interest. "We do not take interest into consideration as we were prevented by the Embargo from sending him his balance had any been due to him." Nixon and Walker further asserted, "In truth had the Embargo not enabled us to dispose of the Tea, the abatement [owing to the inferior tea] which in that case we should have claimed would itself have cancelled the Bond."[128] Even the reputable Howqua faced similar accusations when he sued some debtors in U.S. courts during the 1810s–20s.[129]

Regardless of the truth or falsity of these claims, the disputes suggested that Chinese merchants pumped considerable monetary resources into the U.S. economy through the tea trade, at least in the North. The Chinese had extended a large amount of credit to their American commercial partners by 1795. In that year, an American named John Howel reported on the default by Thomas Handasyd Perkins and other Boston merchants on Consequa's notes, insisting that it was "absolutely necessary some steps should be taken to retrieve the character [i.e., reputation] of the Americans here. Such villa[i]nies," Howel continued, "have been practised as have sickened the Chinese from having any dealing with them on that liberal scale they would otherwise adopt."[130] The credit relationship and disputes nonetheless continued into the nineteenth century. Although the greatest number of Consequa's debtors were in Philadelphia, he employed an attorney named Sullivan to collect debts in Boston and John Jacob Astor to pursue debtors elsewhere, such as the Rhode Islanders Dr. Whitney and Samuel Snow.[131] Consequa aside, the first two decades of the nineteenth century saw numerous similar lawsuits or disputes concerning the promissory notes written by Americans in favor of Chinese merchants to purchase tea at Canton. Chinese litigants and creditors included the Hong merchants Chunqua, Exchin (Loqua), Howqua, Pacqua, and Yougua, as well as the outside shopmen Cowqua, Eshing, Keetshing, Kingling, Namshing, Syngchong, and Thonching.[132]

Other notes no doubt went unrecorded or undisputed, although how many and for how much cannot be determined. Considering the significance of the Chinese creditors, John P. Cushing, Boston merchant, repeatedly reminded Carrington of paying off his debt to such Chinese merchants as Fouchong, Namshing, Chuqua, Washing, and especially Howqua, after he left China in 1811. "We judged it most for your interest to pay the note to Houqua [Howqua] in preference to those in the hands of Englishmen," Cushing noted in 1812, "as it will make a favourable impression on him," which would prove an advantage "in case you should want any future accommodation."[133]

It is unclear how much of the unpaid debt American merchants eventually settled, but Consequa's tragic ending stands clear. Tired of tedious litigation and sometimes prejudiced court decisions, Consequa petitioned President James Madison personally, lamenting some U.S. traders' unreliability and doubtful credibility at a time of economic difficulties. "If my losses were no greater than what I could well bear, I would," put up with them, and "not complain."[134] Here Consequa might have mimicked the tactics of foreign merchants in China, who, as a last resort, asked the Qing emperor to resolve their financial disputes with Hong merchants. However, in all likelihood Madison never read his petition.[135] The nonpayment destroyed Consequa, who was subject to corporal punishment under Chinese laws that offered limited protection but penalized Hong merchants for indebtedness.[136] Moreover, while Consequa had consigned $50,000 in goods and extended a loan of almost $40,000 in 1809, he was deeply in debt to the EIC.[137] Consequently, the financial difficulties shrank Consequa's business with Americans. As Edward Gray, a Philadelphia merchant, wrote to Chunqua in 1809, "Conseequa will have no more business with this place. You and Houqua [Howqua] will do all."[138] Consequa, facing the imperfect enforcement of international contracts, could only "as usual [growl] at the Americans to whom he attributes all his embarrassments."[139]

Consequa informed President Madison that some American merchants had used his credit as capital in "other Branches of Commercial Speculation, in which they have been unsuccessfull," and that explained why they were "utterly unable to pay" him.[140] The Chinese merchant never clarified which commercial activities his U.S. counterparts participated in, but historical records reveal that the early traders disbursed the profits and credit accumulated in the China trade in three main ways.[141] First, they rechanneled the resources into their international trade or related economic sectors, such as financial institutions and shipbuilding. For example, by carrying Chinese tea to the Netherlands, Carrington had obtained not only handsome profits but also approximately $125,000 in credit from the Dutch company Daniel Crommlin and Sons by 1809. Equal to over $5.25 billion in 2024 in terms of the share of GDP, Carrington amassed a considerable fortune for himself and his trading partners within four years.[142] Somewhat later, Carrington returned to Providence from Canton in 1811 and invested in mercantile trading to China, South America, and Europe.[143] With the profits from the China trade and the slave trade, John Brown, along with other merchants in Providence, founded the Providence Bank in the early 1790s.[144] The Bostonian Perkins also laid the foundation of his fortunes in the voyage to Canton in 1789, which enabled him to establish a commission house there while securing his position as a leading merchant in Boston.[145] The Philadelphian China trader Stephen Girard used his wealth to subscribe a substantial amount of money for the Second Bank of the United States in 1816.[146] In 1787 Shaw sent "home a small property, taken up on credit from the Chinese, as part of the funds for building a large ship, in or near Boston."[147] Philadelphia's shipbuilding industry also expanded in response to the needs of the China trade, particularly for tea clippers.[148] Second, U.S. merchants ventured their resources in unrelated enterprises, such as land speculation, canals, and manufacturing. In 1795 Brown owned 210,000 acres of land in the Adirondacks in New York state,[149] and Carrington invested in the Blackstone Canal in the 1820s, as well as in several textile mills.[150] Additionally, other merchants bequeathed money to public institutions, thus transforming their commercial capital into social capital. Girard's endowment helped found a nonsectarian school for orphans, pave the Philadelphia streets, and improve canal navigation in Pennsylvania. John Cleve Green, a New Jersey China trader, was a notable benefactor of Princeton University, Princeton Theological Seminary, and many New York charities.[151]

Therefore trade with China, including tea, offered a promising avenue for ambitious young men of modest means. As historians Downs and Fichter argued, the China trade garnered considerable capital for the early U.S. economy, reoriented the economic development of New England and the mid-Atlantic states, and produced a class of gentlemen on the East Coast by the 1830s, the entry level of which was generally $100,000. The average time for China traders to amass the fortune was seven to twelve years, and some did so in less than five years.[152] Thus, when reviewing the China trade a century later, Tyler Dennett concluded that its importance "is to be gauged not so much by the net trade returns for each year as by the fact that it offered a means for the accumulation in a few years of a large amount of capital of which the rapidly growing states were in urgent need."[153] Sydney Greenbie and Marjorie Barstow Greenbie also asserted in their 1925 book that "the trade with the Orient is one of the two great economic facts of the history of the United States between the Revolution and the Civil War," the other being westward expansion.[154]

When the War of 1812 ended, Americans entered a new era in the China trade, but Consequa paid the price for his reckless decisions in the credit economy. Individual resident agents, like Shaw and Read, gave way to established commission houses, such as Russell and Company.[155] Many of Consequa's U.S. commercial partners overcame the trials during the economic depression of 1807, the Embargo of 1807–9, and the War of 1812. However, the Hong merchant went bankrupt in 1821 and died two years later, still owing $200,000 to his foreign counterparts. Similar to Consequa's petition to Madison, a party of foreign claimants gathered at the city gate of Canton in 1824 to ask the Qing government for payment. Consequently, the Cohong members promised to settle Consequa's debts in three years.[156] The leading Hong merchant, Howqua, dominated the business with Americans and grew legendary for his credit. Even after Howqua's death in 1843, the Forbes family in Boston continued to invest his wealth in America, including railroad stocks and U.S. public debt, into the 1870s.[157]

The early Sino-American tea trade had faced problems of fluctuant commodity markets in China, the difficulty of procuring and remitting specie from America, and the absence of protection for Hong merchants' credit to foreign merchants, yet this era was also the formative stage of the transpacific credit system. Relying on commodities and silver, Americans were initially disadvantaged in the global tea trade, given that Europeans, and especially the EIC, employed the credit transaction—the advance system—to control tea's supply even before the market was open to Americans. However, at least from the 1790s, Chinese tea merchants extended long-term credit to their

American counterparts. Such credit transactions as bookkeeping, consignments, and respondentia facilitated the tea trade between the United States and China, even when Americans were short of funds. As a proof of debt and a means of remittance, the credit instrument—promissory notes—recorded and undergirded these credit transactions. The notes' negotiability also generated a credit market in Canton and extended credit relations in China to America and even the Atlantic world. Thereafter the transpacific credit network, anchored in credit transactions and credit instruments, bumped new lines of credit to the money-scarce U.S. republic, intertwined the two economies with global financial markets, and conditioned the rise and fall of transpacific commerce in subsequent decades of the nineteenth century.

2

White Gold and Black Gold

WEAVING A GLOBAL NETWORK, 1815–42

After the War of 1812, the leading Hong merchant, Wu Bingjian, better known as Howqua, dominated trade with Americans. While it is unclear whether the litigation brought by Consequa and other Chinese jeopardized Americans' chances in obtaining credit, Howqua reinforced the transpacific credit economy by extending even more credit to his U.S. commercial partners. Paul S. Forbes, head of Russell and Company and the U.S. consul in Canton, noted that Howqua's "unbounded Confidence in Americans has never been equalled," as this Chinese merchant entrusted "to those with whom he had no ties of country, language, or Religion between 2 and 3 millions of Dollars at one time."[1] Howqua grew legendary among Americans for his generosity.[2] In addition to the well-known anecdote that Howqua destroyed a $100,000 promissory note that Benjamin C. Wilcocks owed to him, he exempted the interest on John Murray Forbes's notes, relinquished Bryant and Sturgis's $30,000 debt, and charged zero interest for three years on a $5,000 loan to Peter Snow after already putting $80,000 on Snow's account. He urged his debt collectors in America "by no means to insist on the payment if it should appear that [John L. Bowers] is destitute or that his means are slender."[3] Furthermore, Howqua promised to lend Russell and Company, the largest U.S. commission house in China, "any amo. [amount] [they] may require" in 1833.[4] The Hong merchant and his family likely maintained this practice for years. After losing a critical source of financial resources, Edward Cunningham, a leading partner of the company, deplored in 1861 that "the only real difficulty was the want of money . . . times having changed since we could depend on Houqua for a floating balance of 2 or 300,000 and an extra 200,000 in case of great need."[5] "Charitable, benevolent and just," the *Times* said in a commemoration of Howqua after his passing in 1843.[6]

However, the eulogies failed to mention that some Americans referred to Howqua as "the timid young lady," one of the most derogatory terms to describe a man.[7] Indeed, unlike the manly and reckless Consequa, who was "very lavish of promises" and extended "very liberal credit," Howqua made judicious loans and insisted on punctual repayments.[8] Samuel Russell and Company reported to Carrington that they "could undoubtedly purchase of Mr. Houqua, and obtain as long credits as Mr. C[onsequa] used to do for you," but they could not "buy of [Howqua] on so favourable terms."[9] Even James P. Sturgis, Howqua's close commercial partner, failed to obtain an additional loan from the Hongist, owing to Sturgis's credit history.[10] "We always considered the old debt of yours to Houqua as standing very much in the way of any new loan from him," Robert Bennet Forbes reminded Sturgis. "We had good reason so to consider it, for the old man often alluded to it."[11] Indeed, generosity alone was inadequate to make a successful merchant. Howqua's readily available credit was in no way an easily accessible source of capital.

Nor were Americans merely passive participants in international trade finance. Employing another credit instrument—the bill of exchange—to facilitate the U.S.-China tea trade, Americans not only increased their independence in the credit economy and enhanced their purchasing power of tea, but also played a pivotal role in two monumental historical events: the Panic of 1837 and the Anglo-Chinese Opium War. While the EIC had issued bills of exchange in China when Americans entered the Canton trade, U.S. merchants introduced new sterling bills, generated in the transatlantic cotton trade or issued by the Bank of the United States, during the War of 1812. Having become Americans' chief means of tea purchase by the late 1820s, this paper device maintained its central role in trade finance for subsequent decades, declining only when telegraphic fund transfers rendered this financial mechanism clumsy at the dawn of the twentieth century. When Americans were able to sell millions of dollars' worth of bills to British-Indian opium smugglers in Asia, their silver shipments to Canton declined by 50 to 80 percent during 1820–40. While U.S. merchants had been the chief supplier of silver to China and the second-largest importer of Chinese tea, their new ways of trade finance exhausted China's silver reservoir and, meanwhile, further increased the U.S. specie stock and inflated its economy by the mid-1830s. A decade later, streams of changes in the commercial and credit markets, along with other torrents, accumulated into economic and political floods—the Panic of 1837 and the Opium War of 1839—that swallowed the Pacific and Atlantic worlds. Focusing on the credit economy of the U.S.-China tea trade, this chapter reveals the much less-known but equally critical factor that escalated these economic and political tensions on both sides of the Pacific Ocean.

The existing literature mostly treats these economic and political crises in the United States and China during the 1830s as separate incidents. The Panic of 1837 was America's first financial crisis to feature massive bank and business failures, in this case into the early 1840s.[12] Americanists describe the panic as a transatlantic economic depression, caused by land speculation in the American West, a bank war launched by President Andrew Jackson, or British credit that overheated the U.S. economy.[13] Roughly around the same time, the Qing empire faced a monetary crisis during the so-called Daoguang Depression (1820–50). This economic downturn was characterized by acute silver scarcity.[14] Silver scholars have analyzed the economic crisis by meticulously calculating China's silver reserves based on international trade statistics, global silver flows from Spanish America, or domestic demand for specie.[15] The silver question was also closely tied to the historiography of the Opium War. To purchase Chinese tea without depleting the British stock of silver, the EIC licensed private merchants to smuggle opium into Canton and successfully reversed England's trade imbalance with China. Scholars also portrayed opium as the only specie substitute for Americans in Canton.[16] However, the opium trade caused dramatic silver outflow from China. Plagued by the drug smuggled by British and U.S. traders, the Qing government launched anti-opium campaigns but only triggered the Anglo-Chinese Opium War.[17]

While Peter Temin identified Americans' adoption of bills in the China trade as a contributing factor in both the Panic of 1837 and the Opium War, this chapter elaborates on the credit creation process to illuminate the connection between the U.S.-China tea trade and the transpacific crises.[18] The first section focuses on the changing power dynamics of the international tea trade after the War of 1812. While the influence of continental European companies waned during the war, the EIC consolidated its monopoly over China's tea trade in Canton. Tea also dominated U.S-China commercial relations during this period. Taking advantage of tensions between British and Chinese traders, Americans tried the advance system and forged strong bonds with the senior Hong merchant, Howqua, thus enhancing their competitiveness in the tea market. The second section focuses on the credit system of the tea trade. After the War of 1812, Americans challenged British control over the exchange market by bringing private bills of exchange to China. The new bills not only funded the transpacific tea trade but also created tight connections between the Pacific, Atlantic, and Indian financial systems. Using and trading bills of exchange locally and internationally, Chinese merchants became a crucial nexus in the global credit networks. Furthermore, their tea trade shaped the fluctuations of exchange rates in China throughout the nineteenth century. The last section examines the consequences of the expanding credit system of the tea trade buttressed by bills of exchange. After the adoption of this paper device, Americans reduced their silver shipments to Canton dramatically, which fueled inflation in the U.S. economy but aggravated the silver drain in China. The eruption of the Panic of 1837 and the Opium War revealed not China's isolation under the Canton Trade System but the interconnectedness of the Pacific, Indian, and Atlantic credit networks before the Opium War.[19]

For All the Tea in China

Tea started to dominate U.S.-China trade after the War of 1812, while the power imbalance between American, Chinese, and British tea merchants persisted. The United States consistently ranked as the second-largest importer of tea from China.[20] Moreover, tea's share in total U.S. imports grew significantly, from approximately 38 percent during 1818–19 and over 40 percent during the 1820s to 47–78 percent during the 1830s and over 80 percent in 1840–41 (see figure 2).[21] It remained challenging, however, for Americans to procure high-grade Chinese teas, due to the Cohong's monopoly of the supply and British competition in the market. Deeply engaged in the unpredictable international trade, most of the wealthy Hongists chose to trade exclusively with the EIC, while small Hongs and outside merchants traded with the American upstarts.[22] The advance system granted British traders a competitive edge in acquiring fine teas. Consequently, even though U.S. tea imports grew significantly, the EIC had maintained its control over 70 to 80 percent of China's tea exports since the last decade of the eighteenth century.[23] When British tea shipments from Canton reached more than 34 million pounds in 1833, those to the United States totaled merely over 14 million pounds, or less than half of the British imports.[24]

The company's voracious appetite for teas often brought the tea ventures of other buyers—Americans and Europeans alike—to a halt. This happened not long after the War of 1812, particularly the seasons of 1819–21, when the supply of new teas from the interior was limited.[25] Girard, the Philadelphia merchant who saved the U.S. government from bankruptcy during the War of 1812, failed to obtain tea in Canton, because Howqua "cou'd [could] not give them teas which he considers prime" after the EIC had made selections, even though Girard depended "entirely on his friendship for the quality of the teas which will be shipped."[26] The competition also escalated in open-market purchases. Dorr already lamented in 1799 that the price of the teas he wanted to purchase would be lower "if the English fleet don't arrive [at] all."[27] The competitive pressure remained unabated in the 1820s. Carrington's ship *George* and the brig *Washington* owned by Benjamin Shreve of Salem, Massachusetts, left China in 1820 only with black teas no more than the middling quality, "as the Compy [company] had the choice of all the teas in the market before any of said cargoes were purchased."[28] Americans' tea shipments to Europe also suffered. "We think it very doubtful if there will be any further expeditions either for Europe or the U. States," Cushing reported to John Berenberg Gossler and Company, the famed merchant bank in Hamburg, Germany, "as the English Company have cleared the market of all the teas that they considered possible." Cushing also noticed that "the agent of the *Montesquieu*, the last ship for Holland, had great difficulty to obtain a decent cargo."[29] Tea's scarcity continued into 1821. The EIC took all the teas, including those they rejected the previous season, at prices 30 to 40 percent higher than the previous year. Consequently, in January 1821, several months before the closing of the tea season, American and Dutch merchants were unable to "procure teas eno' [enough] to load the ships which are expected."[30] The competition in China's tea market contributed, at least partially, to the plummet in U.S. tea imports in 1820–21 (see figure 8).[31]

The situation by no means improved after the expiration of the EIC's monopoly over the China trade in 1834, because private British merchants flooded into China. The many English houses engaged in the tea trade included Moffat and Company, Money and Wigram, and Forbes and Forbes, among others.[32] The wealthy Scottish house Jardine Matheson and

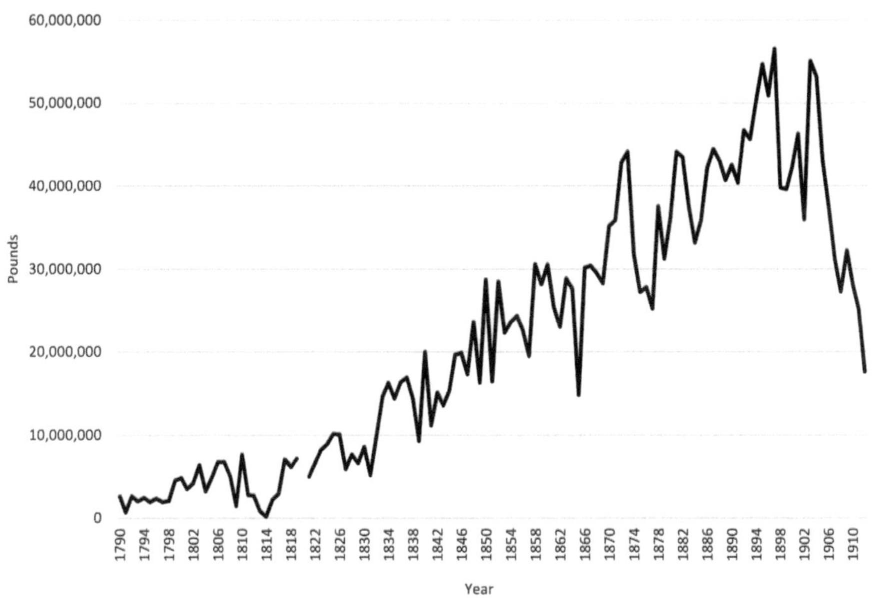

Fig. 8. Quantities of tea imported from China to the United States, 1790–1912. Sources: 1790–1905: U.S. Department of Commerce and Labor (USDCL), "World's Production," 138–40. 1792–94: Flagg, "China," 1:516. 1905–7: USDCL, *Foreign Commerce and Navigation, 1907*, 344. 1908–12: USDCL, *Foreign Commerce and Navigation, 1912*, 356.

Company adopted the advance system to contract tea with Hong merchants at the rates offered by the EIC.[33] Meanwhile, by advancing money to private English dealers, the EIC retained its control even after the abolition of its official monopoly.[34] Facing the "unexpected demand for England" in 1834, Russell and Company retreated from the black tea trade in Canton.[35] So did other Americans. "Our countrymen have avoided Black teas from their comparatively high price," Russell and Company explained in 1835, and "filled up their ships chiefly with green."[36] Hence it is unsurprising that green tea came to dominate the U.S. market. Yet procuring the green teas on Britons' list was a daunting task. John Murray Forbes advised his brother, Bennet, in 1836 that "Hyson, Gunpowder & Imperial of good quality will be run upon by the English in the early part of the season & will be extravagantly high. I think they will also be too high with you to touch."[37] Consequently, young hyson dwarfed other varieties in U.S. tea imports beginning in the 1830s (see figure 3).

Not everyone was confined to the system monopolized by the Cohong and dominated by the British. Some Americans procured tea from shopkeepers, or traders outside the Cohong. For example, Carrington traded regularly with Eshing and Washing, while William Law purchased tea from Hipshing.[38] Although the Qing government's regulated policy under the Canton Trade System confined China's maritime trade to the Cohong, the boundary between outside and Hong merchants was indefinite in on-the-ground activities.[39] The kinship with Hong merchants enabled some shopkeepers to participate in the Canton Trade, such as Consequa in 1784, who was the nephew of the then Cohong's head, Phuankhequa.[40] Others shared the economic burden of inadequately capitalized Hongs and traded with foreigners under their licenses.[41] Outside men Eshing, Namshing, Pouqua (possibly the Paunqua), and Washing had established such high reputations among Westerners that trading with them became an integral part of the Canton Trade.[42] These shopkeepers often sold high-quality products at lower prices for ready money.[43]

Exploiting the power dynamics among Chinese Hong merchants and outsiders, some Americans even participated in the advance system, although they paid high prices for circumventing the Cohong. In 1823 John Renshaw Thomson, the U.S. consul in China, a trader named Rush, and several others contracted with a private Chinese dealer who promised to procure tea at low prices directly from the interior before the tea season began. However, after receiving these Americans' advance payments and delivering a small quantity of tea, the dealer absconded with the rest of the money. Thomson survived the fraud, but Rush lost almost every dollar he had and others suffered heavily, amounting to at least $200,000 in losses. "[Though] perhaps in the first place his intentions were not dishonest," Thomas Tunno Forbes—the first China trader from the Forbes family in Boston—estimated, when fully realizing the difficulty to acquire teas much cheaper than the market price, "he concluded it was best to pocket the whole & be off."[44] The substantial risks of advancing funds to unfamiliar dealers outside the Cohong deterred other Americans from participating in the advance system, as "it is generally admitted that [it] is entirely unavailing to contract for them [teas] in the interior before the markets open here [Canton]."[45]

Others cultivated stronger trust relations with the Cohong, choosing not to challenge the established system but thriving within its framework. The above-mentioned Cushing and Forbes brothers formed an alliance with Howqua, who had, cautiously, consigned tea to Americans before the War of 1812.[46] During the wartime commercial stagnation, Cushing spent his idle time managing Howqua's funds, making investments through his agents in London and Calcutta, and shipping on joint account with Howqua. These financial and commercial collaborations fortified his friendship with this leading Hong merchant.[47] After Cushing returned to the United States, his cousins, John Murray and Robert Bennet Forbes, maintained the rapport with Howqua. The Chinese gentleman was especially fond of the astute and prudent John, who exalted Howqua for taking him "under [his] fatherly care" when he was only eighteen years old.[48] Howqua authorized John to manage his giant overseas commercial empire through Russell and Company.[49] Cushing and generations of the Forbes family were senior partners of the commission house, and Howqua was the most important sponsor.[50]

As Wong's research has demonstrated, Howqua and his U.S. friends strengthened their partnership to counter their mutual rival, the EIC.[51] Referring to the EIC as the "Commercial Monster John's Company," Howqua revealed his antagonism to the company's grip on the Canton trade.[52] Americans' presence gave Howqua a chance to reach overseas markets by sidestepping the EIC. Expanding his business overseas through Cushing's networks in Europe and America, Howqua maintained accounts with Perkins and Company and, later, Russell and Company in Canton, Baring Brothers and Company in London, as well as James and Thomas H. Perkins and Bryant and Sturgis in Boston.[53] The nature of Russell and Company as a commission house, or a broker, further facilitated Howqua's foreign trade.[54] Through the company, he consigned thousands of chests of tea, annually or temporarily, to merchant firms in Amsterdam, Antwerp, Hamburg, and London, as well as the EIC's former agents in Liverpool and Nova Scotia, Canada.[55] Howqua "was always a warm friend to the Americans," John's brother, Bennet, summarized in his book, "and through them was supposed to have carried on a considerable trade, on his own account, both to Europe and the United States."[56]

In exchange, neither the company's monopoly nor other merchants' competitive pressure prevented the Cushing-Forbes alliance from acquiring the choicest teas from Howqua. Cushing admitted that "the old gentleman [Howqua] gives us the privilege of choosing from the teas which he has prepaired [*sic*] for the Company."[57] In 1820, when Howqua refused to furnish Girard's *North America*, Cushing had already secured "the very best description of teas" for his ships *True American* and *Cordelia*.[58] "The whole of the above teas were selected before the Company had their choice," Cushing boasted to their agent in London. "The black teas particularly are of the best possible description." In contrast, "the cargoes of the *Integrity* [of Carrington], *N. [North] America* [of Girard], & *Washington* [of Brown and Ives] were purchased after the Company had made their selections & are consequently very much inferior."[59] Like Girard, other Americans found themselves subordinate to Cushing in the commercial hierarchy. "We are not the first to be served," lamented a report Carrington received in 1821. "If he [Howqua] has a very prime chop of Teas, we might *possibly* be able to purchase it of him provided *another person* did not want it." The person was Cushing.[60]

Bills of Exchange from England and America

However, even the resourceful Cushing, who had to furnish the ship *Cordelia* "principally on credit from various people," regretted that the tea cargo would not "prove so good as if a little more money had been employed in the operation."[61] After all, when Cushing and Forbes procured tea from Howqua, they had to pay for it, and the tea venture was a costly business. Therefore sufficient capital remained the most important factor in securing fine teas.

WHITE GOLD, BLACK GOLD, AND BILLS OF EXCHANGE

To raise enough funds to purchase tea or settle account balances, Americans continued to explore the world, including the "chain trade" in Southeast Asia, for suitable commodities that interested the Chinese.[62] Gradually emerging from the various goods were "the chief mediums of the purchase of teas for this country [America]—exchange upon England and cotton goods."[63] While cotton goods referred to Indian cotton and British manufactures, the "exchange upon England" was a bill of exchange.[64] Like the promissory note, the bill of exchange is a credit instrument recognized by both the Anglo-American and continental European legal frameworks.[65] A bill of exchange is a piece of paper whereby the debtor issues an order to the drawee—either a bank or a merchant firm—to pay a specified sum to the bill holder. Therefore the credit relationship involves at least three parties, distinguishing it from the promissory note that represents the bilateral obligations between two parties.[66] While functioning like a check that circulated domestically, a bill of exchange usually facilitated international transactions and remittance. Figure 9 is a bill of exchange relating to the China trade. Edward Gassett and Company in Boston drew this bill on Augustine Heard and Company at Canton, ordering the latter to pay Anthon and Company of Hong Kong $844.62 no later than three days after December 20, 1851.[67] The Chinese cashier of Augustine Heard and Company translated the value from Arabic numerals, $844.62, to the Chinese commercial numbering system known as the "Suzhou Code." Combining Chinese characters and the Suzhou Code, the Chinese employee also recorded the date of this transaction in both lunar and solar calendars.[68] Therefore, through the bill of exchange handled in China, transnational economic and cultural communications unfolded.

As the first country that adopted paper money in recorded history, China was no stranger to bills of exchange. Indeed, scholars regarded the bill of exchange, *feiqian* (flying cash), better known as *bianhuan* (convenience note), as the prototype of Chinese paper currency. Records about the circulation of the *bianhuan* already appeared in such literary works as *Yinhua lu* (*Recordings of Conversations*) during the ninth century.[69] Introduced during the reign of Emperor Xianzong (reign, 805–20) in Tang China (618–907), convenience notes facilitated merchants' remittance from the capital city to their home circuits (the administrative unit of the Tang dynasty). When a merchant deposited coins, the primary currency of Tang China, with the *jinzouyuan* (the capital liaison office of each local circuit) in the capital city, they received a paper receipt. The merchant held half of the receipt, while the *jinzouyuan* sent the other half to their local government. After returning to their home circuit, the merchant cashed the receipt with the local government if the two halves matched.[70] In the nineteenth century, Chinese bills of exchange preserved the traditional format of the *bianhuan*, as contemporaries describe: "Half of an impressed seal is on the bill and half remains on the docket in the book of the firm which issued it."[71] Thus "the note that matches with the other half is exactly the bill of exchange today,"

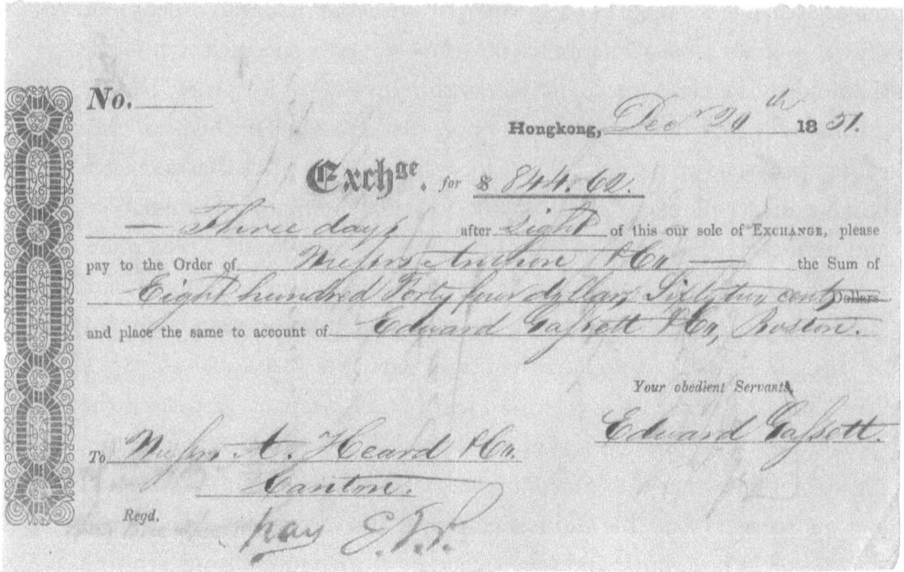
No. ______

Hongkong, Dec 20th 1851.

Exchge. for $ 844.62.

Three days after Sight of this our sole of Exchange, please pay to the Order of Messrs Anthon & Co — the Sum of Eight hundred Forty four dollars Sixty two cents Dollars and place the same to account of Edward Gassett & Co, Boston.

Your obedient Servants

Edward Gassett

To Messrs A. Heard & Co.
Canton.

Regd.

pay E.G.

Fig. 9. A bill of exchange, 1851. The Suzhou Code employs a numerical symbology where the combination of "〨〤〤〦〢" paired with "百十元毛" denotes the monetary value $844.62. Carton 27, folder 2, HFBR, Baker Library, Harvard Business School.

Chinese scholar Feng Liutang explained.[72] Hence Chinese merchants had been familiar with the practice, if not the format, of bills of exchange introduced by foreign merchants.

The British were the pioneers who brought Western bills of exchange to China. On his second trip to China, Shaw noticed that licensed British private traders deposited into EIC's treasury their opium and cotton proceeds, "for which they receive bills on the company in England."[73] Unlike silver and merchandise that incurred substantial transportation fees, insurance, or duty, the paper bill was a cheap means of remittance and settlement, particularly for long-distance trade. Amazed by its convenience, Shaw noted, "This fund has for a number of years rendered it unnecessary for the company to export from Europe any specie for carrying on their commerce with the Chinese."[74] Read also commended this cost-saving and risk-mitigating arrangement in 1806. "It occurred to me that this mode of remittance might possibly answer your purpose to be drawn for from hence," Read wrote to Willings and Francis in Philadelphia. "I have every reason to believe from

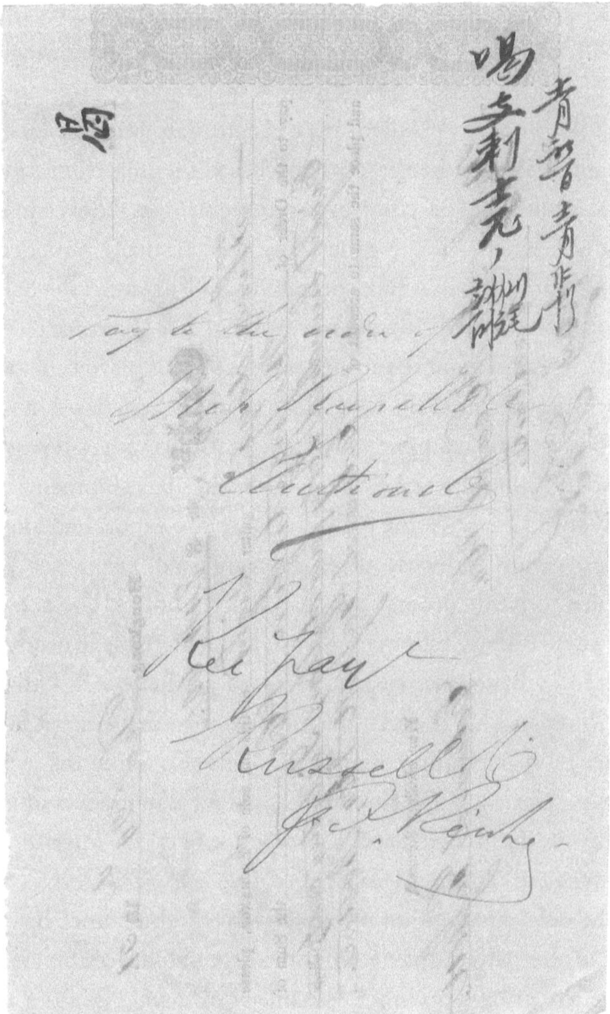

the increased difficulty in exporting specie from hence that Bills on India will be higher in future."[75]

Indeed, when exporting specie grew difficult during the Embargo of 1807–9 and the War of 1812, U.S. merchants started to use bills of exchange to fund their trade in Canton. While the foreign bills available in China were typically issued by the EIC or on India, Americans introduced "private bills" drawn on merchant firms in Great Britain, which were well-established means of payment in the transatlantic trade.[76] In 1811 Carrington had employed private bills to continue his China trade.[77] Waln used four private sterling bills to repay his promissory note to Consequa in 1812 (see chapter 1). In October 1812 Minturn and Champlin of New York also paid Consequa a set of English bills drawn on private companies in London.[78] The large amount of private bills brought by Americans to Canton in 1810–11 even alerted the EIC, as many British-Indian traders purchased the bills from Americans at lower rates, challenging the company's monopoly over the exchange markets in India and China.[79] "If the Americans were annually provided with an extensive Credit on Houses of respectability in England," the Select Committee of the EIC warned, "we are not aware of any Circumstances to deter the Indian Capitalist from remitting the proceeds of his Speculations in the China market by means of the Bills which might be purchased in Canton."[80] To attract buyers, the company lowered their bills' prices. Possibly to the relief of the EIC committee, Americans resumed silver shipments to Canton after the War of 1812 when the embargo on specie export had loosened and the supply of South American silver recommenced.[81]

The return to hard currency puzzled many scholars, but it reveals how much the circulation of bills of exchange, as a negotiable instrument, relied on trust. Hosea Ballou Morse, the Harvard graduate well known for his work in China and his research on the EIC, regarded Americans' continued reliance on specie "unnecessary."[82] Downs also found the revived silver shipments perplexing. "It is not at all apparent why traders of all nations resumed the old-fashioned, expensive practice of specie importing, when a cheap, convenient, and profitable alternative lay within reach."[83] Cheong ascribed the delayed adoption of bills to silver's abundance before 1826.[84] However, an alternative explanation is the negotiability of this credit instrument. Like the promissory note, the bill of exchange is also a negotiable instrument that could be transferred to others beyond the original credit relationship. As figure 9 shows, Augustine Heard and Company endorsed, or sold, the bill to Russell and Company.[85] However, trust is the key to the transference.[86] Confidence in the creditability of the issuers or previous holders determined the negotiability of the bills, because no one was willing to hold a piece of unredeemable paper. As historian Jessica Lepler observed, confidence was the alchemy that transformed paper into gold.[87]

While faith in the Chinese government sustained the circulation of the *bianhuan* and the authority of the English Crown guaranteed the EIC exchange, private bills represented only the credibility of individual firms in

Great Britain, not to mention that American newcomers brought them to Asia. Not all of the private London houses had as high a reputation as the EIC in India or China, thus rendering "their credits less current than those of houses longer known" in Canton.[88] The credibility of U.S. merchants proved insufficient to improve private bills' negotiability in Asia's exchange markets. Even in 1833, when Americans' bill trade had boomed in Canton, "Perkins & Co., Bryant & Sturgis, and John P. Cushing of Boston, who are all of the first standing for respectability & wealth" remained unfamiliar names in Bombay. Howqua, who was "well known throughout India," endorsed their bills.[89] Anyone who had endorsed a bill in India became liable for the debt, if the drawee failed to make payments.[90] Therefore Howqua's endorsement signaled a promise to redeem the bills for his Boston friends, thus enhancing the bills' negotiability in India.[91] Hence not all Hong merchants, Indian traders, and English firms readily accepted the private bills brought by Americans. The bills that failed to find sufficient buyers in the exchange market "would oblige us to be always prepared with a large sum of money to meet Bills which might be drawn upon us at any moment," Cushing analyzed. The risk was counterproductive to the convenience of the credit system.[92] Therefore, without a large credit market to keep their bills circulating after the War of 1812, Cushing and his fellow Americans chose to ship specie instead.[93]

From the season of 1826–27, however, flourishing commerce in cotton, "the white gold," and opium, "the black gold," across the Indian and Atlantic markets rekindled Americans' bill trade in Asia. Despite fluctuations, cotton imports from India to China increased steadily during the late 1820s.[94] More important, the rampant opium smuggling from India to China, particularly via Lintin Island, gained momentum beginning with the season of 1826–27 (see figure 10).[95] The drug traffic generated enormous profits, enabling the EIC not only to eliminate Britain's trade deficit with China but also to reverse the silver flow between the two nations during 1827–40.[96] Meanwhile, the British-Indian demand for a convenient means to remit their cotton and opium sales proceeds from Canton back to India and England soared to an unprecedented level.[97] Seizing this chance, the EIC issued bills on Bengal at a favorable rate, which "does away [with] the necessity of shipping silver or copper."[98] Americans also resumed their sales of private English bills in Canton. In addition to the demand for the credit instrument, American suppliers also found it as a more favorable time than

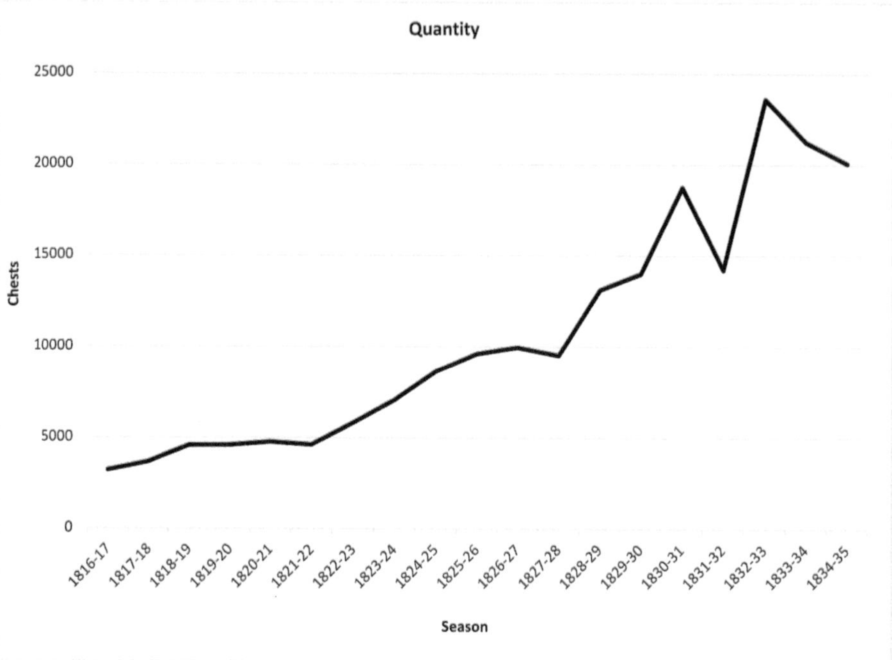

Fig. 10. Quantity and value of Indian opium imported to China, 1816–35. Source: Forbes, *Remarks on China*, 44. Multiple datasets highlight the scale of the opium trade in China. Forbes's records detailed both the quantities and value of smuggled opium over an extended period, while Hosea Ballou Morse, drawing on the statistics of the EIC's Canton branch, provided comparable figures for a shorter span, between 1818 and 1828. Additional sources offer slightly different data. Across all the datasets, 1826–27 was the turning point marking the trade's rapid expansion. See Morse, *Chronicles of the East India Company*, 4:383; Cheong, *Mandarins and Merchants*, 21; Lin, *China Upside Down*, 76–78, 88–89; Yan, *Zhongguo jindaijingjishi tongjiziliao xuanji*, 36; Business Records on the Remission of Funds to the Far East and Packing Goods for the China Trade, 1828–1829, box 1, FFP, Massachusetts Historical Society.

a decade ago. Having become the primary supplier of raw cotton to Great Britain after 1826, the United States dominated 70 to 80 percent of British cotton imports throughout the nineteenth century.[99] Thus the Atlantic cotton trade provided a consistent supply of English bills, establishing Americans' exchange business in China and India as a stable enterprise.[100] In 1832 "Americans had negotiated exchange to the amt. [amount] of at least £500,000," Joseph Archer wrote in November of that year from Canton.

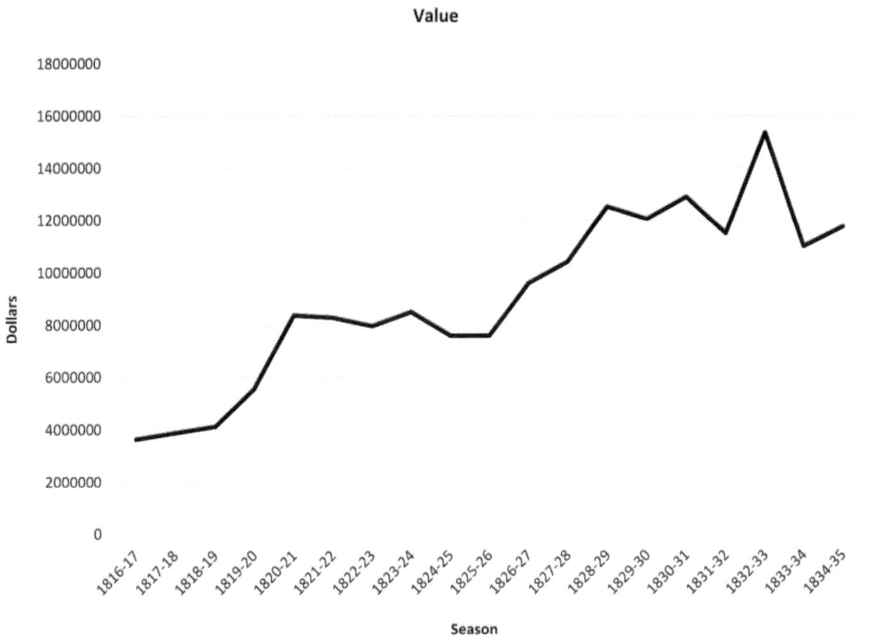

"By far the greater proportion of all the Bills on England negotiated in this market have heretofore been required for remittances to Calcutta and Bombay in payment for Opium and Cotton."[101] Drawing on the extensive experience with the triangular trade in cotton, opium, and bills of exchange across the Pacific, Indian, and Atlantic Worlds, U.S. merchant Gideon Nye concluded, "The rate of exchange in China depends upon the condition of the opium trade chiefly," and "the cost of cotton goods is ruled chiefly by the cost of the raw material here [in the United States]."[102]

The private bills of exchange introduced by U.S. traders developed a financial network that further integrated the monetary and commercial markets in Great Britain, the United States, China, India, and Southeast Asia with global finance, enhancing American merchants' profits and the convenience of the transpacific credit system. Cushing and Forbes bought bills on London at home and sold them in Canton or Calcutta, as the opium traffic drove the rates of bills higher in the latter places. Buying sterling bills, valued at £100,000, in America cost $488,888.88, but selling them in Bengal and Canton, even at the lowest exchange rates in the previous ten years, would yield a net gain of $68,602.12, or a 14 percent profit margin during 1828–29.[103] Facilitated by the chain trade, the Cushing-Forbes alliance also sold English and Second Bank of the United States (BUS) bills in Southeast Asia and then purchased goods for the Chinese market.[104] Since 1825 the newly founded BUS had issued bills of exchange designed specifically for Americans' trade with Asia. Known as "East India Bills," these "180-day sight" bills, drawn on London or Paris, would "not be negotiated, except to the Eastward of the Cape of Good Hope." Americans thereby could simply purchase bills at home using domestic banknotes.[105] The BUS's creditability enhanced the negotiability of the paper device and its circulation in China and Southeast Asia. In 1834, Ebenezer Irving of Boston sent his son in Canton a set of BUS bills as the start-up funds, including investments in tea, because he learned that "the bills of the United States Bank on Baring Brothers & Co., London were the most convenient and safest."[106] Even though "it incurred some expense to procure these [BUS] Bills," Bryant and Sturgis also explained from Batavia, "presuming that they are so undoubted as to preclude the necessity of any endorser at Batavia," the investment could "save us the usual charge for that transaction."[107] The size of the BUS bills circulated in Canton fluctuated, but their value had reached over $750,000 in 1831, when the bills on London brought by Americans amounted to a little less than $1.2 million.[108] It is unclear how many times these instruments were negotiated in China. In truth the world's money market in the nineteenth century dealt largely in bills of exchange, because this financial instrument, unlike stocks and bonds, could be traded many times without the need for an organized marketplace.[109] Hence, when Americans employed private bills to fund their Canton trade, they helped link China with international financial networks.

GREEN GOLD AND PAPER GOLD

The profitable bill trade also facilitated China's tea commerce and strengthened its credit infrastructure. Russell and Company's constituents sent the house bills of exchange, or letters of credit, that authorized them to draw bills of exchange, commissioning the company to invest in tea.[110] Disruptions to routine tea transactions, such as during the 1830s commercial panic in India, highlighted Chinese and U.S. merchants' dependence on the bill trade.[111] In November 1833 the tea trade in Canton should have started several months earlier but was delayed by the difficulty of selling bills. "Money is very scarce with the Chinese. They are I think becoming a little uneasy about the price of Teas," Archer complained, "as they are, as well as ourselves, alarmed about the difficulty in raising funds out of Exchange on England."[112] Even the vessels that had been loaded with a cargo of old teas, such as the brig *Nabob* from Boston, failed to gather sufficient funds to set sail, and "the impossibility of disposing of her Exchange is all that is detaining her."[113]

As Archer implied, Chinese merchants were also integral components of the credit network interwoven by the flow of tea and bills of exchange. Howqua's vast overseas business benefited from this credit system. After selling his tea in North America or Europe, his consignees remitted the net profits to Baring Brothers and Company in London, who invested the proceeds in merchandise and remitted the balance back using bills of exchange on London or Bengal.[114] Howqua's American business partners sold English bills for him in the United States.[115] Other Chinese were also active in exploring this credit network in Canton. "Exchange on England has been sold pretty largely by the Chinese at 4/10d [four shillings ten pence per Spanish dollar]," Russell and Company reported in March 1835.[116] Moreover, these Chinese adeptly weathered the fluctuations in the credit market during the tea season. "Exchange has in some instances been sold to the Chinese at 4/10, they again have given it to Europeans at 5/" in 1833, and "the difference of course goes on to the prices of Teas."[117] In buying bills low (four shillings ten pence) but selling them high (five shillings), these Chinese merchants profited from foreign traders' demand for bills to invest in tea.

Since the need to invest in tea conditioned the demand for bills of exchange, the tea economy shaped the fluctuations of exchange rates in China. Given that the tea season in Canton usually commenced before September and ended in April, the rates of bills stayed low between February and May nearing the end of the tea season but rose high from June to September, when foreign traders sought bills to exchange for silver and purchase tea.[118] The prices of tea and bills synchronized over the coming decades, even as tea centers relocated and the tea season changed dates. The market rates of bills in Shanghai and Fuzhou during the 1860s–70s remained low during January to March, but between May and July, when the market for new teas opened, the exchange rates rose sharply "in consequence of heavy settlements in tea." Declining from July or August, the rates gradually returned to the January levels, "governed throughout by the operations in the tea market."[119] During a particular season, the ups and downs of the tea business also influenced the bill trade. For instance, tea transactions stagnated in December 1836 during the middle of the tea season: "Bills on London are offered at 4/11d, but very little demand for them."[120] Consequently, selling bills at an inappropriate time likely reduced U.S. traders' capital and thwarted their tea ventures.

To avoid the hurdles in the exchange market, British and U.S. houses preferred to pay bills directly for tea, a practice that illuminated the relationship between credit money, silver currency, and barter payment in China's foreign trade. Consequa had accepted EIC's bills on Bengal for tea as early as 1786.[121] In 1830 a member of the Cushing-Forbes alliance, Perkins, also used bills on London to exchange for silk.[122] Unable to sell their bills to obtain silver in 1833 amid the world financial crisis, English merchant C. Gordon attempted to forge "a new system" "to truck Bills of Exchange with the Chinamen for Teas."[123] The term "truck" referred to the barter trade, which the EIC employed to exchange their woolen goods for Chinese tea.[124] Just as with the EIC's handling of unsaleable woolens, William Jardine took pains to promote the new system and to capitalize on the large amount of bills managed by Jardine Matheson and Company.[125] The scale of such operations alerted the prudent Howqua. "There is a heavy amount of Bills on England & letters of Credit already in the market which is accumulating by every arrival," Howqua wrote to John in 1834; "at present there is no sale, except in barter which you know would not suit my purposes."[126] The word "barter" revealed Howqua's conceptualization of bills of exchange as a commodity, rather than a bona fide currency as silver, the "real" money in China. However, the nineteenth-century wording of the barter trade should not camouflage the existence of a modern credit economy.[127]

Although bills of exchange never replaced silver in the Canton trade, Americans' ability to sell bills in China, India, and Southeast Asia or employ the paper to buy tea reduced their silver shipments to Canton. Bills of exchange settled more transactions in the U.S.-China trade during the 1830s than specie and merchandise did. Consequently, although the value of Chinese tea imported into the United States climbed to $4 million to $6 million between 1833 and 1837, Americans' specie exports to China plummeted to less than $1 million during the same period (see figures 22 and 11).[128] As figure 11 shows, the silver flow from America to China reduced by 50 to 80

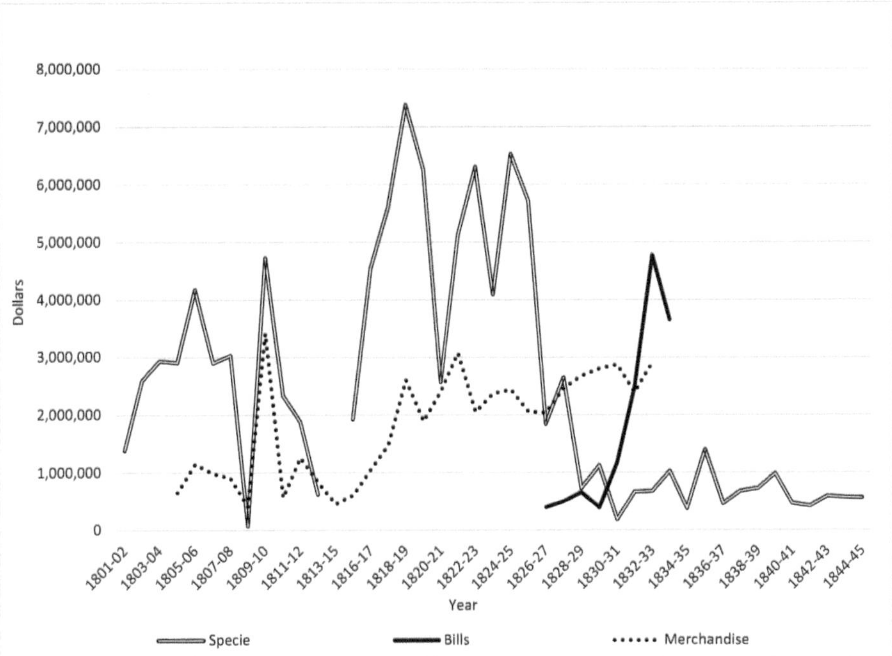

Fig. 11. Value of specie, bills of exchange, and merchandise imported to China by American ships, 1801–45. Sources: Merchandise, 1806–31: Pitkin, *Statistical View*, 303. Merchandise, 1804–5 and bills, 1837–38: Forbes, *Remarks on China*, 24. The value of U.S. merchandise imports into China in 1805 was $2,653,818 in Pitkin's book but only $653,818 in Forbes's table. Given that American imports into China never exceeded $2 million in any other years before 1809, Pitkin's figure is likely a transcription error. Thus this chart adopts Forbes's more plausible figure. Additionally, for the amount of bills introduced into China during 1837–38, this chart also relies on Forbes's data, as the information is lacking in other sources. Specie and bills, 1801–45: Downs, *Golden Ghetto*, appendix 3, 361–63. This chart adopts Downs's data gathered from five sources, as they are more comprehensive than alternative sources. This chart uses most of the data from the first column of Downs's table. The data for 1801–3, 1835–36, and 1838–45, unavailable in the first column, are from the other two columns. For similar datasets, see Irigoin, "End of a Silver Era," figure 2; Wong, *Global Trade*, 90. Despite the varied value of China's specie imports, 1826–27 was the turning point across all datasets.

percent between the 1820s and the 1840s.[129] Undergirded by the multilateral credit network woven by the flow of bills of exchange, China's tea trade proceeded smoothly and efficiently. However, the credit system, without the immediate transfer of silver after each transaction, was a vulnerable loop buttressed by the faith in a promising future. When any link broke under external pressure, chain effects ensued to cripple the entire structure.

The Panic of 1837 and the Opium War

John Forbes left China in December 1836. Writing to Howqua a day after the Chinese New Year, John hailed the "fair winds and pleasant weather" as "/Fong Sue/ [*Feng Shui*]," the Chinese belief that the natural and built environment influences human affairs.[130] However, the winds and water at sea did not bring him good luck on shore. After landing on U.S. soil in March 1837, John felt overwhelmed by reports on the Panic of 1837, one of the worst international financial storms that crumbled the U.S. economy.[131] The first wave of business failures occurred in March, the very moment when John returned, and banks throughout the United States suspended specie payment in mid-May.[132] In letters to his friends in Canton, John lamented that almost no American houses in New Orleans, New York, and Atlantic cities were solvent and the fate of London houses was unknown. The pressure on the Chinese was also tremendous, owing to a chain "reaction of the distress in Great Britain upon the Canton Houses and through them upon the Hongs."[133] The economic crises leading to the panic had discouraged American ships from sailing to China, stagnated the U.S. tea market, and curbed English houses' demand for Chinese tea since January 1837.[134] Even when several U.S. and English ships ventured to Canton that year, they had limited funds and credit, further interrupting the cash flow of Hong merchants, who had already been operating under strained conditions.[135] Sturgis confessed that he "had no confidence in any house East of the Cape [of Good Hope], Chinese, Am'n [American], or English, except Howqua."[136] John shared this sentiment. Fearing that the financially embarrassed British would run on Hong merchants and concerned about the gloomy economy, John sent over a hundred letters between April and July to Russell and Company or their business partners in China and Great Britain. In a dozen of these letters, he repeatedly warned his friends to clear their account balances with the Chinese or to avoid any more transactions in tea.[137]

Economic pressure also resulted from the bills of exchange current in Canton, which were irredeemable or unsaleable because of their issuers' failures. "I should tremble for our debts which may exist from the Hongs, or the English," John wrote to express his concerns to John Green, the new head of Russell and Company. "Many men long thought rich here will go," and "many of the Bills we drew last year were near being sent back by the London houses and some of the parties here would not have been paid."[138] Indeed, beginning in February 1837, bankruptcy hit quite a few prominent houses in England, many of whom had close business relationships with U.S. and British traders in Canton.[139] The failed English houses, which had issued or endorsed bills to Americans and the Chinese, were unable to cash the devices and their papers lost value in the credit market.[140] Even bills drawn by the Second Bank of the United States on their London agents lost favor among merchants in Canton, as the Bank of England rejected the paper.[141] The consequence was reversion to barter and silver payments for the coming years. Europeans preferred barter, whereas Hong merchants "would deal only for cash; and insisted on being paid before the teas were delivered."[142]

While scholars largely attributed the Panic of 1837 to political and economic factors in the Atlantic world, some have linked the crisis to U.S.-China trade. As Norwood argued, Nicholas Biddle issued the BUS bills out of concern that the China trade had exhausted the U.S. specie stock.[143] Adopting English and BUS bills of exchange in the U.S.-China trade dramatically reduced Americans' exports of silver to China. Temin estimated that the bills circulated for China trade helped replenish the U.S. specie reservoir with $4 million annually in the 1830s (also see figure 11). Meanwhile, a large amount of British capital flowed into America. The two lines of monetary resources substantially fueled inflation in the U.S. economy during the mid-1830s, leading to the Panic of 1837.[144] Thus the multilateral credit networks across the Pacific and Atlantic worlds worked together to foment the crisis in America.

On the other side of the Pacific Ocean was the aggravated silver drain, especially in silver-dependent southern China.[145] After direct trade with Canton unfolded in 1784, Americans supplied 97 percent of the silver flowing into China in most of the years between 1807 and 1833 (also see figure 12).[146] However, this source of silver drained away beginning in the late 1820s after Americans sold bills in Asia to finance their tea trade. Silver shipped by Americans reduced from an average of $5 million during 1815–25 and $2.4 million in 1825–30 to less than $0.6 million from 1830 to 1835 (also see figure 12). It is unsurprising that Temin calculated that American traders who used bills in the China trade saved $4 million annually for the U.S. economy. Meanwhile, Americans increased their sales of private bills from less than $0.5 million in the 1820s to an average of over $2.7 million during 1830–35.[147] Bennet recalled in 1842, "While there were four millions of Company's bills negotiated, about three millions of dollars' worth of American bills drawn on London" circulated in Canton.[148] In other words, by using and selling private bills, American merchants annually extracted a massive amount of silver, equivalent to $11–$119 billion in 2024, without transferring South American specie to refill the Chinese silver reserves.[149] Furthermore, silver steadily flowed out of China through the opium trade. Thus the depletion of China's silver stock, visualized by the widened gap in figure 12, became substantially exacerbated after the season of 1826–27. The last time a similar silver shortage occurred was during the Embargo of 1807–9, which crippled Consequa's finances.

Contemporaries, both Americans and Chinese, had felt the heavy toll of the silver drain on China's money market and economy. John noted in 1836 that "we have never known before such a scarcity of money among both Chinese and foreigners at this season of the year."[150] Consequently, the price of silver rose in Canton, because broken, cut, and Spanish dollars "vary in value from par to 15% advance with the supply."[151] In addition to foreign specie, the ratio between the currencies of China—sycee and copper coins—had climbed to 1:1,400–1,600 in 1837, although the rate had been around 1:1,000 during the eighteenth century and the first decade of the nineteenth century. The most abrupt increase in the exchange rate of sycee and coins occurred after 1827, when Americans' private bills of exchange altered the credit structure of the tea trade.[152] The high price of all forms of silver placed heavy burdens on the Chinese political economy. Although coins circulated in Chinese daily lives, native and foreign silver was used to pay taxes to the imperial treasury of the Qing government. Thus local governments and chief taxpayers lost heavily when exchanging coins for silver.[153] Hong merchants also employed silver to pay duties, contributions, and debts to the government and foreign creditors. The Cohong had owed 1,464,283 taels to the Qing court from 1836 to 1839.[154] The amount was massive, given that the aggregate contributions paid by Hongists to the Qing

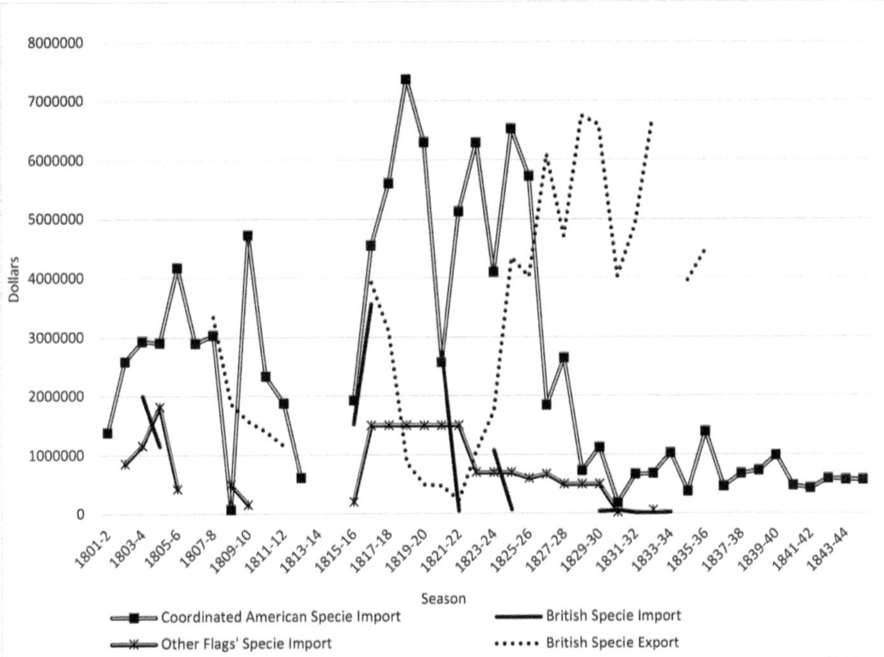

Fig. 12. China's import and export of silver through Canton, 1802–45. Source: Downs, *Golden Ghetto*, 359–62. Both tables on pages 360 and 362 document U.S. silver shipments to China, but some figures are inconsistent. Downs's table on page 360 contains transcription errors in the seasonal entries for 1816–17 to 1832–33 when compared with the data on page 362. Additionally, the figure for 1839–40 on page 360 also slightly differs from the corresponding entry on page 362. This chart adopts the data on page 362 where discrepancies arise.

government in the six decades from 1773 to 1832 amounted to 3,950,000 tales.[155] Meanwhile, Hong merchants also owed heavily to foreign merchants. Eight of the eleven Hongs were indebted in 1837. Two failed Hongists left 2,376,000 taels for their colleagues to clear, an amount of unprecedented magnitude in the history of the Cohong.[156] Some British traders distributed pamphlets at home in 1838–39, promoting an incoming war with China to recover the debts owed by Hong merchants.[157]

"Some disease was eating away the vitals of the Co-Hong," historian T. F. Tsaing lamented, without clarifying the causes of the disease.[158] While some Chinese who had extensive experience with China's maritime trade, such as Liang Tingnan, noticed the reduced silver flow from America to Canton, most Qing officials and scholars paid closer attention to the disease of opium smuggling.[159] "Everyone under Heaven knows it is opium that is siphoning off China's wealth," Huang Juezi, a Chinese minister, famously stated in his memorial to Emperor Daoguang in 1838.[160] To solve the troubles created by opium and silver, Emperor Daoguang held conferences beginning in 1836 to discuss whether to legalize or ban opium smuggling.[161] Prohibition policies eventually triumphed over the legalization attempts. In 1839 the emperor sent Commissioner Lin Zexu to Canton to remedy the evil. A staunch supporter of anti-opium campaigns, Lin wasted little time in interrogating Howqua and confiscating over twenty thousand chests of the drug from British and U.S. traders. For each chest of opium, Lin offered to reward its owners at least 6.5 pounds of tea.[162] Russell and Company submitted about four thousand chests to the commissioner.[163] Under the supervision of more than sixty officials at Humen, five hundred workers destroyed the opium by mixing it with water, lime, and salt, eventually discarding the decomposed drug liquid into nearby creeks flowing to the ocean.[164]

Lin's actions further agitated the belligerent parties and helped foment the Anglo-Chinese Opium War. British traders had consistently voiced their discontent with or animosity toward Qing China's regulated trading policy in Canton. Lin's siege of foreign companies and destruction of their opium, together with Cohong's debts, only intensified the already fragile Anglo-Chinese relations. The ensuing confrontations between English captain Charles Elliot, Lin, and other Qing representatives, starting in September 1839, escalated into skirmishes and eventually erupted into the full-blown Opium War, which lasted three years.[165] When the war ended with the defeat of Chinese troops in 1842, the Qing government signed the Treaty of Nanjing, promising to settle Hong merchants' debts, pay $21 million indemnity to the British government, abolish the Canton Trade System, and open four more cities, namely the "treaty ports," to British traders. Although never involved in the war, the U.S. and French governments signed similar treaties with China in 1844, reaping equal benefits from the troubles caused by opium, silver, and credit.

The treaties also ended the Cohong. Howqua's feelings about the changes were complicated. When British troops blockaded Canton, all Hong merchants but Howqua and Monqua escaped. Howqua decided to stay, as he believed that his presence would hasten negotiations with the English and the resumption of trade.[166] This decision cost him millions of dollars. Having paid over $3 million for the ransom of Canton, Howqua lost over $2 million by English looting in the city.[167] After the war, the Qing government pressured Hong merchants "to pay large sums of money before [they] are let fall."[168] Howqua blamed Lin for his "mistaken policy," which "has got his country into a dilemma," and remonstrated English troops, who "seem bent on plunder & murder."[169] Meanwhile, he heartily rejoiced at the abolition of the Cohong. "I look forward with pleasure to the time when I shall be a freeman," he wrote to Cushing in December 1842.[170] Several months later, this senior merchant passed away, eventually freed from all worldly burdens.[171] The Cohong system and Old China Trade went to the grave with him.

In the Canton Trade era, tea became predominant in U.S.-China trade in the 1820s. Exploiting the power struggles among British and Chinese merchants, Americans were able to procure tea from Chinese shopkeepers or cultivate close bonds with leading Hong merchants. The credit system that financed tea transactions also underwent a pivotal change that greatly enhanced Americans' purchasing power. While credit transactions and promissory notes had established a transpacific credit network in the late eighteenth century, the widespread use of bills of exchange in the early nineteenth century reshaped the financial structure of the tea trade. Engaged with the triangular trade in Chinese tea, Indian opium, and American cotton, U.S. merchants introduced bills of exchange from England or America to Canton, which invigorated the bill trade in China, India, and Southeast Asia and interlinked the credit markets in the Atlantic, Indian, and Pacific Oceans. Some Chinese merchants even accepted bills of exchange as payments for their tea. While enabling U.S. merchants to earn more profits and enjoy greater convenience in the credit economy of the tea trade, the structural change in trade finance also reduced Americans' silver shipments to Canton to a half or even a tenth of what it had been during the 1820s and 1830s. The expanded credit system fueled inflation in the U.S. economy but depleted China's silver stock, ultimately providing another stepping stone for the Panic of 1837 and the Anglo-Chinese Opium War in 1839. Silver and barter payments thereby resumed, and the tea trade stagnated. Nevertheless, credit transactions and instruments would proceed into the treaty ports after the Opium War, forming a coastal credit system that incorporated more Chinese tea and credit markets into the global financial system.

PART 2 *Oolong Tea*

Amid the military chaos in China during and following the Opium War, an increasing number of U.S. consumers were able to enjoy the aromatic oolong, a new type of Chinese tea that marked Americans' distinctive taste in the latter half of the century. While "Congous, Indias and Ceylons are the favorites of Great Britain, Russia, Australia and Canada," an American journal declared in 1904, "Oolongs are popular in our country only."[1] The popularity of oolongs arose during the 1840s. As early as 1843, New York importer Samuel Wetmore and Company had found that oolongs were "liked for family use."[2] The *United States Economist* noted in 1852 that "Young Hyson and Oolong are the most inquired after at full prices."[3] The quantity of oolongs imported into America exceeded that of black tea in 1852, surpassed that of young hyson in 1869, and overshadowed the aggregate amount of green tea imports by 1883 (see figures 3 and 4). The emergence of oolongs as the star products among U.S. consumers reflected the changing landscape of the U.S.-China tea trade, shaped by military and economic unsettlement during and after the Opium War.

Part 2 explains the new commercial setting of the transpacific tea trade after the end of the Canton Trade. Tea commerce between Chinese and U.S. merchants extended to the treaty ports, notably the green tea districts in the Yangzi River Valley (Shanghai, Ningbo, and Jiujiang) and the oolong tea ports on the southern coast of China (Fuzhou, Xiamen, and Danshui) (see figure 13). The eras of the Taiping Rebellion (1851–64) and the Second Opium War (1856–60) were the most critical formative years for the post-Opium-War tea trade. Besides green tea, U.S. merchants also dominated the oolong tea trade in the newly opened treaty ports, while the British remained the largest buyers of Chinese black tea. However, controlling the supply of oolongs from Taiwan to America, British houses competed with Chinese tea merchants and undermined the U.S. advantage in the transpacific tea trade.

The following two chapters analyze the financialization of the U.S.-China tea trade and the power structure of the credit economy beyond Canton. Credit transactions and instruments employed by both the Chinese and Americans facilitated expansion of the transpacific credit system into newly opened tea ports after the Opium War. The financialization process started when banking resources began supporting the tea trade's credit economy. From the 1850s onward, Chinese traditional banks supplied tea traders, Chinese and Americans alike, with native promissory notes and bills of exchange, thus transforming the basis of the credit system from merchants' relationships in Canton to banking services in the treaty ports, particularly in the regions around Shanghai. Relying on native banking facilities, Chinese tea warehouses, namely *chazhan,* emerged as professional tea brokers after the abolition of the Cohong. These middlemen sustained post–Opium War tea transactions and maintained the credit economy between the tea ports and interior producing districts in China. On the U.S. side, the dominance of commercial credit persisted during the first two decades after the Opium War. American commission houses, acting as their own banks, introduced another credit instrument—checks—into the southeastern treaty ports and issued inland bills to develop credit networks along the east coast of China, where the trade in green and oolong teas concentrated. While neither Chinese nor U.S. merchants solely relied on British credit instruments, Europeans banks were also ascendant during wartime in China and America, further financializing the credit system of the transpacific tea trade in the 1860s. However, foreign banks would take another decade to dominate the tea trade's credit system. A cup of oolong thus reflected shifts in the financial landscape and power dynamics of U.S.-China tea commerce.

The fashion of drinking oolong tea in America, the green tea country, merits close examination. Nineteenth-century Americans considered oolong, the "black dragon," a type of black tea.[4] Historical statistics also included oolong in the black tea category.[5] Yet the rise of oolong was compatible with U.S. consumers' preference for green tea. Nineteenth-century American literature described oolong as a "Black Tea with Green Tea flavor" or an unfermented black tea.[6] Nonetheless, the concept "unfermented black tea" is paradoxical, because the chief distinction between green and black tea is fermentation, a term employed by the Chinese to refer to the scientific concept of oxidation.[7] Green tea, the earliest type of Chinese tea, is unfermented. The most critical skill to make green tea is the first step, "fixation" or "de-enzyming," in which the heat produced by firing or steaming raised the temperature of the leaves to over 149 to 158 degrees Fahrenheit to deactivate the enzymes responsible for oxidization. The process preserves the green color of the tea leaves.[8] By contrast, black tea is fully fermented. Black tea production, invented after that of green tea, skips the "fixation" step. The most critical technique, instead, is oxidization—a chemical change that transforms the catechins in tea polyphenols into theaflavins or thearubigins. This process alters the taste and color of tea leaves, and directly contributes to the astringency and red tone of the tea's liquor.[9]

Oolong, also named *qingcha* (cyan tea), is a variety between green and black tea, because it is partially fermented.[10] Tea producers in Fujian, and later Taiwan, produced oolong by combining the techniques of processing green and black teas.[11] The first step in manufacturing oolong is to wither fresh leaves, as in black tea fermentation, but is followed by the most critical step, "tossing and rocking." This skill, which entails cycles of shaking and resting, bruises and oxidizes the margins of fresh leaves but leaves the center part unoxidized, so an American tea book described some oolongs' infused leaves as "bright-green in color, having a brown edge, caused by fermentation."[12] After tossing and rocking, tea leaves go through the pan-firing or steaming step, which was originally employed in processing green tea, to halt oxidization and stimulate the aromatic substances. Therefore oolongs combine the freshness of green tea and the mellowness of black tea. The number of times of tossing, differing widely from four to twelve, and the degree of oxidation determine the color and aroma of the final products.[13] Some oolong products manufactured in Fujian and Taiwan, which are about 30 to 50 percent oxidized, resemble green tea in color, while the Oriental Beauty of Taiwan is 70 percent oxidized and thus more akin to black tea.[14] Many oolongs consumed by nineteenth-century Americans were lightly oxidized, as the liquor yielded a golden-yellow color.[15] Americans also bought heavily oxidized oolong, because after importing black teas in the original boxes from China, U.S. dealers often refaced the printed label "Souchong" into "Fine Oolong" or "Ningyung [Ningyang Oolong]," thus selling the black tea at twelve to twenty cents higher than its original value.[16]

Given oolong's resemblance to green tea, it may not be a coincidence that the tea's popularity in the U.S. market arose during wartime, when the supply of Chinese greens was limited. Oolong had emerged as an independent denomination of tea in America during the 1830s.[17] This tea appeared as frequently as young hyson in New York, Baltimore, and Connecticut newspapers during 1839–40 and grew statistically significant in the 1840s, even though initially oolong's price was two to three times higher than any other teas (see figure 4).[18] The Opium War erupted at the same time. Although military clashes never terminated China's tea exports, which had "gone on much as usual," the warfare temporarily restricted supplies from the green tea districts.[19] Owing to the six-month British blockade of the Canton River, overall U.S. tea imports dropped dramatically from 250,000 chests in 1839–40 to 108,000 chests in 1840–41.[20] More specifically, "green teas were very scarce in market" in 1841, "having been kept back and large quantities sent away when the British approached the city [Canton]."[21] The quantity of good country green tea was especially limited in 1841, a quarter short of the previous year's supply.[22] It is likely that oolong's aromatic similarity to green tea relieved consumers' thirst for the latter. The advertisement in the *Cincinnati Daily Nonpareil* still categorized oolong as a type of green tea in 1836, although it fell under the umbrella of black tea during and after the Opium War.[23] The oolong districts' geographical proximity to Canton also eased wartime supply shortages. Indeed, the oolongs favored by Americans came primarily from Fujian and Taiwan, which were closer to Canton than the green tea districts (see figure 13).[24] U.S. merchants' business correspondence specified their favorite oolongs as "Kohn Oolongs," the "Sha Yuen kinds," and especially the "Ning Yong Oolong."[25] Named after the districts of origin—Gaoqiao, Shaxian, and Ningyang—all these oolongs were produced in Fujian province.[26] From Fujian, a Chinese named Ke Chao brought oolong tea plants to Taiwan early in the nineteenth century. Since the 1820s, people in the island had manufactured the leaves into oolong tea and sold the final products to Fujian.[27]

Further propelling oolongs to America was the warfare after the Opium War, which forced the development of oolong ports in Fujian and Taiwan. Although China opened four more treaty ports—Xiamen, Fuzhou, Ningbo, and Shanghai—to foreign traders in 1842, tea continued to pour into Canton.[28] Out of the four new ports, only Shanghai had developed into a

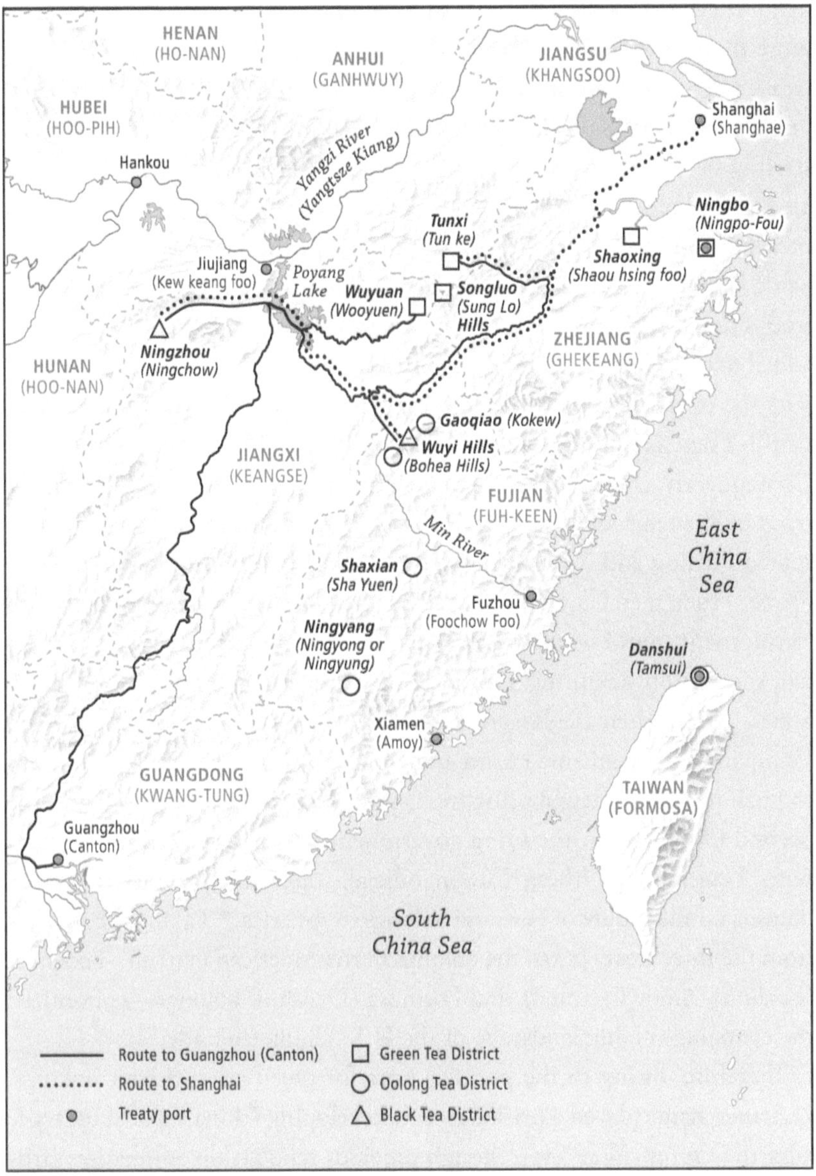

Fig. 13. Major districts and ports for the U.S.-China tea trade after 1843. Map created by Erin Greb Cartography, based on the "Map of Tea Districts with Various Routes to Canton & Shanghae" in Rutherford Alcock, "Report on the Tea Trade of Shanghae and Its Prospects," in House of Commons, *Returns of the Trade, 1847 and 1848*, 62–63.

major tea center by 1850. A major supplier of green tea, Shanghai "furnished more than three-fourths of the American trade in tea" by 1855. The other treaty ports had little share in the trade, even though they were situated in tea-producing regions.[29] Nonetheless, the political and economic crises starting in 1851 recast the trading landscape. The Taiping Rebellion, initiated as a religious movement led by a Confucian scholar turned Christian preacher, Hong Xiuquan, evolved into one of the bloodiest civil wars in world history. The battles between the insurgents and the Qing government's troops devastated most parts of China between 1851 and 1864.[30] Worse still, added to the domestic turmoil was international warfare. Failing to renegotiate the treaties signed with the Qing government after the Opium War, British-French joint forces waged the Second Opium War during 1856–60.[31] Consequently, chaos, uncertainty, and anxiety constantly halted Americans' trade in Shanghai and Canton for a decade.[32] However, the military action spared Fuzhou and Xiamen for most of those years.[33] In 1853, advised by former Hong merchant Samqua, Russell and Company experimented with "a shipment from Foochow [Fuzhou]" to alleviate tea shortages in Shanghai, successfully acquiring a cargo of high-quality oolongs for the United States.[34] Thereafter, the largest American commission houses, Russell and Company and Augustine Heard and Company, extended their operations to Fuzhou and the neighboring treaty port, Xiamen.[35] After China lost the Second Opium War, the Qing government had to open ten more treaty ports. Danshui in northern Taiwan, officially opened to Americans in 1860, dominated the supply of Formosa oolongs to America.[36] Taking their names from the three treaty ports, the oolongs in the American market—Foochow (Fuzhou), Amoy (Xiamen), and Formosa (Danshui) oolongs—epitomized the changing trading landscape of the U.S.-China tea trade.[37]

Therefore, owing to the peculiar taste for green tea and later oolongs, U.S. merchants played a pivotal role in developing China's global tea trade after the Opium War, even though previous scholarship emphasizes British dominance.[38] In 1853 U.S. commission houses initiated the commercial development of Fujian's oolong ports, while British firms, such as Jardine Matheson and Company and Dent and Company, followed their lead.[39] Furthermore, while British purchases in Fuzhou focused on black teas, oolongs were "chiefly to America."[40] When reporting on the oolong trade in Fuzhou, China's Imperial Maritime Customs usually detailed "the oolong market for America" but rarely mentioned British operations on this tea.[41] Xiamen developed primarily for the U.S. tea market. Oolongs constituted 70 to 90 percent of Xiamen's tea trade during 1862–73, and Americans were the largest buyers.[42] In the late nineteenth century, Americans also consumed "95 per cent of the total output" of Formosa oolong, either transshipped from Xiamen or exported directly from Taiwan, and only a fraction of this tea went to England "for mixing purposes entirely."[43]

However, the power dynamics in the commodity chain of Formosa oolong reveal an underlying crisis in Americans' tea trade with China. Despite American consumers' exclusive demand for oolongs, British firms controlled the tea's supply from Taiwan to the United States. American vessels seldom touched Danshui before 1869, even though fifteen British and an equal number of North German vessels had arrived in that single year.[44] The British firm Dodd and Company initiated the direct shipment of Formosa oolong to New York in 1869.[45] Major tea companies in Danshui during the 1870s—Dodd and Company, Tait and Company, Elles and Company, Brown and Company, and Boyd and Company—were all British houses.[46] In 1872 Francis Blackwell Forbes, the new leader of Russell and Company, promoted a "Formosa Scheme" to extend their operation to Danshui, on joint account with the New York tea importer and the house's major constituent, E. W. Corlies.[47] However, with capital as the bottleneck for the commission house and other partners' interest in opening a branch in Xiamen, the visionary Forbes had to abandon the project. Corlies also lost heavily in the tea ventures in 1873, the year the global Long Depression began.[48] This was the era when Americans were fighting a financial battle with European banks, attempting to maintain their position in the credit economy of transpacific tea trade (chapter 4).

In contrast, Chinese financial influence remained strong during this period. Bringing commercial and financial capital from the mainland, Chinese merchants were the major rivals of English houses in Taiwan. In addition to transshipping most Formosa oolong to America via Xiamen, Chinese merchants brought tea plants, funding, and manufacturing techniques to the island during the 1860s.[49] The number of establishments opened by tea merchants from mainland China grew from 33 in 1876 and 50 in 1884 to 95 in 1892 and 131 in 1895, while that of foreign establishments increased only from five to six during the two decades. In at least one year, 1892, thirteen of the ninety-five Chinese tea companies rivaled their foreign counterparts in the size of capital.[50] Around the 1890s, twenty Chinese brokers from Canton and Fujian, who operated on native banks' loans, advanced 80 percent of their goods' value and furnished Taiwan tea producers with substantial operating capital.[51] Chinese capital from Fujian also founded twenty to thirty tea manufactories on the island, "thus vigorously boosting Taibei's economy."[52] The ready credit provided by native capitalists of Xiamen even fanned the tea mania in Taiwan in 1872 (see chapter 4). "In the early days of the Formosa trade, the foreigners controlled almost exclusively the packing and firing," James Wheeler Davidson noted in his book on Taiwan, "but afterwards Chinese gradually entered the field, and have absorbed the larger share of the business," although he added that foreign establishments, primarily the British companies, still handled most of the better-quality teas by 1903.[53] Thus oolongs, the tea that defined American taste in the latter nineteenth century, opened a new arena for the transpacific tea business. The three players' contestation in international trade and its trade finance intensified during the three decades after the Opium War. The following two chapters will examine the financialization of the transpacific tea trade and the power dynamics among American commission houses, Chinese merchant-bankers, and European financial institutions.

3

From Canton to the Coast

RESTORING TRUST, 1843–65

While Captain Cole prepared for his trip to Shanghai in April 1857, his employer, William Appleton and Company, furnished him with the statistics of the U.S. tea trade and a long letter explaining how to purchase tea in China. Boston merchants and statesmen William Appleton and Samuel Hooper managed the company. They usually sent bills of exchange, letters of credit, specie, or cotton goods to China and commissioned Russell and Company to procure tea for them.[1] After the Opium War, the major challenge for their tea business was the complex exchange rates across the treaty ports, which significantly affected the cost of the company's operations at different places in China. "We think this is not always remembered by purchasers," William Appleton and Company explained. "They have sometimes forgotten that when they paid 16½ Taels at Canton it was no more than paying 11½ Taels at Shanghai."[2] The complicated exchange rates across the treaty ports even baffled Hooper, the seasoned China trader.[3] No wonder a two-year dispute would arise between Captain Cole and Russell and Company over the trade finance of this 1857 tea venture.

Furnished with 100,000 Mexican dollars, Cole arrived in Shanghai amid the Second Opium War and the Taiping Rebellion in 1857. For safety's sake, Cole placed the specie in the vault of Russell and Company before he sailed for Fuzhou to procure tea. The Chinese employee of Russell and Company, the so-called comprador, promised Cole not to open the package without the captain's presence. To acknowledge the receipt of the silver dollars, Mr. Reiche, the bookkeeper of Russell and Company in Shanghai, recorded the 100,000 Mexican dollars as 81,000 Shanghai taels in a pro forma entry, which was a note before he formally placed the amount into William Appleton and Company's account with the company. "Shanghai taels" was the local monetary unit adopted by Chinese and foreign merchants in 1857. Even though the market rate between Mexican dollars and Shanghai taels was $73 per 100 taels, Reiche granted a more favorable exchange rate, $82, to Cole, with a 1 percent commission fee deducted.[4] However, while Cole was in Fuzhou, he found that Russell and Company had used the dollars without his knowledge. Worse still, after he returned to Shanghai in April 1858, not only did Reiche reduce the value of the specie to 72,000 taels on the account book, but Russell and Company in Shanghai intended to deduct the cost of tea in Fuzhou from the Mexican dollars. The different exchange rates across these ports further increased the expenses of Cole's tea ventures.[5] Hence two years of wrangling ensued over the true value of the Mexican dollars in Shanghai and the settlement of the Fuzhou purchase, showcasing the intricate credit economy after the Opium War, which comprised more credit instruments and exchange markets than those existing during the Canton Trade era.

A close look at the credit system of the tea trade in the treaty ports adds complexity to the power dynamics of postwar China trade. Previous research on this era often paints the victory of the West, especially Great Britain, in China: European merchants remodeled the treaty port economic system, foreign capital provided infrastructure for the tea trade before the rise of Chinese competition, modern Chinese financial institutions were absent, and European banks had dominated the exchange business in China by the 1860s.[6] However, the image of the Western, especially European, preeminence portrayed in scholarly works contrasts starkly with the shared frustration that permeated nineteenth-century business records. American and European merchants documented their Chinese counterparts' competitiveness, native merchant-bankers' influence, and the lack of leading foreign banks in the treaty ports.[7] Thus the generalization of Europe's immediate triumph compromises chronological accuracy and underestimates the sophistication of China's credit economy.

Historians have started to revisit these stereotypes by emphasizing Chinese merchants' control over international payments and the interdependence of European financial institutions with native banks.[8] This chapter follows this trend to investigate the tea trade's credit system in the treaty ports. Both Chinese and American merchants employed their own credit instruments to develop intraregional credit networks after the 1850s. Hence their agency in expanding the coastal credit economy and exchange markets was no less significant than European capital. Moreover, Chinese banks started to financialize the credit system of the tea trade before the growth of European banking in China. As the first section shows, initially, credit transactions continued in Canton after the end of the Old China Trade, and sterling bills remained the primary credit instrument for tea trade finance. In the newly opened treaty ports, credit economy also germinated. However, rather than relying on sterling bills or European banks, native banks furnished Chinese and foreign merchants with bills of exchange (money orders) and promissory notes (*Zhuangpiao*, or bankers' orders) to facilitate cashless transactions. The financial resources also empowered Chinese traders to dominate the supply of tea to the treaty ports. Therefore the tea trade's credit system, on the Chinese side, transitioned from a commercial relationship in Canton to a financial network, especially in Shanghai and the Yangzi River Valley. On the U.S. side, mercantile credit still dominated the tea trade. The second section shows that, while relying on Chinese credit instruments in Shanghai, American commission houses introduced checks, known as "Comprador's Order to Pay," to the southern coast of China. These checks, written by Chinese compradors, reflected the instrument's changing formats in America. U.S. commission houses also assumed the function of banks to clear intraregional transactions on their account books and issued inland bills of exchange, in U.S. dollars rather than English pounds, between Chinese treaty ports. Consequently, these credit instruments and transactions restored trust between Chinese and U.S. merchants after the Opium War and developed a coastal credit system for the tea trade. With Shanghai and Hong Kong emerging as financial centers, the new credit economy interlocked more regions in China with the global financial network.

Restoring Trust

After the opening of the four new treaty ports in 1842, the U.S.-China tea trade grew to a new level (see figure 8). Canton, however, remained the tea center for Americans in China. The *United States Magazine* celebrated the Treaty of Wangxia, which granted Americans equal access to the treaty ports open after the Opium War, as "more favorable to commerce than that of England," because they "further excited the hopes of dealers."[9] Indeed,

American tea merchants were enthusiastic about the new China trade, as tea transactions and speculation thrived immediately.[10] Tea accounted for over 80 or even 90 percent of the aggregate U.S. imports from China between 1840 and 1845 (see figure 2). Yet the magnitude of the trade in Canton reduced the operations in other ports to small retail businesses.[11] Robert Bennet Forbes, the staunch and outspoken proponent of British hostility against China, acknowledged in 1844 that the prospect of the new treaty port system was "very much over-estimated;" as "the trade at Shanghai had commenced, after some difficulties, but it had not opened at Ningpo" at all.[12] The other two ports, Fuzhou and Xiamen, failed to develop into tea centers within a decade until the Taiping Rebellion and the Second Opium War wreaked havoc in other ports, particularly Canton and Shanghai. Shanghai's tea export economy developed comparatively fast, eclipsing Canton as the primary hub to send green tea to America in 1851. However, its markets notably specialized in lower-grade products.[13] Despite incurring a 35 to 40 percent higher transportation cost by shipping tea from Shanghai's green tea hinterlands to Canton, tea dealers still preferred the old port as the premier outlet for "the finest and higher grades of tea." After all, the quotations offered in Shanghai were 10 to 20 percent lower than the remunerative prices realized in Canton.[14] Only when Canton lost its dominance as the major trading port after the Taiping Rebellion and the Second Opium War did the commerce in "fine and finest descriptions" of green teas flourish in Shanghai.[15]

OLD CREDIT NETWORK

Contemporaries had pondered why Chinese and foreign merchants maintained the "long prescriptive custom" of trading in Canton while other treaty ports adjacent to the tea country had been open. They found one of the old port's enduring appeals was "derived from capital," mainly in the form of sterling bills.[16] Bills of exchange often accounted for roughly 70 percent of Americans' payments in postwar Canton, along with a minimal portion of silver and commodities. Thus sterling bills remained the primary form of capital and the chief means of tea purchase after the Opium War. For example, in 1845, when U.S. imports from China reached $7,285,914, the exports of American goods amounted to a mere $2,112,585, with three-fourths being cotton and about 8 percent, or $163,410, being specie. Credit, primarily bills on London, filled the $5,009,919 deficit.[17] "The commerce of

China is conducted on the basis of imports, opium, and credits on London," American consul R. W. Murphy reported a decade later, in 1855, but the merchandise from America was a trifle and opium was about 30 percent of the value. Credit instruments remained predominant in balancing Americans' accounts.[18] Noticing the steady increase in U.S. tea imports by 1856, the English magazine *Economist* clarified that "most of the tea sent there is paid for by bills on London."[19] "Of the Teas imported into the United States," William Appleton and Company also noted in 1857, "a large proportion, perhaps four fifths, are paid for in China with Exchange on London."[20] Hence the U.S. constituents of Augustine Heard and Company and Russell and Company adopted English pounds as the monetary unit in their tea orders and instructed the commission houses to buy "Green Teas £5000 Strg [Sterling]," "£1000 or equivalent of same at Canton in Oolong," or "£500 or equivalent of same at Canton in Congou."[21] In contrast the supply of silver to China further shrank until the breakout of the Taiping Rebellion and the American Civil War, when foreign merchants, unable to sell their goods and bills, had to ship silver and gold to China (see figure 14).[22] Before that, the discovery of gold and silver in the United States added another tool for Americans to obtain English bills. The *Economist* noted that Americans had doubled their tea imports from China during the 1850s, "all of which were paid for by means of bills drawn upon London against credits established" for various American produce, including gold from California and the West Coast of America.[23] Therefore it is unsurprising that Augustine Heard and Company's accounts in 1866 and 1867 meticulously documented their shipments of gold to London banks.[24]

Nonetheless, the large amount of sterling bills hardly found a market beyond Canton during the 1840s and 1850s. Even though Shanghai would become the financial hub between Calcutta and San Francisco by 1863, its foreign exchange market developed only slowly during the immediate postwar years.[25] "The Exchange business in Shanghai is evidently only in its infancy," an English house reported in 1850, with most of the firms there "being mere dependencies on Canton or Hong Kong."[26] Others noticed the bill market in Shanghai "beginning to assume a definite form" in 1851, but it had no organizations "where you can meet people you want and find them inclined to talk of business."[27] The volatile exchange rates also reflected the immaturity of Shanghai's market. When Americans, such as Wolcott

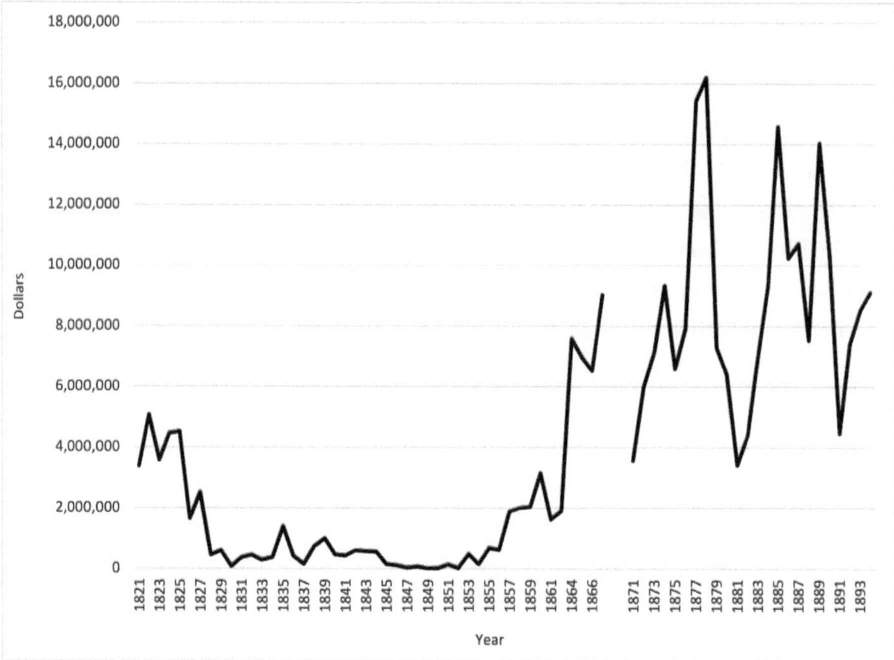

Fig. 14. Bullion and specie exported from the United States to China, 1821–94. The data for 1861 included gold shipments to China. For the shipments during 1863–67, the article "The China Trade: Number I from China" from the *Merchants' Magazine and Commercial Review* fails to specify the proportion of silver versus that of gold. This magazine article also claimed that the annual shipment of bullion had reached a million dollars by 1854, a figure nearly ten times higher than Homans's records of the silver imports to China for the same period adopted in this chart. The figure suggests that the magazine's estimate likely included gold alongside silver or exaggerated the volume of the transpacific bullion flow. Sources: 1821–56: Homans, *Historical and Statistical Account*, 181. 1857–60, 1871–94: Pan, *Trade of the United States with China*, 22, 43. 1861: "China," *Merchants' Magazine and Commercial Review*, August 1, 1862, 134. 1863–67: "The China Trade: Number I from China," *Merchants' Magazine and Commercial Review*, June 1, 1868, 460, ProQuest American Periodicals.

Bates and Company, purchased bills on London and Calcutta in Shanghai during 1851, the rates fluctuated markedly compared to the relatively stable prices in Canton.[28] Fuzhou, the future major tea port, remained devoid of exchange business during the 1850s. Its exchange market developed only in the 1860s following the expansion of the tea trade in 1853. An exchange market also emerged in Hankou, the tea center opened after the Second

Opium War, in the 1860s, but it remained small by the 1870s.[29] Therefore, like contemporary financial centers, the large capital market of Canton, built on its international commercial and financial networks, attracted major companies.[30] All mercantile firms were headquartered at the port after the Opium War, except Jardine Matheson and Company and Dent Company, which relocated their offices to the new British colony Hong Kong.[31] Those moving to Shanghai usually left a house or an agent in Canton to handle the exchange operations, until the old port lost its financial and commercial dominance in the 1860s.[32]

Equally important to the exchange market, the trust relationship and credit economy formed during the Canton Trade era—embodied by the advance system, exchange accounts, and bills of exchange—resumed and sustained the tea business in the old port. For instance, Chinese merchant Yenqua continued credit transactions with Augustine Heard and Company while maintaining exchange accounts with Russell and Company after the Opium War. In 1847, through Augustine Heard and Company, Yenqua's hong, Zhixiangsheng ji, supplied teas to William Appleton and Company in Boston and Baring Brothers in London. These U.S. and British companies advanced approximately 70 to 75 percent of the value of tea, in the form of bills on London, to Yenqua in March and May 1847. After the contracted tea arrived in October 1847, Yenqua received the full payment with advances and fees deducted. The proceeds helped clear Yenqua's account balances with Russell and Company, for the Chinese merchant had transferred the value to the company in July 1847.[33] Thus the two American commission companies engaged in the advance system to contract tea from Yenqua after the Opium War. Moreover, built on the existing credit network, Chinese merchants, like Yenqua, readily accepted bills of exchange as the advance payment and employed account books to clear the transactions with their U.S. counterparts.

In contrast, lacking such well-established trust relationships, the trade in other treaty ports unfolded through barter or silver payments. Some Chinese middlemen chose barter only, selling their teas in exchange for English manufactured goods or opium.[34] Without Cohong's mediation, the sense of insecurity and distrust was mutual for foreign traders. "There being no longer security-merchants to pay the debts and fulfill the engagements of those who are unfortunate, or of those who commit acts of fraud," British

Consuls warned those in Ningbo in 1843, "British subjects are hereby cautioned against giving credit to any large amount. A barter trade will be found the best and safest in the end."[35] Likewise, the trade at Shanghai was "almost exclusively a barter trade" during the 1840s. The earliest Chinese brokers in Shanghai, whom the British report described as "a miserable set of Canton linguists, with no other capital than their own assurance and the tea men's ignorance," secured little trust from Chinese and foreign traders, so opium and cloth sustained the "practical working of a recently introduced system of barter."[36] Opium also initiated small-scale Fuzhou trade during the 1840s.[37] In 1857, three years after Augustine Heard and Company extended its operation to Fuzhou, they still bartered 140 pieces of long-ells woolens for tea.[38] Even though references to barter in the earliest treaty ports declined after the mid-nineteenth century, the pattern repeated itself in the Yangzi River area and Taiwan, which were open to foreign trade after the Second Opium War.[39] The worsened silver shortage after the Opium War reinforced the barter economy (see figure 14).[40] Even specie circulated on trust in the new ports. Following the norms in Canton, the Chinese in the treaty ports and their neighboring regions preferred the extinct Spanish Carolus dollars.[41] Nonetheless, the Carolus dollars were in no way superior to Mexican, Peruvian, and U.S. dollars in terms of purity and weight.[42] British traders thus lambasted the custom as the "foolish preference shown by the Chinese" or "a prejudice," whereas Americans emphasized that large British and Indian houses in Shanghai, notably "Jardine, Sassoon & a few Parsee's," demanded only Spanish dollars as well.[43] All explained the slow development of the treaty ports beyond Canton.

NEW CREDIT NETWORK

However, even at the height of barter and silver payments, the credit economy began to germinate in Shanghai. Credit instruments issued by Chinese banks, including *piaohao* (exchange banks or remittance banks) and *qianzhuang* (copper or cash shops), bolstered the tea trade's credit system in the treaty ports.[44] The well-organized banking sector in China had developed considerably in Canton, Shanghai, and Ningbo by the 1790s.[45] In the nineteenth century, the exchange banks, managed primarily by merchant-bankers from Shanxi province, controlled the remittance business within China, and the cash shops dominated Chinese credit markets.[46] Before

1840, tea and silk merchants in Canton had taken money to native banks, which then purchased native bills of exchange from Shanxi exchange banks for remittance.[47] When this convenient credit instrument was available in Shanghai, tea dealers in the new port turned away from opium. Thus the *North China Herald* reported that "a considerable amount of Money orders in the hands of Tea and Silkmen, caused an immediate and heavy decline" in the prices of opium in September 1850.[48] The "continued fall in prices" persisted into the end of that year, owing to the "the large amount of money orders in circulation." Consequently, opium—"originally taken in barter and bought by the Brokers of the Tea and Silk men"—found few buyers in Shanghai.[49] Defined as "a triple-binding note sent by one native bank (or a merchant) through a merchant (or a native bank) to another native bank," a money order was an inland bill of exchange that involved three parties in the credit relationship.[50] When a merchant purchased commodities at a different place, they bought these bills from Shanxi banks' local branches. Before visiting the marketplace, the merchant sent the bills to their agents in the district, who then exchanged the bills with the branch of the Shanxi bank for local money orders to pay local dealers.[51] Therefore money orders increased the availability of credit to tea traders and facilitated intraregional transactions after the Opium War.

American merchants also used these native bills of exchange to facilitate their China trade. In April 1869 the Shanghai market for foreign imports was stagnant. Unable to sell their commodities, both American merchants and foreign banks sought out Chinese bills to invest in China goods. "That purchase of Chinese bills at 25½ was a lucky one," Forbes celebrated in a letter. "The banks were after those very bills, but while they were haggling I gobbled 'em up and spoilt their little game."[52] The bills were also available to merchants at other ports in the Yangzi River area. In early 1873, when Forbes intended to send Fitz Heinemann, his agent in Hankou, 50,000 taels from Shanghai as advance payments, Forbes proposed to "bargain for Shanse [Shanxi] bills payable with you [Fitz] towards the end of May."[53] Chinese bills from Shanghai thus financed the company's advance system in Hankou, largely for tea. As historian Luman Wang emphasized, even the Hongkong and Shanghai Bank, with branches in only six regions of China, would depend on Shanxi *piaohao*'s branches in about forty localities to make remittance between the treaty ports and interior China.[54]

Promissory notes issued by native cash shops, known as *qianzhuang* in the wider Shanghai area, also developed the tea trade's credit network within the barter or silver economy. As a British report concluded in 1849, Chinese merchants bartered tea in Shanghai for either silver or long cloths throughout the 1840s. If the latter, the tea merchants seldom took the cloth back home but sold it to itinerant Suzhou brokers or Shanghai bankers for promissory notes of twenty days' sight. The native bankers' competitiveness in the trade lay in "the facilities which their paper affords," namely "a banker's promissory note," which answered "his purpose as well as money, and [passed] current from hand to hand for the purchase of goods or payment of debts."[55] Suzhou, a city west of Shanghai, was one of the bases for wealthy cash shops. Nine groups of merchant-bankers originating in Zhejiang (Ningbo, Shaoxing, and Huzhou) and Jiangsu provinces (Suzhou and Zhenjiang) dominated the banking sector of Shanghai during the latter half of the nineteenth century.[56] Even those who sold tea for silver tended to "buy promissory notes from Hang-chow [Hangzhou] merchants," who came from the capital city of Zhejiang.[57] After foreign merchants accepted native promissory notes, the credit network encompassed the entire commodity chain. As early as the 1850s, foreign merchants had employed native banks' promissory notes as means of payment.[58] No wonder when Taiping rebels marched into Hangzhou, Americans' business correspondence paid special attention to the impact on native banks and their facilities. "There has also been some trouble among the Bankers, one of them having broken—and those indispensable to Import trade." Franklin Gordon Dexter, Appleton and Company's agent in Shanghai, received a report in 1860: "Bankers Orders, are not now supplied except to cash depositors."[59] British consular reports also documented foreign traders' purchasing the *zhuangpiao* to pay for Chinese produce before selling their goods in Canton and Fuzhou in 1869.[60]

Known as banker's orders, or *zhuangpiao*, the promissory notes issued by native banks rebuilt the trust relationship and financialized the credit economy in the new treaty ports. "The *zhuangpiao* is a promissory note issued by *qianzhuangs*," Ma Yinchu, Chinese economist, explained.[61] According to Ma, these banks' promissory notes emerged out of distrust between Chinese and foreign merchants in the treaty ports. Commercial promissory notes were nothing new to the China trade, given the dealings of Consequa and Howqua with American traders. However, financial promissory notes arose in the foreign trade after the Opium War. "In the past when foreign merchants traded with Hong merchants, they had credit with each other," Ma noted, "so foreigners were willing to deliver their goods first and accept payments later. However, the mode of trade suddenly changed after the opening of the five Treaty Ports." Foreign merchants distrusted Chinese importers outside Canton, owing to their limited proficiency in foreign languages and dependence on brokers for transactions. Native banks thereby filled the gap. The cash shops issued *zhuangpiaos* to guarantee Chinese buyers' payments within a flexible period, ranging from five to twenty days, or paid for these Chinese clients after their *zhuangpiaos*' expiration.[62] "Since Chinese merchants made payments to the *qianzhuang*, foreigners dealt solely with these native banks," Ma maintained, "so they never trusted their Chinese counterparts."[63] Native banks' credit instruments thus transformed the basis of the credit system from merchants' relationships in the Canton Trade to financial networks in the treaty ports, paving the way for further financialization of the transpacific tea trade.

When foreign banking remained underdeveloped in China during the first two decades following the Opium War, foreign merchants in Shanghai relied heavily on Chinese banks for credit instruments to make payments.[64] As a letter written by a foreign merchant to the *North China Herald* clarified, the "large and wealthy banking establishments of the City, whose ramifications extended over all this section of the country, and whose operations were of a magnitude almost surpassing belief, issued notes in the greatest abundance, which were as well known," the author adding, "and received with as little hesitation as the dollar itself." The circulation of these notes even rendered silver payments unnecessary in Shanghai. "With 'bankers' orders as they were termed, our exchanges were effected, and dollars were rarely used, or seen, save in petty disbursements."[65] However, Taiping rebels' occupation of Shanghai in September 1853 forced many Chinese merchants and bankers to close their businesses, and the Chinese notes suddenly disappeared. Consequently, "foreigners were left with scarcely dollars enough to pay for the necessaries of life."[66] Native banks' failures in the succeeding years also "disinclined Foreigners to accept the unusually current Bank order."[67] As Chinese merchant-bankers suffered heavy losses in Shanghai, money became scarce and the originally stable exchange rate began to rise.[68] Americans' persistent concern—Shanghai's high exchange rate drove tea to other ports—remained an issue into 1856.[69] Amid the financial crisis and the scarcity of bankers' orders, the U.S. consul clarified that "foreigners began to impose the belief on the native Chinese that the Carolus dollar was the most valuable," not the other way around. Thus emerged the silver question in Shanghai among foreign merchants, who proposed to accept Mexican dollars as currency to increase the circulating medium in commerce.[70] When the Taiping Rebellion quieted down, peace returned to Shanghai and "the present system of Chinese Banker's orders" revived in 1860. Despite the wide circulation of Mexican dollars, foreign merchants in Shanghai still believed the paper device "to be inseparable from the Trade of this Port and that it must continue to be in use."[71]

Outside the wider Shanghai area, native banks' promissory notes also became prevalent during the following decades. Foreign merchants in Hankou acknowledged that "the present system of credit and payment" in 1864 was "in bankers orders" handled by their compradors.[72] In 1874 Hankou authorities' attempt to ban native banks from issuing promissory notes and enforce silver payments halted trade in the port until the officials rescinded the prohibition.[73] Native credit instruments also emerged on the southern coast. An article titled "Native Banks in Foochow" traced the circulation of native promissory notes in Fuzhou to the start of the international tea trade during the 1850s. Despite the large amount of specie brought by foreign buyers to the port, merchants demanded a more convenient circulating medium. Thus the notes "drawn on the bank and are payable to bearer" replaced silver coins in this port.[74]

Native banks' credit instruments and financial facilities enhanced Chinese merchants' influence in the tea ports along the Yangzi River, notably Hankou, Jiujiang, Ningbo, and Shanghai, which were also the primary suppliers of tea to the U.S. market (see figure 13). The Hankou Maritime Customs reported in 1864 that "formidable opponents have arisen in the persons of Chinese." The facilities offered by native banks, along with some commission houses in the port, enabled "the Cantonese [sojourners in Hankou] to compete with the foreigner in the tea market."[75] In Jiujiang the branches of ten British and three American houses had extended there by 1863, two years after the port was open to foreign trade. However, despite Jiujiang's proximity to tea-producing districts and the Hankou market, all foreign merchants but one English tea firm had withdrawn from the port by 1869.[76] The Chinese in Jiujiang, supported by advances from Shanghai, dominated the tea trade, whereas foreign houses found "themselves nearly entirely deprived of the benefits of a barter or exchange business," customs commissioners E. De Champs and Edward B. Drew analyzed, "a position which is still further aggravated, by the difficulties which fetter financial operations in the absence of any Banks."[77] Given the resources extended from Shanghai, where native banks concentrated, Champs likely referred to the lack of foreign banks in Jiujiang. Chinese capital also dominated the tea market in Ningbo, where many wealthy native banks originated. Therefore, by 1870, teas shipped from Ningbo to Shanghai had been "entirely on Chinese account."[78] Even when foreign merchants started to describe Shanghai's financial sector as smaller and less transparent than its European counterparts during the 1870s, they conceded that "Chinese banks afford facilities to their customers which a foreign establishment could not do without the certainty of serious loss."[79] For instance, when heavy advances to tea and silk dealers made money scarce and interest rates high in 1877, Shanghai cash shops were able to draw a few lacs of silver from neighboring places to relieve the pressure on Shanghai's money market. The financial resources strengthened "the negotiability of their orders among foreigners" and enabled the Chinese merchant "to hold his produce [to ask for better prices], which he might otherwise be unable to do if the position of the banker from whom he had procured advances became jeopardised."[80]

Forming a Coastal Credit Network

In 1864 foreign merchants in Hankou even tried to lure Ningbo banks to this newly opened port and to "take an immense power away from the compradores," although the scheme would be hard to implement in the tea trade.[81] Indeed, while native banks offered financial resources to traders, Chinese compradors helped American companies build a commercial credit network across the treaty ports. Originally working as servants and house stewards for foreign merchants in Canton, compradors acted as salesmen, cashiers, tea dealers, and partners of foreign houses in other ports, many of them being sojourning Cantonese.[82] The credit system enhanced these Chinese employees' prominence, as foreign firms relied on them to assess and guarantee the credibility of native credit instruments.[83] "All matters from selecting *zhuangpiaos*, assaying silver, to trading bills of exchange passed through compradors' hands."[84] Thus foreign merchants in Hankou deplored their reliance on the comprador, for "the latter is responsible for all banker's orders taken by him."[85] Economist Srinivas Ram Wagel categorized native banks' orders and compradors' guarantee as the double warranties of credit in the China trade.[86] The distrust of compradors but the absence of other facilities, such as foreign banks, prompted some foreign merchants to espouse cash payments or Ningbo banking's expansion into Hankou.[87] Therefore Andrea Lee McElderry argued that the rise of *qianzhuangs* and compradors in facilitating China's international trade after the Opium War shows foreign merchants' inability to fully participate in China's trading system, rather than their financial superiority or immediate triumph.[88]

COMPRADOR'S ORDERS

Compradors also issued checks, known as comprador's orders to pay, to facilitate Americans' tea trade in the treaty ports.[89] The comprador's order resembled a modern bank check, defined as a written order request addressed to a bank to pay a third party on demand.[90] Augustine Heard Jr. explained that "orders, or cheques, were drawn on" compradors in China, "precisely as on a modern Bank."[91] After all, foreign banks were still establishing themselves in China during the first two decades of the treaty system.[92] Four British-Indian banks and the French Comptoir d'Escompte de Paris were open in China during the 1850s. Among them the British-owned Oriental Bank remained the leading foreign bank for decades.[93] However, the *Economist* lamented in 1856 that "India, and especially China, are beyond the influence of those banking operations."[94] Heard asserted that even the Oriental Bank was "one most conservative, and exercising really but little influence."[95] Consequently, mercantile capital dominated Americans' commerce in China, commission houses acted as their own banks, and they "sought no facilities outside of its own resources."[96] The commercial checks written by their compradors functioned like official bank drafts in China. Even in 1905 a U.S. consul in China still found that "in many foreign business houses bills are paid by the representative of the business office in an order on the comprador of the firm, and this order is banked as a bank check or draft,"[97] showing the long-term influence of the paper instrument on the credit economy in China's treaty ports.

"Comprador's Order to Pay" financed the U.S.-China tea trade in Canton after the Opium War. Yenqua accepted comprador's orders from Augustine Heard Company as payments, advances, or returns on tea in the 1840s–50s.[98] The American house also issued a large amount of comprador's orders to finance its active and massive transactions. The extant orders document their business with over two dozen Chinese tea sellers between the 1840s and the 1850s.[99] Simply presenting the orders to pay, compradors advanced tens of thousands of dollars, each time, to Footae, Chuenqua, Cumwoe, and Ahming for their green or black tea.[100] The company also used comprador's orders to settle account balances, such as the $21,206.01 with Moushing or the $556.75 with Kincum, in their tea transactions.[101] In addition to these large transactions, compradors also wrote orders with small face value, such as the $189.88 to Tingqua for the dividend of tea received in New York or the $7.50 to Yatchong for a box of tea, suggesting the wide circulation of the check in daily dealings.[102] Moreover, standardized orders emerged. Printed comprador's orders replaced hand-written ones during the 1850s. Many Chinese merchants stamped their seals, rather than left signatures, on these paper devices (also see figures 15 and 16).[103] All demonstrated that this credit instrument gained growing currency in Canton's tea trade.

When Americans adopted comprador's orders to finance their tea trade in China, the check was arguably a newly standardized financial instrument in the United States. Many comprador's orders in China adopted and adapted the format of English or early American checks, reflecting the ongoing evolution of this instrument in the United States. Despite the emergence of checks in continental Europe around 1400 and its limited use in seventeenth-century London, standardized checks drawn on banks grew into general use only during the 1830s in England and the 1840s in the United States.[104] English and early U.S. checks were "bearer instruments," which clarified no ownership and required no endorsement when being transferred to a third party. Since any holder could cash the check or transfer it by mere delivery, this instrument was less secure and more challenging to document than promissory notes and bills of exchange. From the 1820s to the 1830s, the mainstream American check transitioned to a more secure instrument payable to "a particular person or order," so the named person could either cash or endorse it to a third party.[105] A small number of the comprador's orders at the Heard Family Business Records

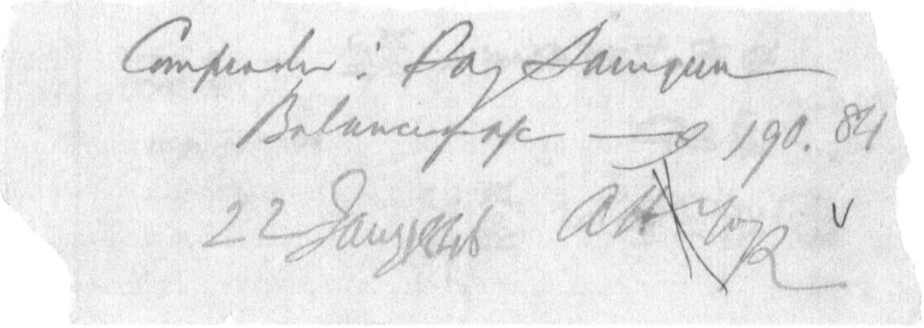

Fig. 15. Comprador's orders to pay Samqua balance on account, January 22, 1846. While the English inscriptions on the draft only mention Samqua and its face value, the Chinese text on the reverse side provides crucial transactional details. The rightmost line left by Samqua's store states, "Tongshun Hong received 190.84 dollars from Heard to pay for the balance of tea." Adjacent lines added by the comprador of Augustine Heard and Company specify the date and identities of both parties. Notably, the inscriptions on Comprador's orders gradually gave way to Chinese hongs' seals in the coming decade (see figure 16). Bills of exchange, 1844–1866, reel 86-3147 R-56, HFBR, Baker Library, Harvard Business School.

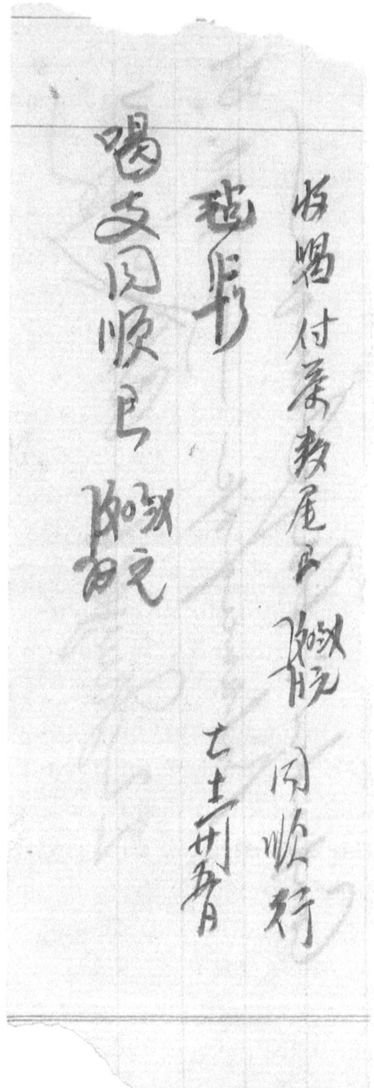

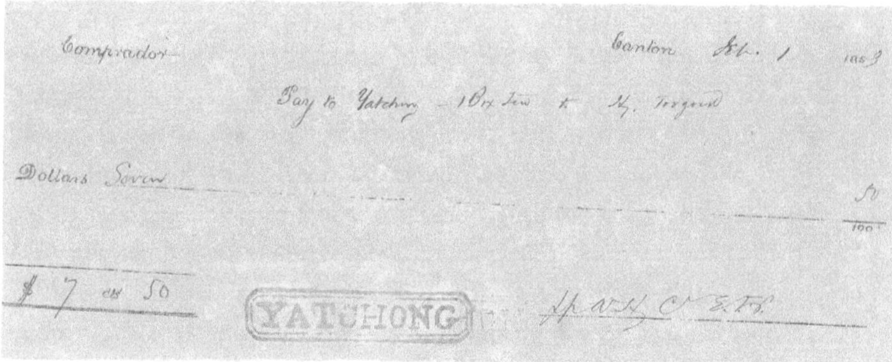

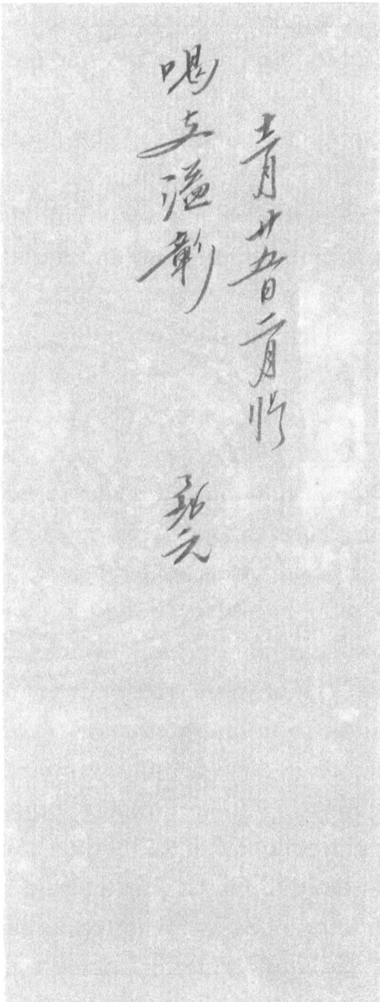

Fig. 16. Printed comprador's order to pay with Yatchong's seal, February 1, 1853. Bills of exchange, 1844–1866, reel 86-3147 R-60, HFBR, Baker Library, Harvard Business School.

were bearer instruments. One was drawn on the company to "pay bearer six dollars and 68 cents for three chests fine Oolong."[106] Most comprador's orders employed in the tea trade before the 1860s have neither "bearer" nor "order" written on them, but were in the "pay to a particular person" format. Therefore the orders were more secure than the bearer orders but less liquid than "pay-to-order" checks (see figures 15 and 16). It is unclear whether the instrument in China was transferrable by endorsement. The role of Chinese employees as drawees also rendered comprador's orders distinct from standardized American checks. After the 1840s, U.S. checks were increasingly drawn on banks and only occasionally on cashiers of these financial institutions. In contrast, most of the orders to pay were still drawn upon compradors—cashiers of Augustine Heard and Company—and only occasionally on the company.[107]

When the tea trade extended to Fuzhou, Augustine Heard and Company also issued comprador's orders in this treaty port, but they remodified its format for local use. In 1854, the first year when American houses operated in Fuzhou, a large number of comprador's orders emerged to pay for tea from over thirty Chinese stores in this port. The company's compradors used the paper device with the face value from several hundred taels to tens of thousands of dollars, each time, to pay over thirty suppliers of green, black, and oolong tea, such as Fook Hoong (Fook Hung), Hop Chun, Tong Chun, or Tong Mow.[108] Comprador's orders also facilitated the upcountry system, in which American and English houses sent compradors into the interior to purchase or contract tea directly from producers, because the company's checks also paid for manufacturing green tea in the countryside around Fuzhou.[109] While the value of the orders in Canton was in Spanish or Mexican dollars, those circulating in Fuzhou adopted taels as the monetary unit. Moreover, many Fuzhou orders clarified "chopped dollars" or "small sycee" as the standard of value.[110] Thus this paper device reflected the distinct forms of silver adopted across the treaty ports. The variances in monetary units generated extra work for the compradors handling printed orders. Appearing in Fuzhou from 1859, the preprinted compradors' orders adopted dollars and cents as the monetary units. While compradors needed to fill out only the payees' names and the amount of money on a printed order, they had to cross out the standardized monetary units and replace them with the Chinese tael, mace, and candareen.[111] Nonetheless, the printed orders issued in the 1860s adopted taels more frequently as the monetary unit, suggesting the process of localizing this instrument for the local monetary system of Fuzhou.[112]

Beyond Canton and Fuzhou, comprador's orders also made intraregional payments, but primarily along the southern coast, rather than the Shanghai and Yangzi River region. A comprador's order issued in Fuzhou to pay "Amoy Coolies" implied payments made to the adjacent treaty port, Xiamen.[113] The branch of Augustine Heard and Company in Hong Kong drew on their comprador to pay for a "Foochow Godownman," who sold forty rattan to the company in 1859.[114] After the Heards extended to Shanghai in 1847, the office also made some comprador's orders, in Canton, to pay the expenses in Shanghai, such as the salaries of tea tasters and workers. However, none were issued locally within Shanghai and the Yangzi River area to finance the company's extensive tea business there.[115] In truth, the commercial credit network woven by comprador's orders seldom went beyond the southeastern coast of China—particularly Canton, Fuzhou, and Hong Kong.[116] The absence of orders in Shanghai and the tea centers along the Yangzi River—including Ningbo, Jiujiang, and Hankou—likely attest to the influence of native banks and Chinese credit instruments in these regions. As Chinese banker Pan Jiufen recalled, the cash shops in Shanghai managed intraregional clearing in the Yangzi River Valley and middle China.[117] Therefore it is likely that American commission houses employed Chinese banking facilities, rather than their commercial checks, to pay tea sellers in these treaty ports.

COASTAL EXCHANGE MARKETS

While comprador's orders issued by Augustine Heard and Company illustrated the use of a single credit instrument in the U.S.-China tea trade, years of wrangling between Russell and Company and William Appleton and Company illustrated the function of the entire coastal credit network. After Captain Cole reported disputes regarding the 1857 tea venture, the new head of Russell and Company, Thomas Walsh, maintained intensive correspondence with William Appleton and Company to justify how they handled trade finance. Their disagreements highlight the role of American commission houses as banks for foreign buyers in the tea trade with China, the complexity of the coastal exchange system, and the rise of Hong Kong and Shanghai as new credit centers for the treaty ports.

In their letters, Russell and Company took pains to dismiss Cole's assertion about his ownership of the Mexican dollars in Shanghai by highlighting the commission house's role resembling a bank that absorbed deposits and settled tea transactions on account books. First, while Cole insisted that he placed the dollars in Russell and Company's temporary care, Walsh countered that "Captain Cole must somewhat misapprehend the nature of the *deposit* [emphasized by the author] he made." Walsh treated the 100,000 Mexican dollars as a formal deposit—evidenced by Russell and Company's crediting the sum on William Appleton and Company's account—rather than a temporary safekeeping arrangement, in which case, Russell and Company would only present Cole a receipt. Clarifying the transaction's financial nature nullified Cole's demand that "the packages not to be opened" and justified the company's use of the dollars before Cole's return to Shanghai.[118] Second, after procuring teas via the branch of Russell and Company in Fuzhou, Cole thought that the Shanghai office would ship the dollars to Fuzhou to settle the transactions. Nonetheless, Reiche, the bookkeeper, directed the Fuzhou office to transfer the account balance to Shanghai.[119] Therefore, relying on bookkeeping, the house made payments via different branches "without actual remittances," and "if one account was credited for the same amount that was debited to the other." Commission fees incurred in the process.[120]

Varying exchange rates across the treaty ports complicated the internal clearance between different branches of the same company. Consequently, another dispute arose between William Appleton and Company and Russell and Company over the silver valuation of the Fuzhou tea purchase in Shanghai, demonstrating the necessity of adopting the credit economy—including account books mentioned above and the inland bills explained below—to clear intraregional balances. Owing to the Qing government's liberal economic policy, local monetary systems complicated the actual value of silver in different places.[121] During the Taiping Rebellion, Chinese bankers and merchants made "Shanghai tael" the unit of account for all transactions in the port, with one "Shanghai tael" equaling 98 percent of sycee—the imaginary pure silver in China.[122] While merchants in Shanghai converted the value of other forms of silver into Shanghai tael, those in Hong Kong adopted Mexican dollars as the standard.[123] Chopped Spanish dollars, or Spanish dollars with stamps, remained an accepted currency in

Fuzhou.[124] While the value of a Mexican dollar was worth only 72–78 percent of the Shanghai tael, it equaled 86–90 percent of the chopped dollars in Fuzhou.[125] The value of silver in Canton also differed from that in Shanghai, and Xiamen adopted the Canton standard.[126] The monetary system was equally complex in the Yangzi River area. For instance, the local silver of Hankou, named *yangli*, was worth less than Shanghai taels.[127] Consequently, a major contention arose between the two companies over how to convert the value of the Fuzhou tea purchase, priced in Spanish dollars, to Mexican dollars or Shanghai taels. The fluctuating market rates of silver over the span of several months further complicated the disputes.[128] Other U.S. tea buyers faced the same problem of varying exchange rates across the treaty ports. Thus Augustine Heard and Company documented the "Coast Exchange" in their account books to trace the changing value of goods and services, such as the rates of "teas from Foochow" respectively in Hong Kong dollars and Shanghai taels.[129] Using account entries to settle the transactions, rather than physically transferring different forms of silver between the ports, helped streamline the tea trade.

Aside from the silver value of tea, William Appleton and Company protested the settlement of the Fuzhou purchase in Shanghai, because this practice violated the regular procedure of intraregional clearance: Hong Kong should be the credit center. According to Hooper and Appleton, the Shanghai office of Russell and Company seldom directly settled the account balance in Fuzhou. "Every account we have had at Foochow has been made up and settled by drafts on the Hong Kong house," Hooper explained, "and if our funds are at Shanghae [Shanghai], remittances have been made from there [Shanghai] to settle the Hong Kong a/c [account] and the rates of Exchange advised."[130] Therefore Hong Kong, as the financial center for the coastal tea trade, should have been the place to settle the 1857 Fuzhou transaction. Indeed, in August 1859, Russell and Company in Shanghai "remitted $64,000 to Hong Kong" to pay "the drafts from Foochow" for Cole's tea purchase.[131] The Shanghai branch of this company continued to remit bills on Hong Kong to pay for other Fuzhou tea purchases during 1859–60.[132] Samuel Hooper and Company's account with Russell and Company in Fuzhou also showed that Russell and Company drew drafts on the Hong Kong office to fund tea cargos from Fuzhou in July to October 1860.[133] When examining Russell and Company's tea accounts in August

1869, Forbes also clarified that "the subsidiary accounts connected with the shipments of this term [the season of 1868–69]" in Shanghai "have been closed lately in Hong Kong," highlighting the Shanghai office's reliance on Hong Kong to clear their trade balances.[134]

Indeed, Hong Kong sustained the credit system of the coastal tea trade through its exchange market and the bills drawn on this port. Colonized by the British after the Opium War, Hong Kong initially served as a transiting port between China, Great Britain, and India. Amid the Taiping Rebellion, nonetheless, wealthy Chinese merchants migrated to Hong Kong, bringing their commercial networks with Southeast Asia and the United States to the colony.[135] With a large number of brokers and merchants concentrating in Hong Kong, its exchange market developed considerably. During the 1860s, Augustine Heard and Company and Russell and Company recounted a wide variety of bills of exchange sold in Hong Kong, including "sterling exchange" (bills on London), American bills (drawn on San Francisco), "Bank paper," and "private Bills."[136] Therefore even the commission houses in Shanghai settled their account balances in Hong Kong with bills of exchange, bank drafts, or silver.[137] For Captain Cole's tea venture, Hooper and Appleton expected the Shanghai office to purchase bills on Hong Kong to settle the Fuzhou balance, as they customarily did for other tea ventures, rather than clearing the transaction directly in Shanghai.[138] Moreover, bills on Hong Kong were then sold at 24 percent discount in Shanghai.[139] Thus following the regular clearance route would have saved them a substantial amount of money, although Walsh claimed that the result "would have been the same, since the Exchange between Hong Kong & Foochow would have been still 10 @ 12%."[140]

More important than whose decision was more cost-effective was the broader shift in financial centers underpinning the credit system of the Sino-American tea trade. Cole and Hooper originally remembered Canton as the place to settle the 1857 Fuzhou tea purchase. However, Russell and Company clarified in 1860 that their office in Hong Kong was the first point of contact to clear the transaction.[141] Canton remained the financial center by the late 1850s, when Shanghai's exchange market still offered bills on Canton for sale to facilitate the remittance between the two treaty ports. During the Taiping Rebellion, American and English firms trucked a large amount of bills on Canton to exchange for tea in Shanghai.[142] Similar to English bills, bills on Canton interconnected with the tea trade cycle. On

Shanghai's exchange market, the rates of bills on Canton fluctuated with tea transactions, commanding a 1.5–4 percent premium before and during the tea season and falling to a 0.25–0.5 percent discount during the December-to-April trade suspension.[143] Yet in 1856, enraged over the British-French aggression toward China on the verge of the Second Opium War, a Chinese mob set the commercial districts in Canton on fire, thus terminating the lingering influence of the old port in China's international commerce.[144] After being "held by the Allied forces of England and France for nearly three years" during the Second Opium War, Canton had "become almost the last important place in China as regards trade" with Americans in 1861.[145] Consequently, on Shanghai's exchange market, bills on Hong Kong replaced those on Canton. Traders remitted funds to Hong Kong more frequently than to Canton.[146] The British colony thereby encompassed the former credit center within its financial orbit.[147]

Drawn upon different financial centers, inland bills continued to circulate and expand the intraregional credit network across Chinese treaty ports. In addition to sterling exchanges and American dollar bills, Hong Kong's exchange market offered bills on Shanghai for sale.[148] A credit market was formed in Fuzhou in the 1860s, selling inland bills on Shanghai along with English bills on London.[149] The intraregional credit network also extended to the Yangzi River region. In Hankou's exchange market, bank and mercantile bills on Shanghai (demand bill or ten-day-sight bill), Hong Kong (demand bill), and London (six-month-sight bill) were all available in the 1870s.[150] Hence, during 1859–66, Augustine Heard and Company issued considerable bills of exchange among Chinese treaty ports, primarily between Hong Kong and such cities as Shanghai, Fuzhou, Xiamen, and Macao.[151] The inland bills, like bills on London, extended U.S. traders' financing periods for their tea transactions, as Forbes calculated for Edward King, who conducted business at Fuzhou: "If we had the credits here [Shanghai] for your tea purchases we should have 30 days use of the proceeds of the sterling, before Hongkong bills [on Shanghai] in reimbursement of your drawings would mature."[152] Apparently, the adoption of the inland bills across Chinese treaty ports enriched Americans' monetary resources beyond what English and American bills could afford.

Along with American commission houses, the Chinese also employed the available credit instruments to tighten the network across the treaty ports.

Native banks were a key component of the coastal credit system. For instance, among the ninety cash shops in Fuzhou in 1867, two of them drew on other ports for their clients at the rate of 2.5–4.5 percent.[153] In the 1870s Chinese merchants in Xiamen shipped dollars to Hong Kong to buy bills drawn by foreigners.[154] The business with American houses involved more Chinese into the credit network. Augustine Heard and Company in Canton wrote repeatedly to the branch in Hong Kong in 1868, sending "Tea, Rice and General Market Reports" and advising them to issue thousands of dollars' drafts on many Chinese merchants, such as Aleen, Ayue, and particularly Akarm. Some of the transactions were in tea.[155] The Chinese also accepted the inland bills endorsed by their American trading partners. As figure 17 shows, the Fuzhou branch of Augustine Heard and Company drew a ten-day-sight bill on Hong Kong, valued at $2,040, on October 27, 1859. The Hong Kong office accepted the bill four days later and clarified the sum would be "due November 10/13 [November 10–13]," 1859, roughly within ten days. The bill was then endorsed to a Chinese firm, Guang Changlong, possibly located in Canton (i.e., Guang). The Chinese inscriptions on the back indicate that Guang Changlong accepted the bill on November 12, 1859 (or October 18, 1859, in the lunar calendar), before its due date, thus providing the Hong Kong office funds to pay the Fuzhou branch.

Consequently the U.S.-China tea trade integrated the newly developed treaty ports with global financial networks. U.S. commission houses received bills on London from their constituents to fund their tea trade and then sold the bills in the exchange markets across Chinese treaty ports. The fluctuations in Fuzhou's bill market were "governed throughout by the operations in the tea market," as were those in Shanghai and Hong Kong.[156] In turn the varying sizes and uneven development of the exchange markets reshaped the English bills' value and, accordingly, the tea trade's cost. For instance, before the 1857 tea season was open, the price of the sterling exchange in Canton and Fuzhou was four shillings nine pence per Spanish dollar, lower than the rate of six shillings nine pence per Spanish dollar in Shanghai.[157] Likewise in September 1869 when the tea trade initiated, the rates of sterling bills remained lower in Fuzhou than Shanghai. "But when your Oolong market opens, your sterling market which is a smaller one than ours will advance more rapidly," Forbes wrote from Shanghai to Fuzhou. Thus Forbes suggested the Shanghai office, rather than the Fuzhou branch, to handle the

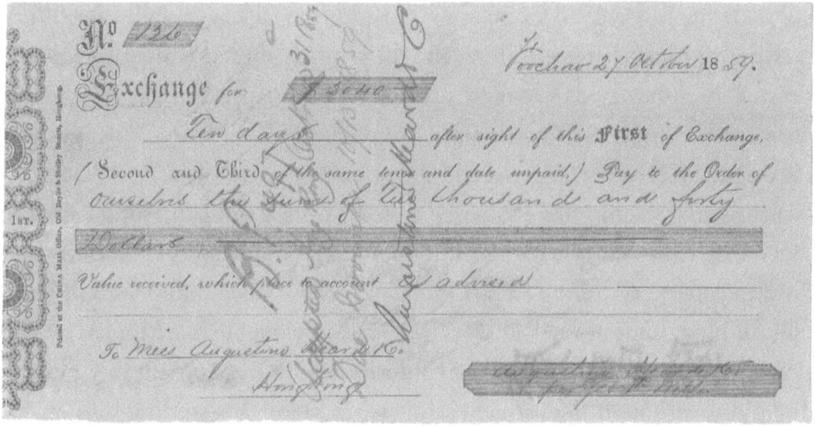
No. 136
Exchange for $3040
Foochow 27 October 1859.
Ten days after sight of this First of Exchange, (Second and Third of the same tenor and date unpaid,) Pay to the Order of ourselves the sum of three thousand and forty Dollars
Value received, which place to account as advised
To Messrs Augustine Heard & Co. Hongkong
Augustine Heard & Co. per Geo. F. Weller

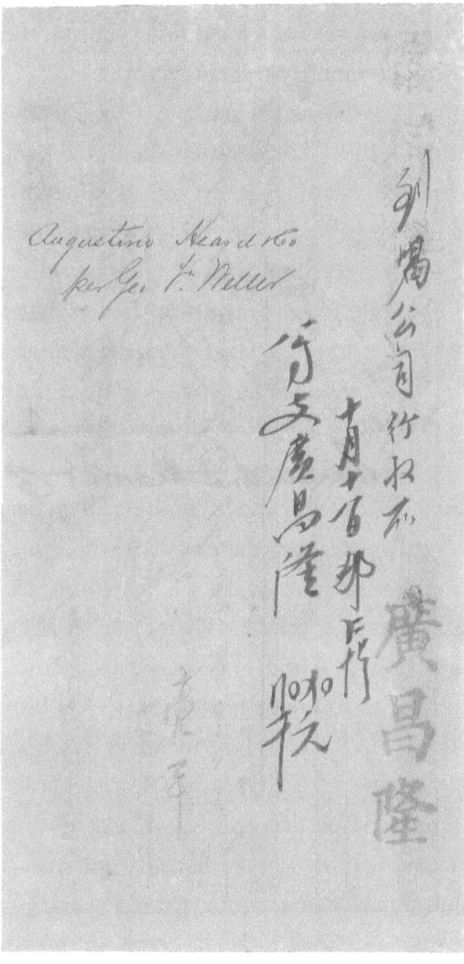

Fig. 17. Bills of exchange endorsed to Guang Changlong, 1859. Bills of exchange, 1844–1866, reel 86-3147 R-62, HFBR, Baker Library, Harvard Business School.

bill trade for Russell and Company.[158] In addition to English bills, the direct exchange business between China and the United States was also developing. From September 20 to October 5, 1859, William Appleton and Company drew from Boston on Russell and Company in Hong Kong.[159] Augustine Heard and Company also issued bills of exchange on New York, Boston, Washington DC, and San Francisco to settle transactions in Hong Kong.[160] The transpacific credit network built upon dollar bills was by no means confined to Americans. Hong Kong's exchange market offered four-month-sight bills on New York in 1867, and such bills were available in Shanghai by the 1880s, indicating the growing demand for the U.S. instrument in China.[161] Therefore, although the existing scholarship highlights sterling bills as the credit instrument for Americans to settle "virtually all their international debts" before World War I, American houses had issued dollar bills in the trade with and within China during the nineteenth century.[162]

In sum, the credit system of the U.S.-China tea trade extended to the newly opened treaty ports after the Opium War. Despite the initial slow development of commerce and finance outside Canton, the credit economy of the tea trade germinated in Shanghai during the 1850s, expanded to the southern coast amid the Taiping Rebellion, then extended to other tea ports in the following decades. While U.S. commission houses acted as their own banks, Chinese banks began to financialize the trust relations and credit networks between U.S. and China tea merchants. Rather than solely relying on bills on London and European financial institutions, the commercial and financial bills, notes, and checks issued by both the Chinese and Americans sustained the post–Opium War credit system. Shanghai, in the Yangzi River area, and Hong Kong, along the east coast of China, emerged as the centers undergirding the credit networks. Tightly connected across Chinese treaty ports, the exchange markets—initially in Canton and later in Shanghai, Hong Kong, Fuzhou, and Hankou—transformed the transpacific tea business into a series of credit transactions. The process involved selling English sterling or U.S. dollar bills for silver in China (mostly for payments upcountry); paying tea sellers with Chinese banks' bills of exchange or promissory notes, comprador's orders, inland bills on major treaty ports, or money on account (primarily in the treaty ports); and selling tea for U.S. dollars or international currencies (in overseas markets). The tael-dollar-sterling exchange rates in global financial markets, mostly calculated on commission houses' account books, determined the profitability of the tea trade in China. Rather than paying silver for each transaction, tea merchants employed credit transactions and instruments to translate the international commerce into a numbers game.[163]

As for the disputes between William Appleton and Company and Russell and Company, the two U.S. houses likely dropped the issue without resolution. Walsh ascribed their disagreements to the misconceptions of Cole, "who seems not to have clearly apprehended matters of Coast Exchange."[164] Cole accused Reiche the bookkeeper of not only cheating him out of 9,000 taels but also robbing Russell and Company several years before by wielding his supreme power of pen over account books, although the house claimed their Chinese comprador to be the defaulter.[165] Trusting their long-term captain, Appleton and Hooper suspected that the former head of Russell and Company, Paul S. Forbes, had embezzled their 100,000 Mexican dollars and Walsh simply fabricated new numbers to conceal the theft.[166] Nonetheless, Hooper refrained from pushing further, to avoid unpleasant feelings with Russell and Company.[167] After all, American importers relied on these commission houses, as both commercial and financial institutions, to carry out their tea ventures in China. After the 1860s, however, European banks would financialize Americans' tea trade and undermine commission merchants' influence, thus implementing another change to the credit system and power structure of the transpacific tea business.

4

From Commerce to Finance

TRANSFORMING THE CREDIT NETWORK, 1865–73

After decades of uncertainty caused by the Opium Wars, the Taiping Rebellion, and the American Civil War, peace finally returned to both sides of the Pacific Ocean. While William Tecumseh Sherman marched to Atlanta, Georgia, in 1864, the Qing troops took over Nanjing, the capital city of the Taiping rebels. It seemed "now probable that the Insurgents may be driven from the Green Tea and Silk districts," exulted Augustine Heard and Company.[1] The more-than-a-decade-long military actions of both Taiping rebels and Qing troops completely depopulated the green tea districts and destroyed some oolong regions, but the supply of tea gradually rebounded in the late 1860s.[2] On the other side of the Pacific Ocean, the demand for tea also soared. The interruptions of foreign trade during the American Civil War depleted U.S. tea stock, which was "entirely bare of greens and with a lower stock of blacks than the trade has been in the habit of carrying" (also see figure 8).[3]

Consequently, waves of mania swept China's tea markets across the treaty ports for almost a decade. Prices of the small stocks of green tea in Canton climbed shortly after the end of the American Civil War in 1865.[4] The news that the U.S. tea market was improving had also stimulated competition in Shanghai and Jiujiang by October 1865.[5] "If export figures may be taken as a test of prosperity," the *North China Herald* declared in 1868, "then nothing can be more flourishing than the trade in Tea."[6] Indeed, the Hankou Maritime Customs' report in 1869 vividly captured the speculative intensity: "when the market opened for the new season on 27th May at about 10 o'clock at night, by 2 o'clock in the morning, every chop which had arrived (about 50) had been settled at hourly advancing prices," Commissioner G. W. Caine noted, "and to those who waited for the morning to buy, nothing remained!"[7] The feverish buyers did not distinguish different varieties of tea. "The teamen continue to speculate in Congous" in Shanghai when the crop of Moyune (the best green tea manufactured in Wuyuan, Anhui province) remained short in August 1869, and "one chop had changed hands three times in one day."[8] The mania had also spread to Xiamen and Taiwan by 1872. Emboldened by the loans extended by Chinese capitalists from Xiamen, not only tea traders but also shroffs, tea boys, and men without capital all rushed into the market, showing absolute indifference to prices. Finding the market frenzy amusingly chaotic, a foreign merchant in Taiwan declared that "the Tea business had a great fascination for cooks, whose souls you would think could never rise above an omelet."[9]

This chapter traces how European banks and Chinese brokers, the latter supported by native banks, financialized the tea trade and fanned the decade-long tea mania. The existing scholarship on China's global tea trade has highlighted foreign capital, especially European banks, in organizing China's tea supply after 1853.[10] However, as previous research that reconsiders foreign capital's dominance in China's treaty ports, this chapter revisits the Eurocentric narrative by uncovering the complex power dynamics between native *qianzhuangs*, U.S. commission houses, and European banks in Chinese tea and credit markets.[11] The first section affirms foreign banks' growing influence on the U.S. side of the transpacific tea trade. Employing bank credit as working capital, small traders from America imported Chinese tea directly from the treaty ports. Even U.S. commission houses relied on European banks to invest in tea, participate in the advance system, and operate in China's exchange markets. However, foreign banks were by no means the only financiers of the transpacific tea trade. In the second section, native banks' credit funded Chinese tea brokers, known as *chazhan* or tea warehouses, and, through them, trickled down to tea dealers in the treaty ports and interior districts. The third section disentangles the power dynamics of the three players during 1865–73. Despite their growing influence on native banks and American mercantile capital, European banks failed to achieve full dominance over the financial system and the exchange markets essential to bolster the transpacific tea trade. The effects of the ongoing financialization of the tea trade, nonetheless, were evident. The liberal credit from banks fueled waves of speculation and planted seeds of crises beneath the prosperity, paving the way for the declining tea trade after 1873.

As the English newspaper in Shanghai, *The Celestial Empire*, concluded, the collapse of European and American tea markets around 1873 resulted from both "the managers of banks" and "the ever-thickening array of brokers."[12] Both helped transform the credit economy of the U.S.-China tea trade from a commercial system to a financial one.

Financing U.S. Buyers

The arrival of a female tea trader from America, Susan Ann King, in 1870 was met with fanfare. Even the Chinese newspaper *Shenbao* (*Shanghai Daily*) reported on King's adventure.[13] A successful merchant, King accumulated a substantial fortune before arriving in Asia. King's company had processed blackberry and raspberry leaves from the American South into various commercial teas before the American Civil War. Amid the wartime supply shortages, King remanufactured imported black tea into high-priced greens for the U.S. government. After the war, King cofounded the Woman's Tea Company with female fashion entrepreneur Madam Ellen Louise Curtis Demorest in 1872.[14] King's widely publicized tours to China and Japan in 1870 would serve as a powerful advertisement for her new enterprise.[15]

However, her arrival also alerted some old China hands, including Francis Blackwell Forbes of Russell and Company. Forbes dedicated two paragraphs to "Miss King, the female tea taster" in his normally terse reports on the tea trade in China. To Forbes, King represented a new generation of dealers who started to challenge the dominance of U.S. commission houses in China. "I don't know whether she will create any great revolution on the tea trade," Forbes wrote to his constituent in New York, "but there is no doubt that she is one of a class which is gradually effecting a change in China business," which rendered it "almost impossible to execute" the orders received from America.[16] For decades, like William Appleton and Company in Boston, even the largest importers in New York had to commission brokers in China, particularly Russell and Company or Augustine Heard and Company, to purchase tea before they distributed it to domestic wholesalers or grocers.[17] Now the importers or even grocers, like King, sailed directly to China. If "every Yankee peddler is really going to import his own pound of tea," Forbes grumbled, "first class houses like R & Co. [Russell and Company] will have to pass out of the trade, and employ their money in shaving the pedlers' [*sic*] bills!"[18]

While the accurate number of these "peddlers" is unavailable, the claim of selling tea imported directly from China was trending in American grocers' advertisements. The founder of the Pekin Tea Company, Henry "Chevalier" Wikoff, was among the first to declare purchasing tea directly from Canton and Beijing, in 1847. While this claim only became a subject of ridicule among Wikoff's rivals during the 1840s, the Great American Tea Company—later renamed the Great Atlantic and Pacific Tea Company—announced in 1867 that their ships, *Golden State* and *George Shotton*, returned with the finest teas from Japan and Fuzhou.[19] Given the company's ostentatious manner, researchers have questioned their claims.[20] Whether the company's flamboyant rhetoric contained a grain of truth is less important than the possibility or expectation for grocers to directly enter the tea trade, bypassing brokers. As the Great American Tea Company declared, its goal was to contract tea before its picking and to target "the 'middlemen' in the Tea trade," including the U.S. commission houses in China and bankers that made "large profits upon the foreign exchange used in the purchase of Teas."[21] King's trips to China actualized the plan in 1870. Ultimately, Carter, Macy, and Company, starting as a grocery store in New York during the 1850s, extended its operation to China and Japan by the 1890s.[22]

Contemporaries' observations attested to the possibility for grocers to enter the tea trade. The English consul in China, B. Robertson, noticed that the trade once "in the hands of the few" had "drifted into those of the many" during the 1860s.[23] Forbes was among the loudest complainers. "Every body now-a-days want fine teas," he grumbled in 1870, "and every year more and more men come out here with the idea that they can get what they want more cheaply and easily than through resident mercha [merchants]."[24] Chinese scholar and journalist Wang Tao also reported on the dramatic changes in foreign merchants' wealth in the latter nineteenth century. "Foreign merchants used to be highly ambitious and arrogant owing to their abundant capital and rare goods. Nothing short of substantial profits and enormous returns could sway their hearts," Wang observed in the 1880s. However, while their number increased steadily, their goods declined in quality and value, and "they rushed to contest razor-thin profits."[25]

If the opening of new treaty ports after the Opium War inspired Wikoff's claims of importing tea directly from China in the 1840s, the postbellum communication revolution offered grocers the infrastructure support. Wang attributed the changing demographics of foreign traders to lowered oceanic shipping expenses.[26] Forbes agreed, adding that "the opening of steam & rail routes between China and our continent has drawn into the tea trade a lot of small fry who formerly purchased in New York."[27] Indeed, technologies revolutionized long-distance trade during this era.[28] Tea clippers gave way to steamers, and a steamer line ran regularly from Shanghai and Hong Kong to San Francisco beginning in 1862. The Suez Canal, opened in 1869, reduced the three- to six-month voyages via the Cape of Good Hope to thirty to sixty days.[29] The telegraph cable between Shanghai and Europe, first used in 1871, compressed the time for transmitting information and remitting funds from two months to several days.[30] "The shortening of the passage and lowering of the price of passage brought increasing numbers to the field," Heard Jr. recalled in his 1891 memoir, titled "Old China and New."[31]

The communication revolution also aided the proliferation of European banks in Asia.[32] As the growth of financial institutions spawned speculation in exchange and liberal credit, small dealers were able to obtain working capital. "Formerly capital was an essential element of commerce," Robertson noted in 1873. "Now it is not, for the banks replace it by advancements on shipments."[33] Americans had already grasped the changing tide brought about by financial capital. Forbes complained in 1869 that banks "with their eager desire to get more than London interest for their money, have granted credits to Tom Dick & Harry, men without means," thus resulting in the oversupply of tea.[34] Heard concurred. In the early years of the new China trade, "the old Houses with large capital, had a practical monopoly of the business." However, "by the establishment of Banks, little capital for the transaction of regular business was necessary," and "the new-comer, almost without money and without the expense of heavy establishments, had a great advantage."[35] The local English newspaper in Shanghai, *Celestial Empire*, also reported that the low interest rate and abundant banking facilities in Europe and America stimulated "men of buckram" to enter the trade during the 1870s.[36]

Therefore the rise of banks greatly facilitated the U.S.-China tea trade, which reflected the trend of global financial expansion. The era from the mid-nineteenth century to World War I saw the first phase of increased international capital movements, undergirded primarily by bonds, bills of exchange, and, later, bank deposits.[37] China was a key component of the trend. During the Taiping Rebellion, the large number of wealthy refugees in Shanghai and the opening of Yangzi River ports attracted foreign banks into China. The U.S. Civil War also spawned a large number of small European banks in India, tasked with financing the country's cotton export in the absence of American cotton. These banks extended branches into China and treated this place as their future source of profit.[38] Consequently, in addition to the five European banks formed during the 1850s, twelve foreign banks opened in China's major treaty ports after 1861, all originating from either London or India, except the Hongkong and Shanghai Bank. Only half of these banks survived the financial panic erupting in 1865–66 that haunted the world's economy for years.[39] However, the survivors grew powerful, since foreign companies in China increasingly relied on bank loans for working capital after the depression.[40] While every commission house was their own bank during the 1840s–50s, Augustine Heard and Company had begun employing bank drafts to settle account balances between its branches and relying on various banks for credit since the 1860s, such as the Agra Bank Hong Kong, the Asiatic Banking Corporation, and the Imperial Bank, as well as the Hongkong and Shanghai Bank.[41] Therefore the tea trade in China was closely interlinked with the advance of foreign banks. Five European banks were in full operation in Fuzhou in 1868, and two of them—the Comptoir d'Escompte and the Chartered Bank of London, China, and Australia—"withdrew from the port after the termination of the tea season, having only come to operate while the tea market was open."[42]

Interest-bearing loans from European banks also bolstered Americans' engagement with the advance system in the tea trade. Evidence of Americans' participation in the advance system before the Opium War was extant but scant, such as the disastrous dealings of Thomson and Rush with the absconded Chinese dealer (chapter 2).[43] After the war, Americans started to contract tea with Yenqua in Canton (chapter 3) and tea dealers in regions around Shanghai, Fuzhou, Hankou, or Jiujiang.[44] However, paying for tea before the market was open required substantial floating capital. For example, Russell and Company employed $100,000 to contract Formosa oolong in 1872.[45] Yet the return was slow. "We at Shanghai for advances last year on shipments, not yet returned," Cunningham cautioned. "Two years are required generally to get back surplus proceeds from America."[46] Facing the problem of cash flow, European banks became a dependable source of advance payments for U.S. houses. In 1868, Russell and Company's agent in Hankou "talked the cash advances matter over with" Hermann Wallich, manager of Comptoirs d'Escompte in Shanghai, "who promises to do the business at [a] 10%" interest rate.[47] This French bank maintained close connections with several American commission houses in the advance system; as Forbes warned his colleagues in 1870, "The Comptoir's would willingly transfer that business to Heard [Augustine Heard and Company] or Olyphant [Olyphant and Company], if we decline it."[48] Therefore it was detrimental to the Shanghai office of Russell and Company when they had already "commenced advancing on the usual understanding" by July 1870 but Wallich rejected their application for credit. Russell and Company had to seek loans from other banks, withdraw 80,000 taels from their "Yangtse" deposits, and practically close their accounts in the region. "That Wallich should so foolishly lose one of his best constituents, and a business which must have yielded very handsome returns," Forbes grumbled, suggesting the large size of bank loans afloat in the advance system.[49] However, the profits of tea and money easily amended the relationship. Three years later, the bank once again sent 600,000 taels for the company to procure exchange and invest in tea.[50] Meanwhile, the German Deutsche Bank was vying for Russell and Company's tea advance business in Hankou and Fuzhou.[51] Forbes suggested Seligmann to "wait till China New year was over," when "the losses and gains of the past season settled among the teamen, before making any decision."[52] The instruction demonstrated the cruciality of the tea trade in determining the company's credit relationship with European banks. In March and April 1873, when Russell and Company started to contract tea, the Deutsche Bank had obtained a good part, if not all, of their Fuzhou advance business.[53]

Aside from loans and advance payments, foreign banks engaged with the credit economy of the U.S.-China tea trade through bills of exchange. Foreign financial institutions in China started as exchange banks, whose main business included handling silver and trading bills of exchange for foreign merchants in China.[54] "This bullion business has fallen almost entirely into the hands of the banks," Forbes explained in 1866, "who thus lay down funds for the purchase of mercantile paper," or merchants' bills of exchange.[55] Indeed, the Oriental Bank and the Commercial Bank of India traded bills on England, India, Ceylon, Singapore, Hong Kong, and Fuzhou in Shanghai's exchange market during the 1850s–60s.[56] Formerly Americans acquired bills by selling goods to Great Britain or purchasing them at home; now they could obtain bills from European exchange banks in China. Augustine Heard and Company had employed compradors' orders to purchase bills from the Commercial Bank of India and the Oriental Bank, as well as the Mercantile Bank of India, London, and China since the 1850s.[57] Thus the growth of European banking increased the supply of bills of exchange in China, which were critical to facilitate its international tea trade. Chinese tea guilds sensed foreign banks' crucial role in handling this credit instrument and sustaining the tea trade. "Foreign merchants need a large amount of silver to buy tea. Borrowing from banks for only one day, they purchase tens of thousands of products; when lacking cash, Westerners customarily ask banks to remit bills of exchange," secured by teas obtained in China.[58]

Financing Chinese Brokers

After King's arrival, the Woman's Tea Company announced that, having made an arrangement with a Chinese plantation owner, King "remained a year among the Celestials personally inspecting the gathering and packing of the herb."[59] The Great American Tea Company made similar claims about working directly with Chinese tea growers.[60] However, their engagement with tea production, even if probable, was rarely possible. In truth, European and American merchants rarely left the treaty ports, even though the Treaty of Tianjin signed between China and Great Britain in 1858 allowed foreigners to take business or leisure trips into the interior with passports issued by their consuls.[61] In contrast to Europeans and Americans, foreign commissioners at China's Imperial Maritime Customs often commended Russians for their direct interactions with "Chinese tea-growers," using the only tool they had but Euro-American merchants lacked: "the medium of the Chinese language."[62] Even when some foreign buyers visited the interior tea country, Chinese historical records depicted their hasty departure. "During Spring and Summer every year, itinerant traders gather here; Westerners also come sometimes," *Yining zhouzhi* (Gazetteer of Yining District) noted in 1873, "but they are so different from us that everyone gawks at them along the way, so they stay only several days before leaving."[63]

According to contemporaneous Maritime Customs' reports, foreign merchants' rare visits to the tea country also resulted from the omnipresence of Chinese middlemen.[64] Gone were Hong merchants as the agents. Yet a group of professionalized Chinese brokers, known as *zhan* (warehouse) in Chinese or as teamen in English records, had emerged to orchestrate the foreign tea trade.[65] Wang Tao noted in the late 1850s that "specialized silk and tea warehouses recently emerged within and without Shanghai."[66] Chinese scholar Ge Yuanxu recounted twenty tea warehouses at Shanghai in 1876.[67] Specialized tea warehouses also began appearing in other treaty ports within a decade of their development. In the 1850s the "custom of the trade in Foochow [was] for the teas to be settled by the broker—the owner of the property never appearing," so English and American importers rarely met their Chinese counterparts.[68] In Jiujiang, "eight large Hongs and an equal number of Brokers divide amongst them the different kinds of Tea" by 1867, six years after the opening of this port.[69] About a dozen tea warehouses existed in Hankou during the 1870s–80s.[70] With the rising popularity of Formosa oolong, the 1890s marked the golden age for the over twenty brokers in Taiwan.[71] Hence, when shipping tea to the treaty ports, interior dealers usually sought accommodations and information about foreign buyers at these *zhans*. Warehouse owners hired salespeople to look for and negotiate with foreign buyers. Working as linguists in the Canton Trade, these salespeople spoke foreign languages, or at least "pidgin English," fluently.[72] "Receiving silver after the delivery of goods, the itinerant dealers never have to worry about their business."[73] Thus the emergence of these tea brokers minimized direct contacts between Chinese owners and foreign buyers. Their operation also rendered the upcountry system—the major means for foreign companies to directly control tea's supply—expensive and defunct after the 1860s; instead of traveling to the tea country, their compradors made arrangements with the brokers, who bought the leaf in the interior and prepared the tea for them.[74]

With brokerage concentrated in their hands, tea warehouses arose to demonstrate the prosperity of China's foreign tea trade and the development of the credit economy in the treaty ports. Before the Opium War, most tea *zhans* were merely warehouses that stored and manufactured tea for exportation, whereas the *hangs* were the middlemen.[75] However, in 1915, tea merchant Yu Xie identified two groups of tea brokers—*hangs* and *zhans*. While the *hang* catered to Chinese sellers and buyers, the *zhan* had emerged to serve Chinese sellers and foreign buyers.[76] The flourishing tea trade in the treaty ports prompted and sustained the division of labor.[77] The credit economy in the treaty ports further entailed the specialization of tea warehouses in international commerce. Immediately after Shanghai was open, such warehouses as the Dunli Zhan had been "accommodating silk and tea merchants and storing their goods."[78] Operating in a barter economy, the earliest brokers had to prepare a wide variety of goods, notably textiles, silk, and tea for barter payments.[79] The widespread use of native banker's notes as the principal instruments of payment and exchange enabled brokers to specialize in a single commodity, whether tea or silk. Specialized tea warehouses thus emerged during the 1850s when the credit economy was burgeoning in Shanghai. Moreover, tea warehouses, grander in size and style, guaranteed Chinese sellers' credit in the face of skeptical foreign buyers.[80]

As in many cash crop economies in the world, Chinese tea brokers "are also the financial institution of the tea trade," extending credit to interior tea districts.[81] Since the eighteenth century, interior tea manufacturers and dealers had relied on Hong merchants' advances to cover their shipping expenses and provide working capital.[82] After the abolition of the Cohong, tea warehouses paid their clients' transportation fees, known as *shuijiao yin* (freight), which "was a loan by nature."[83] The cost of transportation remained a substantial burden to those supplying tea to the treaty ports. An 1888 Maritime Custom Report hinted at the cruciality of the advances. Wenzhou, a prominent tea district in Zhejiang province, failed to develop into a major tea center for China's foreign trade, as local dealers lacked sufficient capital to afford shipments and especially the duties en route to Shanghai, while brokers' interest charges were too high. Unwilling or unable to rely on brokers, six out of ten tea firms in Wenzhou closed their establishments within a year, while the other four had a gloomy outlook on their future business.[84] In contrast, dealers from the famed green tea country in Anhui province accepted tea warehouses' charges and deployed the advances as their working capital. Thus "tea warehouses had the power to determine the number of tea firms and the price of raw teas," Yu Xie concluded, "evidenced by the growing number of tea firms and the rising price of tea that resulted from the generous freight extended by tea warehouses in recent years."[85] Vying for more business, tea warehouses often competed with each other to offer a higher percentage of freight at more favorable interest rates.[86] Some dealers also maneuvered the credit system by securing advances from many brokers without disclosing their borrowing history to any of them.[87]

While attracting itinerant dealers to the treaty ports with freight, tea brokers also sent capital directly to interior tea traders and growers. A Cantonese sojourner, Tang Qiaoqing, founded a famous *zhan*, Qianshen'an, and developed it into the largest tea warehouses in Shanghai and Hankou. To procure green tea for his warehouses, Tang entrusted Jiang Mingheng, a tea peddler in Anhui, when extending loans to key green tea districts from 1867 onward. Born into a family of tea traders, Jiang was well acquainted with local dealers' credit history.[88] Tang's Qianshen'an, along with another tea warehouse named Taihehe, also opened offices in the black tea district, Hefeng subprefecture of the Hubei province, after 1867. Originally a poor area lacking arable lands, the place developed an increasingly booming local economy bolstered by the tea trade.[89] Competition among tea brokers in extending advances to the tea districts was so fierce that the Shanghai Tea Guild stipulated in 1871 that when middlemen brought funds to interior tea growers, they should work for only one tea firm and the advances should not exceed the goods' value.[90] Brokers from the mainland also introduced the advance system to Taiwan in 1872, altering the structure of direct trade between local and foreign traders on the island.[91]

Tea warehouses' financial power was inseparable from the Chinese banking sector. As Liu explained, tea warehouses' credit was a collateral loan, extended on the condition of the delivery of teas.[92] Having exclusive rights to the leaves prepared by their debtors, brokers secured not only new teas but also steady credit from native banks.[93] "In truth the advances paid by warehouses were loans from banks and *qianzhuangs*, upon the promise to repay the debts in summer and fall," tea merchant Yu Heyan explained. "Fearing that they would lose credit with *qianzhuangs* and banks, warehouse owners monopolized the supply and disallowed the dealers to sell their tea to others."[94] Robertson had noticed the credit transaction among the Chinese in 1873, asserting, "The teamen at the Treaty ports are not as a rule men with capital," for "they, like foreigners, resort to their own banks for advances to pay for the teas in the interior."[95] The Bank of Shanghai's report clarified: "Tea manufactories in interior China relied on tea warehouses' advances, and the warehouses depended on *qianzhuangs* or banks for financial resources."[96]

Aside from advance payments, native banks also provided Chinese tea brokers with working capital. According to late nineteenth-century reports, the tea trade required a significant amount of start-up funds, second only to those to open banks and pawn shops.[97] Moreover, Chinese warehouses boasted spectacular office buildings adorned with rare items to attract clients.[98] These brokers also "fraternized with foreign merchants, spent lavishly on socialization activities and daily lives, and borrowed from *qianzhuangs* to cover the cost."[99] The expenses, estimated by Chinese official Ma Jianzhong, amounted to 60 to 70 million taels, which had already been a heavy burden on tea warehouse owners. Once facing cash-flow problems, these brokers had to borrow more from native banks.[100] Bankers were clear about the potential in this lucrative tea trade, so "whenever a new *zhan* was formed, *qianzhuangs* were well aware of the owner's actual wealth," *Shenbao* reported. "Vying for their business, every banker promised a ready amount of loans between 10,000–20,000 taels and 30,000–40,000 taels." Consequently, the broker easily raised 100,000 taels within a month or less.[101] When the trade flourished, warehouses gained tenfold their borrowed capital by extending loans to tea manufactories and earning commission fees. Once the trade stagnated, their property shrank by 20–30 percent to 60–70 percent. Some managed to persevere and retain *qianzhuangs*' trust, waiting for new teas coming to the market in the successive season, when native banks offered new loans and speculated on another lucrative tea season.[102] Given that most of these newspaper reports on native banks' extensive credit to tea brokers surfaced after 1873, when China's tea trade had already begun to decline, it is easy to envision the exuberance of such credit transactions during the golden age of 1865–73, when tea prices were extravagantly high and the trade was exceptionally remunerative.

Financialization

Bills and loans provided by Chinese and European banks further financialized the U.S.-China tea trade, in which financial resources marginalized merchants' capital as the foundation of the credit system. The process had started when Chinese banks issued native credit instruments and provided banking facilities in the 1850s (chapter 3). Their loans also expanded tea transactions and speculation. "Money was easily obtained from the Native banks," Francis W. White, customs commissioner in Ningbo, stated, "and the Tea season of 1872 was opened with an eager competition that augured ill for the prospects of the year."[103] In the same year, Xiamen native capitalists extended generous loans to tea dealers in Taiwan, "the only condition being that the Tea obtained should be consigned to them." The consequence was the craze for Formosa oolong in 1872.[104] Noticing that tea and silk merchants at the treaty ports mostly relied on cash shops for funding, paid usurious interest rates to these native banks, and lost heavily during the tea season, the writer of an 1873 *Shenbao* article wondered, "Why were people so willing to borrow to trade?"[105] On the demand side, foreign banks boosted Americans' capital and fanned the tea mania after 1865. As Heard summarized, banking was one of "the most potent instruments in revolutionizing businesses" in the China trade.[106] After banks offered easy credit, the tea trade was "thrown open to all comers."[107] While resident merchants and commission houses relied on the financial resources to expand their regular business, newcomers from the United States, with little of their own to lose, aimed for the finest green teas without any price limits.[108] Consequently, these small traders, who "simply add to the number of competitors, and having come so far are not disposed to go back empty handed," ignited more purchase frenzies in an already overheated tea market.[109]

Despite the expansion of the tea market, the extent of foreign capital's dominance over the credit economy of the transpacific tea trade had been uncertain by the 1870s. Indeed, in the late nineteenth century, many Chinese cash shops relied on European banking facilities, particularly the "chop loans," which were interbank credit extended from foreign banks with only native bank orders as security.[110] However, direct contacts between foreign and Chinese banks were initially rare. Extant historical documents trace the origin of the "chop loans" to 1869, when Wang Huaishan, the first comprador of the Hongkong and Shanghai Bank, initiated the practice of interbank lending between foreign and native banks.[111] Foreign exchange banks originally had a specialized and limited role in China's credit system. While Chinese exchange banks controlled the remittance business and native cash shops dominated credit markets within Shanghai's hinterland, foreign banks in China primarily discounted foreign merchants' bills of exchange and promissory notes, granted loans, and absorbed their deposits.[112] Even in 1893, "most of the business done by Foreign banks is confined to money transactions in connexion with the export of tea and other Native goods," R. B. Moorhead, commissioner of the Hankou Customs, reported.[113] While foreign merchants obtained credit from European banks, Chinese traders maintained close business ties with their cash shops. "According to a leading tea merchant, tea *zhans* obtained three-fourths of their loans from *qianzhuangs*, while one-fourth from [modern] banks."[114] On the southern coast, even though foreign commercial capital, including Russell and Company and Augustine Heard and Company, made heavy advances to Chinese brokers who brought tea from the interior to Fuzhou, a British consul clarified that foreign capital controlled "over 40 per cent," rather than a predominant share, of the "business of advances to the native teamen" in 1876. Furthermore, the business "seems to be steadily falling into the hands of the native banks and financiers" in the 1870s, with "the amount advanced by foreigners for 1881 being less than 10 per cent. of the total amount, as against some 18 per cent. in 1880."[115] Hence, already dominating the finance of Shanghai and the Yangzi River Valley, native capital made great strides into the southern coast. Cash shops' massive influence on China's commercial world, at least in the regions around Shanghai and Fuzhou, persisted into the early twentieth century.[116] Therefore Chinese financial credit likely remained fundamental for native tea dealers during most years between 1865 and 1873.

Meanwhile, European banks attempted to exert more control over the tea trade through bills of exchange—Americans' chief means of tea purchase in China—by shortening the term of the credit instrument. Six months had been the standardized term for most bills of exchange circulating in the China trade, such as the 180-day BUS bills issued in the 1830s, which were negotiable only east of the Cape of the Good Hope (chapter 2). In contrast, the term in New York was generally sixty to seventy-five days; in the Anglo-American trade, it rarely exceeded four months.[117] Discussions of shortening the bills' term from six months to four months had emerged occasionally during the 1840s and 1850s but eventually evaporated.[118] Amid the depression of 1865, European banks revisited the policy.[119] London- and Paris-based banks in Shanghai, such as the Oriental Bank, the Chartered Mercantile Bank, and the Comptoir d'Escompte, revived "an old hobby of theirs—to shorten the usance of China bills on London from <u>six</u> to <u>four</u> months sight," Forbes reported in 1866.[120] However, the six-month bills provided invaluable resources for the long-distance tea trade, as, with a six-week grace period included, Americans had seven and a half months to make monetary arrangements. The voyage from China to New York still averaged four months during the 1860s, since not every merchant commissioned steamers to replace slower clippers. After receiving the tea cargo in America, U.S. importers managed to sell the commodity within two months and then have another two weeks to deliver their bills to London. Hence, even if suffering losses in their tea ventures, American merchants still had another month to find money and pay the bills before the expiration dates.[121] Although the long-term credit furnished gamblers with substantive resources to speculate in the market, reducing the term to four months would severely constrain financial flexibility and leave limited time to make ends meet.[122]

Unsurprisingly, influential mercantile groups in China, even those who had abundant resources to expedite bills' redemption, opposed the change initiated by European banks. "In old times, when the banks tried this same game," Forbes plotted with Cunningham in 1866, "R & Co. [Russell and Company] put a spoke in their wheel by receiving remittances from Barings & Rothschilds and buying up all the good bills in the market. Can you not make a similar arrangement now?"[123] It is likely that Forbes and Cunningham actualized the scheme in Fuzhou the following year, as six-month bills of well-known houses and local banks were in such overwhelming demand that the European banks which implemented the four-month policy lost significant exchange business on both England and Chinese treaty ports. Even the newly established Hongkong and Shanghai Bank refused to join their European counterparts, citing its mission to serve local mercantile communities. Continuously and actively handling six-month bills, this fledgling exchange bank secured merchants' trust, enhanced its influence, and leveraged its position to profit from the jostling between financial and mercantile capital. The outcome was the revival of six-month bills in China throughout the 1870s.[124]

The rivalry in the six-month bill market revealed ambiguities in the power balance between American commission houses and European financial institutions during the 1860s–70s. European banks' triumph over mercantile capital was not immediate. After all, the exchange market in Shanghai had still sold more merchants' bills on London than bank papers by 1864–66, even though bank papers dominated the bills on Hong Kong.[125] Many private buyers considered the bills of the Oriental Bank—the leading European financial institution—"as no better than J. M. & Co. [Jardine Matheson and Company] or our own [Russell and Company]," as Forbes put it in 1866.[126] Yet European banks' influence was on the rise. The Oriental Bank and numerous new banks vying for the exchange business at slim profit margins had caused Russell and Company severe losses in the bill market by 1858–59.[127] In the undeveloped exchange markets of the newly opened treaty ports, such as Hankou, merchants relied chiefly on foreign banks to sell bills, since the number of private purchasers was limited.[128] European banks' influence on the credit economy grew more swiftly during economic and political crises, aided by the stagnant commerce and merchants' decreased demand for credit instruments. In 1860, when the approach of Taiping rebels halted the import trade and bill market in Shanghai, "the Banks [were] almost the only buyers of Bills, while there [were] many sellers."[129] The principal bill buyers in Hong Kong during the American Civil War were banks, "which have done nearly all the business [of Sterling exchange], very few private Bills being in the market."[130] "The cessation of tea purchases and the inaction in the northern silk market" during the depression of 1865 also produced "a great scarcity of bills" and "the general distrust of nearly all commercial paper." The Oriental Bank thus offered low prices for even first-class merchants' bills, including those of Russell and Company.[131] After the economic panic in 1865, as Stephen Lockwood argued, European exchange banks began to regularize the exchange market, which had provided a steady source of revenue and the primary means of tea purchases for large American houses in China.[132] Capitalizing on merchants' need for loans and bills, European banks further promoted their papers over commercial bills. When remitting bills to Russell and Company and Augustine Heard and Company for payments in 1867, the Bank of Rotterdam emphasized that "'its own bills are preferred' as returns!"[133] Ultimately in 1872, the China Imperial Maritime Customs adopted the relative prices of Shanghai taels and bank bills on London, rather than merchants' bills, as the standard exchange rate, suggesting European banks' ascendancy over foreign mercantile capital in China.[134]

Tea Mania

In sum, after the civil wars, European and Chinese banks continued to financialize the credit system and expand the U.S.-China tea trade in the treaty ports. European exchange banks' influence arose globally. Their liberal credit not only enabled small traders to enter the direct tea trade with China but also financed U.S. commission houses' tea purchases and advance payments. These banking institutions also supplied financial bills of exchange and competed with American commission merchants in China's exchange markets, but they failed to shorten six-month bills or outcompete U.S. mercantile capital before the 1870s. Meanwhile, Chinese banks continued to finance the domestic credit system by extending loans to specialized tea warehouses and, through them, to interior dealers and producers. Therefore the power dynamics of the credit economy remained complex during 1865–73. American mercantile capital, Chinese cash shops, and European financial institutions collaborated and competed to shape the credit transactions and instruments that sustained the transpacific tea trade, until the global Long Depression altered their power structure after 1873. The three powers collectively developed the era of 1865–73 into the golden age of the U.S.-China tea trade. Easy financial credit pushed the volume of trade to an unprecedented level (see figure 8). Moreover, the trading environment was peaceful, communication technologies advanced, the price of bills on London lowered significantly after the depression of 1865, and the United States abolished the duty on tea in 1871, further fueling waves of tea speculation (see figure 18).[135] Tea arrived in London and New York markets several months before the six-month bills expired, so traders accumulated a substantive surplus of cash when the tea season closed.[136] During the tea season, the resources enabled them to speculate in the market.

The decade-long tea mania ensued, defined by exorbitant prices and ceaseless demands. "People are equally mad about Tea," Forbes wrote in 1866, startled by the high rates that foreign merchants paid in Hankou and Fuzhou.[137] The customs commissioner in Xiamen noted that, when the tea season commenced in 1868, "purchases [of oolongs] were made at extreme rates for rapid shipment via California to New York," thus incentivizing Chinese teamen to send "orders into the interior for extensive supplies at extravagant rates."[138] Forbes reported from Shanghai that Olyphant and Company, Augustine Heard and Company, "and Littles ([Fitz] Heinemann's friends) have paid absurd prices, and discounted more than their profits for the benefit of the Heathen Chinese."[139] Tea price also kept climbing in the home market, for New York and London competed for low-grade teas "at prices higher than were ever known before."[140] The tea mania even

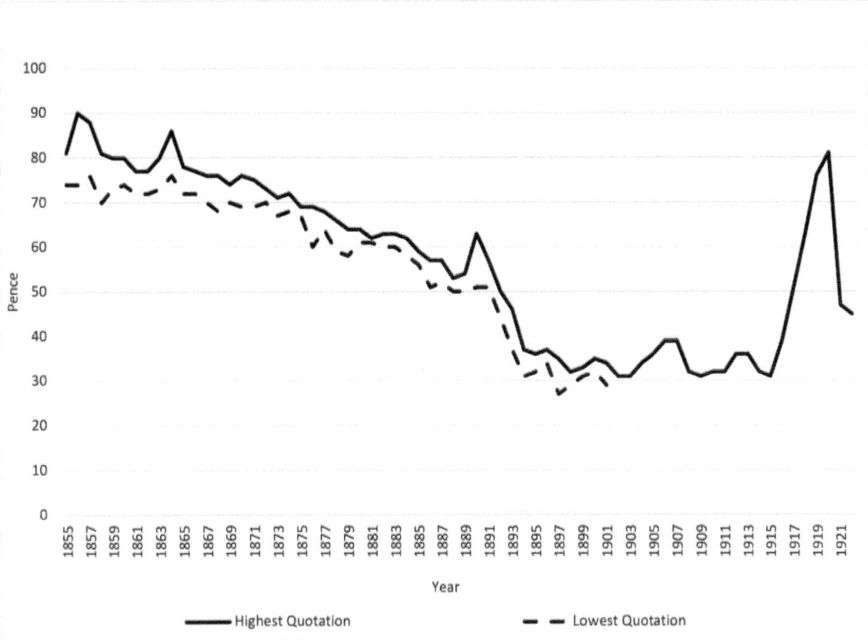

Fig. 18. Exchange rates between English bills of exchange (in pence) and silver (in Haiguan taels) in Shanghai, 1855–1922. Haiguan tale (Hk. Tls) was the monetary unit used by the China Imperial Maritime Customs. One Haiguan tale equals 111.40 Shanghai taels. Sources: 1855–71: *Six Essays*, 67–68. The document does not clarify whether the monetary unit of silver was Haiguan taels or Shanghai taels. Comparing the data for 1872–74 in this document and other datasets shows that the value was in Haiguan taels. 1872–91: "Highest and Lowest Rates of Exchange at Shanghai for Bank Demand Drafts on London, 1872–91," in Inspector General of Chinese Maritime Customs, *Decennial Reports on the Trade, 1882–1891*, "Appendix I.—Trade Statistics," xvi. 1892–1901: "Highest and Lowest Rates of Exchange at Shanghai for Bank Telegraphic Transfers on London," in Inspector General of Chinese Maritime Customs, *Decennial Reports on the Trade, 1892–1901*, vol. 2, *Southern Ports, with Appendices*, xix. 1902–22: Hamashita, *Zhongguo jindai jingjishi yanjiu*, 2:551–52. The data compiled by Hamashita do not distinguish the highest and lowest exchange rates. The exchange rates across all treaty ports, including Hong Kong, followed a pattern consistent with that of Shanghai. See "Annual Average Equivalent of the Haikwan Tael in English Money at Sight Rate of Exchange for 21 Years, 1868 to 1888," in Zhonguo jiuhaiguan shiliao bianji wenyuanhui, *Zhongguo jiuhaiguan shiliao*, vol. 14, illustration 14-1; and King, *History of the Hongkong and Shanghai Banking Corporation*, 1:274, 401.

temporarily pushed the price of sterling bills up in 1872.[141] Yet the craze persisted despite the rising cost of the trade. George Hughes, the customs commissioner who reported on Xiamen's tea trade with the United States for years, captured the tea frenzy in his 1872 report. "The law of supply and demand which must necessarily govern every produce market, seemed for a time disregarded," Hughes bemoaned. "Prices, high as they were at the commencement of operations, rapidly advanced until they had attained a figure never before reached in the annals of this trade."[142]

Crises lurked beneath the surface of prosperity. Gambling spirits characterized the golden age, for when tea prices were exorbitant, heavy losses were frequent. Early shippers typically earned profits or suffered limited losses, while latecomers—Chinese and Americans alike—in overstocked markets faced devastating consequences.[143] A more underlying impact was the systemic deterioration of Chinese tea, owing to "the eagerness to buy irrespective of price or quality."[144] The growing evils of selling tea different from or worse than the samples resulted in various lawsuits brought by foreign traders to Chinese officials in Fujian and Hankou during the 1860s–70s.[145] In the meantime, adulterated products proliferated. The black teas offered on the Shanghai market in 1870 were with "much dust and broken leaf which should certainly not appear in Teas of the first crop." Unsold old green tea was also mixed with Japanese or Huzhou leaves.[146] In addition, dusty tea jeopardized the appearance and reputation of Chinese green and oolong tea, driving buyers in New York to procure Japanese greens.[147] The *Celestial Empire* even reported on heavily dyed, or faced, green teas mixed with inferior leaves, which fraudulent dealers in Shanghai exploited to meet rampant demand during 1872–73.[148] Robertson attributed these quality issues to "a fault of system rather than individuals," for "the native dealers will be tempted to badly pack and prepare their teas for the sake of hurrying them off their hands so long as they observe the eagerness of the foreign buyer to possess himself of the produce."[149] Financial credit also played a critical role. "The easy terms on which money is procured from the numerous foreign banks is another incentive to speculation that is rather damaging to the trade," a British consul complained.[150]

The outcome was saturated tea markets in America before the 1870s. However, despite the extravagant prices, constant failures, and deteriorated quality, the speculators were still eager to buy. Green teas shipped from

Shanghai to America by the end of November 1868, several months before the end of the tea season, had reached "a whole year's consumption for the United States!"[151] The number kept climbing in 1869, when "an export of greens to America [reached] quite six millions [*sic*] in excess of last year."[152] In Xiamen, the major supplier of oolongs to America, "it appeared as if buyers hurried into the market with little thought save that of securing the Tea, and shipping it off with, so to speak, the greatest possible haste," so "before the end of September the export was represented by most formidable figures."[153] Not only were Americans buying for the U.S. market, but "the English having already oversupplied their own markets with tea," along with other European merchants, also shipped tea from Shanghai and Xiamen to New York.[154] Consequently, in 1871, only a year after King's arrival in China, the U.S. tea market began to collapse, initiating the decline of the U.S.-China tea trade during the global depression after 1873.

PART 3 *English Breakfast Tea*

The history of English breakfast tea reflected the decline of the U.S.-China tea trade. In this green and oolong tea country, black tea, particularly congou and souchong, comprised only a third or less of U.S. tea imports from China before 1900 (see figures 3 and 4). Yet featuring a special denomination—"English breakfast tea"—American black tea culture was by no means insignificant. Invented for or in the United States, this brand designated to England only distinguishes Americans' distinctive taste for tea from that of their British counterparts. "English breakfast tea" was the generic term for Chinese black tea among nineteenth-century Americans, to whom green tea was simply known as "tea."[1] Already detached from the Chinese categorization of tea, the label was flexible enough to accommodate black teas from other regions into the family. Consequently, after Americans' tea imports from China plummeted in the twentieth century, English breakfast tea morphed from pure Chinese black teas into a blend with Indian, Ceylon, or African blacks. While green tea represented the fledgling U.S.-China tea trade and oolong signaled its expansion, the rise and fall of English breakfast tea, as a Chinese black tea, crystalized the eventual decline of the transpacific commerce.

While part 3 investigates the changing identity of English breakfast tea to illustrate the changing trading landscape in the late nineteenth century, chapter 5 explains the function of the credit economy after 1873 and its effects on the declining transpacific tea business. The credit system sustained efficient and cashless transactions between American and Chinese tea merchants for a century. Yet the adversity of the fragile credit network became increasingly evident during the global Long Depression of 1873–97, which arguably resulted from the adoption of the gold standard in Germany and the

United States. The ensuing decades-long silver depreciation, tea devaluation, and shrinking profits drained the vitality of tea commerce. Both Americans and the Chinese, who operated on credit, suffered heavily. Lamenting their reliance on British financial capital, Americans withdrew from the tea trade in China. The thinly capitalized Chinese, who faced urgent credit repayment deadlines and shrinking profit margins on tea sales, had to scale down their tea economy by producing inferior quality teas at faster speeds. In contrast, their competitors from British colonies and Japan launched advertising and lobbying campaigns to seize the U.S. tea market. Thus, despite its convenience and efficiency, the transnational credit system paved the way for the decline of the U.S.-China tea trade and the rise of English breakfast tea as a blended product in the twentieth century.

Albeit the designation of "English" breakfast tea, "no such name is known in England," Heard Jr. emphasized in 1891, "and, indeed, no such thing."[2] A 1904 magazine article also clarified that "the term is unknown in England."[3] Thus nineteenth-century literature satirized those mistaking "English breakfast tea" for an English tradition. The anecdote about a young Mrs. Vasearline who insists on serving her guests from London English breakfast tea appeared in a collection of jokes published in a British newspaper.[4] In a cartoon published in *Harper's Bazaar*, an American lady, labeled an Anglomaniac, declared that her "consistency's the gem," and "that makes [her] English Breakfast tea decline at 5 P.M."[5] The irony is that this tea was neither "English" nor consumed at "breakfast," making her boast of consistency self-contradictory and heightening the satire of her Anglophile pretensions. Given the tea's conflicted identity, an American tea merchant who stayed in China for twenty years found it hard to conceptualize after he returned to Washington DC in 1890. "Is it a green or black tea?" he asked the host. "And do the English drink anything different at breakfast from what they have in the afternoon?"[6] It is unclear whether the merchant received a satisfactory answer, but it is certain that this tea had grown into a recognizable, independent brand in the United States by the late nineteenth century.

In truth, the tea was an American invention, and many vied for the title of inventor. A Scottish immigrant in America, named Drysdale, won credit for blending Ceylon, Indian Assam, and Chinese Keemun (祁門紅茶 *Qihong*) into English breakfast tea, which remains one of the most popular recipes today.[7] However, Drysdale's tea could only appear after the production of

Indian tea in 1833, Ceylon in 1875, and Keemun in 1876 (see chapter 5). Earlier records exist, as some claimed that Richard Davies, an English merchant in New York City who founded the Canton Tea Company, employed congou as the base, mixed with a bit of pekoe and pouchong, to make this tea in 1843.[8] Pekoe, or *Baihao*, meaning the white hair of young leaves, was a superior Chinese black tea.[9] Packed in half-pound paper, "pouchong" or *Baozhong* was also Chinese tea, as its name was derived from the rectangular- or square-shaped packages used by tea merchants from Anxi, Fujian province. While the Taiwan tea industry would popularize the term as a particular type of oolong at the start of the twentieth century, the nineteenth-century pouchong could be any kind of Chinese tea in bags, but it usually referred to souchong or oolong.[10] The tea-retailing pioneers—Canton Tea Company and Pekin Tea Company—had repeatedly marketed Chinese teas as "English Breakfast Tea" in New England, New York, and Maryland during the 1840s.[11]

Indeed, English breakfast tea, as a pure black tea from China, appeared frequently in historical documents from the 1840s. From that period, U.S. importers designated the term as a rank of Chinese black tea. Heard Jr. maintained that a U.S. supercargo in China created the term in 1849 to classify, and give novelty to, his black tea products. Instead of marking tea chests conventionally from the lowest "fair" and "good" to "superior," "fine," and "curious," the supercargo devised a number of special labels, such as "English Breakfast Tea" and "Old Company's Congou," to distinguish various grades of black tea. However, "'English Breakfast' was the only one that struck the fancy of the public and it remains to this day," Heard recalled in 1891.[12] Moreover, the term "English breakfast tea" was often associated with the higher classes of Chinese black tea. Russell and Company only labeled the best black teas as "a fine Breakfast Tea" but ranked the cheaper ones as "ordinary," "good," and "medium quality."[13] The New York firm Beebe and Company was more particular with the use of "English." In 1859 they ordered their agents in China to designate the congous costing fifteen to twenty cents more than others as "Choicest English Breakfast Souchong" and the cheaper congou and souchong as fine and finest "Breakfast Souchong."[14]

To U.S. tea sellers and consumers, English breakfast tea was a kind, rather than a rank, of Chinese black tea. An American journal designated the term to Chinese congou, the most popular black tea in England. The "heavy-liquored, black-leafed Congou, which forms the staple of the mixture sold in England under the generic name of Black," the author declared in 1869, "sometimes finds its way to this country as English Breakfast Tea."[15] Oscar Riggs, writing in 1883, also characterized English breakfast tea as "the Congou tea of commerce."[16] When Chinese tea merchant Yu Xie visited the United States in 1915, he still interpreted "English Brerkfast [*sic*]" as a synonym for congou.[17] The soaring importation of congou into America at the start of the twentieth century likely demonstrated and reinforced the success of this seller's brand (see figure 3). Others referred to English breakfast tea as other varieties of Chinese black tea. An American medical report published in 1877 identified "English breakfast tea" as Chinese "Souchong."[18] An 1888 magazine also instructed hostesses to use "good quality of English breakfast tea, that is, a pure Souchong," for afternoon tea.[19] The term was also an umbrella concept for all black teas picked in China's Hubei and Hunan provinces. They were "best known to us as English breakfast tea," the *Youth Companion* explained in 1870.[20] Joseph M. Walsh asserted in 1884 that English breakfast tea included "Caper, Pekoe, Souchong, Congou and Pouchong," all being Chinese black tea.[21] An American lady concluded in 1905 that English breakfast tea was "a general name for all Chinese black teas on account of their popularity in England."[22]

In the final decades of the nineteenth century, English breakfast tea had begun to incorporate blacks from other regions. Indian tea had rarely been on sale independently in the United States by the 1880s. American dealers mixed it with weaker-bodied, lighter-flavored Chinese tea to improve the aroma and taste of the drink, because Indian tea possessed strength and fragrance but lacked the smoothness and softness of high-rank Chinese blacks.[23] It is unclear whether this blended tea was named "English breakfast tea," but being black qualified Indian tea for the term. It is unsurprising that in 1873, a magazine article on the export of Indian tea to London claimed that "in America this tea is known as 'English breakfast tea.'"[24] By 1904 Americans had also accepted Ceylon black tea into the category. A magazine article published that year named the "malty, heavy flavor" of all fermented teas from China, India, and Ceylon an "English Breakfast" flavor, regardless of their origins.[25] When William Ukers published *All about Tea* in 1935, the term had acquired its modern usage as a mixed black tea. Ukers explained that English breakfast tea was "originally applied to China Congou in the

United States, and now used to indicate blends of black teas in which the China flavor predominates."[26] Black teas from India, Ceylon, and Africa are the kinds that support and augment the Chinese flavor in present-day English breakfast tea.

The changing ingredients of English breakfast tea reflected the importance of advertisements and the decline of Chinese tea in the U.S. market. The latter half of the nineteenth century was an era when retailers invented their own store brands to market tea products. For instance, "Houqua's celebrated black tea" of the Canton Tea Company or the Thea-Nectar of the Great Atlantic and Pacific Tea Company replaced the strange-sounding names transliterated from Chinese.[27] The marketing of English breakfast tea, as an American seller's brand, capitalized on U.S. consumers' imagination of the English taste to promote Chinese blacks in this green and oolong tea country. Already detached from the genuine contents, the fluid concept easily morphed when Indian and Ceylon black tea outcompeted Chinese products. In 1915 Americans consumed 20 million pounds of Indian and Ceylon black teas annually, whereas the aggregate amount of Chinese green and black tea imported to the United States was a little over 20 million.[28] Thus English breakfast tea's transitioning from pure Chinese blacks to a blend with Indian and Ceylon teas signaled the decline of the U.S.-China tea trade (chapter 5).

In the century-long tea trade, the power dynamics in the credit economy constantly reshaped U.S. tea consumption after the American Revolution. Unable to compete with European companies in the advance system and British traders in black tea market, Americans began importing more green tea early in the nineteenth century, especially the young hyson disregarded by the EIC. The distinctive taste nonetheless helped Americans find a niche in the tea trade with China and paved the way for the rise of oolongs in the United States. This was also the time when American upstarts became major players in China's credit markets. However, the rise of new tea suppliers undermined the U.S.-China tea trade. Japanese, Indian, and Ceylon products, which "were unknown to the world," began to challenge those from China in the 1860s. "Up to 1862 the Northern States of our country consumed fully 80 per cent of green teas," Thomas A. Phelan of the National Tea Association observed. "Since the above date green teas have given way to Japans in the West." Oolongs remained favorable in the eastern states.[29]

However, British capital controlled the supply of Formosa oolong, the mainstay of the oolong tea trade, to the United States. After Japan colonized Taiwan following the Sino-Japanese War (1894–95), Formosa oolong tea became a Japanese brand. Although black tea had become the most popular tea in the South by 1915, Chinese products lost their dominance to Indian and Ceylon blacks.[30] The changing identity of English breakfast tea mirrored the historical trend of the declining U.S.-China tea trade. While consumers had flexibility in selecting their favorite tea brands, competitions between American, British, Chinese, and other Asian merchants determined the varieties available in the U.S. market. A teacup displayed the color and flavor of the leaves; behind it was the power structure of the credit economy that financed the global supply chain. Hence the last chapter will place the shifting consuming and trading patterns into the credit economy and power dynamics of the U.S.-China tea trade during 1873–1911.

5

Booms and Busts

LOSING THE TEA TRADE, 1873–1911

A newspaper article titled "China Losing Tea Trade" appeared in the *London Daily Mail* and the *Washington Post* in 1902, declaring that "the trade was slipping out of China's hands—hands that used to supply the world."[1] Chinese scholars Huang Yanpei and Pang Song echoed the idea. When Huang and Pang compiled the statistics of China's foreign trade between 1876 and 1916 into a book, they simply titled it *The History of China's Failures in the Commercial War.* "Tea has been the specialty of our country," the two scholars lamented, but "the overseas market was captured. The Chinese tea economy will collapse if no one takes effective measures."[2] On the other side of the Pacific Ocean, George H. Macy, an American tea importer and grocer, testified before the U.S. Congress in 1902, painting a similar picture of the gloomy tea trade but focusing on Americans' failure in it. "We started business there [China] after our war, and then lost our vessels, and the merchants were driven out, and one after another dropped out," Macy asserted. "With one or two exceptions, we [Carter, Macy & Company] are about the only American house represented at those different ports."[3] Therefore the decline of tea trade at the dawn of the twentieth century marked a mutual failure for both Chinese and Americans facing international competition.

Historians have identified two primary causes of the decline of China's global tea trade: external factors, like foreigners' market manipulation and negative marketing campaigns against Chinese tea, and internal weaknesses, including Chinese teas' deteriorating quality, uncompetitive pricing, outdated production methods, inefficient business practices, and excessive taxation of tea merchants.[4] However, this chapter reveals the decline of the U.S.-China tea trade as a consequence of broader structural shifts in the global monetary system. The dynamic credit economy, which facilitated efficient international settlements and stimulated transpacific commerce, caused significant economic suffering during the late nineteenth century, as Chinese and U.S. tea merchants operated against the protracted global recession after 1873 and increasingly depended on banking facilities. The first section of this chapter reconstructs the troubled times for the transpacific tea trade. The world's conversion to the gold standard contributed to the global Long Depression of 1873–97, depreciated the value of silver in China, and deflated the price of tea in America. While the transpacific credit system had been interlocked with waves of economic crises for a century, the decades-long meager profits caused by high local price and low market rates of tea were unprecedentedly devastating to both Chinese and American tea merchants. Relying on borrowed capital and fragile credit networks, tea traders' financial embarrassment worsened even after the quantity of tea shipped from China to America recovered in the 1880s and spiked in the 1890s. The following two sections detail the impacts of the new financial landscape on both sides of the tea trade. U.S. merchants lost heavily in tea and exchange markets. Owing to the absence of U.S. banks in China, Americans' dependence on European banking institutions, with London as the financial center, grew to be a pressing matter. Undergirded by the fragile credit network, the Chinese tea economy shifted to a model of thinly capitalized operation, small-scale manufacturing, lower-end products, and faster-pace turnouts. Taking advantage of the downgraded Chinese tea economy, the newly arising tea producers in other parts of Asia launched advertising campaigns to capture the U.S. market. The U.S.-China tea trade ultimately withered. The last section of this chapter integrates the decline of the transpacific tea trade with the status of the United States and China in the world at the beginning of the twentieth century, thus highlighting the significance of this research on tea, credit, and U.S.-China relations.

Depression

The underlying crisis of the U.S.-China tea trade became evident in 1873, when the tea market collapsed, tea prices plummeted, and the exchange rate depreciated. American tea merchants were "feeling the effects of a period of overtrading" that year. However, easy credit from England resumed against the panic and sustained tea imports into America.[5] "Of course, trade was overdone; losses came." The U.S. tea market eventually collapsed, and many banks "were compelled to wind up."[6] The panic soon spread back to China. Forbes described the tea season of 1872–73 in Shanghai as "a massacre of many of the lesser teamen"; even larger tea firms lost 10 to 15 percent on their settlements.[7] "This year [1873] there seems a chance of fewer tea hongs being established," Forbes analyzed, "but nothing short of a miracle seems likely to give us really cheap tea!"[8] Miracles occurred at times. Tea prices plummeted after 1873. The market value of green tea, dominated by Americans, almost halved. Moreover, after the cliff drop following 1874, tea prices in China never returned to their previous level until the early part of the twentieth century (see figure 19). The exchange market also experienced a similar downturn. The value of silver against sterling bills, in gold standard, had already been depreciating in China after the depression of 1865. The trend only accelerated between the 1870s and the 1880s; the price of silver against sterling further plunged during the 1890s; and the exchange rate continued to fluctuate at a low level into World War I (see figure 18).

In theory, cheap tea and exchange could benefit many merchants. While the commodity's price dropped, the lowered exchange rate devalued silver, enabling importers to make more purchases without increasing the laying-down cost of the trade. Writing in the late nineteenth century, a Chinese scholar viewed the change as an opportunity to develop China's tea economy, because the silver currency's depreciation would incentivize both foreign and native merchants to increase their investments in Chinese tea.[9] Economist Charles Frederick Remer echoed this analysis. The decrease in trade expenses should heighten competition among tea importers, thereby creating "an opportunity for unusual trading profits." Although the competition would drive up demand and eventually restore the price of tea, the uncertain timing of the market's invisible-hand recovery made prolonged unusual profits possible.[10] Precedents exist: the low exchange rate after 1865 had fueled tea speculation across Chinese tea ports (chapter 4). Historical statistics from the post-1873 period also support these theories: after a temporary retrogression during 1873–78, the quantity of tea exported from China to America recovered in the 1880s and spiked in the 1890s before its ultimate fall after 1905 (see figure 20).

However, neither Chinese nor American tea traders remembered the post-1873 era as a time of unusual trading profits. Chinese-language records point

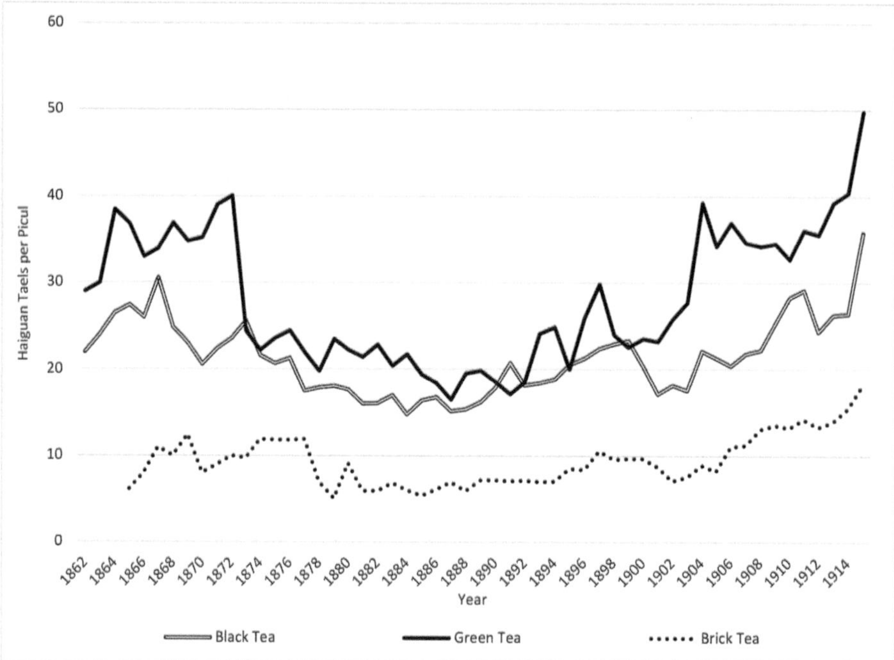

Fig. 19. Average price of tea in China, 1862–1915. The price reflects the value of tea excluding duties. Sources: 1862–1901: "Forty Years Values of the Principal Articles of Chinese Produce," in Inspector General of Chinese Maritime Customs, *Decennial Reports on the Trade, 1892–1901*, vol. 2, *Southern Ports, with Appendices*, xxiv. 1876–1915: Huang and Pang, *Zhongguo shangzhan shibaishi*, 94–97. Huang and Pang provided more comprehensive annual records of both the value and quantity of tea exports. Their data align with those in the Chinese Imperial Maritime Customs' decennial reports, except for the average price of brick tea in 1889, green tea in 1892, and black tea in 1897. Given the greater completeness of Huang and Pang's dataset, this chart uses their figures when discrepancies arise. Hamashita's data for 1882–1921 and Yao's records from 1862 to 1894 provide additional verification. See Hamashita, *Zhongguo jindai jingjishi yanjiu*, 2:557; Yao, *Zhongguo jindai duiwaimaoyishi ziliao*, 3:1654.

to the years around 1873 as the beginning of the tea trade's decline. "Chinese tea merchants all amassed wealth during the reigns of Emperors Xianfeng and Tongzhi (1850–1875), but the business largely became debilitated after Emperor Guangxu's enthroning (1875)," *Shenbao* reported. "The situation even deteriorated year over year after 1880."[11] Yu Xie also categorized the tea trade of Anhui province, the major supplier of green tea to the United

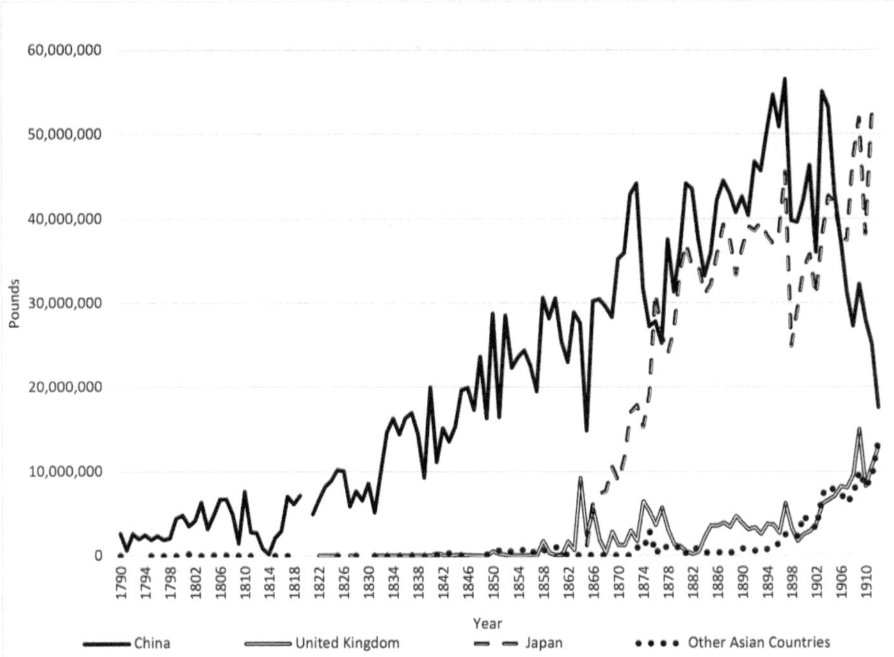

Fig. 20. Quantities of U.S. tea imports by country of origin, 1790–1912. Tea imports from China for 1862–64 included Japanese tea. The category "Other Asian Countries" for 1905–12 refers to the British East Indies. Sources: 1790–91 and 1795–1904: U.S. Department of Commerce and Labor (USDCL), "World's Production," 138–41. 1792–94: Flagg, "China," 1:516. 1905–7: USDCL, *Foreign Commerce and Navigation, 1907*, 344. 1908–12: USDCL, *Foreign Commerce and Navigation, 1912*, 356.

States, into three phases: the prosperous years before the Opium War, the transitional and still profitable period during the 1840s, and the lost decades after 1875.[12] Indeed, despite temporary revivals, the tea trade with America between 1873 and 1911 experienced constant downturns for decades.[13] Even the revival of tea shipments to America after the 1880s failed to save most Chinese merchants from heavy losses, although some individuals earned profits in particular years. Hence *Shenbao* summarized in 1889: "The tea trade declined so dramatically in the past ten years that countless people lost their businesses and even lives."[14]

The situation of U.S. tea traders was equally devastating after 1873. Augustine Heard and Company and Olyphant and Company, both investing aggressively in tea, suffered catastrophic losses in 1873. "Oolongs of [Augustine Heard & Co.'s] shipment have been sold at 15 @ 20 [fifteen to twenty] cents a pound loss!"[15] Augustine Heard and Company soon failed in 1876.[16] Olyphant and Company continued shipping tea to the United States when the Heards withdrew from the trade. However, the stagnant demand meant only three parties—all relatives or affiliations of the house—absorbed their imports.[17] Olyphant and Company also went bankrupt in 1878, two years following the Heards' exit from the trade.[18] Russell and Company persevered before its eventual fall in 1891, but its Hong Kong branch and partners lost heavily on tea.[19] The house's major consignee of tea in America—John M. Forbes and Company—lost $80,000 within three years, between 1873 and 1876, the 2024 equivalent being more than $2 million.[20] Cunningham also wrote from Massachusetts in 1876–77, repeatedly lamenting losing "about 10%" on teas, large profits being "very exceptional now-a-days," and "constantly decreasing rates" of tea.[21] In "the last ten years there have been only two seasons which have given a margin for profit to the American or European merchants engaged in the tea trade," M. M. De Lano, U.S. consul in Fuzhou, summarized in 1880, "while native dealers have been steadily sinking under financial embarrassments."[22] American importers also faced a dire situation. By 1882 green tea had "been rushed off in New York—by auctions held weekly—to the lowest bidder." While grocers obtained cheaper teas, many importers went out of business. A few companies with large capital grasped the business into their hands, because they could afford to earn no profits beyond commissions.[23]

Consequently, the decline in U.S.-China trade recast the landscape of China's tea production after 1873. Hu Yuanlong, the Chinese merchant who received the most credit for inventing Qimen (Keemun) black tea, was originally engaged in the green tea trade. The gloomy market forced him to convert to black tea production in 1876.[24] His home province, Anhui, started to manufacture more black teas, although the project often met with discouraging results.[25] Xiamen, the primary port for the U.S. market, also saw "the decrease in the exportation of Oolong Teas" in 1875, "which has sensibly diminished owing to the low prices ruling in the American market which have not even covered the cost of production." Some tea farmers thus remanufactured their oolongs into congous for the English market.[26] Around the same time, Taiwan teamen had their unsold oolongs reprocessed into pouchongs for China's domestic market. Initially having little knowledge of the technique and solely relying on Fuzhou tea workers, Taiwan tea traders developed pouchongs into a signature tea of the island in the coming decades.[27]

The massive losses on both sides reflected the dramatically changed commercial and financial landscape after 1873. Unlike the golden age of the 1860s and early 1870s, when the exchange rate was low in China but the tea price was high in the United States, tea prices on American markets deflated for decades during the global Long Depression. Dubbed by scholars as "the first truly international crisis," the depression started as a financial panic at the Vienna stock market in May 1873 and then spread to the United States after the failure of the banking house Cooke and Company in the same year. Other countries experienced recessions at different times and rates. Despite the ongoing debates over the causes and extent of the Long Depression, researchers agree that price deflation was one of the elements that defined this international crisis.[28] As part of the broader Long Depression, the U.S. market experienced an unprecedented sharp decline in tea price after 1874, a historic low that persisted for three decades (see figure 21). Chinese products aside, the value of teas from Japan and other Asian countries all depreciated in the United States.[29] Thus "it is curious to notice how low the price [of tea] now is," Americans exclaimed in 1883, "and how easy it is even for persons in very moderate circumstances to indulge a taste" for tea.[30]

The global depreciation of silver sustained tea's diminished value, as tea was priced by silver. The global Long Depression ended in 1879 in the United States, while the year 1897 marked its end in Europe.[31] However, tea prices in the U.S. market never returned to prerecession levels until the early twentieth century (see figure 21). Therefore the low rate of the commodity in the United States even outlasted the Long Depression, indicating that a structural change occurred, leading to the systemic and persistent depreciation of tea's value. Contemporaries had contemplated the connections between the depreciation of silver and the simultaneous fall in tea prices. Thus "a great number of people we may say took it for granted that values in China declined as they have done in every part of the world," an article published in *North China Herald* noted in 1886, "and that the fall in the price of silver, and consequently in exchange, had reduced the price of tea and silk here." The author aimed to refute the connection between tea and

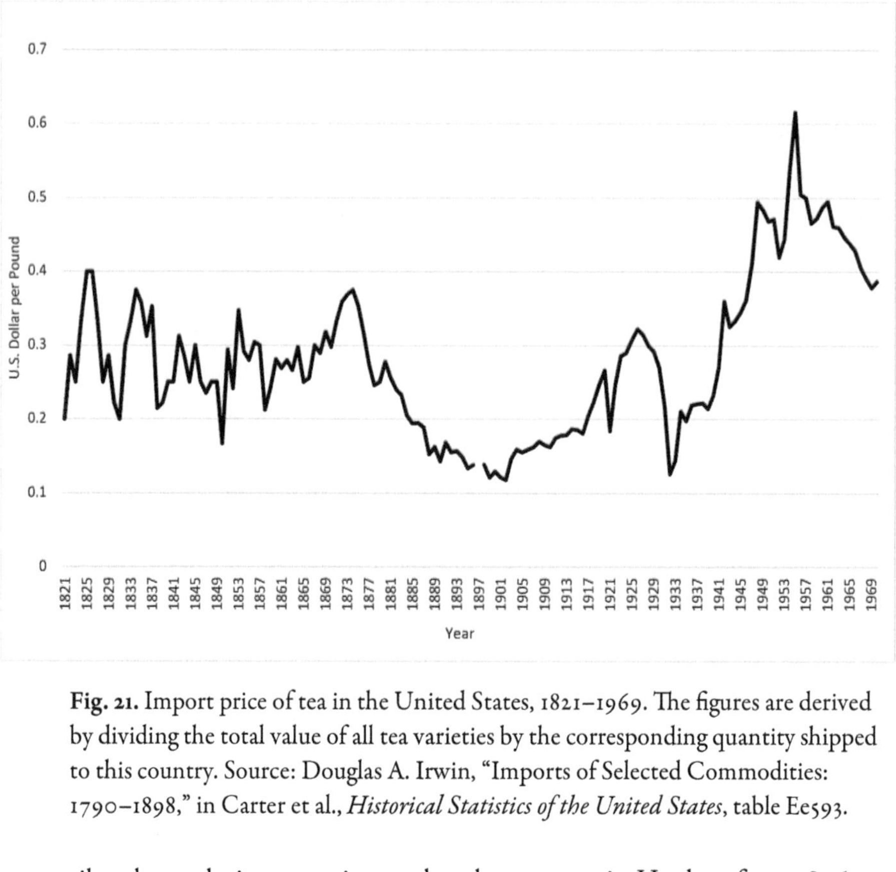

Fig. 21. Import price of tea in the United States, 1821–1969. The figures are derived by dividing the total value of all tea varieties by the corresponding quantity shipped to this country. Source: Douglas A. Irwin, "Imports of Selected Commodities: 1790–1898," in Carter et al., *Historical Statistics of the United States*, table Ee593.

silver by analyzing tea prices and exchange rates in Hankou from 1876 to 1888. However, as figures 18, 19, and 21 demonstrate, 1873 was the actual turning point in these markets. Missing the earlier shift, the author found only remarkably steady commodity and exchange prices.[32] C. Lenox Simpson, commissioner of Jiujiang Customs, explicitly blamed the unprecedentedly disastrous tea season of 1886 on "the depreciation of silver" or, conversely, "the appreciation of gold, which has lowered the prices of all commodities" in China.[33] The U.S. congressional report in 1905 also focused on the correlation between tea and silver. Sold at "the highest import price marked during the last seventy-five years" in 1873, the market value of tea shrank steadily afterward. "How far this fall in price was due to the depreciation of silver (the monetary standard in most of the tea producing countries at the time), which set in about the same time, would be hard to answer," the authors of the report pondered; however, "it is sufficient to state that, but for the rapid decline of the value of silver since 1875, tea prices, on the whole, would have probably maintained a higher level."[34]

Indeed, the adoption of the gold standard in Europe, the United States, and Asia caused a structural change in world monetary systems, which devalued silver and sustained the global Long Depression, thus depreciating the market price of tea in the United States from the 1870s onward. The value of silver remained stable for half a century after Great Britain adopted the gold standard in 1815, when Asia, particularly China and India, absorbed the surplus silver in Europe. However, in 1871 Germany started to coin gold and demonetize silver when this empire received a substantial amount of gold indemnities following the Franco-Prussian War (1870–71). The United States, passing the Coinage Act of 1873, also ceased silver coinage. Other European countries followed suit, adopting gold as the basis of their monetary systems. The trend also began in Asia, as India terminated free coinage of silver in 1893 and Japan converted to the gold standard in 1897.[35] Meanwhile, the world output of silver continued to expand, from fifteen times the gold production in 1881 to twenty-three times in 1890, thus accelerating the global depreciation of silver.[36] Some scholars ascribed the global Long Depression of 1873–97 to the world's adoption of the gold standard and silver's devaluation, which reduced the amount of currency in circulation, depreciated the value of assets and capital stock, and eventually slowed investment, manufacturing, and industrial production.[37] It is also well known that the gold standard and the collapse of commodity prices, such as that for grain and cotton, caused massive hardships among U.S. farmers, ultimately stimulating the populist movement in America during the 1890s.[38]

Less known was how the structural change in global monetary systems impoverished those engaged in the U.S.-China tea trade. The devaluation of silver after the adoption of the gold standard was unprecedented.[39] Compared to the silver-gold exchange rate in China over the past five centuries, silver's value depreciated by three to eight times after 1873.[40] Measured by the value of silver in China, the price of tea also deflated dramatically. Hence, while Fuzhou merchants exported 87,780,000 pounds of tea to earn $23,979,000 during 1874–75, they had to ship an extra 9.5 million pounds in 1881–82 to make $23,765,000. The income was even $200,000 less than that of seven years before.[41] On the micro level, prices of oolongs in Xiamen,

Fuzhou, and Taiwan fell below the cost of production for "almost the whole season" of 1873.[42] Green tea was also devalued. The finest gunpowders and young hysons used to command 80 taels per picul in China, but the price dropped to 50 taels and later to 40 taels in the 1880s; the price of the lower ranks of green tea, sold at 12 to 16 taels per picul, reduced to 6 to 9 taels.[43] Consequently, although the quantities of Chinese tea exported to America began to recover in 1878 and even exceeded the predepression level after the 1890s, the value realized on the American market shrank, failing to generate profits or cover the cost of the tea trade (see figures 20 and 22).

Worse still, while exchange rates between gold and silver further plummeted and the market value of tea in the United States kept deflating, tea's average prices rose in China (see figures 18 and 19). The persistent depreciation of silver fueled inflation in the Chinese economy and increased costs of domestic tea production and trade. Therefore, in 1896, Qing reformist and intellectual Chen Chi noted silver's value had grown "lighter" relative to commodity prices.[44] Indeed, since the late 1880s, Chinese newspapers and official reports had recounted the exorbitant cost of manufacturing or shipping tea in the interior, which surpassed even the market value realized in the treaty ports. In Fujian, while tea growers' earnings had plummeted to 7 or 8 taels per picul by 1887, they had to pay 20 taels per picul for tea production and transportation.[45] Likewise, the cost to produce the first crop of Ningzhou black tea was 30 taels per picul, whereas the quotation offered in the Hankou market was merely 20 taels. The cost of the second crop was lowered to 19 taels, and yet the market price dropped to 17 to 18 taels.[46] The price of raw teas, which usually accounted for about 70 percent of the cost of the tea trade, grew even higher at the dawn of the twentieth century. The Jiang family in Anhui procured crude leaves at an average of $0.206 per catty in 1845 and $0.185 in 1846, but the same amount cost $0.192 in 1897 and $0.297 in 1905.[47] U.S. consuls and the customs commissioners at major tea ports—including Ningbo, Fuzhou, Danshui, and Xiamen—also noticed elevated costs incurred in the interior tea districts, which often surpassed contemporaneous market quotations in Chinese treaty ports, London, and New York during the 1880s and 1890s.[48] Indeed the value of tea in the United States remained stubbornly low after the Long Depression. When the cost of shipments from China to America had reached more than nine cents per pound in 1890, the market price of tea in New York was merely

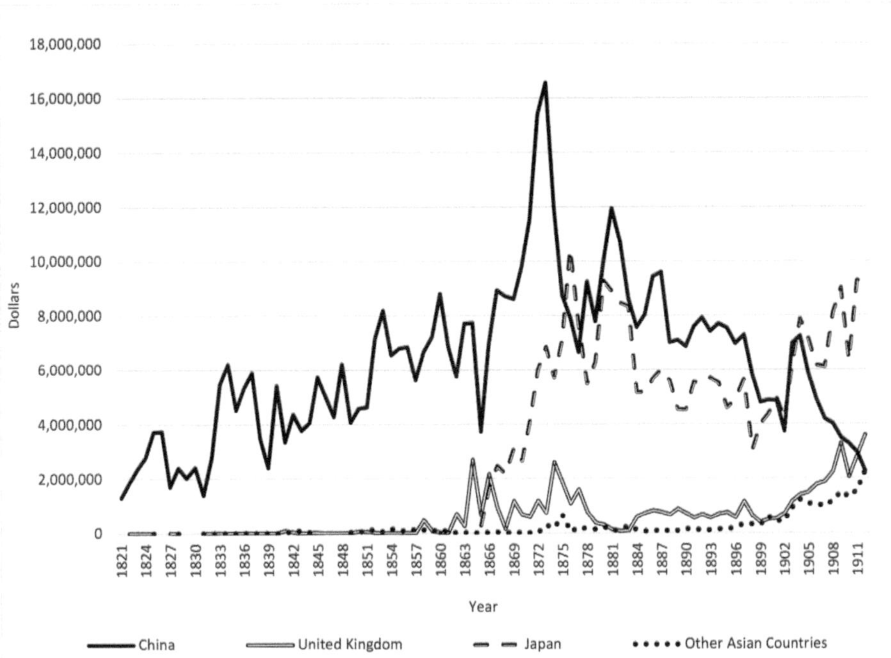

Fig. 22. Value of U.S. tea imports by country of origin, 1821–1912. Tea imports from China for 1862–64 included Japanese tea. The category "Other Asian Countries" for 1905–12 refers to the British East Indies. Sources: 1821–1905: U.S. Department of Commerce and Labor (USDCL), "World's Production," 139–40. 1905–7: USDCL, *Foreign Commerce and Navigation, 1907*, 344. 1908–12: USDCL, *Foreign Commerce and Navigation, 1912*, 356.

ten to twelve cents per pound.[49] Thus C. H. Oliver, deputy commissioner at Ningbo, attributed tea merchants' losses in 1903 to "the high local prices and the decline in the market values abroad," well summarizing the state of the business in the preceding decades (also see figures 19 and 21).[50]

Consequently, facing the global crisis, the gold standard, a low market price abroad, and a high local cost, the U.S.-China tea trade began to wither after 1873. Worse still, the decline in the aggregate value of the tea trade took place decades before the prolonged reduction in the quantities of Chinese tea exports to the United States (see figures 20 and 22).[51] The illusion of a flourishing commerce enticed traders, but most returned with empty purses. Thus China's Imperial Maritime Customs at Hankou, Jiujiang, Shanghai, and Fuzhou all complained that "while the quantity of the export has indeed been great, the result of the year's transactions has been extremely disastrous to the Chinese tea-brokers and to the Foreigners."[52] The depreciation of the green tea trade in Ningbo during 1891, which was directly associated with the U.S. market, was also "due rather to lower prices than to less business."[53] Consequently, although low exchange rates stimulated a steady increase in China's overall export, "almost every item, except Tea, has shared in the expansion."[54]

Dependence

"One wishes we could return to tea & silk & cotton goods & make simple trade money," Cunningham complained when the global depression began. Tea's devaluation forced Russell and Company to diversify their investment portfolio in China, yet "this guerilla style of business, nibbling at everything, is disorganizing, demoralizing & other de's."[55] Another "de" that should appear in Cunningham's list was dependence, particularly on the increasingly unstable credit system during the global depression. Russell and Company still thrived on the verge of the crisis, but a large amount of their assets remained tied to bills of exchange.[56] Owing to the commercial stagnation, the demand for these papers dwindled and their prices dropped fast. For instance, within the week of January 9–15, 1873, the exchange rate fell from 6 shillings to 5 shillings 11¼ pence, greatly depreciating the value of the house's intangible property.[57] Augustine Heard and Company's finance was in a more dire situation. The "entire stagnation in trade & the losses in the Tea trade probably reduce the demand for Bills." As it was "very difficult, almost impossible to sell Bills" in China, John Heard's mounting frustration saturated his business correspondence.[58] Heard attempted to sell some in New York, but a broker informed Heard that "all China Bills are & have been worked on with suspicion on a/c [account] of the heavy losses in the trade."[59] Nonetheless, the company's outstanding debts on the exchange accounts kept accumulating, with £135,767 due by late September 1873. With his bills of exchange unsalable in America, Heard turned to his friend in London. "I hope you understand clearly that all our resources are now exhausted," Heard pleaded. "Unless we can sell Bills, we have nothing, literally not one cent to provide for the exchange a/c [account]."[60]

American houses' financial embarrassment only bolstered the financialization process dominated by European banks in China, including the

Hongkong and Shanghai Bank, which was local but dependent on London to operate its exchange business.[61] Facing the recession starting in 1873, John Heard made a special arrangement with the Hongkong and Shanghai Bank to pay Fearon and Company in London, with teas shipped to New York as the collateral.[62] While the Heards' account books during the 1860s recorded the sales of exchanges and commodities along with the purchase of tea, Imperial Bank's credit appeared more frequently in the company's tea purchase book during 1873–74.[63] Despite the financial arrangements, this second-largest U.S. commission house in China ended its operation in 1876. Russell and Company survived, but the devaluation of silver in China and "the depreciation caused in property upon which we depend to pay our obligations" delivered a heavy blow to the house.[64] After 1873 the company's capital reduced "at the rate of from $50,000 to $70,000 a year" while "making nothing beyond household expenses."[65] Partners of the company started to borrow from banks. However, it was not always successful, for the French bank was disinclined to offer any loans in 1875.[66] Banks' influence was one of the direct causes of the company's failure in 1891, as the Hongkong and Shanghai Bank refused to accommodate Russell and Company's unsuccessful speculation in silver in 1890.[67]

European exchange banks were not unscathed during the depression, because the value of their assets also shrank with silver's devaluation.[68] However, taking advantage of the financial unsettlement, survivors further controlled the exchange market and the tea trade. European banks finally shortened and standardized the term of bills from six months to four months in 1880, demonstrating a victory over mercantile capital in China's exchange market.[69] Thus, in 1891, against their tea shipments to New York, American house Purdon and Wiggin drew four-month bills on John M. Forbes and Company and then sold the bills to the Hongkong and Shanghai Bank.[70] The fluctuating exchange rates in China further empowered European banks to control the bill trade, because these financial institutions assumed the risk in the exchange market for merchants.[71] While America and Europe made efforts to fix the exchange rate between silver and gold during the 1890s, "the instability of silver [was] utterly disorganising to the export trade" in China.[72] Indeed, while Macy considered even 1 percent fluctuation in exchange to matter considerably to his tea business in Asia, the exchange rate in China fluctuated over 11 percent in 1895.[73] Therefore, although the

U.S. commission houses served as their own banks and handled the complex coastal exchanges during the 1850s and 1860s, Macy's tea companies, which extended to China in the final decade of the century, relied on international banks to weather the fluctuations in the credit market. The U.S. Congress asked Macy in 1902 whether it was challenging for Carter, Macy, and Company to make exchanges and conduct business in Asia, since the currency in Taiwan and Xiamen were Mexican silver dollars but the Japanese wanted gold. "Not [in] the least," Macy replied. "When we buy the goods from the producers we very often settle with the banks on the rate of exchange."[74] The tea company maintained bank credits payable primarily in London and occasionally in New York. Its Chinese branches drew bills of exchange on these financial centers and commissioned exchange brokers to identify banks—whether English, French, Russian, Japanese, or Chinese—that offered the most favorable rates on their bills, thus generating funds for their tea procurement.[75]

Consequently, a great portion of the transnational tea trade in the late nineteenth century was translated into settlements facilitated by banks' credit instruments and account books. European banks financed the China trade by issuing bills of exchange to foreign importers and purchasing bills from exporters, profiting from the changing exchange rates and commission fees.[76] For example, key to the operations of the Hongkong and Shanghai Bank was the account difference between "bills receivable," which financed the purchase of China goods—primarily silk and tea—and "bills payable," which financed imports to China. The bank's sterling deposits in London and New York settled the account balances.[77] Account books and credit instruments also interwove tea suppliers within China into global financial networks. Interior Chinese tea dealers "either pays himself, or arranges with the native bank to finance his purchase"; they then sold tea to foreign merchants in large treaty ports, such as Shanghai, and received either native banks' promissory notes or foreign banks' checks as payments.[78] If these Chinese merchants used foreign checks to repay their loans from the cash shops, these native banks could use the papers to clear their account balances with foreign banks and thus complete the financial circle.[79]

The growing reliance on European banks, with London as the financial center, and the absence of U.S. banks in China imposed additional burdens on Americans' tea trade, especially as profits dwindled after 1873. By 1880 the number and variety of bills of exchange passing through London solidified its status as the international financial center.[80] In contrast, even though dollar bills drawn directly between the United States and China had circulated before the depression, the direct exchange business remained relatively small by 1873.[81] Moreover, some principal New York banking houses, with headquarters located in London, rejected dollar bills or purchased them "with considerable restrictions."[82] Even though the idea "to emancipate themselves from their dependence on English bankers" had emerged in the minds and discussions of Forbes and the Heards as early as the 1860s, U.S. banks were absent from China for the entire nineteenth century.[83] Consequently, after Russell and Company failed in 1891, Carter, Macy and Company, the major tea firm in China during the last phase of the trade, confessed that by 1902 "as much as 90 per cent of [their] business is financed through London." By sending millions of dollars' credit to finance their tea trade in the East mostly through London, Macy's tea company incurred a significant amount of expenses each year.[84] After all, London bankers charged 2 percent commission fees on processing Americans' bills. Moreover, American traders paid additional 4 to 6 percent fees to acquire bullion, ship gold or silver from America to London, negotiate bills of exchange, and pay bank charges in Asia. In other words, despite record-low tea prices in the last decades of the nineteenth century, U.S. importers had to pay an average of 3 to 4 percent more to European banks to facilitate their extensive tea business, owing to the absence of American banking facilities in China.[85] "At present, all the vast sums of money passing between America and Asia," Consul David H. Bailey warned in 1873, "are paying enormous tribute to London."[86] The discourse of financial tribute to London persisted into the first decade of the twentieth century when English banks still dominated Americans' international trade finance, as S. D. Scudder declared at the Pennsylvania Bankers Association in 1908: "London gets a tribute on business which never originated there."[87]

Thin Capitalization

While London overshadowed American merchants in the credit economy, native banks—a major source of credit for Chinese tea dealers—also increasingly relied on foreign banks' loans and credit instruments. Taking advantage of the unprecedented silver depreciation after 1873 and the financial panic in China during the 1880s, European banks increased their loans to native banks, secured by the latter's promissory notes.[88] "Chinese remittance banks, silver shops, pawn shops, and copper shops all depended on foreign capital," a Chinese lamented in the late nineteenth century, "because it is easy to exchange gold pounds for sycee, but more difficult the other way around."[89] Therefore, by 1888, all of the sixty-two large cash shops in Shanghai had received foreign bank loans approximating several million taels in total.[90] When cash shops in Hankou and Shanghai failed in 1908, they owed over 4 million taels to foreign banks, an unprecedented financial panic that startled every treaty port and caused bank runs even in China's capital city.[91] Bank loans aside, native banks also employed foreign banks' credit instruments in tea transactions. In 1893 not only were native banks "more willing to make their remittances to Shanghai in drafts on Foreign banks" in the tea trade, but "Foreign bank notes, which at the beginning of the decade were held in distrust by the Natives, are now readily accepted by banks and merchants."[92] Chinese cash shops obtained credit from foreign banks and native remittance banks at lower interest rates. They then lent to Chinese merchants at higher rates even after the global Long Depression unfolded.[93] Hence the credit economy that fostered China's tea trade remained robust during the crisis, sustaining the illusion of a thriving commerce.

Relying on financial credit, Chinese tea dealers adopted a thin-capitalization model after 1873, in which brokers, dealers, and manufacturers possessed only a fraction of their working capital but borrowed heavily from banks or warehouses. Xu Run, who founded one of the earliest tea warehouses in 1867, refocused on tea after his failed silk speculation in the 1880s. With limited capital to restart his tea business, Xu secured six-month loans, totaling approximately 200,000 taels, from Chinese banks in 1886.[94] Like Xu, financed by bank credit, a large number of tea dealers were thinly capitalized. *Shenbao* noticed that tea peddlers were mostly destitute during the 1880s. They possessed a capital of less than 10,000 or even 5,000–6,000 taels but borrowed 30,000–40,000 taels from warehouses to defray the cost of shipping and selling tea. In other words, native tea dealers typically owned only a third or even less of their working capital.[95] Likewise to tea manufacturers, Jiang, the Anhui merchant who worked for Tang Qiaoqing's warehouse, raised only 2,000 taels for his tea manufactory Lianshunchang in 1900, while Tang provided 4,000 taels as the paid-in capital and promised more loans for its operation. Six years later, Jiang and his partners gathered 8,000 taels to cofound another tea manufactory, Qianhengtai. Tang lent 10,000 taels, and two native banks furnished Jiang with 6,000 taels and 2,000 taels, respectively.[96] "Most of the small manufactories did not have their own paid-in capital," the Anhui tea merchant Yu Xie concluded in 1916, because "they borrowed from others, such as local dealers or tea warehouses."[97]

Although credit was nothing new to the tea trade, the profitability of the commerce dwindled after 1873, so the economic pressure of the credit economy kept mounting on tea dealers. Despite the ready credit for his operation, Xu, together with the great majority of the well-established tea brokers, lost heavily in the 1886 tea venture. However, his tea warehouses in Shanghai and Hankou had to pay fees and interests to banks, totaling tens of thousands of taels.[98] The annual interest rate of loans in China, ranging from 12 percent to 40–50 percent during 1872–85, was much higher than the 2.49–4.82 percent rate in Europe.[99] Even during the prosperous years, two-thirds of Chinese brokers in Fuzhou, who had to repay their bills at 4 percent monthly rate, had gone bankrupt by 1870, not to mention that selling tea became an increasingly uphill battle after 1873.[100] Moreover, the term of the credit was short. The customary term of native banks' promissory notes—the *zhuangpiao*—had been standardized into ten days by 1876, and bank bills also expired in ten days after the delivery of tea.[101] Therefore, after manufacturing and packing tea within two weeks, tea dealers had to seal a deal with foreign buyers within ten days; "up to ten days after tea's delivery, *piaohaos* chased after [them] day and night to collect the bills."[102] However, well aware of the cruciality of time to Chinese dealers, foreign buyers were slow to offer bids or wait for the best exchange rates to settle their transactions.[103] When the trade paused, "the teamen feel it at once, for the interest of their loans is running and their anticipated profits are risked," the Maritime Customs reported.[104] Thus it grew customary for the Chinese to force sales at reduced prices, compete against each other, and therefore incur more losses.[105]

Operated on the credit economy with slim profits, high interest rates, and short credit terms, manufacturers and merchants downgraded China's tea economy, favoring producing small amounts of tea at a faster pace. Xu piloted the trend in the late 1860s, and others accelerated it after 1873. Since the early nineteenth century, Chinese tea had been classified according to their distinct market channels: *yangzhuang* tea for international export and *tuzhuang* tea for domestic consumption. "Zhuang" means a category of tea. "The *yangzhuang* was distributed to the United States, Great Britain, and Russia, whereas the *tuzhuang* catered specifically to domestic consumption."[106] Chinese suppliers usually packaged the *yangzhuang* tea into big chops, or *dabang cha*, which comprised 400–3,000 chests with a wide variety of tea products.[107] For instance, a big chop from Anhui usually included eight to twelve varieties of green tea, chiefly four classes of hyson, five varieties of young hyson, and five ranks of gunpowder.[108] The big chop from Zhejiang consisted of approximately twenty varieties, primarily gunpowder and some hyson-series tea.[109] Hubei and Hunan factories also manufactured over a thousand chests of black tea into a big chop.[110] However, the distinction between the *yangzhuang* and *tuzhuang* became increasingly blurred in the late nineteenth century. As early as 1868, Xu had begun manufacturing *tuzhuang*-style tea to simplify export production. Rather than processing six hundred to a thousand piculs of fine teas into a big chop, Xu purchased two to three hundred piculs of cheap crude leaves to manufacture only five of the most popular varieties of green tea, notably three grades of gunpowders and two ranks of young hyson.[111] This method reduced not only expenses but also the time cost of tea production. While it took around twenty days to make a big chop, manufacturing two to three hundred piculs only required fourteen to fifteen days, thus shortening the cycle of output by nearly a week and greatly easing the pressure of the credit economy on tea merchants.[112] Unable to compete with the small-scale production, others followed suit and the trend spread widely after 1875.[113] The narrowed profit margin also prompted U.S. merchants to cope with, and incentivize, the change to smaller chops. "The business is self killing because in these small importations," Cunningham complained in 1876, "profit for years has depended on getting especial chops suited to certain wants, such chops are not one in ten to the whole amount of tea."[114]

Consequently, small factories and firms mushroomed. These "wildcat tea manufactories," as named by Yu Xie, often produced a hundred chests, in total, only for quick sales.[115] While the firms' size shrank, their number swelled in many tea centers. In Jiujiang, tea manufactories increased from 252 in 1881 to 344 in 1882, but most were small and insignificant ones.[116] In Hankou, owing to heavy losses in the tea trade during the 1880s, large tea firms closed, dragging large banks, such as a well-established branch of the Shanxi remittance bank, Yuanfengjiu, to failure. The consequence was "the establishment of a number of small Native hongs in place of some of the larger ones"; the number of small banks also doubled, tasked with financing these small tea firms.[117] Likewise in Anhui, during the heyday of the green tea trade, only about twenty to forty tea companies existed in the tea districts, a number that was even less than 20 to 30 percent of that in the early twentieth century.[118] Hence, as the quantities of tea exported to the United States increased, many established companies and old brands disappeared from the trade.[119]

The quality of Chinese tea further deteriorated, and the inferior varieties drove the trade with America after 1873. The Bureau of the Economic Inspection of Republican China (1912–49) traced rampant green tea adulterations in Zhejiang Province to the post-1875 era, when newly founded small tea warehouses purchased raw leaves on credit with little consideration of the quality, and manufactories cut or ground coarse leaves to hasten tea production.[120] Careless preparation and adulteration of oolong and black teas with other leaves, dust, sweepings, or dirt were also common in Hankou, Xiamen, Fuzhou, and Danshui.[121] Noting "even the popularity of Formosa Teas will not ensure business" in 1891, the commissioner of Danshui Customs deplored that "the Native producer sacrifices quality for the sake of quantity."[122] While coloring green tea with indigo and Prussian blue was a nineteenth-century norm, Chinese manufactories invented another technique, *yinguang*, which further damaged the reputation of Chinese tea. This tactic improved the appearance of cheap green tea by adding powders of talc and wax into the coloring matter to form a coat of glossy, greenish color over dried leaves.[123] Americans named it "coating" or "facing," because the coloring matter was so heavy that it coated the tea inspector's hand.[124] Among the nearly three hundred tea firms in Anhui, only a dozen old brands—Lixiangji, Guangsheng, and Yongda, among others—refused to adopt the scheme. Reports on highly faced green tea had emerged during 1872–73 (see chapter 4), but according to the investigation of the governor-general of Huguang province, Zhang Zhidong, the fraud grew rampant after 1875, when the profitability of the tea trade grew slim.[125] Cheap teas also dominated the U.S.-China tea trade. While green tea remained crucial to the transpacific tea trade, from the year 1879, the U.S. market received more Pingsueys—chiefly cheap gunpowders from Pingshui, Zhejiang province—than Fychows, the latter mostly referring to higher-grade hyson-series tea manufactured in Anhui (see figure 3).[126] After all, owing to the exorbitant cost of production and the low market price of tea, only "those who bought the cheapest class of Teas" made a little money.[127] After tea arrived in America, U.S. merchants repacked the cheap grades in fancy packages and sold them at the same price, further disincentivizing the supply of higher-quality teas.[128]

However, no longer monopolizing the global tea trade, Chinese tea growers and traders met increasingly fierce competition in U.S. markets. The attempts to challenge China's monopoly over the tea trade had started early in the nineteenth century. From Dutch Java in 1825 and British India in 1833 to Ceylon in 1875 and Natal, Africa, in 1887, Europeans experimented with tea cultivation in their colonies.[129] Black teas from India entered the U.S. market during the American Civil War.[130] Lacking colonies to grow tea, U.S. merchants imported Japanese green tea from Nagasaki and Yokohama as early as 1859.[131] When Russell and Company was struggling with the high price in China before 1873, its commercial partners "made much money . . . on Japan teas."[132] While Forbes claimed that "successful operations in teas must be initiated in China" in 1866, the quantity of green tea shipped from Japan to America doubled that from China ten years later, in 1876.[133] As scholars have elaborated, capitalizing on late nineteenth-century American anxieties about food purity and health, British companies and Japanese enterprises vied for U.S. consumers by waging massive advertising and lobbying campaigns against adulterated and dyed Chinese tea.[134] While the *New York Times* still asserted that "the best was the Chinese" and "the India teas were of poor quality" in 1870, Chinese tea increasingly became the target of negative advertisements during the following decades.[135] Thus, claiming that "every pound of China tea he had been able to find was colored and faced," the New York Tea Association decried as a national scandal that the U.S. federal government allowed the importation of fabricated Chinese tea and urged all importers "to deal only in Japans and Ceylons."[136]

Outraged by the advertisements against Chinese tea encountered in the United States, Yu Xie, whose family ran a green tea business for generations, denounced the claims as "deceitful, guileful lies designed to smear the reputation of Chinese tea."[137] In addition to admonishing his Chinese counterparts to strictly avoid fraudulent practices, Yu Xie recommended establishing direct advertising channels in foreign markets.[138] Indeed, when silver depreciation similarly reduced the value of Japanese tea, contemporaries likewise blamed the falling prices on Japanese merchants' careless processing methods and widespread adulteration.[139] Nevertheless Japanese tea brands maintained their reputation at least partially through their direct advertising campaigns in the American market. By 1915 Yu Xie noticed that Japanese tea companies were spending annually $30,000–$50,000 on advertisements in the United States, which was an equivalent of $0.97–$1.61 million in 2024 dollars. British tea companies like Lipton and Ridgway also lavished at least $400,000–$500,000 per year, or $12.9–$16.1 million in 2024 dollars, promoting Indian and Ceylon teas in America.[140] Against the busyness of Japanese, British, Indian, and Ceylon companies was the sound of silence among Chinese tea merchants. "A dozen virtues might be predicated of China teas without overstepping the bounds of truth, and it seems a pity no one has taken the matter in hand," an article published in both English and American newspapers lamented in 1902, when "advertisement is the life-blood of commerce at the present day."[141] Indeed, despite the Qing government's efforts to showcase Chinese tea at U.S. World's Fairs, the now thinly capitalized native merchants invested nothing in tea advertisements in America.[142]

Losing the Trade

Thus the dynamic credit economy, which bolstered the growth of the U.S.-China tea trade for a century, led to its decline in the post-1873 trading environment. The adoption of the gold standard dramatically depreciated the value of silver, triggered a global depression, and decreased the profitability of the transpacific tea trade. The credit economy became a heavy burden on the impoverished tea merchants, Americans and Chinese alike. Unable to sell their bills of exchange or rely on U.S. banks in China, American commission houses increasingly depended on European banks for credit to conduct business. Their transnational tea trade, no longer lucrative, benefited London bankers through the credit network formed in the past decades, which Americans deemed as a tribute paid to Great Britain. Chinese brokers, dealers, and manufacturers also found it increasingly challenging to sell tea at remunerative prices. Relying on bank credit, they downgraded their tea economy, sped up the pace of tea production, and in doing so let the quality of their products deteriorate. These thinly capitalized tea merchants were unable to maintain their negotiating power with foreign tea buyers or market their products in America, whereas Japanese and British companies spent lavishly on advertising and lobbying activities against Chinese tea. The U.S.-China tea trade ultimately withered.

Roughly a century after the expedition of the *Empress of China* to Canton reinforced the pride of liberty, Americans mourned their loss of independence in the tea trade. Noticing the increase of teas from British colonies by 1895, the *New York Times* warned that "Great Britain has been striving for several years to change the taste of the tea-drinkers of the world."[143] The financial reliance on London further intensified Americans' wariness. Bemoaning the failure of Russell and Company in 1891, John Russell Young claimed that "British policy, British money, and British financial influence are prompt towards the destruction of American commercial power in the East."[144] "At one time it poured a stream of wealth into our land, but somehow or other we grew careless and allowed the channel to be diverted to other nations," the *New York Times* also complained in the same year. "The heavy capital with which the crops [of tea] are raised, the experts who taste and the dealers who buy the leaf, the lead in which it is cased, the steamers in which it is carried, the companies which insure it, and the banks which attend to the financiering are all foreign," the newspaper lamented, "chiefly British."[145]

Nonetheless, Heard Jr. regarded the discourse of "the opposition of British interests" as American politicians' excuses. "The trouble is that the business is no longer profitable," Heard simply put.[146] When Heard Jr. left Boston for China in 1846, a steamer passed by with Warren Delano, the maternal grandfather of Franklin Delano Roosevelt, on board. "There is Warren Delano, just home from China, with $600,000," his fellow passengers exclaimed. "In ten years we will do the same thing." Yet in the late nineteenth century, success was uncertain even if Americans spent their entire lives in China.[147] Moreover, the relocation of tea trade hubs to the treaty ports north of Canton made the already busy work more unpleasant. Tea came to Canton in late autumn, and traders saw little urgency in preparing shipments absent steam and telegraph. "The opening of Shanghai and Foochow made a vast difference in this respect, and now the busiest season is the hottest," starting in the summer months, not to mention the work's faster pace to cope with steamers and telegraph communications.[148]

More important, the economic and political status of the United States had changed dramatically through the nineteenth century, thus changing Americans' means and mindset to accumulate wealth. Life at home was relatively comfortable, and economic opportunities abounded. "The struggle for life is not so urgent here as in England or Germany," Heard Jr. asserted, "and the American prefers to remain at home."[149] Thus Norwood described the Gilded Age as the death of the China trade and the birth of the China market, when an increasingly industrialized America sought overseas outlets for its surplus capital and commodities, rather than startup funds from the golden ghetto in China.[150] Even though the tea trade with China declined, the United States emerged as a new imperialist power and joined the Eight-Nation Alliance to invade China during the Boxer Uprising (1899–1901). The New York–based International Banking Corporation finally extended to Shanghai in 1902, to receive the indemnity from the defeated Qing government rather than financing the shrinking tea trade. Other U.S. banks would extend to China when Europeans' influence waned during World War I.[151]

While U.S. influence was on the rise, the failing tea economy further impoverished Qing China. Before its decline began in the 1870s, the tea trade was a pillar of the Qing government's income and military spending, especially when the backbone of its national revenue transitioned from land tax to commercial tax during the latter half of the nineteenth century.[152] However, as tea's market value shrank, so did the tariff revenue of the Qing government. In Fuzhou eight-tenths of the decrease in duties resulted from the diminished export of tea.[153] Formosa oolong, the most popular tea in the United States, became a Japanese product after 1895, further eroding China's duty revenue. Worse still, the U.S. Congress passed "An Act to Prevent the Importation of Impure and Unwholesome Tea" in 1897, targeting cheap teas of inferior quality.[154] Zhang Zhidong distributed copies of the entire U.S. tea act among Anhui merchants, urging them to improve the quality of their products. "The times are fraught with difficulties, and the military funds are severely strained," Zhang deplored. "Tea is vital to China's tax revenue, so we must take concrete measures to sustain it."[155] Nonetheless, American merchants' interest in Chinese greens kept waning, so "selling big-chops to the United States grew hopeless in the past decade," Yu Xie complained in 1915.[156]

The Qing government faced a dilemma when handling the tea economy. On the one hand, thinly capitalized Chinese tea merchants had already paid exorbitant taxes at home, whereas their counterparts in Japan, India, and Ceylon paid no duties or received subsidies for their tea production.[157] On the other, more than devaluing tea and compressing the duty revenue, silver depreciation also aggravated the Qing court's deficit and increased the actual amount of war indemnities owed to foreign countries, the great majority having adopted the gold standard. The debts reached as high as fifty times the Qing government's regular expenditure at the beginning of the twentieth century.[158] When the state was hampered by empty coffers while the people were impoverished and resentful, rebellions are inevitable and unstoppable, Qing official Zhang Jian predicted in 1895, when China lost the Sino-Japanese War and had to pay unprecedentedly massive reparations.[159] Within less than two decades, the Revolution of 1911 erupted and ultimately terminated the Qing regime. Following that year—127 years after the initiation of U.S.-China trade—teas shipped directly from Great Britain to America once again surpassed Chinese tea imports (see figure 22).

Conclusion

In a pamphlet titled *Tea Is an American Drink*, Lipton Tea Company promoted Indian and Ceylon teas to U.S. consumers by aligning tea consumption with American identity. "Granted, tea is not a tradition in the United States as it is in some countries," the advertisement claimed. However, Lipton reminded American consumers, "perhaps we should reminisce back to the days of 1773, when those of us on this side of the ocean drank as much tea as the English." Thus this British company sought to revive Americans' interest in tea by invoking their colonial memory. Lipton's rhetoric reveals that tea consumption had become a forgotten tradition among Americans in the twentieth century, although the advertisement also admitted, "America is the second largest importer of tea in the world."[1] In the gap between Americans' significant tea imports into the United States and vague memory of their tea culture, this book fits.

This World in a Teacup restores the importance of tea in U.S. history throughout the nineteenth century. Despite American independence, the Anglo-American power dynamics in China continued to influence U.S. tea consumption patterns well after the American Revolution. Initially, American traders in China's global tea trade struggled to compete with well-established European companies and British merchants, who employed the advance system to acquire tea before the tea season or invested heavily in their favorite teas on the open market. Yet the United States grew to be the second-largest importer of Chinese tea as early as the 1790s, when Chinese merchants extended long-term, high-value credit to these upstarts in the Canton Trade. Cultivating trust and credit relations in China, American tea merchants enhanced their purchasing power and eventually dominated green and oolong tea ports in China, even though the British remained the largest buyers of black tea. The power dynamics in China reshaped tea consumption in America. U.S. tea drinkers replaced black teas and old-brand green teas with young hyson and oolong in the nineteenth century, thus distinguishing themselves from their British counterparts and colonial ancestors. A new denomination, "English breakfast tea," also emerged in the United States to market premium and pure Chinese black teas in the American market. However, with the decline of the U.S.-China tea trade after 1873 and the influence of British capital on the tea supply chain in Asia, English breakfast tea morphed into a blend of Chinese, Indian, and Ceylon teas in the early twentieth century.

Tea consumption patterns in America were entwined with trade finance in China. Highlighting the two dimensions of credit—credit transactions and credit instruments—in China's arguably largest export business during the long nineteenth century, this book challenges the divergence, duality, and linear monetary hypotheses that reinforce the stereotype of China's foreign trade as an inherently cumbersome hard-money system. This conclusion offers a preliminary comparison between the credit economy of the transpacific tea trade and American credit practices in the Atlantic world. While more nuanced analogies are beyond this book's scope, this comparative perspective only aims to revisit Orientalist assumptions and contribute to broader discussions about global credit systems.

The dynamics of the credit economy in China did not diverge from that in the Atlantic world. Instead, from the earliest stage of the U.S.-China tea trade, credit transactions were as common as that in Americans' Atlantic commercial activities. Before English bills of exchange emerged as the principle means of international payments in the early nineteenth century, bookkeeping sustained the monetization process in the Atlantic world to fill the gap of barter and specie payments.[2] Likewise, exchange accounts buttressed the early U.S.-China tea trade, rendering physical movements of silver only necessary to clear account balances. As the dominant form of trade and credit in Europe and America during the nineteenth century, consignment sales bolstered de facto transactions between Chinese and American tea merchants without requiring immediate full payments. Credit instruments documented and facilitated these credit transactions in the international tea trade. Like in the early U.S. economy, promissory notes had been facilitating tea settlements between the Chinese and Americans since the late eighteenth century.[3] Bills of exchange then arose to support transnational commerce. During 1815–25, when regional credit markets for sterling bills emerged across the Atlantic ports and an international payment system burgeoned for the transatlantic trade, American, British-Indian, and Chinese merchants also started to trade bills of exchange in Asia, supporting China's tea trade and integrating Canton with global financial markets.[4] The last type of credit instruments, bank checks, became standardized in the United States during the 1840s, when compradors' orders to pay buttressed regional tea transactions between U.S. companies and Chinese sellers. In addition to commercial credit, Chinese banks had financialized the transpacific tea trade through native bills of exchange and promissory notes since the 1850s. While the global movement of financial capital accelerated in the latter nineteenth century, European banks entered China, vying for both the finance of the tea trade and the influence on China's exchange markets. Placed in this comparative perspective, the China trade was not absent from or late in developing the credit economy.

While the chronology of the credit system helps reconsider the divergence narrative, examining the relationship between silver and credit revisits the duality and linear monetary theories. It is plausible that the sustained demand for silver in the China trade distinguished it from U.S. Atlantic commerce, where the precious metal played only a secondary role to account transactions and sterling bills in balancing payments.[5] However, while silver scarcity rendered credit indispensable in Atlantic commerce, the massive amount of silver shipped by Americans to China in no way evinced credit's absence or underdevelopment in the latter region.[6] China's silver influx reflected trade imbalances rather than underdeveloped credit mechanisms. The limited Chinese demand for American goods, combined with the exorbitant costs and risks of silver transportation, made credit equally vital, if not more quintessential, to transpacific commerce.[7] Therefore, since at least the 1790s, American and Chinese traders cultivated trust relations and developed the transpacific credit system through credit transactions (bookkeeping, consignments, and respondentia) and instruments (promissory notes, international and inland bills of exchange, as well as comprador's orders to pay). Therefore the vicissitudes of the silver flow never thwarted the growth of the U.S.-China tea trade. Even as Americans' silver shipments to China declined, U.S. tea imports continued to grow substantially. Moreover, credit was not confined to international payments. Like the transatlantic cotton trade, which connected international and internal credit relations through advance payments and bills of exchange, U.S. and Chinese tea traders, brokers, and bankers also employed the advance system, promissory notes, bills, and bank facilities to translate the transpacific credit economy into domestic credit relations.[8] Therefore investigating the credit economy of the U.S.-China tea trade invalidates the West-East duality. The research also challenges the linear monetary theory. Rather than following a linear path of development, commodity money, silver currency, and credit instruments were all integral components of China's commercial ecosystem. It was hard for any forms of payment to completely supplant the other. While silver was the real money that liquidated trade balances, credit conveniently settled de facto transactions. Thus credit transactions and instruments complemented hard-money and barter payments, especially when international trade was stable and mutual trust sustained merchants' long-term cooperations. In the event of economic crises or lost trust, the return to silver and barter was frequent, such as during the international financial crises or in the newly opened treaty ports, yet credit was by no means absent in China. Likewise in the Atlantic world, merchants preferred specie when facing economic depressions or exchange rates' fluctuations.[9] Foreign merchants in Shanghai were no less eager than the Chinese to adopt hard-money payments during the Taiping Rebellion, after the disappearance of native credit instruments. In short, both Atlantic and Pacific trading systems were hybrid forms that allowed merchants to make flexible decisions in real-world trade finance.

By emphasizing the importance of credit in financing the U.S.-China tea trade, this book both acknowledges and complicates the distinct power dynamics of the transatlantic and transpacific trade. The prevalence of English bills of exchange in tea transactions between American and Chinese merchants demonstrated the influence of British credit on the transpacific commerce. However, rather than simply relying on sterling bills, Americans issued dollar bills in China's treaty ports. Their comprador's orders facilitated regional tea transactions. Chinese tea merchants also employed promissory notes, before the widespread use of sterling bills, and native financial instruments, after the Opium War, to develop the transpacific credit system. Despite the growth of European banking in China after the

1860s, Chinese merchant-bankers and U.S. commission houses still counterbalanced their influence on credit instruments and exchange markets for about a decade. Only after the adoption of the gold standard and the depreciation of silver in the 1870s did European banks, with London as the financial center, dominate the credit economy of the U.S.-China tea trade. The nuanced power dynamics portrayed in this book, therefore, present a more complete picture of global credit systems than the narratives centering on a single power.

Disentangling the multilateral power relations of the transpacific credit economy, anchored in tea transactions, this book also enhances historical understanding of foundational developments in U.S.-China relations, which have become so essential, and controversial, to the world today. Tea and credit interlocked Chinese and U.S. economies from the beginning of their encounter. Chinese merchants extended new lines of substantial monetary resources to their American counterparts through credit transactions and instruments generated in the tea trade, thus lubricating the money-scarce early U.S. economy. American tea buyers were equally important, as they supplied over 90 percent of China's silver imports. After 1826, U.S. merchants prioritized bills of exchange as the primary means of tea purchases and reduced silver shipments to China, thus exacerbating the monetary crisis in China and inflation in America. Tea speculation after both nations' civil wars and the global Long Depression once again demonstrated the interdependence of the two economies. Liberal financial credit sustained the golden age of the transpacific tea trade in a peaceful trading environment. Yet after the global adoption of the gold standard in the 1870s, American property's value shrank when the tea trade was stagnant, bills of exchange were unsalable, and silver's value depreciated. Chinese traders also downscaled their tea economy in response to tea's falling prices in the United States and the pressure of the credit economy in China. Therefore the decline of the U.S.-China tea trade both represents a bilateral commercial breakdown and reflects the interconnectedness of global financial networks. Relying on credit transactions and instruments, Chinese and American merchants built a sophisticated credit system that constantly reshaped the power structure of the international tea trade. In turn, their tea transactions interwove regional credit networks into the global credit economy, which was so fragile as to collapse under speculation, economic crises, or lost hopes in one place or time, yet resilient enough to revive and thrive through reciprocal trust. When the system functioned well, the underlying force was both sides' confidence in a promising future, which remains an invaluable asset for today.

Acknowledgments

My research on the U.S.-China tea trade began at the University of Georgia (UGA). When I first proposed this dissertation project, people often asked, "Was there any tea trade between the United States and China?" Even though having encountered scholarship mentioning the trade in passing, I originally shared similar doubts. In conversation with my adviser, Dr. Allan Kulikoff, I confessed that I considered this topic simply because of my habit of drinking tea and my fascination with anything about tea culture. Allan encouraged me to pursue this project. As he told me, the dissertation, which was also my first book project, usually took about ten years of work, so choosing a subject of genuine passion was important. Thus I embarked on the decade-long journey to uncover this pivotal yet overlooked transpacific commercial exchange. This single case demonstrates Allan's insight as both an accomplished historian and a thoughtful adviser. Before that, Allan had helped me find my master's thesis topic at Nankai University, China, where he was a Fulbright visiting scholar and I was a graduate student. After Allan recruited me to UGA in 2009, the kindness of him and his wife, Lihong Xie, was indispensable for me to navigate the challenges of adapting to life in a foreign country. Throughout the eight years of the PhD program at UGA, Allan's perceptive critiques, steadfast support, and tireless patience with me, a non-native speaker, made the research and writing of the dissertation a much less daunting task. I can never express enough of my respect and gratitude to him.

This book also owes its birth to the generous support of the institutions that awarded me research fellowships and grants. This project was funded by the New England Regional Fellowship, Peabody Essex Museum Phillips Library Research Fellowship, Program in Early American Economy and

Society (PEAES) Short-Term Fellowship, Smithsonian Institution Predoctoral Fellowship, Gilder Lehrman Fellowship, Short-Term Fellowship from Winterthur Museum, Garden, and Library, Chinese Government Award for Outstanding Self-Financed Students Abroad 国家优秀自费留学生奖学金 granted by the China Scholarship Council 国家留学基金委员会, Franklin Research Grant from the American Philosophical Society, and the National Endowment for the Humanities (NEH) Long-Term Fellowship at the Massachusetts Historical Society. UGA, Wake Forest University, and the University of North Carolina at Charlotte offered internal funding—such as the Gregory Research Award, Willson Center Graduate Research Award, Paul N. Howard III Dissertation Writing Award, Excellence-in-Research Award, Faculty Research Grant, Junior Faculty Development Award, and Frances Lumsden Gwynn Award—that provided precious release time for me to complete archival research and the writing of the manuscript. I'm grateful to the librarians and curators at Baker Library of Harvard Business School, Rhode Island Historical Society, Mystic Seaport Collections Research Center, Peabody Essex Museum Phillips Library, Library Company of Philadelphia, National Museum of American History, Gilder Lehrman Institute of American History, Winterthur Museum and Library, Massachusetts Historical Society, Historical Society of Pennsylvania, American Philosophical Society, Van Pelt Library at the University of Pennsylvania, Athenaeum of Philadelphia, National Archives in College Park, the Hagley Museum and Library, Massachusetts Historical Society, National Library of China, and Shanghai Library. They frequently assisted me in discovering new sources relevant to my project. Their expertise regarding the collections proved an invaluable resource to me.

Numerous professors and colleagues read my manuscript and provided constructive comments. My dissertation committee members—Stephen Mihm, Ari Levine, and Scott Nelson—asked insightful questions about Americans' preference for green tea and the transpacific silver flow, thus reorienting my research and inspiring me to explore new questions. Mark Wilson read the entire book manuscript, directed me to the scholarship on the Atlantic credit economy, and provided productive comments on the subtitle, historiography, arguments, and structure of this book. Nick Guoth proofread a chapter and urged me to further clarify the technical aspects of tea production. John David Smith, Jurgen Buchenau, and Amanda Pipkin read my book proposals and guided me through the publication process. Other colleagues who attended my brown-bag presentation—Benny Andres, Dan Dupre, Maren Ehlers, Peter Ferdinando, Ella Fratantuono, Willie Griffin, Christine Haynes, Carol Higham, David Johnson, Jason Newton, Ritika Prasad, Tina Shull, Carmen Soliz, and Peter Thorsheim—read chapters of my manuscript and offered constructive feedback for revision. I restructured the entire book after discussions with them.

I am also deeply in debt to professors, colleagues, and friends for their unwavering encouragement and generous sharing of resources essential to this book. I extend my sincere gratitude to my professors at UGA—Diana Morrow, John Morrow Jr., Michael Kwass, Timothy Cleaveland, Shane Hamilton, and John Inscoe—who opened my eyes to cutting-edge historical theories and methodology. More important, their kindness and generosity toward me, an international student, provided the crucial encouragement that I needed to persist and complete my dissertation. Qiong Zhang, Rais Rahman, Jake Ruddiman, and Barry Trachtenberg at Wake Forest University were both friends and mentors. My conversations with them helped me find the broader historical context of my project. I owe a lot to my colleagues at the Chinese Historians in the United States (CHUS) for their wholehearted support. The talks, events, and discussions we had at CHUS significantly broadened my understanding of diverse historical subjects. I appreciate the generosity of John Bazelow, DONG Yu, David Sicilia, Yi Sun, Xi Wang, Scott Abel, Samuel Segura Cobos, Rafael I. Pardo, William Clarence-Smith, Robert Hellyer, Andrew Liu, Dael Norwood, Kenneth Pomeranz, Michael Aldous, Christopher Sherwood Davis, Rebecca L. Yurman, and Xiaoyu Gao, who shared insights and resources critical to develop my research. My thanks also go to the colleagues who shared sources and ideas after my conference presentations. I regret not recording all of their names, but I deeply appreciate the inspiration gained from our discussions.

Last but not least, special thanks to my parents, DU Shuzhong and FU Yanying, and brother, DU Boyu! The past years were anything but easy. Only they know how long the road has been.

Notes

INTRODUCTION

1. Jefferson, *Notes on the State of Virginia*, 181.
2. Shaw and Quincy, *Journals of Major Samuel Shaw*, 231, 350.
3. To keep the narrative consistent with the concept of the "Canton Trade System," this book retains "Canton" but employs modern pinyin to romanize other Chinese cities' names. Shaw and Quincy, *Journals of Major Samuel Shaw*, 200, 337; Smith, *Empress of China*, 3, 201.
4. The figure is from the East India Company's report. Other accounts compiled by Americans differ greatly, especially for the value of silk. However, tea remained among the most valuable commodities in all accounts. See Morse, *Chronicles of the East India Company*, 2:95; Smith, *Empress of China*, 172–73. Regarding 1 tael = $1.39, see Joseph Archer to G. and S. Higginson, October 21, 1833, JAL, Collection of the Historical Society of Pennsylvania; Grant, "Failure of the Li-ch'uan Hong," 246.
5. Yen-p'ing Hao's article is the primary English-language study of the tea trade between the United States and China. See Hao, "Chinese Teas to America." Chinese-language journal articles examine a particular phase of the transpacific tea trade, rather than the entire nineteenth century. See Li and Ding, "Qingmo zhongmei chaye maoyi"; Shi, Dong, and Wei, "Shijiu shiji shangbanye zhongmei chaye maoyi"; Tao, "Zhongmei chaye maoyi de xingqi" and "Zhongmei chaye maoyi de fazhan." For the research on British or Dutch tea trade, see Ch'en, "1760–1833 nianjian Zhongguo chaye chukou" and "Tianxin chashang"; Ellis, Coulton, and Mauger, *Empire of Tea*; Liu, *Dutch East India Company's Tea Trade*; Macfarlane and Macfarlane, *Empire of Tea*; McCants, "Poor Consumers"; Nierstrasz, *Rivalry for Trade*; Van Driem, *Tale of Tea*.
6. Chen, *Jindai Zhongguo chaye*, 30–32, 99–100, 103–4, 108–12, 184–89; Downs, *Golden Ghetto*, 65–71, 94–95, 98–101, 201, 212; Fichter, *So Great a Proffit*, 88–92; Gardella, *Harvesting Mountains*, esp. 36, 52–69; Grant, "Failure of the

Li-ch'uan Hong"; Lin, *Cha, tang*, 22–23; Liu, *Tea War*, 53, 190–93; Lockwood, *Augustine Heard and Company*, 15–26; Shi, *Jinshi yilai shijie chayeshichang*, esp. 141–70; Wong, *Global Trade*, 73–74, 80–82, 93, 101; Zhong, *Chaye yu yapian*, 71–74; Zhuang, *Tea*, 164–83.

7. Roth, "Tea Drinking in 18th-Century America"; Fichter, *Tea*; Merritt, *Trouble with Tea*.
8. Carter, "Oong (Charles) Ar Showe"; Haddad, *Romance of China*; Rappaport, *Thirst for Empire*; Hellyer, *Green with Milk and Sugar*.
9. Kent Deng reconsidered the silverized Chinese economy and provided a detailed summary of silver scholarship. See Deng, "Miracle or Mirage?," esp. 320–43. For works representative of silver scholarship, see Frank, *ReOrient*, 131–64; Hamashita, *China*, 39–56; Irigoin, "End of a Silver Era"; Lin, *China Upside Down*, esp. 57–68; Von Glahn, *Fountain of Fortune*, 70–141, and "Cycles of Silver," 35–44.
10. On the research challenging the portrayal of the barter economy dominant in China, see Hamashita, *China*, 114–44; Frank, *ReOrient*. The stereotypes of Chinese credit economy are cited from Homer and Sylla, *History of Interest Rates*, 607; Downs, *Golden Ghetto*, 86; Cheong, *Hong Merchants of Canton*, 269; Fichter, *So Great a Proffit*, 34; Irigoin, "End of a Silver Era," 212–14; Perkins, *Financing Anglo-American Trade*, 5; Wagel, *Finance in China*, 124–27.
11. The quote is from Dennett, *Americans in Eastern Asia*, 21.
12. For popular histories, see Berdichevsky, "Coffee or Tea?"; "Why Most Americans Drink Coffee Not Tea"; Regelski, "Revolution of American Drinking"; Carp, "7 Myths"; Pettigrew, *Tea Companion*, 25. For academic challenges to the claim, see Fitcher, *So Great a Proffit*, 17; Hellyer, "1874," 191–92; Topik, "How Mrs. Olson Got Her Full-Bodied Coffee," 4–5.
13. For tea consumption during and after the American Revolution, see Merritt, *Trouble with Tea*, 111–46; Fichter, *Tea*.
14. See this assumption in Dennett, *Americans in Eastern Asia*, 21.
15. Thurber, *Coffee*, 204–5; Topik, "How Mrs. Olson Got Her Full-Bodied Coffee," 4–5.
16. "Concerning Tea," *Massachusetts Ploughman and New England Journal of Agriculture* 63, no. 46 (August 6, 1904): 6; "Advertisement 15," *Maine Farmer* 67, no. 13 (January 26, 1899): 5, ProQuest American Periodicals. An advertisement of the Berry-Hall Company in Burlington, Vermont, in the late nineteenth century claimed that "300 cups of the most delicious Tea in the World can be made from one pound of Gold Star Oolong" sold by them, thus helping quantify the cups of hot beverage made from 1 pound of tea leaves. Berry, Hall Company, "Gold Star Oolong Tea," 1875–99, Trade Card olvwork81706, Baker

Library, Harvard Business School, Historical Collections, accessed November 1, 2024, http://hollis.harvard.edu/fullrecordinnerframe.ashx?itemid=|misc/via|olvwork81706&imageid=HBS.BAKER.TC:1894&embed=false (site discontinued). These statements should not be considered an exaggeration. The Royal Society of Chemistry asserts that two grams of loose tea is enough to make a cup of the hot beverage, although they did not clarify the size of the cup. Therefore one pound of loose black tea makes 227 cups of tea. See Royal Society of Chemistry, "How to Make a Perfect Cup of Tea."

17. Oscar W. Riggs, "The Tea Commerce of New York," *Frank Leslie's Popular Monthly* 16, no. 3 (September 1883): 299–300, ProQuest American Periodicals.
18. Philanthropus, *Lady & Gentleman's Tea-Table*, 26–27.
19. "Description of the Tea Plant; Its Name; Cultivation; Mode of Curing the Leaves; Transportation to Canton; Sale and Foreign Consumption; Endeavors to Raise the Shrub in Other Countries," *Chinese Repository* 8 (May 1839–April 1840): 143, Hathitrust.
20. "One Good Cup of Tea," *Washington Post*, February 23, 1890, 9, ProQuest Historical Newspapers.
21. Flagg, "China," 1:519.
22. Macgregor, *Commercial Statistics*, 5:66–67. Nye, *Tea*, 49.
23. "Tea and Coffee," *Sanitarian* 4, no. 35 (February 1, 1876): 76, ProQuest American Periodicals; U.S. Department of Commerce and Labor (hereafter cited as USDCL), "World's Production," 143–49.
24. Waln made his trip to China in 1819. Commerce: Introductory Remarks, Robert Waln, Jr.'s Notes on China, WFP, Collection of the Historical Society of Pennsylvania.
25. J. B. W., "Thea Orientalis: Part First," *Southern Literary Journal and Magazine of Arts* 1, no. 6 (February 1836): 383, ProQuest American Periodicals.
26. "Our Tea-Table; Or, Tea-Growing in the Celestial Empire," *Eclectic Magazine of Foreign Literature, Science & Art* 40, no. 4 (April 1, 1857): 544, American Antiquarian Society Historical Periodicals.
27. For the tea and silk exports before 1833, see Von Glahn, "Economic Depression," 101, figure 9. For the data on 1867–94, see Yao, *Zhongguo jindai duiwaimaoyishi ziliao*, 3:1609, table 4. For 1900–1920, see Li, *China's Silk Trade*, 77.
28. The quote is from "Adulterated Chinese Tea," *New York Times*, July 11, 1897, ProQuest Historical Newspapers. For quantities of Chinese tea exported to the world, including Great Britain, Russia, the United States, Australia, and continental Europe, see Yao, *Zhongguo jindai duiwaimaoyishi ziliao*, 2:1204–5. For the data on tea consumption in major countries during 1884–1905, see USDCL, "World's Production," 143–51.

29. Irigoin, "End of a Silver Era," 210–11.
30. Moulton, *Principles of Money*, part 2, 13–30; Ray, "Medieval Islamic System," 49. While these scholars emphasize the transfer of the ownership of commodities when conceptualizing credit, this book adopts a broader definition with the primary focus on the time element of transactions.
31. Goetzmann and Rouwenhorst, "Introduction," 5.
32. A similar idea about the distinction between commercial and monetary credit can be found in Lapavitsas, *Marxist Monetary Theory*, 24.
33. Cheong, *Hong Merchants of Canton*, 59–62, 110, 278–79; Ch'en, "Transaction Practices," 749–50; Van Dyke, *Merchants of Canton and Macao: Politics and Strategies*, 18–19.
34. Chen, *Jindai Zhongguo chaye*, 30–32, 65–67, 188, 191–95, 266–67; Gardella, *Harvesting Mountains*, 54–57, 65–69, 123; Hao, "Chinese Teas to America," 26. Basing his work on Gardella's research, Pomeranz mentions the importance of credit to Chinese tea trade. Pomeranz, *Great Divergence*, 173–74.
35. Lin challenges the previous research's emphasis on foreign credit by detailing the growth of Chinese capital in Taiwan after the 1870s. In contrast, the arguments of Ch'en, Chen, Rowe, and Van Dyke spotlight foreign monetary resources, especially different forms of British funding, to Chinese middlemen, although these scholars, particularly Gardella, also mention the credit extended by Chinese merchants and bankers. Paul Van Dyke's research emphasizes Chinese credit to foreign merchants, but focusing on the eighteenth-century China trade, his publications mention the U.S.-China trade relationship only in passing. Lin, *Cha, tang*, 105–11; Ch'en, "Transaction Practices," 750–51; Chen, *Jindai Zhongguo chaye*, 191–95, 53, 69, 266–67; Gardella, *Harvesting Mountains*, 65–69, 123; Liu, *Tea War*, 52, 248–53; Rowe, *Hankow*, 135–36; Van Dyke, *Merchants of Canton and Macao: Politics and Strategies*, 18–21.
36. For bills of exchange in China, see chapter 2. For promissory notes in Europe, see Orrell and Chlupatý, "Virtual Money," 64–65; Quinn and Roberds, "Evolution of the Check," 8.
37. Ogden, *Law of Negotiable Instruments*, 1. For different philosophies regarding checks being a credit instrument or simply a means of payment in the continental European and Anglo-American legal systems, see Effros, "Problem of Postdated Checks," 113–15; Quinn and Roberds, "Evolution of the Check," 6–7; Rabel, *Conflict of Laws*, 224–29.
38. Quinn and Roberds, "Evolution of the Check," 2–5; Esteves and Nogues-Marco, "Monetary Systems," 451; United Nations, "United Nations Convention," 1–2.
39. Quinn and Roberds, "Evolution of the Check," 3n4; Chitty, *Practical Treatise*, 3a.
40. Given the great proliferation of the works in this field, here are only some examples. Some extend the scope of research to Jewish and Islamic practices,

but the major focus remains Europe. Burns, *Money and Monetary Policy in Early Times*; Freyer, "Negotiable Instruments"; Geva, *Payment*; Johnson, *Promissory Notes*; Lapavitsas, *Marxist Monetary Theory*; Moulton, *Principles of Money*; Ogden, *Law of Negotiable Instruments*; Perkins, *Financing Anglo-American Trade*; Quinn and Roberds, "Evolution of the Check"; Redlich and Christman, "Early American Checks"; Rogers, *Early History*; University of California, *Dawn of Modern Banking*.

41. Ogden, *Law of Negotiable Instruments*, 8; Lapavitsas, *Marxist Monetary Theory*, 35–38; Moulton, *Principles of Money*, part 2, 16. Burns recognized the ancient forms of credit instruments but claimed Jews and Italians reinvented the modern ones. See Burns, *Money*, 284–85.
42. Burns, *Money*, 284–85; Zadok and Zadok, "Promissory Note"; Van De Mieroop, "Invention of Interest," 21. For more details, see Du, "'Flying Cash,'" 239–40.
43. Neal, "Introduction," 5; Ray, "Asian Capital," 452, 458–63; Du, "'Flying Cash.'"
44. Dai, "Qingdai huipiao"; Li, "Shanghai jindai zhuangpiao"; Liu and Xie, "Mingqing minjian shangyexinyong"; Miao, *Songdai xinyong piaoju*; Lou, "Jindai Zhongguo changjiangshangyoudiqu," 118–19; Peng, *Zhongguo huobi shi*, esp. 290, 395–97, 459, 462, 554; Yu Hongchang, "Guangxu huipiao," "Qingdai huipiao gailun," and "Qingdai huipiao de hanzimiya."
45. For more details about the credit instruments in China, India, and the Islamic Empire and the European legal system, see Du, "'Flying Cash.'"
46. Dai, "Qingdai huipiao," 13; Effros, "Problem of Postdated Checks," 114; Rong, "Jindai Tianjin boma," 76; Sommers and Phillips, "P.R.C.'s Negotiable Instruments Law," 318n1.
47. Chen, *Jindai Zhongguo chaye*, 232; Dennett, *Americans in Eastern Asia*, 72–73; Downs, *Golden Ghetto*, 108–12; Fitcher, *So Great a Proffit*, 108, 210; Greenberg, *British Trade*, esp. 152–70; Hidy, *House of Baring*, 190–92; Lockwood, *Augustine Heard and Company*, esp. 15–26, 37–38; Norwood, *Trading Freedom*, 59–72; Wong, *Global Trade*, 89–92.
48. Cheong, "Beginnings of Credit Finance"; Hao, "Chinese Teas to America," 24–26; Hamashita, *China*, 114–44.
49. Grant, "Hong Merchant Litigation," "Failure of the Li-ch'uan Hong," "April 1820 Debt Settlement," and *Chinese Cornerstone*, 173–84; Wong, *Global Trade*, 93–100.
50. Hao, *Comprador*, 72–74; Lockwood, *Augustine Heard and Company*, 41–42; Ray, "Asian Capital," 486–93; Moazzin, *Foreign Banks*, 77–93.
51. The publications of PENG Xinwei 彭信威, RONG Xiaofeng 荣晓峰, and YANG Duanliu 楊端六 as well as the English-language works of Linsun Cheng, Richard Von Glahn, Luman Wang, among others, describe Chinese credit instruments in detail. Some adopt Western terms to explain Chinese

financial techniques. However, as LOU Min 娄敏 argues, these works usually provide limited information on the real-world trade finance. Other research zooms in on specific Chinese credit instruments in de facto transactions, such as the *duipiao* 兑票, *huipiao* 汇票, or government voucher examined by DAI Xuewen 戴学文, LIU Qiugen 刘秋根, William N. Goetzmann, and Elisabeth Koll, among others, but they rarely touch on the international trading environment. Qiao mentions Shanxi merchants' trade finance on the frontier with Mongolia and Russia, but the use of credit instruments is not the primary focus. See Peng, *Zhongguo huobi shi*; Rong, "Jindai Tianjin boma"; Yang, *Qingdai huobi*; Cheng, *Banking in Modern China*; Horesh, *Chinese Money*; Ji, *History of Modern Shanghai Banking*; McElderry, *Shanghai Old-Style Banks*; Von Glahn, "Origins of Paper Money"; Wang, *Chinese Hinterland*, 63–64, 101–2; Yang, *Money*; Dai, "Qingdai huipiao"; Deng, "Miracle or Mirage?," 343–45; Goetzmann and Koll, "Paying in Paper"; Li, "Shanghai jindai zhuangpiao"; Jones, "Finance in Ningpo"; Liu and Xie, "Mingqing minjian shangyexinyong"; Lou, "Jindai Zhongguo changjiangshangyoudiqu"; Miao, *Songdai xinyong piaoju*; Qiao, "Rise of Shanxi Merchants," 309–26; Yu, "Guangxu huipiao," "Qingdai huipiao gailun," and "Qingdai huipiao de hanzimiya."

52. Moulton, *Principles of Money*, part 2, 16; Von Glahn, "Origins of Paper Money," 66; Gelderblom and Jonker, "Enter the Ghost," 3.
53. For a review and refutation of the theory, see Ray, "Asian Capital," 449–52.
54. Goetzmann and Rouwenhorst, "Introduction," 10–13; Rosenthal and Wong, *Before and beyond Divergence*, 129–66.
55. Temin, *Jacksonian Economy*, 80–82; Irigoin, "End of a Silver Era," 228; Lockwood, *Augustine Heard and Company*, 14–15, 26.
56. Downs, *Golden Ghetto*, 86, 152; Lockwood, *Augustine Heard and Company*, 35; Perkins, *Financing Anglo-American Trade*, 5; Moazzin, *Foreign Banks*, 108.
57. Deng, "Miracle or Mirage?," 331; Liu and Xie, "Mingqing minjian shangyexinyong," 10; Horesh, *Chinese Money in Global Context*, esp. 147.
58. Gardella, "Squaring Accounts," esp. 322–23; Hamashita, *China*, 46–49; Liu, *Tea War*; Pomeranz, "'Traditional' Chinese Business Forms"; Ray, "Asian Capital"; Rosenthal and Wong, *Before and beyond Divergence*, 129–66.
59. Hunt, "Americans," 277–80.
60. Downs, *Golden Ghetto*; Fichter, *So Great a Proffit*; Grant, *Chinese Cornerstone*; Morrison, *True Yankees*; Norwood, *Trading Freedom*; Wong, *Global Trade*.

PART I

1. "Poetry," *Atkinson's Saturday Evening Post* 14, no. 705 (January 31, 1835): 3, ProQuest American Periodicals.
2. Irving and Larkin, *Dear Will*, 140–41.

3. EIC's data show that black tea was predominantly popular in England during 1740–1834. See House of Commons, *Tea*; Mauger, "Charting the East India Company's Tea Trade."
4. Robert Waln Jr., Commercial Memo, Book of Prices, Canton 1819, 17, WFP; Morse, *Chronicles of the East India Company*, 2:95.
5. Ingersoll, *View of the Rights and Wrongs*, 50–51.
6. USDCL, "World's Production," 138; Waln, Commercial Memo, Book of Prices, Canton 1819, 17, WFP.
7. For the complete list of various teas imported by EIC, see House of Commons, *Tea*.
8. "Nantes, July 29," *American Weekly Mercury* (Philadelphia), no. 626 (December 28, 1731): 2–3, America's Historical Newspapers; Roth, "Tea Drinking," 68, 89; Fichter, *Tea*, 139–41.
9. Smith, *Empress of China*, 228, 267–97.
10. Goldstein, *Stephen Girard's Trade*, 77; Fichter, *So Great a Proffit*, 93. For the long debate over whether Bohea was oolong, black, or dark tea, see Huang, "Tea Processing," esp. 535–50; Huang, "Cha Chuanru Ouzhou," 10, 13–16; Ch'en, "Tianxin chashang," 396.
11. "Wonders of a Cup of Tea," *Ariel: A Literary & Critical Gazette* 2, no. 23 (March 7, 1829): 182, American Antiquarian Society Historical Periodicals.
12. Phipps, *Practical Treatise*, xiii.
13. Latourette, *History of Early Relations*, 77.
14. "China and Its Prospective Trade: Trade of British India with Canton," *United States Magazine, and Democratic Review* 18, no. 95 (May 1846): 387, ProQuest American Periodicals.
15. *Retrospect*, 123.
16. Williams, *Chinese Commercial Guide*, 196. This book was reprinted at least five times during the 1830s–60s, and this statement appears in the 1856 version.
17. "About Green Tea," *Pall Mall Gazette* (London), February 1, 1886, British Library Newspapers.
18. Downs, Hellyer, and Rappaport have emphasized the American preference for green tea. See Downs, *Golden Ghetto*, 67; Hellyer, *Green with Milk and Sugar*, esp. 93; Rappaport, *Thirst for Empire*, 141.
19. "About Green Tea."
20. "A Dish of Tea: In Two Parts: Part Two," *Knickerbocker; Or New York Monthly* 13, no. 3 (March 1839): 232, ProQuest American Periodicals. Pindar Cockloft, Esq., was among the pseudonyms that Washington and William Irving and J. K. Paulding used to publish satirical essays and poems during 1807–8. This piece thus reflects New York's taste in tea during the early nineteenth century. See "Salmagundi."

21. Epicurus, “Maxims to Feed by Tea,” *Philadelphia Monthly Magazine* 1, no. 9 (July 1829): 597–98, ProQuest American Periodicals.
22. *Boston News-Letter*, March 12, 1710, America’s Historical Newspapers.
23. *Federal Gazette, and Pennsylvania Daily Advertiser*, November 20, 1793; *Baltimore Daily Intelligencer*, September 3, 1794, America’s Historical Newspapers.
24. Henry R. Schoolcraft, “Journal of a Tour into the Interior of Missouri and Arkansaw,” *Belles-Lettres Repository, and Monthly Magazine* 3, no. 2 (April 1, 1820): 400, ProQuest American Periodicals.
25. J. & T. H. Perkins & Son to Perkins & Co., May 5, 1824, Loose Business Papers, 1824–25, THPP, Massachusetts Historical Society.
26. Forbes, *Remarks on China*, 22.
27. J. F. Davis, “Manufacture of Tea,” *Family Magazine; Or, Monthly Abstract of General Knowledge* 4 (1836): 379, ProQuest American Periodicals. Many claimed that Hyson adopted the name of a rich East Indian merchant who first imported it. “Observations on Tea,” *Boston Weekly Magazine*, January 23, 1841, 150, ProQuest American Periodicals. Philanthropus, *Lady & Gentleman’s Tea-Table*, 19.
28. “Wuchan-Cha” 物产 茶 [Local products—tea], *Duyun xianzhi gao* 都匀县志稿 [Draft gazetteer of Duyun County], edited by Dou Quanzeng 窦全曾 and Chen Ju 陈矩, vol. 6, comp. 1925; “Fengtu-Tuchan” 风土 土产 [Local environment and products], *Baling xianzhi* 巴陵县志 [Gazetteer of Baling County], edited by Pan Zhaokui 潘兆奎 and Wu Minshu 吴敏树, vol. 11, comp. 1872, in Wu, *Zhongguo difangzhi*, 723, 435; “Yanshan zhi” 雁山志 [Gazetteer of the Yan Mountain], in *Zhejiang tongzhi* 浙江通志 [Gazetteer of Zhejiang province], vol. 170, comp. ca. 1722–35, Erudition 爱如生中國方志庫; Jiang Xiling 江锡龄, “Qingchengshan xingji” 青城山行纪 [A trip to the Qingcheng Mountain], comp. 1873, in Chen and Zhu, *Zhongguo chaye*, 415; “The Tea Plant and Varieties of Teas,” *American Quarterly Register & Magazine* 2, no. 2 (June 1, 1849): 414, American Antiquarian Society Historical Periodicals. *Guyu* is also the time to make the best black tea. See “Zhengdun chawu shi” 整頓茶務示 [Notice on reorganizing tea affairs] and “Zicha jiangtou” 子茶將頭 [The second crop of tea will arrive soon], *Shenbao* 申報 [Shanghai news], February 15, June 18, 1895; Yu Heyan 愈鹤岩, “Hongcha jingying zhi mijue” 红茶经营之秘诀 [The secrets of black tea business], *Shangye zazhi* 商业杂志 5, no. 11 (March 1931): 4.
29. Canton, China, May 2, 1801, Sullivan Dorr’s Memorandum Book at Canton, China, 1801, SDP, Rhode Island Historical Society.
30. Davis, “Manufacture of Tea,” 378; Blankaart, *Physical Dictionary*, 289.
31. The EIC imported gunpowder only four times during 1740–1837, but the total amount, 93,842 pounds, was still larger than that of young hyson; House of Commons, *Tea*, 3–5.

32. "Comparative Statement of the Quantities of Tea Imported into the United Kingdom in the Season 1833–4," *Companion to the Newspaper*, October 1, 1835, 492, American Antiquarian Society Historical Periodicals.
33. J. M. Forbes to Perkins & Co., November 28, 1836, Letter Book 1833–35, folder 7, FFBR, Baker Library, Harvard Business School.
34. Davis, "Manufacture of Tea," 379.
35. Davis, "Manufacture of Tea," 379.
36. Jianshe weiyuanhui jingji diaochasuo, *Zhejiang zhi pingshui cha*, 13.
37. William L. Scruggs, "Upper Yang-Tse Valley; Tea and Silk Industry," *Atlanta Constitution*, December 26, 1909, 7, ProQuest Historical Newspapers.
38. "Tea and Tea Drinkers," *Russell's Magazine* 1, no. 2 (May 1857): 176, ProQuest American Periodicals.
39. Davis, "Manufacture of Tea," 379; Ball, *Account of the Cultivation*, 376.
40. Wu, *Wanzhe xin'anjiangliuyu*, 18–19; Ball, *Account of the Cultivation*, 224–33, 244–45, 374–76; "The Tea Plant," *Farmer & Gardener, and Live-Stock Breeder and Manager* 1, no. 28 (November 11, 1834): 217, ProQuest American Periodicals.
41. Chen, *Zhongguo chajing*, 2:305–15.
42. Forbes, *Remarks on China*, 15.
43. Davis, "Manufacture of Tea," 379.
44. J. M. Forbes to Joshua Bates, April 20, 1835, Letter Book 1833–35, folder 6, FFBR.

1. PAPER GOLD AND GREEN GOLD

1. Shaw and Quincy, *Journals of Major Samuel Shaw*, 337.
2. Shaw and Quincy, *Journals of Major Samuel Shaw*, 341.
3. "Monday; Governor," *New Jersey Gazette*, May 16, 1785, America's Historical Newspapers; Smith, *Empress of China*, 225.
4. Smith, *Empress of China*, 224–25; Fichter, *So Great a Proffit*, 45–46; Merritt, *Trouble with Tea*, 125, 133.
5. For the tea sale, see Smith, *Empress of China*, 230–31.
6. Some scholars use the term "green gold" to describe tea. See Etherington, *Green Gold*. For a description of the French Wars, see Fichter, *So Great a Proffit*, 56–64.
7. See Cheong, "Beginnings of Credit Finance"; Hidy, *House of Baring*; Greenberg, *British Trade*; Hanser, *Mr. Smith Goes to China*. Research on credit from the Atlantic trade to Americans is abundant. For some examples, see Price, *Capital and Credit*; Price, "Joshua Johnson in London"; Matson, *Merchants & Empire*; Anderson, "Money"; Nash, "Organization of Trade"; Van Winter, *American Finance*.
8. Benton, "Chinese Mission," 120.

9. Cheong, "Trade and Finance," esp. 34–42; Dennett, *Americans in Eastern Asia*, 20–21; Lockwood, *Augustine Heard and Company*, 21; Fichter, *So Great a Proffit*, 34, 88, 108, 120–21, 205–6; Perkins, *Financing Anglo-American Trade*, 5; Stelle, "American Trade in Opium, Prior to 1820," 425; Zhuang, *Tea*, 177–95.
10. Shaw and Quincy, *Journals of Major Samuel Shaw*, 231, 233.
11. Smith, *Empress of China*, 34–36.
12. Goldstein, *Stephen Girard's Trade*, 31–34.
13. Shaw and Quincy, *Journals of Major Samuel Shaw*, 231–32.
14. Shaw and Quincy, *Journals of Major Samuel Shaw*, 232.
15. Merritt, *Trouble with Tea*, 134.
16. Shaw and Quincy, *Journals of Major Samuel Shaw*, 218; Smith, *Empress of China*, 61.
17. The value of goods procured by Perkins and Company in 1820 and 1821 shows the cost of a tea cargo typically ranged from $120,000 to $180,000. The tea cargoes of *Cordelia*, *Ophelia*, and *R. Edwards* were valued at $123,948.53, $129,530.30, and $175,000–$200,000, respectively. The mixed cargoes of *True American*, *Nautilus*, *Canton Packet*, and *Houqua*—comprising some combination of tea, nankeen, sugar, silk, and cassia—were valued at $184,058.28, $170,372.50, $112,716.38, and $113,766.48, respectively. See Perkins & Co. to James & T. H. Perkins, September 1, September 27, November 26, 1820, February 2, 1821; Perkins & Co. to F. W. Paine, December 5, 1820, vol. 19, Letter Book, 1820–21, RCR. For the relative value of the cargo in the most current data, see Williamson, "Seven Ways." The website Measuring Worth provides three ways of calculating the relative value—its relative price worth (in terms of the consumer price index or GDP deflator), wage or income worth (in terms of unskilled wage, production worker compensation, and nominal GDP per capita), and output worth (in terms of the relative share of GDP). This chapter adopts the "relative share of GDP," because it measures not only the expenditure of the ventures but also the wealth that the investments would generate for the economy. The estimated value is not completely accurate. The monetary unit of the value should be Spanish dollars. I convert it into the U.S. dollar value with the nominal exchange rate, 1 U.S. dollar = 1 Spanish dollar, although admittedly the market rate of exchange changed over time. For the nominal exchange rate, see White, "Archaic Monetary Terms," 98–99.
18. Thomas H. Perkins Jr. to R. B. Forbes, December 31, 1830, box 1, folder 19, FFBR.
19. Smith, *Empress of China*, 64, 189–94; Shaw and Quincy, *Journals of Major Samuel Shaw*, 218; Haddad, *America's First Adventure*, 13.
20. For the various goods, see Downs, *Golden Ghetto*, 105–6, 112–28; Fichter, *So Great a Proffit*, 211–22, 227–31; Stelle, "American Trade in Opium, Prior to

1820," 425; Forbes, *Remarks on China*, 27–29, 44–46; "Advertisement," *New-York Packet*, January 2, 1790, America's Historical Newspapers.

21. Merritt, *Trouble with Tea*, 135.
22. Sullivan Dorr to Ebenezer Dorr, October 28, 1799. In this letter, Dorr mentioned two ships—D and H—which should refer to *Dispatch* and *Hancock*, as clarified in other letters, such as Sullivan Dorr to Jos & Jno Dorr, November 1, 28, 30, 1799, series 1, box 1, folder 1, SDP.
23. Wong, *Global Trade*, 74.
24. Cheong, *Hong Merchants of Canton*, 61, 157–58; Van Dyke, *Canton Trade*, 154; Chen, *Jindai Zhongguo chaye*, 52–53; Hung, "Imperial China," 496.
25. Forward contract is an unstandardized form of futures trading. For these concepts, see Birla, "Speculation Illicit and Complicit," 393; Gottesman, *Derivatives Essentials*, 3–4, 19–20; Schaede, "Forwards and Futures," 498–99; Michie, "Financial Capitalism," 234.
26. For the tea season, see Downs, *Golden Ghetto*, 71; Consequa v. Willings and Francis, Circuit Court of the United States, Pennsylvania District, March 22, 1811, series 1, box 1, folder 7, WFR, Collection of the Historical Society of Pennsylvania; Perkins & Co. to James & T. H. Perkins, September 27, 1820, and Perkins & Co. to F. W. Paine, April 17, 1820, vol. 19, Letter Book, 1820–21, RCR. For the advance system, see Forbes, *Remarks on China*, 15; Cheong, *Hong Merchants of Canton*, 61–62, 157–58; Ch'en, "Transaction Practices," 749–51; Ch'en, "1760–1833 nianjian Zhongguo chaye chukou," 312–13; Grant, *Chinese Cornerstone*, 202–3; Morse, *Chronicles of the East India Company*, 2:53, 126–27. Varied in de facto contracts, the advance payment could also be only a portion of the aggregate value, such as 58–66 percent of the expected market price of bohea tea. Van Dyke, *Merchants of Canton and Macao: Politics and Strategies*, 18–19.
27. Forbes, *Remarks on China*, 15; Waln, "Tea Market," Book of Prices, Canton 1819, 56–57, WFP.
28. Consequa v. Willings and Francis, March 22, 1811, series 1, box 1, folder 7, WFR.
29. Cheong, *Hong Merchants of Canton*, 61–62, 157. Van Dyke, *Merchants of Canton and Macao: Success and Failure*, 21.
30. Cheong, *Hong Merchants of Canton*, 151, 163.
31. J. K. Cunningham to Augustine Heard & Co. Shanghai, June 2, 1870, May 1869–June 1870 Letters Received by A. H. & Co. Constituents to A. H. & Co., Shanghai, reel 87-1762 R-176, HFBR, Baker Library, Harvard Business School; Peters, *Reports of Cases*, 1:89; Chen, *Jindai Zhongguo chaye*, 50.
32. For debates over the relative importance of Japanese and South American silver in China, see Irigoin, "End of a Silver Era," 208; Lin, *China Upside Down*, 66–68; Melitz, "Some Doubts."

33. Phipps, *Practical Treatise*, 167–70; A Shanghai Merchant, "To the Editor of North-China Herald," *North China Herald*, July 28, 1855, 209; Peters, *Guide to, or Descriptive Catalogue*, 72–73; Spalding, *Eastern Exchange*, 404; Perkins & Co. to F. W. Paine, March 26, 1820, vol. 19, Letter Book, 1820–21, RCR, Baker Library, Harvard Business School; Irigoin, "End of a Silver Era," 234.
34. "American Silver Legislation," *North China Herald*, April 8, 1892, 465; Irigoin, "End of a Silver Era," 225–26; White, "Archaic Monetary Terms," 98; Elwell, *Brief History*, 2; Purtle, "Money Making Nation," 107n8.
35. Frank, *Objectifying China*, 105–6; Irigoin, "End of a Silver Era," 210–11; Dudden, *American Pacific*, 5; Norwood, *Trading Freedom*, 192, figure A5; Von Glahn, "Cycles of Silver," 54; Von Glahn, "Changing Significance," 568; "Perkins and Company, Canton 1803–1827," 3.
36. Phipps, *Practical Treatise*, 167.
37. Business Records on the Remission of Funds to the Far East and Packing Goods for the China Trade, 1828–29, box 1, FFP, Massachusetts Historical Society.
38. Downs, *Golden Ghetto*, for the "ready money" claim, see 107–8; for Carrington's identity, see 89, 224.
39. Benjamin Hoppin & Son to Edward Carrington, July 15, 1803, box 9, folder 2, ECP, Rhode Island Historical Society.
40. Benjamin Hoppin to Edward Carrington, October 19, 1803, box 9, folder 2, ECP.
41. Benjamin Hoppin Jr. to Edward Carrington, July 1804, box 9, folder 3, ECP.
42. Invoice of Fifteen Kegs Specie Dollars Shipped by King & Talbot on Board the Ship *Aeolus*, April 29, 1805, box 9, folder 2, ECP.
43. Benjamin Hoppin & Son to Edward Carrington, April 5; William Shaler to Edward Carrington, May 15; King & Talbot to Edward Carrington, May 16, 1806, box 9, folder 4, ECP; Willings & Francis to William Read, April 14, 1806, series 1, box 1, folder 5, WFR.
44. Peter W. Snow to Edward Carrington, April 30, 1807, box 9, folder 4; Benjamin Hoppin & Son to Edward Carrington, April 23, 1809, box 9, folder 5; King & Talbot to Edward Carrington, May 16, 1809, box 9, folder 6, ECP.
45. Benjamin Hoppin & Son to Edward Carrington, April 23, 1809, box 9, folder 5, ECP.
46. John Parker & Sons to Edward Carrington & Invoice of Dollars p. *Ganges* & Sales of Exchange, September 1, 1810, box 10, folder 1, ECP.
47. "Pennsylvania Impost," *Essex Journal and the Massachusetts and New-Hampshire General Advertiser*, November 9, 1785, 4, America's Historical Newspapers; Frank, *Objectifying China*, 111–13.
48. Van Winter, *American Finance*, 1:418.

49. Shaw and Quincy, *Journals of Major Samuel Shaw*, 171.
50. Macgregor, *Commercial Statistics*, 5:55–56; Mui and Mui, "William Pitt," 447.
51. Macgregor, *Commercial Statistics*, 5:57; Fichter, *So Great a Proffit*, 82–93.
52. Macgregor, *Commercial Statistics*, 5:57.
53. For the data on the re-export of tea, see U.S. Treasury Department, *Statements of Imports of Tea and Coffee*, 420–28. Also see Fichter, *So Great a Proffit*, 90.
54. For data on U.S. imports versus those of other countries in the mid-nineteenth century, see Macgregor, *Commercial Statistics*, 5:66–67; Nye, *Tea*, 49. For data during 1863–72: "Tea Trade," in Inspector General of Chinese Maritime Customs, *Trade Statistics*, 44. For the years during 1868–1911, see Zhonguo jiuhaiguan shiliao bianji wenyuanhui (hereafter cited as ZGJHGSLBJWYH), *Zhongguo jiuhaiguan shiliao*, vols. 1–55; see figure 3 for specific page numbers.
55. Downs, *Golden Ghetto*, 148.
56. Descriptions of the Cohong abound. For example, Forbes, *Remarks on China*, 15; Downs, *Golden Ghetto*, 21–22. For the Canton Trade System, see Cheong, *Hong Merchants of Canton*, 37; Hung, "Imperial China and Capitalist Europe," 479–82; Grant, *Chinese Cornerstone*, 31–53.
57. Charles Hummel, "'John Richardson Latimer and the China Trade': Lecture and Article by Charles Hummel," 1958, box 3, folder 1, LFP (W), Joseph Downs Collection of Manuscripts and Printed Ephemera, Winterthur Museum, Garden, and Library.
58. JGR, Kislak Center for Special Collections, Rare Books, and Manuscripts, University of Pennsylvania. The receipt shows that Green bought tea from Conqua. Another Chinese merchant, Fat Hunqua's son, was also named Conqua. He was older than Consequa and had fallen out of the official trade in the 1760s, even though he was still active in the 1780s. See Cheong, *Hong Merchants of Canton*, Conqua as Consequa: 161–62, 188n144, 261; older Conqua: 188n137, 258–59, 293n51. Also see Chen Conqua in Van Dyke, *Merchants of Canton and Macao: Success and Failure*, xxvii.
59. Ch'en, *Insolvency of the Chinese Hong Merchants*, 330–31.
60. Corning, "Sullivan Dorr," 159.
61. Waln, "Standing, Character, Articles of Trade & Residence of a Number of Canton Native Merchants," Book of Prices, Canton 1819, 27–31, WFP.
62. Seaburg and Paterson, *Merchant Prince of Boston*, 101; Grant, "Failure of the Li-ch'uang Hong," 245.
63. Gibson qtd. in Hummel, "'John Richardson Latimer and the China Trade.'"
64. Many studies published before the 1990s tend to portray Hong merchants as debtors who depended on foreign capital. The most representative work is Ch'en, *Insolvency of the Chinese Hong Merchants*. For a more complicated portrayal of the debt relationship or Chinese merchants as creditors, see Cheong,

Hong Merchants of Canton, 58–60; Downs, *Golden Ghetto*, 81, 86–88; Grant, *Chinese Cornerstone*, esp. chaps. 3–7; Wong, *Global Trade*, esp. 66–70, 177–204.

65. Letter of Instructions to William Read, May 3, 1805, series 1, box 1, folder 1, WFR.
66. William Read to Willings & Francis & Willing & Curwen, November 9, 1805, series 1, box 1, folder 2, WFR.
67. William Read to Willings & Francis, November 9, 1805, series 1, box 1, folder 3, WFR.
68. "Memorandum of Notes Given by William Read, James Tatim Jr. & Edward M. Donaldson to Mr. Conseequa," December 12, 1805, series 1, box 1, folder 1, WFR. Since Willings and Francis might have reinvested the money in more China goods or other ventures, the output worth in terms of the relative share of GDP is the best indicator of the value, measuring current market value or the influence of their investments. See Williamson, "Seven Ways."
69. Grant, "Failure of the Li'chuan Hong," 251–52.
70. William Read to Willings & Francis, November 27, 1805, series 1, box 1, folder 3, WFR.
71. Shaw and Quincy, *Journals of Major Samuel Shaw*, 231.
72. Sullivan Dorr to Ebenezer Dorr, October 28, 1799, series 1, box 1, folder 1, SDP.
73. Sullivan Dorr to Jos & Jno Dorr, November 30, 1799, series 1, box 1, folder 1, SDP.
74. Forbes, *Remarks on China*, 16–17.
75. George W. Talbot & Co. to Edward Carrington, March 25, 1812, box 10, folder 4, ECP.
76. Grant, "Failure of the Li-ch'uan Hong," 246.
77. For research on money of account in Europe, see Oscar and Jonker, "Enter the Ghost." For research on Chinese accounting and bookkeeping methods, see Gardella, "Squaring Accounts"; Lowenstein and Cao, "Business Accounting"; Yuan, Macve, and Ma, "Development of Chinese Accounting."
78. Gardella, "Squaring Accounts," esp. 317, 321–26, 332; Wang, *Chinese Hinterland Capitalism*, 66–76.
79. Smith, *Empress of China*, 265, appendix B.
80. Shaw and Quincy, *Journals of Major Samuel Shaw*, 346.
81. For Europeans' and Americans' bookkeeping techniques in the China trade, see Van Dyke, "Bookkeeping as a Window."
82. HHCTL, Phillips Library, Peabody Essex Museum. For the transcription of Hollingsworth's account book, see Du, "Green Gold," 186–90.
83. Quinn and Roberds, "Evolution of the Check," 5. For the format of a modern promissory note, see Ogden, *Law of Negotiable Instruments*, 1–5; United Nations, "United Nations Convention," 1–2.

84. Orrell and Chlupatý, "Virtual Money," 64–65; Du, "'Flying Cash,'" 239–45.
85. Cheong, *Hong Merchants of Canton*, 141–42; Van Dyke, *Merchants of Canton and Macao: Politics and Strategies*, 100; Van Dyke, *Success and Failure*, 103. Cheong used the term "IOU" to refer to the note Coqua wrote to the EIC.
86. "Buddha Head silver coins" was the Chinese term for Carolus dollars. See Von Glahn, "Changing Significance," 573.
87. Consequa v. Willings and Francis, March 22, 1811, series 1, box 1, folder 7, WFR.
88. Memorandum of Notes Given by William Read, James Tatim Jr. & Edward M. Donaldson to Mr. Conseequa, December 12, 1805, series 1, box 1, folder 1, WFR.
89. Downs, *Golden Ghetto*, 53, 71; Augustine Heard Jr., "Old China and New," 22, folder GQ-2-2, HFBR.
90. For instance, on February 14, 1810, a New York firm, Lawrence and Whitney, remitted 13,211 Spanish dollars to pay several notes to Chinese merchants Consequa and Washing. With the $198.16 freight deducted, the dollars should be enough to pay the prime amount and the interest due on June 24, 1810, since the passage usually took four months. Lawrence & Whitney to Edward Carrington, February 14, 1810, box 10, folder 1, ECP.
91. King & Talbot to Edward Carrington, May 25, 1804, box 9, folder 3, ECP.
92. "Shanghai, Friday, June 5, 1885," *North China Herald*, June 5, 1885, 638.
93. "Shanghai, Friday, June 5, 1885."
94. "Shanghai, Friday, June 5, 1885."
95. Van Dyke, *Merchants of Canton and Macao: Politics and Strategies*, 21; Marriner, *Rathbones of Liverpool*, 53–54; Zhuang, *Zhongjianshang*, 217; Woodman, *King Cotton and His Retainers*, 6; King, *History of the Hongkong and Shanghai Banking Corporation*, 1:456.
96. As mentioned in note 30 in the introduction, it is open to question whether consignment is a type of credit owing to the retention of ownership. However, Woodman described the brokers' power in disposing the assignment. See *King Cotton and His Retainers*, 6–7. In this case of the tea trade, the use of promissory notes also helped define the transactions as a credit relationship.
97. Prudent merchants regarded both a larger and a lesser proportion as speculative and unsound, even though some traders consigned without receiving any advances. Marriner, *Rathbones of Liverpool*, 58; Wong, *Global Trade*, 103.
98. Downs, *Golden Ghetto*, 88–89, 398n88; Greenberg, *British Trade*, 158; Habib, "Merchant Communities," 395–96; Van Dyke, *Canton Trade*, 151.
99. Van Dyke, *Canton Trade*, 154.
100. Johnson, *Reports of Cases*, 3:587–89.
101. King & Talbot to Edward Carrington, June 13, 1809, box 9, folder 6; George W. Talbot to Edward Carrington, February 24, 1810, box 10, folder 1, ECP.

102. Waln, "Tea Market," Book of Prices, Canton 1819, 78–80, WFP.
103. Liang, *Yue haiguan zhi*, 25:6b–7b.
104. Grant, *Chinese Cornerstone*, 88–90.
105. For details about how to estimate the value of the notes and the compound interest, see Du, "Green Gold," 175.
106. Johnson, *Reports of Cases*, 3:606; Grant, "Failure of the Li'chuan Hong," 258.
107. William Read to Willings & Francis, November 9, 1805, series 1, box 1, folder 3, WFR.
108. Johnson, *Reports of Cases*, 3:607; Grant, "Failure of the Li'chuan Hong," 245n8.
109. For the one-half interest arrangement, see March 13, HHCTL, cited in Du, "Green Gold," 189.
110. The value was calculated in terms of the relative share of GDP. Williamson, "Seven Ways."
111. White, "Convention on the Uniform Law," 225. For the origin of negotiability in Europe, see Ogden, *Law of Negotiable Instruments*, 9, 14; Quinn and Roberds, "Evolution of the Check," 6.
112. For the roles of money, see Pamuk, *Monetary History*, 1–2. For the meaning of "exchange," see Johnson, *Promissory Notes*, 58.
113. Minturn & Champlin to Edward Carrington, July 9, 1806, box 9, folder 4, ECP.
114. King & Talbot to Edward Carrington, June 23, 1806, box 9, folder 4, ECP.
115. William Shaler to Edward Carrington, June 22, 1806, box 9, folder 4, ECP.
116. Willings and Francis to George W. Biddle and Thomas Willing Jr., May 13, 1809, series 1, box 1, folder 7, WFR.
117. Robert Waln to Stephen Dexter; Robert Waln to Edward Carrington, March 20, 1813, Robert Waln Letterbooks, vol. 19, WFP.
118. The terminal value of these notes had amounted to $17,147.54 on October 25, 1812, and $17,968.66 when transferred to Waln in 1813. The two notes were due on June 20 and September 24, 1811, after which Carrington had to pay compound interest on the notes. George Blight's letter on October 20, 1812, clarified the terminal value on October 25, 1812, and I calculated the amount in 1813. If the rate was 12 percent, the customary rate at Canton, the terminal value of the two notes totaled at least $17,827.47 ($6,977\,[1 + 0.12]^{1.75} + 8,000\,[1 + 0.12]^{1.48} = 8507.46 + 9461.20 = 17,968.66$) on March 20, 1813, when Waln's letters were sent to Carrington. Even though Waln charged 13 percent remittance and insurance fees on the terminal value in October 1812, $17,147.54, he insisted that the transaction was advantageous. After all, if Carrington were to liquidate the notes with his Chinese creditors after the war, he would pay more than the price that Waln charged. See George Blight to Edward Carrington, October 20, 1812, box 10, folder 7, ECP, and Robert Waln to Edward

Carrington, March 8 and March 20, 1813, Robert Waln Letterbooks, vol. 19, WFP.

119. Robert Waln to Coutts & Co., January 5, 1813, Robert Waln Letterbooks, vol. 19, WFP.

120. A Power of Attorney between Consequa and Edward Hallowell, October 31, 1803, private collection.

121. Grant, "Failure of the Li-ch'uan Hong," 248–49.

122. Peters, *Reports of Cases*, 1:87–89, 95.

123. Grant, "Failure of the Li-ch'uan Hong," 252.

124. Consequa v. Willings and Francis, March 22, 1811, series 1, box 1, folder 7, WFR.

125. Grant, "Failure of the Li-ch'uan Hong," 252.

126. Sullivan Dorr to Ebenezer Dorr, September 10, 1799, series 1, box 1, folder 1, SDP; Grant, "Failure of the Li-ch'uan Hong," 246.

127. Consequa, "To James Madison."

128. Nixon & Walker to George W. Biddle, May 12, 1809, box 10, folder 4, ECP.

129. Wong, *Global Trade*, 100–103.

130. Grant, "Failure of the Li-ch'uan Hong," 246.

131. Grant, "Failure of the Li-ch'uan Hong," 246–48; Benjamin Hoppin & Son to Edward Carrington, June 4, 1807, box 9, folder 4, ECP.

132. Grant, "Hong Merchant Litigation," 49, 55; Wong, *Global Trade*, 95–103; Power of Attorney between Syngchong and Edward Carrington, January 31, 1812, box 10, folder 1, ECP.

133. John P. Cushing to Edward Carrington, March 12 and April 16, 1812, box 10, folder 4, ECP.

134. "若虧些小本錢, 自能承當." Consequa, "To James Madison."

135. Grant, "Failure of the Li-ch'uan Hong," 254–55. For the role of the Chinese emperor in settling Hong merchants' foreign debts, see Liang, *Yue haiguan zhi*, 25:2b–7b.

136. Johnson, *Reports of Cases*, 3:607; Liang, *Yue haiguan zhi*, 25:1b–7b.

137. Grant, "Failure of the Li-ch'uan Hong," 249.

138. Qtd. in Grant, "Failure of the Li-ch'uan Hong," 249.

139. John P. Cushing to Edward Carrington, November 15, 1811, box 10, folder 2, ECP.

140. Consequa, "To James Madison."

141. For details, see Goldstein, *Philadelphia and the China Trade*, 40–45; Downs, *Golden Ghetto*, 236–55.

142. See Williamson, "Seven Ways." For Carrington's carrying trade of tea with Daniel Crommelin and Sons, see Du, "Green Gold," 163–68.

143. Historical note, ECP, http://www.rihs.org/mssinv/Mss333.htm.

144. Historical note, JBP, www.rihs.org/mssinv/Mss312.htm.
145. Hunt, *Lives of American Merchants*, 2:60.
146. Fichter, *So Great a Proffit*, 257–64.
147. Shaw, *Journals of Major Samuel Shaw*, 252.
148. Goldstein, *Philadelphia and the China Trade*, 41.
149. Historical note, JBP, www.rihs.org/mssinv/Mss312.htm.
150. Historical note, ECP, http://www.rihs.org/mssinv/Mss333.htm.
151. Goldstein, *Philadelphia and the China Trade*, 44–45.
152. Downs, *Golden Ghetto*, 83–86; Fichter, *So Great a Proffit*, 1–6, 257–77.
153. Dennett, *Americans in Eastern Asia*, 18. This book was originally published in 1922. Fichter also argues that the early East Indies trade facilitated a financial transformation of the Anglo-American world. See Fichter, *So Great a Proffit*, 4–5, 279–81.
154. Greenbie and Greenbie, *Gold of Ophir*, xiii. Also cited in Johnson, *Narratives of Free Trade*, 6.
155. Dennett, *Americans in Eastern Asia*, 71–72.
156. Forbes, *Remarks on China*, 38.
157. Downs, *Golden Ghetto*, 82. Wong, *Global Trade*, 177–204.

2. WHITE GOLD AND BLACK GOLD

1. Qtd. in Downs, *Golden Ghetto*, 82.
2. Wong, *Global Trade*, 93.
3. Hunter, *"Fan Kwae" at Canton*, 43–44; Downs, *Golden Ghetto*, 82; History of Business Done for Houqua by J. M. Forbes, January 1, 1833, reel 88-3878 R-513, HFBR; Houqua to John P. Cushing, June 1, 1840; Houqua to Cushing, December 23, 1842; L. H. Perkins & Co. to James & T. H. Perkins, February 7, 1821, vol. 19, Letter Book, 1820–21, RCR.
4. J. M. Forbes to Russell & Co., August 21, 1833, Letters from Russell and Co. to Their Constituents; Houqua Letters Written by A. Heard, 1832–35, reel 88-3878 R-513, HFBR.
5. Cunningham to P. S. Forbes, June 14, 1861, cited in Liu, *Anglo-American Steamship Rivalry*, 180n12. This Houqua was also likely to be Howqua's son.
6. "Foreign Articles: Russia. Pacific Islands. China," *Niles' National Register* 16, no. 4 (March 23, 1844): 1, Proquest American Periodicals.
7. Downs, *Golden Ghetto*, 154.
8. Grant, "Failure of Li'chuan Hong," 245; Wong, *Global Trade*, 93–94.
9. Samuel Russell & Co. to Edward Carrington, March 6, 1821, cited in Downs, *Golden Ghetto*, 154.
10. For the family and company history, see Downs, *Golden Ghetto*, 150–51, 224.

11. R. B. Forbes to James P. Sturgis, September 11, 1842, LH, Massachusetts Historical Society.
12. Lepler, *Many Panics*, 2–7.
13. Temin, *Jacksonian Economy*, 15–22; Temin, "Economic Consequences of the Bank War"; Engerman, "Note on the Economic Consequences"; McFaul, *Politics of Jacksonian Finance*; Rousseau, "Jacksonian Monetary Policy"; Lepler, *Many Panics of 1837*, esp. 12–13, 18–23, 43–66, 150–56; Roberts, *America's First Great Depression*, 38–42; Knodell, "Rethinking the Jacksonian Economy."
14. Von Glahn, "Economic Depression," 81–82.
15. Irigoin, "'Trojan Horse'"; Lin, *China Upside Down*, 72–114; Von Glahn, "Cycles of Silver," 54–58; Von Glahn, "Economic Depression," esp. 98–108; Von Glahn, "Changing Significance," 575–78.
16. Fichter, *So Great a Proffit*, 227–31; Stelle, "American Trade in Opium, Prior to 1820," 425.
17. The existing literature on the Anglo-Chinese Opium War, including opium smuggling as its causes, is abundant. For some examples, see Chang, *Commissioner Lin*; Derks, *History of the Opium Problem*; Chen, *Merchants of War and Peace*; Polachek, *Inner Opium War*; Wakeman, *Strangers at the Gate*, 11–58; Platt, *Imperial Twilight*; Downs, *Golden Ghetto*, 131–40.
18. Temin, *Jacksonian Economy*, 79–82. Lin and Cheong have also noticed the sharp drop in the volume of specie carried by U.S. ships to China during 1833–56, but they ascribe the trend to other factors than Americans' use of bills for the China trade. Lin claims that the silver scarcity resulted from the declining demand for Chinese tea and silk, but Americans' demand for tea was growing while their silver shipments decreased. Cheong assumes Americans withdrew capital for their internal development during the late 1820s and early 1830s, but this presumption is anachronistic. See Lin, *China Upside Down*, 288; Cheong, "Trade and Finance," 41.
19. The conventional scholarship often portrayed the Canton Trade System as corrupt, isolationist, and conservative. Thus the Opium War that ended the regulated trading system opened China to the world and modernized China's foreign trade. However, researchers started to challenge this Western-centric assumption as early as the 1990s. See Downs, *Golden Ghetto*, 72–80; Wakeman, *Strangers at the Gate*, 44–45; Zhong, *Chaye yu yapian*, 345–48; Rawski and Naquin, "New Look at the Canton Trade"; Cheong, *Hong Merchants of Canton*, esp. 11; Grant, *Chinese Cornerstone*, esp. 31–39; Hung, "Imperial China and Capitalist Europe," esp. 473–91; Van Dyke, *Canton Trade*; Van Dyke, *Merchants of Canton: Politics*; Van Dyke, *Merchants of Canton: Success*; Van Dyke and Schopp, *Private Side*; Wong, *Global Trade*, esp. 6–9.

20. Macgregor, *Commercial Statistics*, 5:66–67.
21. Also see Hao, "Chinese Teas to America," 16; Phipps, *Practical Treatise*, 314; Latourette, *History of Early Relations*, 76; Flagg, "China," 1:518.
22. Joseph Archer to John Creyder, October 21, 1833, JAL; Li, Tan, and Li, *Qingchao yangshang midang*, 69; Wong, *Global Trade*, 73–74, 79–81.
23. Wong, *Global Trade*, 36–37.
24. For the 1833 data on the British imports, see Morse, *Chronicles of the East India Company*, 4:343. The value in piculs was converted to pounds with the ratio of 1 picul = 133.3 pounds. The data on U.S. imports in 1833 can be found in U.S. Treasury Department, *Statements of Imports of Tea and Coffee*, 423; and USDCL, "World's Production," 140.
25. Perkins & Co. to F. W. Paine, March 23, 1820; Perkins & Co. to Henry Cary & Co., January 14, 1821; Perkins & Co. to James & T. H. Perkins, January 14, 24, 27; Perkins & Co. to James & T. H. Perkins, February 27, 28, 1821; Perkins & Co. to F. W. Paine, January 22, vol. 19, Letter Book, 1820–21, RCR.
26. Perkins & Co. to James & T. H. Perkins, February 25, 1820, vol. 19, Letter Book, 1820–21, RCR; Goldstein, *Stephen Girard's Trade*, 68–69.
27. Sullivan Dorr to Ebenezer Dorr, October 7, 1799, series 1, box 1, folder 1, SDP.
28. Perkins & Co. to James & Thomas H. Perkins, March 27, 1820, vol. 19, Letter Book, 1820–21, RCR.
29. Perkins & Co. to John Berenberg Gossler & Co., May 1, 1820, vol. 19, Letter Book, 1820–21, RCR.
30. Perkins & Co. to F. W. Paine, January 22, 1821, vol. 19, Letter Book, 1820–21, RCR.
31. Perkins & Co. to James & T. H. Perkins, January 24, 1821, vol. 19, Letter Book, 1820–21, RCR.
32. Cheong, *Mandarins and Merchants*, 185–86.
33. Cheong, *Mandarins and Merchants*, 190–91.
34. Grant, *Chinese Cornerstone*, 202.
35. J. M. Forbes to John P. Cushing, December 22, 1834, series F, vol. F-6, FFBR.
36. Russell & Co. to Brown & Ives, January 25, 1834, Letters from Russell and Co. to Their Constituents, reel 88-3878 R-513, HFBR.
37. J. M. Forbes to R. B. Forbes, September 28, 1836, series F, vol. F-6, FFBR.
38. Edward Wilson to William Shaler, June 11, 1806; George W. Talbot to Edward Carrington, September 6, 1806, box 9, folder 4; Peter W. Snow to Edward Carrington, March 10, 1811, box 10, folder 2, ECP; Purchase of Tea of Hipshing, June 27, 1816, Bills of Sale, Accounts, Contracts, etc., 1816, box 1, WLP, Rare Books and Manuscripts Division, New York Public Library.
39. Van Dyke, *Merchants of Canton and Macao: Politics and Strategies*, 12; Cheong, *Hong Merchants of Canton*, 37.

40. Cheong, *Mandarins and Merchants*, 161.

41. Grant, *Chinese Cornerstone*, 15–16, 137–38; Ch'en, "Tianxin chashang," 417.

42. Peter W. Snow to Edward Carrington, March 11, 1812, box 10, folder 4, ECP; J. L. Smith to William. H. Smith, May 12, 1810, Robert Waln Letterbooks, vol. 19, 1808–14, WFP; Waln, Standing, Character, Articles of Trade & Residence of a Number of Canton Native Merchants, Book of Prices, Canton 1819, 27–31, WFP; Goldstein, *Stephen Girard's Trade*, 68.

43. "On China: Of the Tea Leaf. Black Teas. Green Teas," *Port-Folio* 7, no. 2 (February 1819): 97–98, ProQuest American Periodicals; Grant, *Chinese Cornerstone*, 137; Grant, "Failure of the Li-ch'uan Hong," 256.

44. Thomas Tunno Forbes to T. H. Perkins, November 1, 1824, series D, vol. D-3 China Letters, FFBR.

45. Thomas Tunno Forbes to T. H. Perkins, November 1, 1824.

46. Wong, *Global Trade*, 73–74, 80–81.

47. Downs, *Golden Ghetto*, 154; Wong, *Global Trade*, esp. 1, 86, 125–34.

48. John Murray Forbes to Houqua, December 31, 1832, series G, box 4, folder 6, FFBR.

49. Wong, *Global Trade*, 107.

50. Liu, *Anglo-American Steamship Rivalry*, 12, 16; Wong, *Global Trade*, 177–204.

51. Wong, *Global Trade*, 72–104.

52. Qtd. in J. M. Forbes to J. P. Cushing, October 17, 1834, series F, vol. F-6, FFBR.

53. Perkins & Co. to James & Thomas H. Perkins, April 22, 1820; and Perkins & Co. to Samuel Williams, September 30, 1820, vol. 19, Letter Book, 1820–21, RCR; History of Business Done for Houqua by J. M. Forbes, December 29, 1832, reel 88-3878 R-513, HFBR; Order by Direction of Houqua to Baring Brothers & Co., October 15, 1832, series F, vol. F-5, FFBR.

54. For the function of commission houses, see Lockwood, *Augustine Heard and Company*, 6–10.

55. History of Business Done for Houqua by J. M. Forbes, December 29, 1832; Russell & Co. to George Wildes & Co., August 15, 1834; George W. Wildes & Co. to Russell & Co., June 24, 1836, Letters to Samuel Russell from Russell and Co., Canton; Baring Brothers, London; George W. Wildes and Co., reel 88-3878 R-513, HFBR; R. B. Forbes to James P. Sturgis, September 11, 1842, LH; Houqua to John P. Cushing, January 13, 1834, vol. F-5; J. M. Forbes to Samuel Cunard & Co., June 11, July 6, July 18, 1837; J. M. Forbes to Houqua, June 16, 1837, series F, vol. F-7; Russell & Co. to J. M. Forbes, October 20, 1838, series F, box 1, folder 24, FFBR.

56. Forbes, *Remarks on China*, 14.

57. Downs, *Golden Ghetto*, 415n42.

58. Perkins & Co. to James & T. H. Perkins, February 25; Perkins & Co. to James & Thomas H. Perkins, March 11, 29, 1820, vol. 19, Letter Book, 1820–21, RCR.
59. Perkins & Co. to F. W. Paine, March 23, 1820, vol. 19, Letter Book, 1820–21, RCR. For the owners of the other ships, see Perkins & Co. to James & T. H. Perkins, February 25, 1820; Perkins & Co. to F. W. Paine, March 23, 1820, vol. 19, Letter Book, 1820–21, RCR.
60. Qtd. in Downs, *Golden Ghetto*, 154.
61. Perkins & Co. to F. W. Paine, March 2, 1820, vol. 19, Letter Book, 1820–21, RCR.
62. For the chain trade, see Shaw and Quincy, *Journals of Major Samuel Shaw*, 233, 351–52; Dudden, *American Pacific*, 6; Fichter, *So Great a Proffit*, 218–22.
63. Nye, *Tea*, 31.
64. For cotton goods, see Business Records on the Remission of Funds to the Far East and Packing Goods for the China Trade, 1828–29, box 1, FFP; Phipps, *Practical Treatise*, 167.
65. Effros, "Problem of Postdated Checks," 113–15. For more details about varied forms of credit instruments, see Du, "'Flying Cash.'"
66. Furniss, *Foreign Exchange*, 3.
67. This Anthon and Company in Hong Kong might be Williams, Anton, and Company. See *Abridged Work*, 23; "Perry Expedition to Japan."
68. To convert the Suzhou Code to Arabic numerals, see http://thdl.ntu.edu.tw/suzhou/ and Williams, *Chinese Commercial Guide*, 296–97.
69. Peng, *Zhongguo huobi shi*, 291n6.
70. Peng, *Zhongguo huobi shi*, 290; Yang, *Money and Credit*, 51–52.
71. Edkins, *Banking and Prices in China*, 3.
72. Feng Liutang 馮柳堂, "Qianzhuangye youlai zhi tuice" 錢莊業由來之推測 [Contemplation on the origin of Chinese native banking], September 1943, in Shanghai Branch of the People's Bank of China (hereafter cited as SBPBC), *Shanghai qianzhuang shiliao*, 8.
73. Shaw and Quincy, *Journals of Major Samuel Shaw*, 169.
74. Shaw and Quincy, *Journals of Major Samuel Shaw*, 169.
75. William Read to Messrs. Willings & Francis, March 10, 1806, series 1, box 1, folder 5, WFR.
76. Cheong, "Beginnings of Credit Finance," 90, 92; Downs, *Golden Ghetto*, 359; Fichter, *So Great a Proffit*, 185.
77. L. Roy Bayard & M'd Evan Letter on Exchange from London to Chinese, March 2, 1811, box 10, folder 2, ECP.
78. Robert Waln to Minturn & Champlin, March 8, 1813, Robert Waln Letterbooks, vol. 19, 309, WFP.

79. Downs, *Golden Ghetto*, 110; Cheong, *Mandarins and Merchants*, 30–31; Cheong, "Beginnings of Credit Finance," 94.
80. Morse, *Chronicles of the East India Company*, 3:179; Greenberg, *British Trade*, 161–62.
81. Cheong, "Beginnings of Credit Finance," 92, 96–101.
82. Morse, *Chronicles of the East India Company*, 3:337; Irigoin, "End of a Silver Era," 213.
83. Downs mentions the relations between the circulation of bills of exchange in Canton and the triangular trade in opium, tea, and cotton in passing. Downs, *Golden Ghetto*, 110, 108.
84. Cheong, "Trade and Finance," 44–45.
85. The Chinese and English inscriptions on the reverse side of the bill indicate the endorsement to Russell and Company. The wording "Pay to the Order of" shows that this was a special endorsement. For the general and special endorsement, see Poovey, *Genres of the Credit Economy*, 39.
86. For the two theories about the basis of credit, confidence, and property, see Moulton, *Principles of Money*, part 2, 15–16.
87. Lepler, *Many Panics*, 28.
88. Augustine Heard to Russell & Co., February 29, October 3, 1836, Original Drafts of Letters from Augustine Heard to Russell and Co., reel 88-3878 R-513, HFBR.
89. Russell & Co. to Forbes & Co., November 27, 1833; Houqua to Jamsetjee Jejeebhoy & Mohamed Ally Rogny, November 23, 1833, series F, vol. F-5, FFBR.
90. Habib, "Merchant Communities," 393–94.
91. Cheong, *Mandarins and Merchants*, 40–42.
92. Although the letter discussed the purchase of tin with bills of exchange in Batavia, the reasoning could be applied to all transactions in bills of exchange. Perkins & Co. to James & T. H. Perkins, February 28, 1821, vol. 19, Letter Book, 1820–21, RCR.
93. For details about the infant bill trade and the EIC's control of the exchange markets in India and China, see Cheong, *Mandarins and Merchants*, 27–43.
94. Bowen, "British Exports," 127; Lin, *China Upside Down*, 76–78.
95. Van Dyke, "Smuggling Networks," esp. 63–64; "Yangwu quanyu ji shang" 洋務權輿記上 [The beginning of foreign affairs, volume 1], 1860, in *Wangqing yangwu yundong shiliaohuibian* (hereafter cited as *WQYWYDSLHB*). Research on the opium trade is extensive. See Morse, *Chronicles of the East India Company*, 3:330–64; Stelle, "American Trade in Opium to China, Prior to 1820"; Stelle, "American Trade in Opium to China, 1821–1839"; Stelle, *Americans and the China Opium Trade*; Janin, *India-China Opium Trade*; Downs, *Golden*

Ghetto, 112–31; Lin, *China Upside Down*, 88–89; Norwood, *Trading Freedom*, 66–67.

96. For nuanced discussion of China's silver outflow, see von Glahn, "Economic Depression," 99–102.
97. Downs, *Golden Ghetto*, 111.
98. Copper could be more readily sold in India than in China. Thomas Tunno Forbes to Sargent & Brooks, January 20, 1828, series D, vol. D-3, China Letters, FFBR.
99. Ellison, *Cotton Trade of Great Britain*, 86; Temin, *Jacksonian Economy*, 103.
100. Cheong, *Mandarins and Merchants*, 112; Hamashita, *Zhongguo jindai jingjishi yanjiu*, 1:347; Lepler, *Many Panics*, 27–30; Roberts, *America's First Great Depression*, 27–31.
101. Joseph Archer to John N. Gossler, November 8, 1833, JAL.
102. Nye, *Tea*, 31.
103. Business Records on the Remission of Funds to the Far East and Packing Goods for the China Trade, 1828–29, box 1, FFP.
104. Business Records on the Remission of Funds to the Far East and Packing Goods for the China Trade; J. M. Forbes to Captain Henry Bancroft, August 22, 1834; J. M. Forbes to R. B. Forbes, March 28, 1835, series F, vol. F-6, FFBR.
105. Memorandum of an Agreement, box I:4, folder 6, JRLP, Manuscript Division, Library of Congress; Downs, *Golden Ghetto*, 111–12; Hidy, *House of Baring*, 74; Norwood, *Trading Freedom*, 59.
106. Irving and Larkin, *Dear Will*, 231, 223–25.
107. Qtd. in Hidy, *House of Baring*, 74.
108. Norwood, *Trading Freedom*, 192, figure A6.
109. Michie, "Financial Capitalism," 238.
110. Augustine Heard to Russell & Co., August 27, 1835, February 29, 1836, April 27, 1836, Original Drafts of Letters from Augustine Heard to Russell and Co., reel 88-3878 R-513, HFBR. For the definition of letters of credit, see *Indian Stamp Act*, 6; Lockwood, *Augustine Heard and Company*, 22–23. For a sample of letters of credit, see Letter of Credit, May 31, 1859, box 2, FGDP, Massachusetts Historical Society.
111. For different explanations of the panic in India, see Cheong, "China Houses," 65–66; Downs, *Golden Ghetto*, 110.
112. Joseph Archer to Foster & Co., November 7, November 8, 1833, JAL.
113. Joseph Archer to Philip and William R. Thompson & Co. and Samuel Parker, November 8, 1833, JAL.
114. History of Business Done for Houqua by J. M. Forbes, December 29, 1832, reel 88-3878 R-513, HFBR; Russell & Co. to J. M. Forbes, March 14, May 2, May 12, 1838, box 1, folder 22; Consignment of Tea and Silks per "Levant,"

August 11, 1838, series F, box 1, folder 23, FFBR; Houqua to John M. Forbes, June 28, 1840; Houqua to Robert B. Forbes, December 27, 1840, LH.

115. Wong, *Global Trade*, 91–92.

116. Russell & Co. to Rogers & Brothers, March 30, 1835, Letters from Russell and Co. to Their Constituents, reel 88-3878 R-513, HFBR.

117. Augustine Heard to John P. Cushing, December 22, 1833, January 4, 1834, series F, vol. F-5, FFBR.

118. Ray, "Asian Capital," 481.

119. "Course of Exchange—1867, 1868, and 1869," *Zhongguo jiuhaiguan shiliao*, 4:1; "Annual Report on Foreign Trade at Foo-chow-foo, for the Year 1868," in *Commercial Reports from Her Majesty's Consuls in China* (hereafter cited as *CRHMCC*), *1869*, 15; W. H. Medhurst, "Shanghae," in *CRHMCC, 1875–76*, 32.

120. J. M. Forbes to Forrestier & Co., November 28, 1836, series F, vol. F-7, FFBR.

121. Van Dyke, "Smuggling Networks," 183n47.

122. Thomas H. Perkins Jr. to R. B. Forbes, December 31, 1830, series E, box 1, folder 19, FFBR.

123. Joseph Archer to Jabez Jenkins, November 9, 1833, JAL. Hao also mentions that Hong merchants accepted bills on London from American commission houses as payment for tea and silk, without citing the sources of the information. Hao, "Chinese Teas to America," 24.

124. For the meaning and practice of "truck," see Grant, *Chinese Cornerstone*, 134; Greenberg, *British Trade*, 7; Wong, *Global Trade*, 38.

125. Joseph Archer to Jabez Jenkins, November 9, 1833, JAL.

126. Houqua to John M. Forbes, May 22, 1834, series F, vol. F-5, FFBR.

127. Hamashita has made a similar argument in 1976. See Hamashita, *China*, 131–32.

128. Also see Irigoin, "End of a Silver Era," 231–32.

129. As figure 11 shows, the value of silver shipped by Americans to China fluctuated significantly after 1826. According to the data compiled by Downs, the five-year average stood at $4,921,468 in 1820–25, then fell to $2,412,302 (1825–30), $588,287 (1830–35), and $735,145 (1835–40), so the percentage decreases were 50.98 percent (1825–30), 88.05 percent (1830–35), and 85.06 percent (1835–40) against the 1820–25 baseline. These statistics align with Dennett's findings, which estimate an 80 percent reduction in Americans' shipment of specie to China during 1831–40 compared to the previous decade. See Dennett, *Americans in Eastern Asia*, 73.

130. J. M. Forbes to Howqua, February 7, 1837, series F, vol. F-7, FFBR. Contemporaries also transliterated the term as "Fung Shuy" or "Fung Shuey." See Hunter, *"Fan Kwae" at Canton*, 45; De Lano, "China," 74. For scholarly research on the concept of *fengshui*, see Bruun, "Fengshui Resurgence," 48–52; He and Luo, "Fengshui and the Environment of Southeast China."

131. Forbes's last letter on the ship *Laconia* was dated March 28, 1837. He clarified in the letter to Edward King that he landed on the night of March 29. See J. M. Forbes to Edward King, May 18, 1837, series F, vol. F-7, FFBR. For the description of the Panic of 1837 as one of the first worst financial crises, also see Lepler, *Many Panics*, 2; Roberts, *America's First Great Depression*, 7–8, 13–47.
132. Lepler, *Many Panics*, 3, 5; Temin, *Jacksonian Economy*, 141–46.
133. J. M. Forbes to Russell & Co., April 5, May 15, May 18, July 7, 1837, series F, vol. F-7, FFBR.
134. J. M. Forbes to Russell & Co., April 5, 1837; J. M. Forbes to Unknown, May 16, 1837, series F, vol. F-7, FFBR.
135. J. M. Forbes to Russell & Co., June 14, 1837; J. M. Forbes to Houqua, June 16, 1837; J. M. Forbes to Russell & Co., July 14, series F, vol. F-7, FFBR.
136. J. M. Forbes to [John C.] Green, May 29, 1837, series F, vol. F-7, FFBR.
137. J. M. Forbes to Russell & Co., April 5, 1837; J. M. Forbes to A. A. Low, May 18, 1837; J. M. Forbes to J. C. Green, April 5, May 18, May 19; J. M. Forbes to [William] Hunter, June 27; J. M. Forbes to Edward King, June 27; J. M. Forbes to Baring Brothers & Co., July 11; J. M. Forbes to Unknown [Howqua?], July 24; J. M. Forbes to Russell & Co., June 1, June 14, July 7, 1837, Letter Book, August 1836–April 1837, series F, vol. F-7, FFBR.
138. J. M. Forbes to John C. Green, April 5, 1837, series F, vol. F-7, FFBR.
139. Cheong, *Mandarins and Merchants*, 248–49; Temin, *Jacksonian Economy*, 138–39; Lepler, *Many Panics*, 96–101, 133.
140. Lepler, *Many Panics*, 130.
141. Russell & Co. to J. M. Forbes, May 22, 1838, series F, box 1, folder 22, FFBR.
142. "Foreign Articles: Great Britain. Robert Peel's Speech," *Niles' National Register* 10, no. 23 (August 7, 1841): 354, ProQuest American Periodicals; Cheong, *Mandarins and Merchants*, 199.
143. Norwood, *Trading Freedom*, 57.
144. Temin, *Jacksonian Economy*, 59–88; "Economic Consequences of the Bank War," 270; Irigoin, "End of a Silver Era," 218 (figure 2), 227 (figure 3), 240 (appendix 1).
145. Owing to the regionalized monetary uses in China, the impacts of international silver and credit on different regions should be examined with more nuance. Thus the analysis here may be applied only to silver-dependent southern regions, especially those under the influence of China's foreign trade. For regional differences in money uses, see Von Glahn, "Economic Depression," 103.
146. Irigoin, "End of a Silver Era," 210–11.
147. Downs, *Golden Ghetto*, 362. Lin also mentioned that the substitution of bills for silver prevented the actual flow of silver from America into China. Lin, *China Upside Down*, 79.

148. Forbes, *Remarks on China*, 43.
149. The estimation is based upon the lowest and highest value of bills sold in Canton during the 1820s–30s, respectively $393,650 in 1829–30 and $4,772,516 in 1832–33. See Downs, *Golden Ghetto*, 362. The relative value in 2024 uses the relative share of GDP; see Williamson, "Seven Ways."
150. J. M. Forbes to Perkins & Co., November 28, 1836, series F, vol. F-7, FFBR.
151. J. M. Forbes to Bevan & Humphreys, July 10, 1837, series F, vol. F-7, FFBR.
152. "Bingkejishizhong Xu Qiu qingjinyapianzhe" 兵科給事中許球請禁鴉片摺 [Supervising Censor of the Office of Scrutiny for War Xu Qiu's memorial on prohibiting opium smuggling]; Yan, *Zhongguo jindaijingjishi tongjiziliao xuanji*, 37; "Daoguang shibanian Huang Juezi zou" 道光十八年黃爵滋奏 [Huang Juezi's memorial in 1838], in Yao, *Zhongguo jindai duiwaimaoyishi ziliao*, 1:342–43, 346–47; "Yangwu quanyu ji shang," in *WQYWYDSLHB*; Lin, *China Upside Down*, 83, 86–87.
153. "Daoguang shibanian Huang Juezi zou," in Yao, *Zhongguo jindai duiwaimaoyishi ziliao*, 1:347.
154. Tsaing, "Notes and Suggestions," 602–7.
155. Ho, "Salt Merchants of Yang-Chou," 153–54.
156. Grant, *Chinese Cornerstone*, 202–3, 206. Also see Russell & Co. to J. M. Forbes, October 19 and December 27, 1837, box 1, folder 21, FFBR.
157. Inglis, *Chinese Security Merchants*; Grant, *Chinese Cornerstone*, 215.
158. Tsaing, "Notes and Suggestions," 607. For representative research on Hong merchants' indebtedness and insolvency, see Ch'en, *Insolvency*; Cheong, *Hong Merchants of Canton*, esp. 59–62, 152, 246–89, 269–70; Downs, *Golden Ghetto*, 77; Grant, *Chinese Cornerstone*.
159. Lin, *China Upside Down*, 75; "Bingke jishizhong Xu Qiu qingjinyapianzhe"; *Guangxu daqing huidian shili* 光緒大清會典事例 [Collected statutes of the Qing dynasty edited during Emperor Guangxu's reign], vol. 630, 7; "Daoguang shibanian Huang Juezi zou"; "Daoguang sihliunian Xu Naiji zou" 道光十六年許乃濟奏 [Xu Naiji's memorial in 1836]; "Daoguang shibanian wuyue Lin Zexu zou" 道光十八年五月林則徐奏 [Lin Zexu's memorial in May 1838]; Bao Shichen 包世臣, *Anwu sizhong* 安吳四種 [Four works of Bao Shichen], vol. 26, 4–5, in Yao, *Zhongguo jindai duiwaimaoyishi ziliao*, 1:342–43, 345–46, 347–48.
160. "今天下皆知漏卮在鴉片." "Liezhuan yibailiushiwu, Huang Juezi" 列傳一百六十五 黃爵滋 [Biography 165—Huang Juezi], in Zhao, *Qing shigao*.
161. Haddad, *America's First Adventure*, 121–22.
162. Chang, *Commissioner Lin*, 173; "Yangwu quanyu ji shang," in *WQYWYDSLHB*; Liang, *Yifeng wenji*, 1:8.
163. Extracts from a Communication Addressed to the Secretary of State, 1854, box 2, folder 20, FFBR.

164. Chang, *Commissioner Lin*, 173–74.
165. Lovell, *Opium War*, 55–108.
166. Houqua to R. B. Forbes, April 12, 1841, LH.
167. Houqua to John C. Cushing, November 21, 1841; Houqua to W. H. C. Plowden, April 2, 1843, LH.
168. Houqua to A. A. Low, April 4, 1843, LH.
169. Houqua to John P. Cushing, October 4, 1841; Houqua to John M. Forbes, November 22, 1841, LH.
170. Houqua to John P. Cushing, December 23, 1842, LH.
171. Forbes, *Remarks on China*, 14.

PART 2

1. "Concerning Tea," *Massachusetts Ploughman and New England Journal of Agriculture* 63, no. 46 (August 6, 1904): 6.
2. Samuel Wetmore [?] to Nathanial Kinsman, March 22, 1843, box 3, folder 5, NKP, Phillips Library, Peabody Essex Museum.
3. *United States Economist, Dry Goods Reporter, and Bank Railroad and Commercial Chronicle* 2, no. 34 (December 11, 1852): 141, ProQuest American Periodicals.
4. "The Tea Plant and Varieties of Teas," 416; "To Consumers of Teas," *Baltimore Sun*, December 5, 1845, 2, America's Historical Newspapers; "Extract from John Caswell & Co.'s Orders for Tea," 1854, and "Indent for the Purchase of Black Teas," 1861, series 2, 1847–75 Sundry Tea Orders, Indents, reel 86-4543 R-137, HFBR; Walsh and Saunders, *"Cup of Tea,"* 104; Williams, *Chinese Commercial Guide*, 193.
5. *Zhongguo jiuhaiguan shiliao*, see figure 3 for specific page numbers.
6. "Interesting to Tea Drinkers," *Tea Cup* (Boston: Oriental Tea Company), July 1876, 2. "Concerning Tea," 6.
7. For the processing techniques used to make the six types of tea in China, see Chen, *Zhongguo chaye dacidian*, 220, 265, 267, 272, 274, 324.
8. Chen, *Zhongguo chajing*, 2:291–92.
9. Chen, *Zhongguo chajing*, 2:325–26; Chen, *Zhongguo chaye dacidian*, 329, 332–33, 367.
10. Chen, *Zhongguo chaye dacidian*, 267; Gardella, "Min-Pei Tea Trade," 325.
11. Chen, *Zhongguo chajing*, 1:314, 2:362.
12. Walsh and Saunders, *"Cup of Tea,"* 106.
13. Chen, *Zhongguo chajing*, 2:368–69, 372; Chen, *Zhongguo chaye dacidian*, 324–25, 374; Qian, *Huacha zhi yanjiu*, 4.
14. Chen, *Zhongguo chajing*, 2:363–64; Chen, *Zhongguo chaye dacidian*, 267, 270.
15. Walsh and Saunders, *"Cup of Tea,"* 104.
16. "China and Its Prospective Trade," 387; Levinson, *Great A&P*, 17.

17. John Matthews Apparatus Company, *Book of Directions*, 50; *Cincinnati Daily Nonpareil*, January 1, 1836, 1; "Importations," *Commercial Advertiser*, October 21, 1837. Thanks to Christopher Sherwood Davis for sharing the sources. "Commercial-Imports," *Boston Daily Atlas*, July 26, 1838, 2, America's Historical Newspapers.
18. For the price of oolongs, see *Baltimore Commercial Journal, and Lyford's Price-Current*, May 18, 1839, May 9, September 6, November 21, 1840; *American and Commercial Daily Advertiser* (Baltimore), September 18, September 19, October 26, November 14, 1839, August 12, 1840; *Connecticut Courant*, November 28, December 5, 12, 19, 1840; *Connecticut*, November 21, 1840, America's Historical Newspapers; "Chronicle," *Niles' National Register* 11, no. 3 (September 18, 1841): 48. The amount of oolong imported to the United States was still less than most of the other varieties of tea in 1842–44. See "Import of Tea into the U. States," *Niles' National Register* 18, no. 15 (June 14, 1845): 233, ProQuest American Periodicals.
19. Augustine Heard to Joshua Bates, June 21, 1842, Original Drafts of Letters Sent by A. Heard from Canton to Other Foreign Countries, reel 88-3878 R-513, HFBR.
20. Forbes, *Remarks on China*, 30.
21. "Foreign Articles: China," *Niles' National Register* 10, no. 23 (August 7, 1841): 354, ProQuest American Periodicals.
22. Houqua to John M. Forbes, November 22, 1841, LH.
23. For oolong as green tea, see *Cincinnati Daily Nonpareil*, January 1, 1836. For oolong as black tea, see *American and Commercial Daily Advertiser*, September 18, 1839; Augustine Heard to Captain Timothy Bryant, September 20, 1843, Original Drafts of Letters Sent by A. Heard from Canton to Other Foreign Countries, reel 88-3878 R-513, HFBR; "Pekin Tea Company," *New York Herald*, March 19, 1845, Chronicling America.
24. Alfred E. Hippisley, "Part I. Report on the Trade of China, within the Cognizance of the Maritime Customs under the Foreign Inspectorate for the Year 1876," in Inspector General of Chinese Maritime Customs (hereafter cited as IGCMC), *At the Treaty Ports, 1876*, 38; William Appleton & Co. to Captain William Cole, April 19, 1857, box 2, FGDP.
25. Augustine Heard to Samuel T. Dana, Original Drafts of Letters Sent by A. Heard from Canton to Friends in Boston; Augustine Heard to Captain Timothy Bryant, September 20, 1843, reel 88-3878 R-513; Report on the Present Position of the Different Classes of Tea, as a Guide to Future Imports, March 20, 1847, carton 27, folder 37; Simes & Farley to E. G. Low, April 19, 1870, May 21, 1869–June 2, 1870, Constituents to A. H. Co., Shanghai, reel 87-1762 R-176, HFBR; William Appleton & Co. to Captain William Cole, April 19, 1857, and Memo Edith Rose's Tea from Foochow, September 1859, box

2; Russell & Co. to Franklin Gordon Dexter, September 6, 1860, and W. S. Sloan to Franklin Gordon Dexter, October 13, 1860, box 4, FGDP.

26. Kohn, or Kokew 高橋, was a region located northward and near the Wuyi Mountains. "Ningyong" or "Ningyung" refers to Ningyang 寧洋, which was a major tea district in Lung-yen-chow (Longyan), about thirty-seven miles north and west of Xiamen. Shaxian, in the prefecture of Yenping (Yanping), produced a finer kind of oolong than the other two districts. See Williams, *Chinese Commercial Guide*, 193; Rutherford Alcock, "Report on the Tea Trade of Shanghae and Its Prospects," in House of Commons, *Returns of the Trade, 1847 and 1848*, 65.
27. Lien, *Taiwan*, 27:7; Chen, *Zhongguo chaye dacidian*, 270; Gardella, *Harvesting Mountains*, 63–64; Taiwan Tea Exporters' Association (hereafter cited as TTEA), *Historical Brevities*, 4–5.
28. Forbes, *Remarks on China*, 55.
29. Flagg, "China," 3:376; Alcock, "Report on the Tea Trade," 63.
30. Kuhn, "Taiping Rebellion," 264–310; Reilly, *Taiping Heavenly Kingdom*, 3.
31. Fairbank, "Creation of the Treaty System," 243–61.
32. "China," in *Letter from the Secretary of State*, 1857, 186; Doty, "Amoy," in *Letter from the Secretary of State*, 1858, 366–67; Samuel Hooper to Franklin Gordon Dexter, January 24, 1860; [Russell & Co.?] to Franklin Gordon Dexter, March 21, 1860, box 3; H. S. Grew to Franklin Gordon Dexter, August 4, 1860; Samuel Hooper & Co. to Franklin Gordon Dexter, August 10, 1860, box 4; Thomas Walsh to Franklin Gordon Dexter, August 11, August 17, 1860; Samuel Hooper to Franklin Gordon Dexter, November 9, 1860, box 4, FGDP.
33. The military action of the Taiping rebels and Qing forces interrupted the supply of new teas to Fuzhou in 1857, and none of the Guangxi tea workers, who accounted for three-fourths of the labor force in Fujian's tea economy, came to pick and manufacture tea during the military clashes. However, most of U.S. business records show the tea trade proceeded smoothly for much of the civil war. See Teas-Circular Report, April 15, 1857, reel 86-4502 R-136, HFBR.
34. Heard, "Old China and New," 30; Gardella, *Harvesting Mountains*, 52; Rappaport, *Thirst for Empire*, 128; Liu, *Tea War*, 53.
35. The contract between the copartners of Russell and Company, stipulated in 1855, mentioned the company's office in Fuzhou. Articles of Copartnership between Paul S. Forbes, Robert S. Sturgis, Edward Cunningham, Daniel N. Spoones, George Griswold Gray, Charles W. Spoones, and Frederick Reiche, 1855, box 4, folder 12, FFBR; Gardella, *Harvesting Mountains*, 55–56.
36. "China," *Merchants' Magazine and Commercial Review* 48, no. 2 (August 1, 1862): 133, ProQuest American Periodicals; T. H. Hyatt, "Amoy," in *Letter from the Secretary of State*, 1859, 375.

37. Thomas A. Phelan, *Some Secrets of Tea* (National Tea Association of the United States of America, 1905), 11, Tea, box 5, WCBA, Archives Center, National Museum of American History.
38. Chen, *Jindai Zhongguo chaye*, 32. The customs report also clarifies that the United States ranked third in terms of the aggregate import of tea from Fuzhou in 1870, behind Great Britain and Australia. See Bon. De Meritens, "Foochow Trade Report for the Year 1870," translated by P. Piry, in IGCMC, *Reports on Trade, 1870*, 77.
39. Gardella, *Harvesting Mountains*, 52.
40. "Annual Report on Foreign Trade at Foo-chow-foo, for the Year 1868," in *CRHMCC, 1869*, 13.
41. Walter T. Lay, "Foochow Trade Report for the Year 1867," in IGCMC, *Reports on Trade, 1867*, 54; Jas Smith, "Foochow Trade Report for the Year 1868," in IGCMC, *Reports on Trade, 1868*, 65; Bn. De Meritens, "Rapport Annuel Sur Le Commerce De Foochow," in IGCMC, *Reports on Trade, 1869*, 79–80.
42. For the statistics of the tea trade in Xiamen during 1862–66, see *Zhongguo jiuhaiguan shiliao*, 1:232, 233, 326, 697, 2:780. For 1867–69, see Le Gendre, "Amoy," 57. For 1870–73, see George Hughes, "Amoy Trade Report for the Year 1870," "Amoy Trade Report for the Years 1872," and "Amoy Trade Report for the Year 1873," in IGCMC, *Reports on Trade, 1870, 1871–1872, 1873*, 94, 180, 125.
43. Quoted from Washington Letter to the Philadelphia Ledger, "Better and Cheaper Tea," *New York Times*, July 20, 1891, ProQuest Historical Newspapers; W. Elwell Goldsborough, "Trade of North Formosa," in U.S. Department of State, *Commercial Relations of the United States, 1882*, 430. The great majority of the tea exported from Taiwan remained oolong before 1911, although the quantities of pouchongs shipped primarily to Southeast Asia grew steadily after 1897. See Taiwan Tea Exporters' Association, *Historical Brevities of Taiwan Tea Export*, 59, appendix. For the transshipment of Formosa oolong to Xiamen, see H. E. Hobson, "Tamsui (Formosa) Trade Report for the Year 1873," in IGCMC, *Reports on Trade, 1873*, 95. For Americans' dominance in the trade and consumption of Formosa oolong, also see USDCL, "World's Production," 132. Lin, *Cha, tang*, 22.
44. Le Gendre, "Amoy," 55.
45. Ukers, *All about Tea*, 2:230.
46. Davidson, *Island of Formosa*, 175, 374; TTEA, *Historical Brevities*, 13.
47. Francis Blackwell Forbes to King, July 9, 1872, vol. N5; Francis Blackwell Forbes to Paul S. Forbes, November 2, 1872; Francis Blackwell Forbes to Will Forbes, November 7, 1872; Francis Blackwell Forbes to King, November 28, 1872, series N, vol. N-6, FFBR.

48. Francis Blackwell Forbes to Edward Cunningham, November 25, 1872, vol. N-6; Francis Blackwell Forbes to Will H. Forbes, January 2, 1873; Francis Blackwell Forbes to Edward Cunningham, January 12, 1873; Francis Blackwell Forbes to Will H. Forbes, January 15, 1873; Francis Blackwell Forbes to John Forbes, February 18, 1873; Francis Blackwell Forbes to Edward Cunningham, March 11, 1873; Francis Blackwell Forbes to Will H. Forbes, March 25, 1873, vol. N-7, FFBR.
49. Gardella, *Harvesting Mountains*, 63–69.
50. Lin, *Cha, tang*, 109.
51. TTEA, *Historical Brevities*, 49–50.
52. Lien, *Taiwan*, 27:7.
53. Davidson, *Island of Formosa*, 377.

3. FROM CANTON TO THE COAST

1. William Appleton & Co. in a/c Current with Russell & Co., September 25–December 1, 1857; William Appleton & Co. to Captain William Cole, April 19, 1857; Samuel Hooper to Franklin Gordon Dexter, October 25, 1859, box 2; Charles W. Orne to Franklin Gordon Dexter, August 12, 1860, box 4, FGDP.
2. William Appleton & Co. to Captain William Cole, April 19, 1857, box 2, FGDP.
3. When the disputes with Russell and Company began, Hooper was confused about the exchange markets and rates in Chinese treaty ports. See Samuel Hooper to Franklin Gordon Dexter, July 25, 1859, box 2; April 22, 1860, box 3, FGDP.
4. William Appleton & Co. to Franklin Gordon Dexter, September 5, 1859, box 2; Samuel Hooper to Franklin Gordon Dexter, April 22, 1860, box 3, FGDP. It is unclear whether this bookkeeper was Frederick Reiche, a copartner of Russell and Company.
5. William Appleton & Co. to Franklin Gordon Dexter, August 30, September 5, 1859, box 2; Samuel Hooper to Franklin Gordon Dexter, April 22, 1860, box 3, FGDP.
6. Chen, *Jindai Zhongguo chaye*, esp. 30–32, 60–70; Gardella, *Harvesting Mountains*, 54–55; Lockwood, *Augustine Heard and Company*, x; Feuerwerker, "Foreign Presence in China," 198; Tsin, *Nation, Governance, and Modernity*, 21–22; Irigoin, "End of a Silver Era," 236; Marriner, *Rathbones of Liverpool*, 179; Moazzin, *Foreign Banks*, 32–33; Chen, "Cong 'yichazhiyi' dao 'chaye gailiang,'" 113.
7. It is easy to find such comments in Imperial Maritime Customs' reports and American business correspondence, although some foreign commissioners also dismissed the extent of Chinese influence. For examples, see A. Macpherson, "Report on the Trade of Hankow, for the Year 1864," in IGCMC, *Reports on Trade, 1864*, 12; E. De Champs, "Kiukiang Trade Report for the Year 1867," translated by R. W. Halket, in IGCMC, *Reports on Trade, 1867*, 6–8; Heard,

"Old China and New," 38–41; Francis Blackwell Forbes to Fitz, August 24, 1869, series N, vol. N-1, FFBR.

8. Jones, "Finance in Ningpo"; Hamashita, *Zhongguo jindai jingjishi yanjiu*, 1:359–60; Moazzin, *Foreign Banks*, 77–93; Ray, "Asian Capital," 486–91; Wang, *Chinese Hinterland Capitalism*; Zhuang, *Zhongjianshang*, 213, 242–43.
9. "China and Its Prospective Trade," 386.
10. Robert S. Sturgis to Edward A. Low, September 19, 1846, box 1, folder 3, LFP (P), Phillips Library, Peabody Essex Museum.
11. Augustine Heard to A. F. Seebohm, January 14, 1843, Original Drafts of Letters Sent by A. Heard from Canton to Other Foreign Countries, reel 88-3878 R-513, HFBR.
12. Forbes, *Remarks on China*, 55. For Forbes's stance on the Opium War, see Yao, *Zhongguo jindai duiwaimaoyishi ziliao*, 1:369–70; J. M. Forbes to R. B. Forbes, series F, vol. F-8, FFBR.
13. For tea exports from Canton and Shanghai during 1845–52, see Flagg, "China," 3:374, 378. For low-value green tea in Shanghai, see Alcock, "Report on the Tea Trade," 60–61; "Shanghae Market Report, December 20th, 1850," *North China Herald*, December 21, 1850, 81.
14. Alcock, "Report on the Tea Trade," 60–63. The percentage is from Mazumdar, *Sugar and Society*, 347.
15. House of Commons, *Commercial Reports, 1865–66*, 104.
16. Alcock, "Report on the Tea Trade," 61–62.
17. "China and Its Prospective Trade," 386.
18. Flagg, "China," 3:377.
19. A China Merchant, "Why Is Silver Sent to the East?" *Economist* 14, no. 649 (February 2, 1856): 118, Economist Historical Archive.
20. William Appleton & Co. to Captain William Cole, April 19, 1857, box 2, FGDP.
21. Memo of Charles S. Young's Order £1500, circa 1849–52, Extract from J. Caswell & Co.'s Order for Tea, 1854, Indent for the Purchase of Black Teas, 1861, Abstract of S. W. Goodrige's Letter Dated New York 29 May 1862, Memo of Charles L. Young Order for Teas, circa 1867–68, Orders, Indents, etc., 1847–75, reel 86-4543 R-137; Copy of Instructions sent to Mess. Augustine Heard & Co. Hong Kong, May 6, 1858, Grinnell, Minturn & Co. to Albert Farley Heard, October 12, 1858, Kn. Weston to Albert Farley Heard, October 9, 1863, Letters Received from Miscellaneous, Domestic, 1855–64, reel 89-1713 R-616, HFBR; Francis Blackwell Forbes to Edward Cunningham, February 1, 1867, series N, vol. N-1a, FFBR.
22. Nineteenth-century documents and researchers' publications noted the spike in the flow of silver into China after the 1850s, because the civil wars in China

and the United States put the import trade to a halt and the confidence in credit instruments waned during military and economic crises, causing the soaring bullion movement between the two countries. The increase of foreign banks in China after the 1860s also likely augmented the silver flow, and the adoption of the gold standard drove the influx of silver after 1873. For credit and silver, see A China Merchant, "Why Is Silver Sent to the East?," 118. Russell & Co. to Franklin Gordon Dexter, March 21, 1860, box 3, FGDP; Augustine Heard & Co. to D. G. & W. B. Bacon & Co., July 2, 1864, box 2/10, BCL, Manuscripts Collection, G. W. Blunt White Library, Mystic Seaport Museum. For the spike in China's silver imports from Great Britain and the United States during the 1850s–60s, see Irigoin, Kobayashi, and Chilosi, "China Inside Out," 40, figure 2. For European banking and the gold standard, see Hamashita, *China*, 52–56, 114.

23. "The Exchange with the East," *Economist* 14, no. 689 (November 8, 1856): 1229, Economist Historical Archive.
24. Tea from Foochow, Shanghae & Japan, on Joint Account with Messrs. Augustine Heard & Co., in Account Current with Weston & Gray, May 28, October 19, 1867, Orders, Indents, etc., 1847–75, reel 86-4543 R-137, HFBR.
25. Marriner, *Rathbones of Liverpool*, 201.
26. W. S. Brown to Rathbone, August 22, 1850, cited in Marriner, *Rathbones of Liverpool*, 199.
27. T. Moncreiff to Rathbone Bros & Co., June 7, 1851, cited in Marriner, *Rathbones of Liverpool*, 199–200.
28. Marriner, *Rathbones of Liverpool*, 199–201.
29. Marriner, *Rathbones of Liverpool*, 203–4. Augustine Heard and Company's early correspondence in Fuzhou mentions only commodities and bullion but not credit. For example, see William Comstock Jr. to Augustine Heard & Co., August 14, August 18, 1854, March 1854–June 1855 Letters: A. H. & Co., Foochow, to A. H. & Co. Canton and Shanghai, reel 87-1762 R-178; Circular Memo, Teas, February 28th to March 30th, 1857, 1857–60 Sales-Tea, Foochow: Tea Reports, reel 86-4502 R-136, HFBR.
30. The triangular trade with India helped maintain Canton's status as the financial center. *North China Herald*, March 15, 1851, 131; Marriner, *Rathbones of Liverpool*, 86, 188–90, 197, 199–200. For the description of modern world financial centers, see Michie, "Financial Capitalism," 248.
31. Heard, "Old China and New," 26.
32. Marriner, *Rathbones of Liverpool*, 197–98.
33. Memo of Yenqua Shipments, July 31, 1847, Orders, Indents, etc., 1847–75, reel 86-4543 R-137; Sales-Tea, Settlements-Yenqua, 1847, reel 86-4543 R-138, HFBR.
34. Marriner, *Rathbones of Liverpool*, 178–79.

35. "Hints to British Merchants Resorting to Ningpo for Purposes of Trade," in Macgregor, *Commercial Statistics*, 5:25.
36. Alcock, "Report on the Tea Trade," 61, 73–74; "Shanghae Market Report, December 20th, 1850," *North China Herald*, December 21, 1850, 81; Hamashita, *China*, 132–44.
37. "Returns of the Trade of the Various Ports of China, for the Year 1846," in *Accounts and Papers*, 20.
38. Circular Memo, Teas, December 30th, 1856, to January 31st, 1857, Sales-Tea, Foochow: Tea Reports, 1857–60, reel 86-4502 R-136, HFBR.
39. Marriner, *Rathbones of Liverpool*, 178–79. For the barter economy in the Yangzi River Valley, notably Hankou, see Samuel Hooper to Franklin Gordon Dexter, January 8, 1861, box 5, FGDP; "Hankow, June 16, 1870," *North China Herald*, June 16, 1870, 454. For Danshui, Taiwan, see H. Kopsch, "Tamsui Trade Report for the Year 1867," in IGCMC, *Reports on Trade, 1867*, 73.
40. Lin, *China Upside Down*, 104.
41. Marriner, *Rathbones of Liverpool*, 187; Lin, *China Upside Down*, 112; Spalding, *Eastern Exchange*, 404, 408–9.
42. "Meeting on the Currency Question," *North China Herald*, February 2, 1856, 196. A Shanghai Merchant, "To the Editor of North-China Herald," *North China Herald*, July 28, 1855, 209; "The Value of the Mexican Dollar," *North China Herald*, January 5, 1856, 91.
43. A Shanghai Merchant, "To the Editor of North-China Herald," 209; D. N. Spooner to Paul Siemen Forbes, January 23, 1854, box 2, folder 20, FFBR.
44. Native banks acquired different names in various regions. *Qianzhuang*, the term this book adopts, was popular along the Yangzi River, while those in the North or the South were often named *yinhao* (silver shops). See McElderry, *Shanghai Old-Style Banks*, 9–15; Yang, *Qingdai huobi*, 146–48.
45. Ray, "Asian Capital," 463–64; SBPBC, *Shanghai qianzhuang shiliao*, 1–2, 5; McElderry, *Shanghai Old-Style Banks*, 12; Jones, "Finance in Ningpo," esp. 47.
46. Cheng, *Banking in Modern China*, 20.
47. McElderry, *Shanghai Old-Style Banks*, 14.
48. "Shanghae Market Report, September 13th, 1850," *North China Herald*, September 14, 1850, 25.
49. "Shanghae Market Report, December 20th, 1850," *North China Herald*, December 21, 1850, 81.
50. Ji, *History of Modern Shanghai Banking*, 23.
51. Wagel, *Finance in China*, 123.
52. Francis Blackwell Forbes to W. H. Foster, April 22, 1869, series N, vol. N-1, FFBR.

53. Francis Blackwell Forbes to Sheppard, March 22, 1873, series N, vol. N-7, FFBR.
54. Wang, *Chinese Hinterland Capitalism*, 6–7, 41. For more details, see King, *History of the Hongkong and Shanghai Banking Corporation*, 1:500–501.
55. House of Commons, *Returns of the Trade, 1847 and 1848*, 73.
56. SBPBC, *Shanghai qianzhuang shiliao*, 1–3; Jones, "Finance in Ningpo," 73.
57. House of Commons, *Returns of the Trade, 1847 and 1848*, 74.
58. Nie, *Zhongguo maiban*, 41.
59. [Russell & Co.] to Franklin Gordon Dexter, March 21, 1860, box 3, FGDP.
60. Nie, *Zhongguo maiban*, 41–42.
61. "夫庄票者, 钱庄自出之本票也." Ma Yinchu 马寅初, "Huifeng yinhang" 汇丰银行 [Hongkong and Shanghai Bank], *Shangye yuebao* 商业月报 [Commerce monthly] 5, no. 7 (July 1925): 19–20, in SBPBC, *Shanghai qianzhuang shiliao*, 18–19. Linsun Cheng also conceptualizes *zhuangpiao* as a type of promissory note. See Cheng, *Banking in Modern China*, 16.
62. "在昔洋商与行商往来, 彼此都有信用, 故洋商敢将货先交行商, 日后收款. 至五口通商, 华洋商人, 随便贸易, 情形顿变." Ma, "Huifeng yinhang," 18–19.
63. "华商既为钱庄负责, 则洋商只注重于钱庄, 对于华商始终不能信任." Ma, "Huifeng yinhang," 18–19.
64. Marriner, *Rathbones of Liverpool*, 187.
65. A Shanghai Merchant, "To the Editor of North-China Herald," 209; Flagg, "China," 3:376–77.
66. A Shanghai Merchant, "To the Editor of North-China Herald," 209; Flagg, "China," 3:376–77.
67. "Shanghae Market Report," *North China Herald*, December 8, 1855, 74.
68. Flagg, "China," 3:376–77; *North China Herald*, December 22, 1855, 82.
69. "China," in U.S. Department of State, *Report of the Secretary of State, 1856*, 193.
70. Flagg, "China," 3:377.
71. *North China Herald*, March 31, 1860, 50.
72. "The Compradore System," *North China Herald*, January 9, 1864, 10.
73. Jas Mackey, "Hankow Trade Report for the Year 1874," in IGCMC, *Reports on Trade, 1874*, 35.
74. "Native Banks in Foochow," 440, 443.
75. A. Macpherson, "Report on the Trade of Hankow, for the Year 1864," 12.
76. Edward B. Drew, "Kiukiang Trade Report for the Year 1869," in IGCMC, *Reports on Trade, 1869*, 131.

77. E. De Champs, "Kiukiang Trade Report for the Year 1867," translated by R. W. Halket, in IGCMC, *Reports on Trade, 1867*, appendix, 7; Drew, "Kiukiang Trade Report for the Year 1869," 131.
78. Jas. K. Leonard, "Ningpo Trade Report for the Year 1867," in IGCMC, *Reports on Trade, 1867*, 41; Francis W. White, "Ningpo Trade Report for the Year 1870," in IGCMC, *Reports on Trade, 1870*, 61.
79. "The Shanghai Money Market," *North China Herald*, June 15, 1872, 476.
80. W. H. Medhurst, "Shanghae," in *CRHMCC, 1875–76*, 32–33.
81. "The Compradore System," *North China Herald*, January 9, 1864, 10.
82. U.S. Department of Commerce and Labor, Bureau of Manufactures, *Monthly Consular and Trade Reports*, August 1905, 21; "Compradore System," 10; Hao, *Comprador*, 64–82; Liu, *Tea War*, 235.
83. "Compradore System," 10; Wagel, *Finance in China*, 125; Hao, *Comprador*, 71–74; Ma, "Huifeng yinhang," 18; Moazzin, *Foreign Banks*, 83; Nie, *Zhongguo maiban*, 42–43.
84. "舉凡莊票之別擇, 現銀之鑒定, 匯票之買賣, 皆由彼等經手." Wang Liewang 王烈望, "Zhanqian shanghai jinrong shichang" 戰前上海金融市場 [Shanghai financial market before World War II], June 1945, in SBPBC, *Shanghai qianzhuang shiliao*, 36.
85. "The Compradore System," 10. Also see *North China Herald*, September 16, 1865, 146.
86. Wagel, *Finance in China*, 125.
87. *North China Herald*, September 16, 1865, 146; "Compradore System," 10.
88. McElderry, *Shanghai Old-Style Banks*, 2–3.
89. See the comprador's orders issued by Augustine Heard and Company over a decade. This section will discuss those relating to the tea trade in detail. Bills of Exchange, 1844–66, reel 86-3147 R-56 to R-62, HFBR.
90. For the definition of a check, see Quinn and Roberds, "Evolution of the Check," 2; Redlich and Christman, "Early American Checks," 290; Rabel, *Conflict of Laws*, 224–25; Spahr, *Clearing and Collection*, 1.
91. Hao, *Comprador*, 72.
92. Baster, "Origins of the British Exchange Banks," 140–44.
93. Scholars provided different dates for these banks' opening in China. See Baster, "Origins," 143–45; Hamashita, *China*, 142; Moazzin, *Foreign Banks*, table 2.2, 99–101; Purtle, "Money Making Nation," 107.
94. "Exchange with the East," 1230.
95. Heard, "Old China and New," 2. For the assessment of the bank's influence, also see Hamashita, *China*, 142.
96. Heard, "Old China and New," 38.

97. U.S. Department of Commerce and Labor, Bureau of Manufactures, *Monthly Consular*, 1905, 21.

98. Comprador: Pay Yenqua, February 5, March 4, May 3, May 15, 1847, February 2, May 10, December 22, 1848, March 26, 1850, September 29, 1851, Bills of Exchange, 1844–66, reel 86-3147 R-57, R-58, R-59, HFBR.

99. These Chinese traders or their hongs were Ahhue (佐記), Ahoo (亞好, whose hong was 潤和), Ahoy (亞魁), A(h)ming (Mingji 明记), Cheepqua (接官, whose hong was 泰昌 or 祥生), Chuenqua (恆豐), Cumwoe (今和), Footae (孚太 or 孚泰), Hingcheong (興昌), Hingqua (慶官, whose hong was 生泰), Hocheong (浩彰), Kowshing (求盛, whose hong was 洛记), Linching (連彰, whose hong was 天寶行), Mowqua (茂官, whose hong was 會昌), Mowshing (茂盛 or 福興), Sewqua (绍官, whose hong was 暢記), Shingqua (生官, whose hong was 寶興), Shungqua (隆昌), Sicqua (锡官, whose hong was 慎祥), Sunghung (順記), Sunqua (信官), Washing (華盛), Wocheong (和彰), Yatchong (溢彰), Yengchon (裕興昌記), Yeutshing (悦成, whose hong was 南利), and Yingqua (賢官, whose hong was 隆盛). See Bills of Exchange, 1844–66, reel 86-3147 R-56, R-57, R-58, R-60, HFBR.

100. Pay Footae, January 21, 1845; Compradore: Pay Footae, February 3, 1847; Comprador: Pay Ahming, March 7, 1845; Comprador: Pay Aming, November 25, 28, 1846; Comprador: Pay Chuenqua, March 8, 1845; Comprador: Pay Cumwo, March 11, 1845, Bills of Exchange, 1844–66, reel 86–3147 R-56, R-57, HFBR.

101. Comprador: Py Moushing for Balance for Teas, December 22, 1845; Compradore: Pay Kincum, December 22, 1847, Bills of Exchange, 1844–66, reel 86-3147 R-56, 57, HFBR.

102. Comprador: Pay Tingqua, April 24, 1850; Pay to Yatchong, January 11, 1853, Bills of Exchange, 1844–66, reel 86-3147 R-58, R-60, HFBR.

103. In the Heard Family Business Records, preprinted checks appeared at the beginning of 1850. Their number grew larger in the tea trade during the 1850s, while hand-written orders became increasingly uncommon. It also becomes more difficult to track the use of the printed and standardized orders in the tea trade, because they present little information on the commercial transactions other than the payee and the face value of the check. Given the large number of the printed orders, it is hard to cite them individually. For specific examples, see Bills of Exchange, 1844–66, reel 86-3147 R-58, R-59, R-60, R-61, HFBR.

104. Redlich and Christman, "Early American Checks," esp. 285–86, 289–90, 294; Quinn and Roberds, "Evolution of the Check," 7–8, 12. For discussions on whether checks were in common use before the 1840s, see Wright, *Origins of Commercial Banking*, 121–23; Baughman, "Early American Checks," 434–35.

105. For the meaning and negotiability of bearer instruments, see Baughman, "Early American Checks," 434; Chitty, *Practical Treatise*, 578; Poovey, *Genres of the Credit Economy*, 52; Redlich and Christman, "Early American Checks," 286–93; Wright, *Origins of Commercial Banking*, 19–20, 40n54.

106. Pay Bearer for Fine Oolong, April 14, 1849. For other bearers' orders whose connection with the tea trade was unclear, see Compadore: Pay the Bearer, June 23, 1845; Pay Yengfoong or Bearer, March 16, 1848, reel 86-3147 R-56, 58, HFBR.

107. For bank checks, see Redlich and Christman, "Early American Checks," esp. 287–88. For checks drawn on the company and used for the tea trade, see Pay Yatchong, November 21, December 8, 1849; Pay to Yatchong, December 5, 1851, July 22, September 24, 1852; Pay to Asum, December 7, 1851; Pay to Comprador, February 14, 1852 (the latter five are printed checks, on which "Comprador" was crossed out and replaced by company; in other words, it was intentionally drawn on the company, not the comprador); Pay Yenqua, March 9, 1849; Pay Bearer for Fine Oolong, April 14, 1849, reel 86-3147 R-56, R-58, R-59, HFBR.

108. The suppliers documented by comprador's orders include Cheep Kee (捷記), Wo Sun (和順), Aning, Ao Sun, Ching Sua, Com Wu, Cow Sun, Fook Chun, Fook Hoong (Fook Hung), Fook Loey, Ghun Sung, Hip Sun, Hop Sun, Hop Chun, Kingsia, King Sing, Lu Hung, Lop Ty, Saw Yek, Sequa, Sun Ty, Teen Sun (天成), Temsing, Tong Chun, Yok Ee (玉怡), Hook Hong, Hop Loey, Hop Hing, Mau Sun, Kum Cheong, and Tong Mow. Bills of Exchange, 1844–66, reel 86-3147 R-60, HFBR.

109. Compradore: Pay to 1 Contract Man, August 21, 1854; Compradore: Pay Aming A/C 500 pcls Basket Tea from Country, August 21, 1854; Compradore: Pay Sam Yek, October 16, 1854; Compradore: Pay for the Following, December 23, 1854, reel 86-3147 R-60, HFBR. For the upcountry system, see Heard, "Old China and New," 30–32; Marriner, *Rathbones of Liverpool*, 96–97; Lockwood, *Augustine Heard and Company*, 43–46; Zhuang, *Zhongjianshang*, 218, 229; Chen, *Jindai Zhongguo chaye*, 29, 64–66.

110. Compradore: Pay for Box Green Tea, August 16, 1854, is an early example. For more examples, see the orders made in Fuzhou, Bills of Exchange, 1844–66, reel 86-3147 R-60, HFBR. For specific orders that adopted chopped dollars as the currency, see Compradore: Pay to 1 Contract Man, August 21, 1854; Compradore: Pay Aming Account 500 pcls Basket Tea from Country, August 21, 1854; Compradore: Pay Hop Chun, September 16, 1854; Compradore: Pay for the Following Teas, September 21, 1854; Compradore: Pay for the Following Teas, September 21, 1854; Compradore: Pay Hook Loy, September 21, 1854; Compradore: Pay Temsing, October 7, 1854; Compradore:

Pay Aning, October 7, 1854; Compradore: Pay for the Following Chops of Tea, October 11, 1854. Some early orders clarified "taels," "chopped dollars," and "small sycee" as the monetary unit and currency. See Compradore: Pay for 430½ Chs Oolong, August 24, 1854; Compradore: Pay for 105½ C. Oolg, August 24, 1854; Compradore: Pay Hequa for 151 hfchests Congou, August 24, 1854, Bills of Exchange, 1844–66, reel 86-3147 R-60, HFBR.

111. Compradore: Pay to Sung Tai, January 5, 1859; Compradore: Pay to Pow Seu, January 7, 1859; Compradore: Pay to Man Wo, January 7, 1859, Bills of Exchange, 1844–66, reel 86-3147 R-60, HFBR.

112. Compradore: Pay to Com Cheong, February 1, 1860, July 2, 1861; Compradore: Pay to Him Sow, September 22, 1860; Compradore: Pay to Kum Cheong, September 22, 1860; Compradore: Pay to Sun Chum Mow, September 22, 1860; Compradore: Pay to Sun Hop Chun, September 22, 1860, Bills of Exchange, 1844–66, reel 86-3147 R-60, R-61, HFBR. Owing to the limited information offered in the standardized printed orders, it is unclear whether they were all used to settle tea transactions.

113. Compradore: Pay to Amoy Coolie, January 2, 1859, Bills of Exchange, 1844–66, reel 86-3147 R-60, HFBR.

114. Compradore: Pay Foochow Godownman, April 25, 1859, Bills of Exchange, 1844–66, reel 86-3147 R-60, HFBR.

115. For comprador's orders to pay expenses in Shanghai from Canton, see Comprador: Pay Shanghai Coolie, January 12, February 20, April 13, May 13, August 9, September 1, 1847, January 4, March 10, June 8, 1848; Comprador: Pay for Shanghai House, November 11, 1847; Comprador: Pay Ushing Account Shanghai House, December 30, 1847; Comprador: Pay a/c Shanghae House, November 30, 1849; Comprador: Pay to Cannister 500 for Shanghae, August 21, 1851; Comprador: Pay to W. Gilbert Account E. Deacon Shanghae, September 22, 1851; Comprador: Pay (to) Shanghae Tea Boy, September 20, October 23, 1851, March 6, June 14, 1852; Comprador: Pay A/C Shanghae, December 26, 1851; Comprador: Pay to Matting to Shanghae House, May 24, 1852. For payments for tea or accessories charged to the Shanghai branch of Augustine Heard and Company, see Pay Yatchong, January 3, 1851; Comprador: Pay to Yatchong, December 1, 1851; Pay to Asum, December 7, 1851. C. A. Fearon of Augustine Heard and Company in Shanghai also drew on the office in Canton to pay foreign merchants or captains. The check functioned like an inland bill. See the drafts on Augustine Heard & Co., March 27, July 6, 1847, Bills of Exchange, 1844–66, reel 86-3147 R-57, R-58, R-59, HFBR.

116. In addition to the above-mentioned orders, many were written for or in Hong Kong and Macao. See Bills of Exchange, 1844–66, reel 86-3147 R-56 to R-62, HFBR.

117. Pan Jiufen 潘久芬, "Shanghai huihuaqianzhuang ziliao souji zuotanhui jilu" 上海汇划钱庄资料搜集座谈会记录 [Minutes of the Conference on Gathering Information Relating to Shanghai Remittance Qianzhuang], January 26, 1957, in SBPBC, *Shanghai qianzhuang shiliao*, 179. McElderry clarified the stronger influence of Shanxi *piaohaos* in the north and *qianzhuangs* in the south of China. See McElderry, *Shanghai Old-Style Banks*, 12–14. Ray mentioned that *qianzhuangs* also financed trade on the southern China coast without offering much detail. Ray, "Asian Capital," 488.
118. Thomas Walsh to Franklin Gordon Dexter, January 26, 1860, box 3, FGDP.
119. William Appleton & Co. to Franklin Gordon Dexter, September 5, 1859, box 2; Thomas Walsh to Franklin Gordon Dexter, January 26, 1860, and Samuel Hooper to Franklin Gordon Dexter, April 22, 1860, box 3, FGDP.
120. Samuel Hooper to Franklin Gordon Dexter, July 25, 1859, box 2, FGDP. For commission fees charged on transferring funds, also see Francis Blackwell Forbes to Fitz, May 7, 1869, series N, vol. N-1, FFBR.
121. McElderry, *Shanghai Old-Style Banks*, 7–9. For examples of the exchange rates between foreign and Chinese silver, see Forbes, *Remarks on China*, 63.
122. Thomas Walsh to Franklin Gordon Dexter, January 26, 1860, box 3 FGDP; Heard, "Old China and New," 33; Peng, *Zhongguo huobi shi*, 576.
123. Irigoin, "End of a Silver Era," 237.
124. Although the monetary unit was tael or Yang-ping tael in Fujian, the payment was in chopped dollars or "dollar silver." See Thomas Walsh to Franklin Gordon Dexter, January 26, 1860, box 3, FGDP. Also see chopped dollars and small sycee in comprador's orders in note 110. For the definition of "chopped dollars," see Heard, "Old China and New," 32; King, *History of the Hongkong and Shanghai Banking Corporation*, 37.
125. Thomas Walsh to Franklin Gordon Dexter, January 26, 1860, box 3, FGDP. Also see "China," in *Letter from the Secretary of State*, 1857, 197.
126. One hundred taels Canton weight of bar silver were worth 111.30 Shanghai taels in 1870. See "Shanghai, June 16, 1870," *North China Herald*, June 16, 1870, 454. Every 100 Peruvian and Mexican dollars equaled 111 taels of sycee silver in Xiamen, while 100 chopped dollars were valued at 113 taels there. See Macgregor, *Commercial Statistics*, 5:23.
127. Peng, *Zhongguo huobi shi*, 576; Macpherson, "Report on the Trade of Hankow, for the Year 1864," 3–4.
128. Samuel Hooper to Franklin Gordon Dexter, August 30, 1859, box 2, March 22, 1860, box 3; Thomas Walsh to Franklin Gordon Dexter, January 26, April 22, 1860, box 3, FGDP.
129. Coast Exchange, 1859, case 26, folder 49, HFBR.
130. Samuel Hooper to Franklin Gordon Dexter, April 22, 1860, box 3, FGDP.

131. William Appleton & Co. to Franklin Gordon Dexter, August 23, 1859, box 2, FGDP.

132. Russell & Co. A/C Hong Kong, November 25, 1859–March 21, 1860, box 2, FGDP.

133. S. Hooper & Co. in Account Current with Russell & Co. in Foochow, August 18, September 8, October 23, 1860, box 4, FGDP.

134. Francis Blackwell Forbes to Edward Cunningham, August 30, 1869, series N, vol. N-1, FFBR.

135. Zhuang, *Zhongjianshang*, 49–54. Riggs, "Tea Commerce of New York," 296; Le Gendre, "Amoy," 51; "China," in *Letter from the Secretary of State*, 1857, 186, 198.

136. Augustine Heard & Co. to D. G. & W. B. Bacon & Co., January 31, 1862, box 1/8, BCL; Francis Blackwell Forbes to Tyson, September 20, 1866, series N, vol. N-1a, FFBR.

137. Augustine Heard & Co. to D. G. & W. B. Bacon & Co., September 1861, and Augustine Heard & Co. to D. G. & W. B. Bacon & Co., October 14, October [missing], 1861, box 1/2; Augustine Heard & Co. to D. G. & W. B. Bacon & Co., October 24, 1861, box 1/3; Augustine Heard & Co. to D. G. & W. B. Bacon & Co., November 14, 1861, box 1/4; Augustine Heard & Co. to D. G. & W. B. Bacon & Co., December 6, 1861, and Augustine Heard & Co. to D. G. & W. B. Bacon & Co., December 13, 1861, box 1/6, BCL. American companies also settled account balances between its own branches in Shanghai and Hong Kong through bank drafts. See Augustine Heard & Co. in Account Current with Augustine Heard & Co., July 4, August 20, October 24, 1863, Shanghai Account Current: June 1863–May 1864, reel 86-3835 R-87, HFBR; Russell & Co. to Franklin Gordon Dexter, January 14, 1861, box 5, FGDP.

138. Samuel Hooper to Franklin Gordon Dexter, March 22, 1860, box 3, FGDP.

139. Samuel Hooper to Franklin Gordon Dexter, April 22, 1860, box 3, FGDP.

140. Samuel Hooper to Franklin Gordon Dexter, August 30, September 5, 1859, box 2, April 22, 1860, box 3; Thomas Walsh to Franklin Gordon Dexter, January 26, 1860, box 3, FGDP.

141. Samuel Hooper to Franklin Gordon Dexter, August 30, September 5, 1859, box 2; Thomas Walsh to Franklin Gordon Dexter, January 26, 1860, box 3, FGDP.

142. Heard, "Old China and New," 25–26; Bill on Canton, February 4, 1848, Bills of Exchange, 1844–66, reel 86-3147 R-56, HFBR; W. S. Brown to S. G. Rathbone, November 24, 1852, cited in Marriner, *Rathbones of Liverpool*, 179.

143. "Shanghae Market Report, September 13, 1850," *North China Herald*, September 14, 1850, 25; "Shanghae Market Report, October 18, 1850," *North China Herald*, October 19, 1850, 45; "Shanghae Market Report, November

15, 1850," *North China Herald*, November 16, 1850, 61; "Shanghae Market Report, December 20, 1850," *North China Herald*, December 21, 1850, 81; "Shanghae Market Report, February 14, 1851," *North China Herald*, February 15, 1851, 113; "Shanghae Market Report, March 14, 1851," *North China Herald*, March 15, 1851, 130; "Shanghae Market Report, April 11, 1851," *North China Herald*, April 12, 1851, 145. The discount rate was even 28.5–29 percent in December 1855. See "Shanghae Market Report," *North China Herald*, December 8, 1855, 74.

144. Heard, "Old China and New," 26; Chan, *Merchants, Mandarins, and Modern Enterprise*, 43; Mazumdar, *Sugar and Society*, 348; Marriner, *Rathbones of Liverpool*, 203.

145. Augustine Heard & Co. to D. G. & W. B. Bacon & Co., October 31, 1861, box 1/4, BCL.

146. Starting in January 1860, the *North China Herald* published the rates of bills on Hong Kong in Shanghai's money market, but it no longer offered quotations for bills on Canton. See "Quotations (Friday)," *North China Herald*, January 7, 1860, 2; "Quotations (Friday)," *North China Herald*, June 9, 1860, 90; "Shanghai, June 16, 1870," *North China Herald*, June 16, 1870, 454; "Shanghai, October 25, 1870," *North China Herald*, June 16, 1870, 317; Francis Blackwell Forbes to Edward Cunningham, August 19, 1869, series N, vol. N-1, FFBR; Esteves and Nogues-Marco, "Monetary Systems," 455.

147. Marriner, *Rathbones of Liverpool*, 197–98.

148. Francis Blackwell Forbes to King, July 9, 1872, series N, vol. N-5, FFBR.

149. Francis Blackwell Forbes to King, September 4, 1869, series N, vol. N-1, FFBR.

150. "Hankow, June 16, 1870," *North China Herald*, June 16, 1870, 455; J. K. Cunningham to Augustine Heard & Co. Shanghai, May 28, May 31, June 2, 1870, May 21, 1869–June 2, 1870, Letters Received by A. H. & Co. Constituents to A. H. Co., Shanghai, reel 87-1762 R-176, HFBR.

151. Bills of Exchange, 1859–66, reel 86-3147 R-62, HFBR.

152. Francis Blackwell Forbes to King, July 9, 1872, series N, vol. N-5, FFBR.

153. Walter T. Lay, "Foochow Trade Report for the Year 1867," in IGCMC, *Reports on Trade, 1867*, 62.

154. George Hughes, "Amoy Trade Report for the Year 1870," in IGCMC, *Reports on Trade, 1870*, 84.

155. For instance, after sending a box of tea together with other merchandise on October 13, 1868, the Canton office of the company informed the Hong Kong branch of their "Sight Drafts favor Akarm" for $22,000, possibly requesting the latter to pay the Chinese or approve the sum. See Charles W. Orne to Augustine Heard & Co. Hong Kong, October 13, 1868. For the sight drafts in favor of Akarm, see Charles W. Orne to Augustine Heard & Co. Hong Kong,

July 17, 30, August 1, 6, 8, 20, September 6, 21, 26, October 21, 25, November 8, 18, December 9, 24, 1868, January 8, 1869; for others, see August 1, 27, September 1, 2, 21, December 1, 18, 1868, February 9, 1869, June 1868–March 1869 Letters Received by A. H. & Co., Hong Kong from A. H. & Co., Canton, reel 86-1762 R-176, HFBR.

156. The quote is from "Annual Report on Foreign Trade at Foo-chow-foo, for the Year 1868," in *CRHMCC, 1869*, 15. For the exchange rates in Hong Kong and Shanghai, see "Course of Exchange—1867, 1868, and 1869," in ZGJHG-SLBJWYH, *Zhongguo jiuhaiguan shiliao*, 4:1.

157. William Appleton & Co. to Captain William Cole, April 19, 1857, box 2, FGDP. When the letter was written, the company had not yet adopted the Shanghai tael as the monetary unit, a change made later that year. The primary specie circulated in Shanghai were also Spanish dollars, particularly the Carolus, which was also named "Shanghae dollar." See A Shanghai Merchant, "To the Editor of North-China Herald," *North China Herald*, July 28, 1855, 209.

158. Francis Blackwell Forbes to King, September 4, September 15, 1869, series N, vol. N-1, FFBR.

159. Russell & Co., Foochow Account p. *Edith Rose*, October 1859, box 2, FGDP.

160. Bills of Exchange, 1859–66, reel 86-3147 R-62, HFBR.

161. Francis Blackwell Forbes to Edward Cunningham, August 14, 1867, series N, vol. N-1a, FFBR. For the exchange rate of bills on New York sold in Shanghai during the 1880s, see "Commercial Postscript, 14 February, 1883," *North China Herald*, February 14, 1883, 191; "Commercial Postscript, 25 March, 1885," *North China Herald*, March 25, 1885, 368.

162. Officer, *Between the Dollar-Sterling Gold Points*, 61.

163. Lockwood, *Augustine Heard and Company*, 14.

164. Thomas Walsh to Franklin Gordon Dexter, January 26, 1860, box 3, FGDP.

165. Samuel Hooper to Franklin Gordon Dexter, July 25, 1859, box 2, FGDP.

166. Samuel Hooper to Franklin Gordon Dexter, August 30, 1859; William Appleton & Co. to Franklin Gordon Dexter, September 5, 1859, box 2, FGDP.

167. Samuel Hooper to Franklin Gordon Dexter, March 22, April 22, 1860, box 3, FGDP.

4. FROM COMMERCE TO FINANCE

1. Augustine Heard & Co. to D. G. & W. B. Bacon & Co., August 3, 1864, box 3/1, BCL.
2. *Retrospect*, 98. Le Gendre, "Amoy," 52.
3. Francis Blackwell Forbes to E. L. Hales, May 17, 1866; also see Francis Blackwell Forbes to Edward Cunningham, November 23, 1866, series N, vol. N-1a, FFBR.

4. Augustine Heard & Co. to D. G. & W. B. Bacon & Co., June 28, August 26, 1865, box 3/7; September 8, October 15, 1865, box 3/8, BCL.
5. Augustine Heard & Co. to D. G. & W. B. Bacon & Co., October 7, December 23, 1865, box 3/8, BCL.
6. *Retrospect*, 97.
7. G. W. Caine, "Hankow Trade Report," *North China Herald*, September 9, 1869, 488.
8. Francis Blackwell Forbes to Edward Cunningham, September 11, 1869, series N, vol. N-1, FFBR.
9. Davidson, *Island of Formosa*, 375.
10. Chen, *Jindai Zhongguo chaye*, 30–32, 57, 188, 191–95, 266–67; Gardella, *Harvesting Mountains*, 54–69, 123. Gardella places more emphasis on the importance of Chinese capital and native banks than Chen does.
11. Lin, *Cha, tang*, 105–11; Nishimura, "Foreign and Native Banks."
12. *Six Essays*, 6.
13. "Xinü chong chashi" 西女充茶師 [Western woman acting as tea taster], *Shenbao* 申報, January 9, 1873, 3.
14. Stanton et al., *History of Woman Suffrage*, 420, 443n230.
15. Carter, "Oong (Charles) Ar Showe," 17–18.
16. Francis Blackwell Forbes to F. W. Macondray, September 10, 1870, series N, vol. N-2, FFBR.
17. Edward Cunningham to Francis Blackwell Forbes, January 3, 1878, P-55, reel 25, no. 3, folder 2, FFP; Samuel Wetmore to Nathanial Kinsman, May 12, 1842; Samuel Wetmore [?] to Nathanial Kinsman, March 22, 1843, box 3, folder 5, NKP; Levinson, *Great A&P*, 16. Walsh, *Rise and Decline*, 17.
18. Francis Blackwell Forbes to W. M. Clarke, August 10, 1871, series N, vol. N-4, FFBR.
19. Carter, "Oong (Charles) Ar Showe," 16; "Choice New Crop Teas," *American Phrenological Journal* 46, no. 4 (October 1867): 149. For similar advertisements, also see "Albro & Brothers, Wholesale and Retail Dealers in Coffee, Tea, Sugar," *New York Evangelist* 39, no. 17 (April 23, 1868): 5; *Christian Advocate* 43, no. 23 (June 4, 1868): 179, ProQuest American Periodicals.
20. Hoyt, *That Wonderful A & P!*, 33–36; Levinson, *Great A&P*, 20–21, 23–24, 29.
21. "Choice New Crop Teas," 149; "The Great American Tea Company Have Just Received Two Full Cargoes of the Finest New Crop Teas," November 1867, Tea, box 2, WCBA.
22. Hall, *Carter, Macy & Company*, 23–28; Hall, *America's Successful Men*, 132.
23. Robertson, "Report on the Foreign Trade of Canton for the Year 1873," in *CRHMCC, 1873*, 6.

24. Francis Blackwell Forbes to F. W. Macondray, September 10, 1870, series N, vol. N-2, FFBR.
25. "前日之為洋商者, 擁厚貲, 居奇貨, 志高氣豪, 非重酬巨款不足以入其目動其心 . . . 今則爭利者日多, 船舶之價日貶, 運載之費日減, 西來一切貨物日漸薄劣, 而其值較之於前亦少四五倍. 錐刀之末, 無不羣焉赴之." Wang Tao 王韜, "Xiren jianji huashang" 西人漸忌華商 [Westerners are gradually becoming wary of Chinese merchants], 1880, in *WQYWYDSLHB*.
26. Wang, "Xiren jianji huashang," in *WQYWYDSLHB*.
27. Francis Blackwell Forbes to W. M. Clarke, August 10, 1871, series N, vol. N-4, FFBR.
28. Lockwood, *Augustine Heard and Company*, 105.
29. "China Trade for 1862," *Merchants' Magazine and Commercial Review* 49, no. 3 (September 1, 1863): 218; "The China Trade," *Merchants' Magazine and Commercial Review*, July 1, 1868, 29–33, ProQuest American Periodicals; Hippisley, "Part I. Report on the Trade of China," 34–35; Heard, "Old China and New," 1–2, 38; Chen, *Jindai Zhongguo chaye*, 117–20; Ray, "Asian Capital," 476.
30. King, *History of the Hongkong and Shanghai Banking Corporation*, 1:45; Chen, *Jindai Zhongguo chaye*, 31–32, 67; Douglass, *Coming of Age of American Business*, 97.
31. Heard, "Old China and New," 39.
32. *Six Essays*, 65.
33. Robertson, "Report on the Foreign Trade of Canton for the Year 1873," 6.
34. Francis Blackwell Forbes to W. M. Clarke, February 19, 1869, series N, vol. N-1b, FFBR.
35. Heard, "Old China and New," 39.
36. Qtd. in *Six Essays*, 6.
37. James, "International Capital Movements and the Global Order," 2:267, 271.
38. Baster, "Origins of the British Exchange Banks," 145–51.
39. Heard, "Old China and New," 2; Lockwood, *Augustine Heard and Company*, 108; Baster, 145–47. For the effects of the depression of 1865, see Giffen, "On the Fall of Prices," 45; Etherington, "Natal's First Black Capitalists," 34; Lay, "Foochow Trade Report for the Year 1867," 45.
40. Hamashita, *Jindai Zhongguo de guoji qiji*, 202–3; Baster, "Origins of the British Exchange Banks," 146–48; Heard, "Old China and New," 2, 38–39.
41. For account balances, see Augustine Heard & Co. in Account Current with Augustine Heard & Co., July 4, August 20, October 24, 1863, Shanghai Account Current: June 1863–May 1864, reel 86-3835 R-87, HFBR; Russell & Co. to Franklin Gordon Dexter, January 14, 1861, box 5, FGDP. For credit, see Tea from Foochow, Shanghae & Japan, on Joint Account with Augustine Heard & Co., in Account Current with Weston & Gray, October 19, 1867,

1847–75 Orders, Indents, reel 86-4543 R-137; W. Y. Hall to Townend Brother & Bovet, April 5, 1870, Letters of Tea Purchases, 1870, reel 86-3740 R-82, HFBR; Francis Blackwell Forbes to D. O. Clark, October 5, 1866, series N, vol. N-1a, FFBR; Heard, "Old China and New," 38–39; Lockwood, *Augustine Heard and Company*, 108. For the changing relationship between the Heards and the Hongkong and Shanghai Bank, see King, *History of the Hongkong and Shanghai Banking Corporation*, 1:91–93.

42. "Annual Report on Foreign Trade at Foo-chow-foo, for the Year 1868," in *CRHMCC, 1869*, 15.
43. Perkins and Company also planned to contract tea in 1821, but little evidence exists to show the house actualized the plan. Perkins & Co. to James & T. H. Perkins, January 24, 1821, vol. 19, Letter Book, 1820–21, RCR.
44. Heard, "Old China and New," 30; Marriner, *Rathbones of Liverpool*, 96–97; Lockwood, *Augustine Heard and Company*, 44–47; Chen, *Jindai Zhongguo chaye*, 64–67; Russell & Co. to Franklin Gordon Dexter, August 1, 1859, box 2, FGDP; Teas—Report from the 16th to 28th May, 1859; Teas—Report from the 17th to 30th May 1860, 1857–60 Sales, Tea, Foochow: Tea Reports, reel 86-4502 R-136; H. Vaughan to Heard, June 4, 1859, Letters Received from H. Vaughan, reel 89-1713 R-616, HFBR; Francis Blackwell Forbes to Sheppard, January 16, 1873; Francis Blackwell Forbes to Fitz, January 21, March 22, 1873, series N, vol. N-7, FFBR.
45. Francis Blackwell Forbes to Edward Cunningham, November 9, 1872, series N, vol. N-6, FFBR.
46. Edward Cunningham to Paul Siemen Forbes, October 5, 1856, box 2, folder 23, FFBR.
47. Francis Blackwell Forbes to Edward Cunningham, January 31, 1868, series N, vol. N-1a, FFBR. For the identity of Hermann Wallich, see King, *History of the Hongkong and Shanghai Banking Corporation*, 1:46; Moazzin, *Foreign Banks*, 26.
48. Francis Blackwell Forbes to F. W. Pomeroy, April 23, 1870, series N, vol. N-2, FFBR.
49. Hankou was located in the Yangzi River area. Francis Blackwell Forbes to Cordier, July 21, 1870, series N, vol. N-2, FFBR.
50. Francis Blackwell Forbes to Will H. Forbes, April 17, 1873, series N, vol. N-7, FFBR.
51. Francis Blackwell Forbes to Fitz, February 20, April 8, 1873, and Francis Blackwell Forbes to Will H. Forbes, April 17, 1873, series N, vol. N-7, FFBR.
52. Francis Blackwell Forbes to Will H. Forbes, January 23, 1873, series N, vol. N-7, FFBR.
53. Francis Blackwell Forbes to Sheppard, March 22, 1873, and Francis Blackwell Forbes to Will H. Forbes, April 17, 1873, series N, vol. N-7, FFBR.

54. *Six Essays*, 69–71; McElderry, *Shanghai Old-Style Banks*, 4; King, *History of the Hongkong and Shanghai Banking Corporation*, 1:19, 83; Purtle, "Money Making Nation," 107–8.
55. Francis Blackwell Forbes to William M. Clarke, August 24, 1866, series N, vol. N-1a, FFBR.
56. "China Branch of the Oriental Bank," *North China Herald*, December 14, 1850, 77, and January 25, 1851, 102; "Quotations. Commercial Bank of India," *North China Herald*, March 1, 1862, 34.
57. Comprador Pay Commercial Bank of India, September 11, 1854; Comprador, Pay to Mercantile Bank for Bills on England, October 7, 1854; Comprador, Pay to Oriental Bank for Bills on Bombay, November 7, 1854; Comprador, Pay to Mercantile Bank of India for Bills on England & Bombay, November 25, 1854; Comprador, Pay to Mercantile Bank of India for Bills on Bombay, December 11, 1854; Comprador: Pay to Mercantile Bank for Bill on Calcutta, December 28, 1854, Bills of Exchange, 1844–66, reel 86-3147 R-60, HFBR.
58. "蓋西商之辦茶也, 所用銀者多, 銀行所借也一日, 而買數萬之貨已, 無此銖則必託銀行以匯之, 乃西例." "Lun sicha gongli xingui yi congshi" 論絲茶公立新規宜從事 [We should follow the new regulations on silk and tea trade], May 17, 1873, *Shenbao*, no. 322.
59. "New York Letter," *Capital* (Washington DC), October 19, 1872, 3, America's Historical Newspapers; *Cairo (IL) Daily Bulletin*, February 23, 1872, Chronicling America.
60. Levinson, *Great A&P*, 29.
61. M. M. De Lano, "Foochow," October 28, 1874, in *Letter from the Secretary of State*, September 30, 1874, 241–42; Bn. De Meritens, "Rapport Annuel Sur Le Commerce De Foochow," in IGCMC, *Reports on Trade, 1869*, 79; Rowe, *Hankow*, 131.
62. The quote is from H. E. Hobson, "Hankow Trade Report for the Year 1869," in IGCMC, *Reports on Trade, 1869*, 21. Also see Macpherson, "Report on the Trade of Hankow, for the Year 1864," in IGCMC, *Reports on Trade, 1864*, 12; MacPherson, "Hankow Trade Report for the Years 1871–72," in IGCMC, *Reports on Trade, 1871–1872*, 55.
63. "每歲春夏客商麕集, 西洋人亦時至, 但非我族類, 道路以目, 留數日輒去." Tu Jiajie 涂家杰, *Yining zhouzhi* 義寧州志 [Gazetteer of Yining District], comp. 1873, vol. 8 Dili zhi-Tuchan 地理志 土產 [Geographical records—local products], Erudition 爱如生中國方志庫.
64. De Lano, "Foochow," 242; De Meritens, "Rapport Annuel Sur Le Commerce De Foochow," 79.
65. These brokers were known as native "teamen" in English records. See De Lano, "Foochow," 241; Liu, *Tea War*, 53–54.

66. "沪城内外, 近来设有丝茶专栈." Zhuang, *Zhongjianshang*, 23. Wang's book was published in 1871, but he had started drafting it in the late 1850s. See Yu, "Lun Wang Tao," 243.
67. Ge, *Huyou Zaji*, 4:43–44.
68. "H. B. M. Consular Court, Foochow," *North China Herald*, October 13, 1860, 165.
69. De Champs, "Kiukiang Trade Report for the Year 1867," in IGCMC, *Reports on Trade, 1867*, appendix, 8.
70. "Hangao chawu" 漢臯茶務 [Hankou tea economy], March 13, 1889, *Shenbao*, no. 5708; Zheng, "Zhi Tangjun Qiaoqing shu" 致唐君翹卿書, in *Shengshi weiyan houbian*, 6:29. For the descriptions of Hankou tea brokers in previous scholarship, see Rowe, *Hankow*, 130–36; Zhuang, *Zhongjianshang*, 231.
71. TTEA, *Historical Brevities*, 50.
72. Yu Xie 俞燮, "Nigailiang huizhou chaye yijianshu (xu)" 拟改良徽州茶业意见书 (续) [Tentative recommendations on reforming Huizhou's tea trade (continued)], *Zhonghua shiyejie* 中华实业界 2, no. 4 (1915): 19–20. Zhuang, *Zhongjianshang*, 239–47, Chinese Periodical Full-text Database 全国报刊索引. For the role of linguists in the Canton trade, see Downs, *Golden Ghetto*, 22–24. "China," in *Letter from the Secretary of State*, 1842, 67.
73. "货售归银, 不烦客虑." Wang Tao's quote is cited in Zhuang, *Zhongjianshang*, 23.
74. De Meritens, "Rapport Annuel Sur Le Commerce De Foochow," 79; "H. B. M. Consular Court," 166; P. Giquel, "Report on the Trade of Ningpo, for the Year 1864," in IGCMC, *Reports on Trade, 1864*, 3; J. J. Henderson, "Amoy," September 30, 1874, in *Letter from the Secretary of State*, 1874, 229; Wagel, *Finance in China*, 115; Zhuang, *Zhongjianshang*, 218, 231. Scholars have debated the relationship between *zhans* and compradors. A camp of researchers, such as Chen and Liu, presented tea *zhans* as warehouses owned by compradors, who worked for or maintained close connections with foreign companies. However, admitting that many compradors were warehouses owners or managers, the other camp, primarily Zhuang and Gardella, identified the *zhans* as independent and distinct institutions from compradors, as compradors had to purchase from tea *zhans* rather than from growers. See Chen, *Jindai Zhongguo chaye*, 60–63; Liu, *Tea War*, 247–48; Gardella, *Harvesting Mountains*, 57, 123; Zhuang, *Zhongjianshang*, 217–21, 244–45, 250.
75. Zhuang, *Zhongjianshang*, 203–12. Different from Zhuang, Kuo-Tung Ch'en argues that tea warehouses already acted as brokers for the EIC in the 1820s. This book adopts Zhuang's argument. See Ch'en, "Transaction Practices," 746, 751. For the function of a *yahang*, also see Wong, "China before Capitalism," 1:137. For *zhans*, also see Peng, *Zhongguo gongshang hanghui shiliao ji*, 2:850–53; Chen, *Jindai Zhongguo chaye*, 62.

76. Yu Xie 俞燮, "Chaye gailun shangbian I (xu)" 茶業概論上編 (續) [A survey of the tea economy I (continued)], *Shiye zazhi* 實業雜誌 [Industry magazine] 2, no. 2 (1921): 10. Wu, *Wanzhe xin'anjiangliuyu,* 5–6, Chinese Periodical Full-text Database 全国报刊索引.
77. Zhuang, *Zhongjianshang*, 156–57.
78. "Shangren Zhang Xinxian wei bingqing kaishe Dunli hao yi yu yingshang maoyi shi" 商人张新贤为禀请开设敦利号以与英商贸易事 [Merchant Zhang Xinxian's application to open the Dunli Company for trading with British merchants], in Wang, *Xijian qingshi shiliao*, 30–31.
79. Zhuang, *Zhongjianshang*, 227–28.
80. Zhuang, *Zhongjianshang*, 107–8, 132–33, 227–28.
81. "茶棧為茶業買賣機關, 居茶商與洋行之間, 專事介紹輸出貿易, 又為茶業金融機關." Wu, *Wanzhe xin'anjiangliuyu,* 5. Also see Chen, *Jindai Zhongguo chaye*, 62; Liu, *Tea War*, 248–53; Zhuang, *Zhongjianshang*, 132–37.
82. Ch'en, "Transaction Practices," 746–47, 749–51.
83. "以近年放水脚觀之, 不啻暗發資本矣." Yu Xie 俞燮, "Yu Huizhou zhujun shangque gailiangshu" 與徽州茶業諸君商榷改良書 [A discussion with Huizhou tea merchants on reforming the tea trade], *Zhonghua guohuo yuebao* 中华国货月报 [Chinese national goods monthly] 1, no. 1 (1915): 6, 7, Chinese Periodical Full-text Database 全国报刊索引. Also see Zhuang, *Zhongjianshang*, 57, 147–48. The financial role of middlemen was critical to many cash crop economies. See Woodman, *King Cotton*, 8–14, 30–42; Ward, "Cash or Credit Crops?"; Faure, *Rural Economy*, 100.
84. J. Neumann, "Wenchow Trade Report for the Year 1888," in ZGJHGSLBJWYH, *Zhongguo jiuhaiguan shiliao*, 14:254.
85. "蓋茶棧之魄力可以操縱茶號之增減, 山價之貴賤 (如近年茶棧放水脚銀寬則茶號加增, 山價昂貴, 其明證也)." Yu, "Yu Huizhou zhujun shangque gailiangshu," 5.
86. Yu, "Yu Huizhou zhujun shangque gailiangshu," 7.
87. Yu, "Nigailiang huizhou chaye yijianshu (xu)," 18.
88. Zhang, Wang, and Sun, *Huishang yanjiu*, 593–94. The source does not clarify when the cooperation between Tang and Jiang started. However, it mentions that Jiang was only twenty years old at that time. When Jiang's father passed away in the first year of Emperor Tongzhi's reign (1862), Jiang was fifteen years old. Therefore the credit relationship should have started by 1867.
89. Xu Shukai 徐澍楷 and Lei Chunzhao 雷春诏, "Wuchan-Hongcha" 物产红茶 [Local products—black tea], *Hefengzhou zhi xu* 鹤峰州志续 [The sequel to the gazetteer of the Hefeng subprefecture], comp. 1867 and recomp. 1885, vol. 7. The *Hubei tongzhi* also asserts that the establishment of tea warehouses had attracted merchants from afar to the Hefeng subprefecture since the reign

of Xianfeng (1831–61), generating profits for dealers and growers in urban and rural areas. See Yang Cengxi 杨承禧, "Hefengzhou zhi" 鶴峰州志 [Gazetteer of the Hefeng subprefecture], *Hubei tongzhi* 湖北通志 [The complete gazetteer of Hubei], comp. 1921, in Wu, *Zhongguo difangzhi*, 421, 379.

90. Peng, *Zhongguo gongshang hanghui shiliao ji*, 2:21.

91. H. E. Hobson, "Tamsui Trade Report for the Years 1869–72," in IGCMC, *Reports on Trade, 1871–1872*, 159.

92. Liu, *Tea War*, 250; Washington Letter to the Philadelphia Ledger, "Better and Cheaper Tea."

93. TTEA, *Historical Brevities*, 48–50; Zheng, *Shanghai qianzhuang*, 68.

94. "其實栈家放出之款項, 又多由银行錢莊移来, 言明夏季及秋季陸續歸還; 而栈家唯恐失信於银行錢莊, 故不准莊家另投他栈, 獨行消售." Yu, "Hongcha jingying zhi mijue," 8. Also cited in Zhuang, *Zhongjianshang*, 147–48.

95. Robertson, "Report on the Foreign Trade of Canton for the Year 1873," 7.

96. "内地茶号, 赖茶栈予以垫款之便利, 茶栈则赖钱庄银行予以金融之调节." *Cha* 茶 [Tea], December 1931, 62–63, in SBPBC, *Shanghai qianzhuang shiliao*, 176.

97. "Sicha liangye youwu zhuanji shuo" 絲茶兩業有無轉機說 [On the prospect for improving the tea and silk trade], April 27, 1879, *Shenbao*, no. 2149.

98. Zhuang, *Zhongjianshang*, 107–8.

99. "交結洋商, 挹注莊款, 應酬闊綽, 日用浩繁." "Sicha liangye youwu zhuanji shuo."

100. Ma Jianzhong 馬建忠, "Fumin shuo" 富民說 [On enriching the people], 1890, in *WQYWYDSLHB*.

101. "大凡新創一棧, 各錢莊知該東實有家資, 莫不紛紛送摺, 每莊往來動以一二萬或三四萬, 少亦數千金. 故一半月之間, 數十萬籌集不暇." "Chaye youguan guoke yi" 茶業有關國課議 [Tea is essential to national tax revenue], November 21, 1889, *Shenbao*, no. 5961.

102. "Sicha liangye youwu zhuanji shuo"; "Chaye youguan guoke yi."

103. Francis W. White, "Ningpo Trade Report for the Years 1871–72," in IGCMC, *Reports on Trade, 1871–1872*, 139.

104. Davidson, *Island of Formosa*, 375–76.

105. "故常見負重利之賬以圖再獲盈餘之利者, 不但不能還利而且反至虧本, 人亦何樂而爲之乎." "Shanghai yingen jinnian yujin" 上海銀根今年愈緊 [Shanghai's money supply further tightened this year], December 25, 1873, *Shenbao*, no. 511.

106. Heard, "Old China and New," 2.

107. Robertson, "Report on the Foreign Trade of Canton for the Year 1873," 6.

108. Francis Blackwell Forbes to W. M. Clarke, August 10, 1871, series N, vol. N-4, FFBR; *Six Essays*, 6; Heard, "Old China and New," 39.

109. Francis Blackwell Forbes to F. W. Macondray, September 10, 1870, series N, vol. N-2, FFBR.
110. McElderry, *Shanghai Old-Style Banks*, 21.
111. Yao Gonghe 姚公鶴, "Shanghai xianhua" 上海閒話 [Anecdotes from Shanghai], and "Da jiyangjushi caifang hushi gongsi qingxing shu" 答暨陽居士採訪滬市公司情形書 [In response to the Hermit of Jiyang on the state of Shanghai companies], *Shenbao*, January 12, 1884, in SBPBC, *Shanghai qianzhuang shiliao*, 29; Cheng, *Banking in Modern China*, 16; McElderry, *Shanghai Old-Style Banks*, 21–22.
112. "Da Jiyang jushi caifang hushigongsi qingxingshu," in SBPBC, *Shanghai qianzhuang shiliao*, 29; Cheng, *Banking in Modern China*, 20; "China Branch of the Oriental Bank."
113. R. B. Moorhead, "Hankow," in IGCMC, *Decennial Reports, 1882–1891*, 177.
114. "据某茶栈领袖言，茶栈与钱庄往来约占四分之三，与银行往来约占四分之一." *Cha*, in SBPBC, *Shanghai qianzhuang shiliao*, 176. The banks likely referred to Chinese modern banks.
115. De Lano, "Foochow," 241. Also see Chen, *Jindai Zhongguo chaye*, 69; Charles A. Sinclair, "Report on the Trade of Foochow for the Year 1881," in *CRHMCC, 1881*, part 1, 15.
116. "Native Banks in Foochow," 447. "Why Chinese Native Banks Are More Powerful Than Modern Banks," *Chinese Economic Bulletin* 8 (1926): 134–35; Bergère, *Golden Age*, 90; McElderry, *Shanghai Old-Style Banks*, 17–18; Zheng, *Shanghai qianzhuang*, 66–68.
117. For the term of most bills on London employed in the China trade, see Hidy, *House of Baring*, 353–54; Lockwood, *Augustine Heard and Company*, 22–23; Marriner, *Rathbones of Liverpool*, 191–92. For the term in the Atlantic world, see Lepler, *Many Panics*, 28–29; Price, "Joshua Johnson in London," 165; Perkins, *Financing Anglo-American Trade*, 135.
118. Marriner, *Rathbones of Liverpool*, 192–94.
119. Lay, "Foochow Trade Report for the Year 1867," 45; Marriner, *Rathbones of Liverpool*, 193.
120. Francis Blackwell Forbes to William M. Clarke, August 29, 1866, series N, vol. N-1a, FFBR.
121. Francis Blackwell Forbes to William M. Clarke, August 29, 1866. Some importers commissioned steamers to ship new teas to America as early and quickly as possible. However, when time was not so critical, American merchants still employed tea clippers due to their lower cost of shipping. See Ira W. Steward to Hoffman Atkinson, October 25, 1869, IWSL, Rare Books and Manuscripts Division, New York Public Library.

122. Marriner, *Rathbones of Liverpool*, 193; Lay, "Foochow Trade Report for the Year 1867," 45.
123. Francis Blackwell Forbes to Edward Cunningham, August 28, 1866, series N, vol. N-1a, FFBR.
124. Lay, "Foochow Trade Report for the Year 1867," 45; Marriner, *Rathbones of Liverpool*, 194; King, *History of the Hongkong and Shanghai Banking Corporation*, 1:85, 185.
125. For the amount of Merchant and Bank Papers sold in Shanghai, 1864–66, see Charles A. Winchester, "Shanghai," in *Commercial Reports from Her Majesty's Consuls in China, Japan, and Siam, 1865–66*, 107.
126. Francis Blackwell Forbes to D. O. Clark, July 9, 1866, series N, vol. N-1a, FFBR.
127. Forbes, *Personal Reminiscences*, 361.
128. Marriner, *Rathbones of Liverpool*, 204.
129. [Russell & Co.] to Franklin Gordon Dexter, March 21, 1860, box 3, FGDP.
130. Augustine Heard & Co. to D. G. & W. B. Bacon & Co., October 31, 1861, box 1/4; Augustine Heard & Co. to D. G. & W. B. Bacon & Co., January 14, 1862, box 1/7, BCL.
131. Francis Blackwell Forbes to E. Cordier, July 28, 1866, series N, vol. N-1a, FFBR.
132. Lockwood, *Augustine Heard and Company*, 108.
133. Francis Blackwell Forbes to [George] Tyson, October 8, 1867, series N, vol. N-1a, FFBR.
134. "Highest and Lowest Rates of Exchange at Shanghai for Bank Demand Drafts on London, 1872–91," in IGCMC, *Decennial Reports, 1882–1891, Appendix I.—Trade Statistics*, xvi.
135. For low exchange rate in 1867–76, see Lay, "Foochow Trade Report for the Year 1867," 45; Francis Blackwell Forbes to W. F. Babcock, November 14, 1868, Francis Blackwell Forbes to W. M. Clarke, November 14, 1868, vol. N-1b, and Francis Blackwell Forbes to J. Webster, March 19, 1869, vol. N-1, series N, FFBR; De Meritens, "Foochow Trade Report for the Year 1870," in IGCMC, *Reports on Trade, 1870*, 77; Hippisley, "Part I. Report on the Trade of China," 35. For U.S. duty, see *Six Essays*, 33; Francis W. White, "Ningpo Trade Report for the Years 1872" and George Hughes, "Amoy Trade Report for the Years 1872," in IGCMC, *Reports on Trade, 1871–1872*, 140, 180.
136. Marriner, *Rathbones of Liverpool*, 217–18.
137. Francis Blackwell Forbes to E. L. Hales, May 17, 1866, series N, vol. N-1a, FFBR.
138. James Jones, "Amoy Trade Report for the Year 1868," in IGCMC, *Reports on Trade, 1868*, 72.

139. Francis Blackwell Forbes to W. M. Clarke, August 10, 1871, series N, vol. N-4, FFBR.

140. *Retrospect*, 97.

141. Francis Blackwell Forbes to Will H. Forbes, December 19, 1872, series N, vol. N-6, FFBR.

142. Hughes, "Amoy Trade Report for the Years 1872," in IGCMC, *Reports on Trade, 1871–1872*, 180.

143. Francis W. White, "Ningpo Trade Report for the Years 1871–72," in IGCMC, *Reports on Trade, 1870*, 139–40; Hughes, "Amoy Trade Report for the Years 1872," 180–81. For accounts of losses, see Jones, "Amoy Trade Report for the Year 1868," in IGCMC, *Reports on Trade, 1868*, 72; Francis Blackwell Forbes to P. S. Forbes, care of Baring Brothers & Co., April 22, 1869, and Francis Blackwell Forbes to Thomas Walsh, August 19, 1869, series N, vol. N-1, FFBR; H. E. Hobson, "Tamsui Trade Report for the Years 1869–72" and "Tamsui (Formosa) Trade Report for the Year 1873," in IGCMC, *Reports on Trade, 1871–1872*, 159; *1873*, 94–95.

144. The quotation is from Jas. K. Leonard, "Ningpo Trade Report for the Year 1867," in IGCMC, *Reports on Trade, 1867*, 41. For similar comments in the 1860s–70s, see Augustine Heard & Co. to D. G. & W. B. Bacon & Co., January 22, 1862, box 1/8, BCL; J. Alex Man, "Amoy Trade Report for the Year 1867," in IGCMC, *Reports on Trade, 1867*, 70; Jas Smith, "Foochow Trade Report for the Year 1868," in IGCMC, *Reports on Trade, 1868*, 65; "Annual Report on Foreign Trade at Foo-chow-foo, for the Year 1868," in *CRHMCC, 1869*, 12; Francis Blackwell Forbes to King, August 25, 1869, series N, vol. N-1, FFBR; J. K. Cunningham to Augustine Heard & Co. Shanghai, May 28, 1870, A. Heard & Co., Letters Received—May 21, 1869–June 2, 1870, Constituents to A. H. Co., Shanghai, reel 87-1762 R-176, HFBR; Hughes, "Amoy Trade Report for the Year 1870," in IGCMC, *Reports on Trade, 1870*, 95; "Shanghai, October 25, 1870," *North China Herald*, June 16, 1870, 317; Hughes, "Amoy Trade Report for the Years 1872," 180; M. E. Bennett to George Basil Dixwell, May 22, 1872, Documents and Memos of Dust in Oolong, 1871–72, HFBR; *Retrospect*, 97, 118; Hughes, "Amoy Trade Report for the Year 1873," in IGCMC, *Reports on Trade, 1873*, 126.

145. Smith, "Foochow Trade Report for the Year 1868," 65; "Hankou laixin."

146. "Shanghai, June 16, 1870," *North China Herald*, June 16, 1870, 453.

147. For dusty tea, see *Retrospect*, 124–25; Hugh Vaughan to Heard, November 26, 1859, Letters Received from H. Vaughan, 1859, reel 89-1713 R-616, and Sixteen Firms' Petition to the Trade Committee of Fuh Keen, April 10, 1872, Documents and Memos, Dust in Oolongs, reel 86-4543 R-137, HFBR.

148. *Six Essays*, 33.

149. Robertson, "Report on the Foreign Trade of Canton for the Year 1873," 7; and "Annual Report on Foreign Trade at Foo-chow-foo, for the Year 1868," in *CRHMCC, 1869*, 14.
150. "Annual Report on Foreign Trade at Foo-chow-foo," 14.
151. Francis Blackwell Forbes to W. M. Clarke, November 14, 1868, series N, vol. N-1b, FFBR.
152. Francis Blackwell Forbes to P. S. Forbes, care of Baring Brothers & Co., April 22, 1869.
153. Hughes, "Amoy Trade Report for the Years 1872," 180.
154. Francis Blackwell Forbes to W. M. Clarke, November 14, 1868, series N, vol. N-1b, FFBR; Le Gendre, "Amoy," 57.

PART 3

1. "About Green Tea," *Pall Mall Gazette*, February 1, 1886; "The Cup That May Cheer, Yet May Injure," *Christian Union* 39, no. 26 (June 27, 1889): 821; "United States English," *Littell's Living Age* 120, no. 1546 (January 24, 1874): 242, ProQuest American Periodicals.
2. Heard, "Old China and New," 19.
3. "Concerning Tea," 6.
4. "Varieties," *Blackburn Standard* (Lancashire, England), June 12, 1886, 2, British Library Newspapers.
5. "Consistency," *Harper's Bazaar* 31, no. 47 (November 19, 1898): 1008, ProQuest American Periodicals.
6. "One Good Cup of Tea," *Washington Post*, February 23, 1890, 9, ProQuest Historical Newspapers.
7. Anderson, *Breakfast*, 15.
8. Anderson, *Breakfast*, 191n46.
9. May 2, Memoranda Book, Canton, China, 1801, box 1, folder 8, SDP; Philanthropus, *Lady & Gentleman's Tea-Table*, 16–17; Stevens, *On the Stowage of Ships*, 657. While the original Chinese term is 白毫, referring to the white hair leaf, English-language records transliterated it in various ways. The spelling in Sullivan's memoranda book is Pakhoo, and the other two sources used Pekoe.
10. For the meaning of Pouchong, see May 2, Memoranda Book, Canton, China, 1801; USDCL, "World's Production," 132; Chen, *Zhongguo chaye dacidian*, 270. For the descriptions of the Pouchong tea as black tea, see Walsh and Saunders, *"Cup of Tea,"* 109, 113; S. Wells Williams, "ART. I.—The Middle Kingdom," *North American Review* 67, no. 141 (October 1848): 289, ProQuest American Periodicals; Downs, *Golden Ghetto*, 67. For Oolong pouchong, see *American and Commercial Daily Advertiser* (Baltimore), September 18, November 14, 1840, 3; "State of Trade," *New York Herald*, October 25, 1844, 3, America's

Historical Newspapers; Extract from J. Caswell & Co.'s Order for Tea, Order for Teas & Sundries from Cassidy & Cheerer, New York, February 14, 1852, 1847–75 Orders, Indents, reel 86-4543 R-137, HFBR; "Memorandum for an Amoy Cargo," April 23, 1859, box 2, FGDP.

11. *Baltimore Sun*, March 7, 1846, 2; "Teas!" *Pittsfield Sun*, February 25, 1847, 3, America's Historical Newspapers; "Pekin Tea Company," *Mechanic's Advocate* 2, no. 4 (January 1, 1848): 30, ProQuest American Periodicals. The same advertisements usually appeared multiple times throughout the year. For tea retailing, see Carter, "Oong (Charles) Ar Showe," 6–7.
12. Heard, "Old China and New," 18–19. Also cited in Hao, "Chinese Teas to America," 28. For the conventional ranks of tea, also see Copy of Instructions sent to Mess. Augustine Heard & Co. Hong Kong, May 6, 1858, Letters Received from Miscellaneous, Domestic, 1855–64, reel 89-1713 R-616, HFBR.
13. Memo Edith Rose's Tea from Foochow, September 1859, box 2, FGDP.
14. Memorandum for a Foochow Cargo, April 23, 1859, box 2, FGDP.
15. "Tea Leaves," *Overland Monthly and Out West Magazine* 3, no. 6 (December 1869): 540, ProQuest American Periodicals.
16. Riggs, "Tea Commerce of New York," 303.
17. Yu, "Youmei diaocha chaye zhi baogaoshu" 游美调查茶业之报告书 [Investigation report on U.S. tea economy], *Zhonghua shiyejie* 中华实业界 2, no. 10 (1915): 8, Chinese Periodical Full-text Database 全国报刊索引.
18. "Medicines Which Increase the Secretion of Milk," *United States Medical Investigator* 6, no. 5 (September 1, 1877): 261, ProQuest American Periodicals.
19. "Five O'clock Tea," *Harper's Bazaar* 21, no. 15 (April 14, 1888): 244, ProQuest American Periodicals.
20. Helen C. Weeks, "Black and Green," *Youth's Companion* 43, no. 43 (October 27, 1870): 344, ProQuest American Periodicals.
21. Walsh and Saunders, *"Cup of Tea,"* 130, 144, 147.
22. "Household: Over the Teacups," *Christian Advocate*, December 7, 1905, 1970; Katherine Louise Smith, "A Cha-na-yu Party in a Boston Drawing-Room," *Boston Cooking School Magazine of Culinary Science and Domestic Economics* 9, no. 10 (May 1, 1905): 483, ProQuest American Periodicals.
23. Walsh and Saunders, *"Cup of Tea,"* 124–25; *Retrospect*, 120; "For Drinkers of Tea," *New York Times*, December 11, 1870, 8, ProQuest Historical Newspapers.
24. "Editorial Paragraphs," *Baptist Missionary Magazine* 53, no. 5 (May 1873): 158, ProQuest American Periodicals.
25. "Concerning Tea," 6.
26. Ukers, *All about Tea*, 2:512.
27. Carter, "Oong (Charles) Ar Showe," 6–7; "Thea-Nectar Is a Pure Black Tea," *Working Christian* (South Carolina), April 18, 1871, Chronicling America.

28. Yu, "Youmei diaocha," 4.
29. Thomas A. Phelan, *Some Secrets of Tea* (The National Tea Association of the United States of America, 1905), 11, Tea, box 5, WCBA.
30. Yu, "Youmei diaocha," 4.

5. BOOMS AND BUSTS

1. From the *London Daily Mail*, "China Losing Tea Trade: Skillful Advertising Has Turned Taste in Other Directions," *Washington Post*, December 14, 1902, 22, ProQuest Historical Newspapers.
2. "茶為我國特產 . . . 國外銷路之被奪可知, 不謀自振茶市將傾." Huang and Pang, *Zhongguo shangzhan shibaishi*, "出版說明" [note for publication].
3. *Currency in the East*, 13.
4. Chen, *Jindai Zhongguo chaye*, 56–57, 221–55, 267; Shi, *Jinshi yilai shijie chayeshichang*, 148–70; Zhong, *Chaye yu yapian*, 90–92; Li and Ding, "Qingmo zhongmei chaye maoyi," 93–96.
5. Francis Blackwell Forbes to Edward Cunningham, February 11, 1873, series N, vol. N-7, FFBR.
6. Heard, "Old China and New," 39.
7. Francis Blackwell Forbes to Gay, January 25, 1873, series N, vol. N-7, FFBR.
8. Francis Blackwell Forbes to Gay, January 25, 1873.
9. "Lun Hankou chawu" 论汉口茶务 [On the tea trade in Hankou], in *Huangchao jingshiwen tongbian*, Juan 61 Licai bu liu-chawu 卷 61 理财部六 茶务 [Vol. 61, Economics, section 6: Tea sector]. Although this anthology, *Huangchao jingshiwen tongbian*, was published in 1901, the essays in the collection were written through the Qing dynasty. The author's focus on Hankou's deterioration as a major tea port suggests that this article was composed after 1870.
10. Remer, "International Trade," 602–3.
11. "中國之業茶者咸同以前無不致富, 光緒以後多至傾頹, 自庚辰以來, 竟一年不如一年." "Chashang yongyue" 茶商踴躍 [Tea merchants are active], March 13, 1889, *Shenbao*, no. 5708.
12. Yu, "Nigailiang huizhou chaye yijianshu" 拟改良徽州茶业意见书 [Tentative recommendations on reforming Huizhou's tea trade], *Zhonghua shiyejie* 中华实业界 2, no. 2 (1915): 1, Chinese Periodical Full-text Database 全国报刊索引.
13. The tea trade with the United States in Shanghai and its supplying ports (Jiujiang and Ningbo) and Danshui improved slightly in 1888. Tea speculations resurged amidst the Sino-Japanese War. The shipments to America also grew during the Boxer Uprising in 1900, the Chinese government's reduction of the custom duty in 1901, and the abolition of the tea tariff in the United States in 1902. See C. Lenox Simpson, "Kiukiang Trade Report for the Year 1888"; M.

Boyd Bredon, "Shanghai Trade Report for the Year 1888"; F. Kleinwachter, "Ningpo Trade Report for the Year 1888"; J. L. Chalmers, "Tamsui Trade Report for the Year 1888"; Hippisley, "Shanghai Trade Report for the Year 1895"; Hy. Edgar, "Foochow Trade Report for the Year 1895"; James W. Carrall, "Amoy Trade Report for the Year 1895"; F. E. Taylor, "Report on the Foreign Trade of China for the Year 1900" and "Report on the Foreign Trade of China for the Year 1902"; H. B. Morse, "Report on the Foreign Trade of China for the Year 1903," in ZGJHGSLBJWYH, *Zhongguo jiuhaiguan shiliao*, 14:160–61, 223–24, 269–70, 331, 23:253, 366–67, 428–29, 31:14, 35:8, 37:5, 9.

14. "Chaye youguan guoke yi," November 21, 1889. Also see "Lun Zhongguo chaye zhi pi" 論中國茶業之疲 [On China's dull tea economy], *Shenbao*, June 18, 1886. On tea merchants' hardships, see Sheng Xuanhuai 盛宣懷, "Qing jianqing chashui zhe" 請減輕茶稅摺 [Memorial on tea tax reduction], March 1902; "Zunzhi michou jiashui mianli shiyi zhe" 遵旨密籌加稅免釐事宜摺 [Memorial on confidential plans to implement the throne's decree for tax increases and Likin abolition], May 1902, in *WQYWYDSLHB*.
15. Francis Blackwell Forbes to Paul S. Forbes, January 23, 1873. Also see Francis Blackwell Forbes to W. M. Clarke, March 10, 1873, and Francis Blackwell Forbes to Paul S. Forbes, April 10, 1873, series N, vol. N-7, FFBR.
16. Edward Cunningham to Francis Blackwell Forbes, January 21, 1876, P-55, reel 25, no. 3, folder 2, FFP.
17. Edward Cunningham to Francis Blackwell Forbes, June 21, 1876, P-55, reel 25, no. 3, folder 2, FFP.
18. Norwood, *Trading Freedom*, 163.
19. Francis Blackwell Forbes to Will H. Forbes, January 15, 1873, series N, vol. N-7, FFBR; Edward Cunningham to Francis Blackwell Forbes, January 21, 1876, P-55, reel 25, no. 3, folder 2, FFP.
20. For the losses, see Edward Cunningham to Francis Blackwell Forbes, January 21, February 15, 1876; for the close ties between Russell and Company and John. M. Forbes and Company, see Edward Cunningham to Francis Blackwell Forbes, December 21, 1877, January 3, 1878, P-55, reel 25, no. 3, folder 2, FFP; Memo of China Goods, circa July 1860, box 3, FGDP. For the 2024 value, see Williamson, "Seven Ways."
21. Edward Cunningham to Francis Blackwell Forbes, January 21, December 21, 1876, December 1, 1877, January 3, 1878, P-55, reel 25, no. 3, folder 2, FFP.
22. De Lano, "The Tea Trade of Foo-Chow for 1880," 81, box 32, PRWS.
23. "Returns of Trade at the Treaty Ports, for the Year 1882," in ZGJHGSLBJWYH, *Zhongguo jiuhaiguan shiliao*, 9:462.
24. "Zhengshi" 政事 [Political affairs], *Nongshang gongbao* 農商公報 [Agriculture and commerce news], no. 20 (March 1, 1916): 9, in Yao, *Zhongguo jindai*

duiwaimaoyishi ziliao, 3:1476; "Zaji" 杂记 [Miscellaneous], in Zhang and Wang, *Mingqing huishang ziliao xuanbian*, 172. In addition, a Chinese official named Yu Ganchen also received credit for introducing the techniques of making congous from Fujian to Qimen. See Chen, *Zhongguo chajing*, 1:300.

25. E. B. Brew, "Report on the Trade at the Treaty Ports of China, for the Year 1881," in IGCMC, *Reports on Trade, 1881*, 15.
26. Kleinwachter, "Amoy Trade Report for the Year 1875," in IGCMC, *Reports on Trade, 1875*, 244.
27. Starting with Wu Fu-lao, from Tung'an in Fujian province, in 1881, tea merchants from mainland China established tea companies in Taiwan to produce Pouchong tea. TTEA, *Historical Brevities*, 14–15.
28. Giffen, "On the Fall of Prices"; Roberts, *Long Depression*, 32–34.
29. For more nuanced data on tea prices by country of origin during 1821–1905, see USDCL, "World's Production," 141. For 1905–7, see USDCL, *Foreign Commerce and Navigation, 1907*, 344. For 1908–12, see USDCL, *Foreign Commerce and Navigation, 1912*, 356.
30. Riggs, "The Tea Commerce of New York," 295.
31. Roberts, *Long Depression*, 32–35.
32. "Shanghai, Wednesday, Nov. 17, 1886," *North China Herald*, November 17, 1886, 521–23.
33. C. Lenox Simpson, "Kiukiang Trade Report, for the Year 1886," in ZGJHGSLBJWYH, *Zhongguo jiuhaiguan shiliao*, 12:146.
34. USDCL, "World's Production," 13.
35. "American Silver Legislation," *North China Herald*, April 8, 1892, 465; Hippisley, "Part I. Report on the Trade of China," 119; *Commercial Reports*, 1891, Shanghai, 3–4, in Yao, *Zhongguo jindai duiwaimaoyishi ziliao*, 2:1270–71; Fetter and Bratter, "China and the Flow of Silver," 32; Hamashita, *Zhongguo jindai jingjishi yanjiu*, 1:159–60, 349, 367–68; Norwood, *Trading Freedom*, 164–68; Officer, *Between the Dollar-Sterling Gold Points*, 60.
36. "American Silver Legislation," 465.
37. Roberts, *Long Depression*, 32; Giffen, "On the Fall of Prices."
38. Roberts, *Long Depression*, 33.
39. Hamashita, *China*, 53.
40. See figure 1 in Deng, "Miracle or Mirage," 329.
41. Charles A. Sinclair, "Report on the Trade of Foochow for the Year 1881," in *CRHMCC, 1881*, part 1, 16.
42. Hughes, "Amoy Trade Report for the Year 1873," 128.
43. He Runsheng 何润生, "Huishu chawu tiaochen" 徽属茶务条陈 [Memorial on Huizhou's tea affairs], in *Huangchao jingshiwen tongbian*, Juan 61 Licai bu liu-chawu 卷 61 理财部六 茶务 [Vol. 61, Finance VI, Tea Affairs].

44. Chen Chi 陈炽, "Zhuyin tiaochen" 鑄銀條陳 [Memorial on silver coinage], November 25, 1896, in Zhang, *Zhongguo jindai sixiangjia wenku*, 77, 81.
45. Chen, *Jindai Zhongguo chaye*, 50; Yao, *Zhongguo jindai duiwaimaoyishi ziliao*, 3:1464–65.
46. "Hankou chaxun" 漢口茶汛 [Hankou tea]; "Hankou chashi xuwen" 漢口茶市續聞 [Update on Hankou tea market], *Shenbao*, May 13, June 20, 1887.
47. Zhang, Wang, and Sun, *Huishang yanjiu*, 588, 596, 604. Also cited in Liu, *Tea War*, 63. One catty equals 1.13 pounds. See Cheong, *Hong Merchants of Canton*, 242n124.
48. De Lano, "The Tea Trade of Foo-Chow for 1880," 81, box 32, RWSP, Manuscript Division, Library of Congress; Kleinwachter, "Ningpo Trade Report for the Year 1882"; H. Edgar, "Foochow Trade Report for the Year 1882"; Henry J. Fisher, "Tamsui Trade Report for the Year 1882"; J. McLeavy Brown, "Amoy Trade Report, for the Year 1882"; R. E. Bredon, "Hankow Trade Report, for the Year 1886"; C. Lenox Simpson, "Kiukiang Trade Report, for the Year 1886"; H. Elgar Hobson, "Shanghai Trade Report, for the Year 1886"; Bredon, "Shanghai Trade Report for the Year 1892," in ZGJHGSLBJWYH, *Zhongguo jiuhaiguan shiliao*, 9:691, 730–31, 751, 784, 12:113–14, 146, 205, 18:248.
49. "Good Tea to Be Scarce," *New York Times*, July 5, 1890, 3, ProQuest Historical Newspapers.
50. C. H. Oliver, "Ningpo Trade Report for the Year 1903," in ZGJHGSLBJWYH, *Zhongguo jiuhaiguan shiliao*, 37:570.
51. Gardella mentions the prolonged contraction of China's tea trade from the 1890s to World War I. See Gardella, *Harvesting Mountains*, 8.
52. E. B. Drew, "Report on the Foreign Trade of China for the Year 1886," in ZGJHGSLBJWYH, *Zhongguo jiuhaiguan shiliao*, 12:6.
53. H. F. Merrill, "Ningpo Trade Report for the Year 1891," in ZGJHGSLBJWYH, *Zhongguo jiuhaiguan shiliao*, 17:309.
54. F. E. Taylor, "Report on the Foreign Trade in China for the Year 1897," in ZGJHGSLBJWYH, *Zhongguo jiuhaiguan shiliao*, 25:7.
55. Edward Cunningham to Francis Blackwell Forbes, March 4, 1875, P-55, reel 25, no. 3, folder 2, FFP.
56. Francis Blackwell Forbes to Will Forbes, December 5, 1872, series N, vol. N-6, FFBR.
57. Francis Blackwell Forbes to Will H. Forbes, January 9, 15, 1873, series N, vol. N-7, FFBR.
58. John Heard to Fearon, August 1, 4, 1873; John Heard to Gus, August 1, 8, 15, 1873; John Heard to Brothers, August 15, 1873, series I, subseries F, Letters Sent, reel 88-4722 R-554, HFBR.

59. John Heard to Gus, August 4, 1873, series I, subseries F, Letters Sent, reel 88-4722 R-554, HFBR.
60. John Heard to Gus, August 4, 11, 14, 15, 1873.
61. See King, *History of the Hongkong and Shanghai Banking Corporation*, 1:19.
62. John Heard to Fearon, December 29, 1873, series I, subseries F, Letters Sent, reel 88-4722 R-554, HFBR.
63. For examples of the account books in the 1860s, see Purchases and Sales on Accounts of Opium, Teas, etc., reel 86-4720 R-143; for bank credit, see 1873–74 Tea Purchase Book, series II, subseries A, reel 86-4543 R-138, HFBR.
64. Edward Cunningham to Francis Blackwell Forbes, August 9, 1876; the value of Edward Cunningham's property in China was still measured in taels. See Edward Cunningham to Francis Blackwell Forbes, October 15, 1880, P-55, reel 25, no. 3, folder 2, FFP.
65. Edward Cunningham to Francis Blackwell Forbes, February 18, 1875, June 21, 1876, P-55, reel 25, no. 3, folder 6, folder 2, FFP.
66. Edward Cunningham to Francis Blackwell Forbes, February 4, 18, 1875, P-55, reel 25, no. 3, folder 6, FFP.
67. King, *History of the Hongkong and Shanghai Banking Corporation*, 1:405–6.
68. King, *History of the Hongkong and Shanghai Banking Corporation*, 1:19, 273–81, 319.
69. "Shanghai, Wednesday, Nov. 17, 1886," *North China Herald*, November 17, 1886, 522. Chen, *Jindai Zhongguo chaye*, 277.
70. Purdon & Wiggin to John M. Forbes & Co., November 19, 25, 1891, box 9, folder 9, FFBR.
71. Hamashita, *Zhongguo jindai jingjishi yanjiu*, 1:163–64.
72. "The Crisis and the Silver Question," *North China Herald*, April 8, 1892, 451; "Mr. Kopsch's Report on the Foreign Trade of China for 1893," *North China Herald*, March 16, 1894, 390.
73. *Currency in the East*, 7; H. Kopsch, "Report on the Foreign Trade of China, for the Year 1895," in ZGJHGSLBJWYH, *Zhongguo jiuhaiguan shiliao*, 23:5.
74. *Currency in the East*, 3–6.
75. *Currency in the East*, 7–8.
76. Moazzin, *Foreign Banks*, 67–69.
77. King, *History of the Hongkong and Shanghai Banking Corporation*, 1:320.
78. Wagel, *Finance in China*, 124; Hamashita, *Zhongguo jindai jingjishi yanjiu*, 1:207.
79. Ma Yinchu 馬寅初, "Shanghai jinrong zhidu zhi queding yu qi gaige fangan" 上海金融制度之確定與其改革方案 [On the design and reform of Shanghai's financial system], *Shenbao yuekan* 申報月刊 [Shanghai news monthly]

3, no. 1 (January 15, 1934): 13, in SBPBC, *Shanghai qianzhuang shiliao*, 35–36; Hamashita, *Zhongguo jindai jingjishi yanjiu*, 1:208.

80. Poovey, *Genres of the Credit Economy*, 36.
81. Bailey, "Banking Facilities," 3.
82. Bailey, "Banking Facilities," 3.
83. Francis Blackwell Forbes to Edward Cunningham, August 28, 1866, August 14, 1867; Francis Blackwell Forbes to William M. Clarke, August 29, 1866, vol. N-1a; Francis Blackwell Forbes to Cordier, August 17, 1872, vol. N-6, series N, FFBR; King, *History of the Hongkong and Shanghai Banking Corporation*, 1:92.
84. *Currency in the East*, 4, 7.
85. Bailey, "Banking Facilities," 2–3.
86. Bailey, "Banking Facilities," 2.
87. "International Banking," *Bankers' Magazine* 77, no. 5 (November 1908): 756, ProQuest American Periodicals.
88. Hamashita, *Jindai Zhongguo de guoji qiji*, 200–202; Nishimura, "Foreign and Native Banks," 113; Moazzin, *Foreign Banks*, 85–88. For the Panic of 1883, see Hamashita, *Zhongguo jindai jingjishi yanjiu*, 1:384–90; Wang, *Chinese Hinterland Capitalism*, 38.
89. "中國之匯號, 銀號, 典肆, 錢莊無不仰洋商之鼻息, 以金鎊易紋銀易, 以紋銀易金鎊難." Chen Chi used the term "Yangshang" 洋商, which means "foreign merchants," but I translated it into "foreign capital." After all, Chinese banks were not solely relying on foreign merchants' capital but also heavily dependent on foreign banks. Chen Chi, "Zhuyin tiaochen," 78.
90. Cheng, *Banking in Modern China*, 16.
91. Li, *Shanxi piaoshang*, line 32–58.
92. Moorhead, "Hankow," in IGCMC, *Decennial Reports, 1882–1891*, 177.
93. "Da jiyangjushi," in SBPBC, *Shanghai qianzhuang shiliao*, 30–31; Edkins, *Banking*, 1–2, 34; Cheng, *Banking in Modern China*, 16.
94. Xu, *Xu yuzhai zixu nianpu*, 41b.
95. "Chaye youguan guoke yi." Chen Guodong's research shows that the expense of the tea company Tianxin Hong was 40,000–60,000 taels in the 1810s. The comparison suggests the small capital of these tea dealers in the late nineteenth century. See Chen, "Tianxin chashang," 423. On native dealers' thin capitalization, also see "Zhongwai ribao chawu shuaifei shuo" 中外日報茶務衰廢說 [From *Zhongwai ribao*: On the declining tea trade], *Hubei shangwu bao* 湖北商务报 [Hubei commerce], no. 19 (1899): 34–36, Chinese Periodical Full-text Database 全国报刊索引; "Lun zhongguo chaye zhi pi"; Shang Lin 商霖, "Zhengdun sicha ce" 整頓絲茶策 [A plan to reform the silk and tea economy], in Yao, *Zhongguo jindai duiwaimaoyishi ziliao*, 3:1563.
96. Zhang, Wang, and Sun, *Huishang yanjiu*, 594.

97. "這種茶號, 且多不一定是自己真資本. . . . 多由貸於他人或山戶, 或茶棧而來." Yu Xie, "Zhenxing zhongguo chaye qianshuo (minguo wuniandong zhi zuo)" 振興中國茶業淺說 (民國五年冬之作) [A rudimentary proposal on revitalizing China's tea economy (composed in winter 1916)], *Anhui shiye zazhi* 安徽實業雜誌, continued issue 續刊, no. 15 (1918): 3–4, Chinese Periodical Full-text Database 全国报刊索引. See also Liu, *Tea War*, 173.

98. Xu, *Xu yuzhai zixu nianpu*, 41b.

99. Lai, "Li Hung-Chang," 279–80, 305n28. Also see Robertson, "Report on the Foreign Trade of Canton for the Year 1873," 7; Shang, "Zhengdun sicha ce"; "China's Trade as Affected by the War," *New York Times*, January 7, 1901, ProQuest Historical Newspapers.

100. De Meritens, "Rapport Annuel Sur Le Commerce De Foochow," 79.

101. Ge, *Huyou Zaji*, 2:16a; Fu, "Shanghai qianzhuang," 71; Zheng and Chen, "Ningbo qianzhuang," 92; Nishimura, "Foreign and Native Banks," 113.

102. "而各新號匯價之銀券約載明茶到地頭, 至多亦止十日如數兌交, 屆期之日票號執券坐取, 日夜追呼." "Zhongwai ribao chawu shuaifei shuo." Also see "Chaye youguan guoke yi"; Ma, "Fumin shuo," in *WQYWYDSLHB*; Shang, "Zhengdun sicha ce."

103. "Zhongwai ribao chawu shuaifei shuo"; Ma, "Fumin shuo," in *WQYWYDSLHB*; *Currency in the East*, 6; Hamashita, *Zhongguo jindai jingjishi yanjiu*, 1:216.

104. Robertson, "Report on the Foreign Trade of Canton for the Year 1873," 7.

105. Hamashita, *Zhongguo jindai jingjishi yanjiu*, 1:216–17; Ma, "Fumin shuo," in *WQYWYDSLHB*; Yu Xie, "Zhenxing zhongguo chaye qianshuo," 3; Chen Chi, "茶务条陈," January 1896, in Zhang, *Zhongguo jindai sixiangjia wenku*, 63–64; "Echa kuiben" 鄂茶虧本 [Hubei tea trade operating at a loss], *Nongxue bao* 農学報, no. 4 (1897): 6, Chinese Periodical Full-text Database 全国报刊索引.

106. "洋莊是美國英國俄國的, 土莊專供本國吃用." Li Cishan 李次山, "Shanghai laodong zhuangkuang dierlei: shougongye–(4) chaye" 上海勞動狀況第二類手工業 (4) 茶業 [Labor conditions in Shanghai, category II: Handicraft (4) tea sector], *Xin qingnian* 新青年, no. 6 (May 1, 1920): 50–51, Hytung Chinese Periodicals Database 瀚唐近代报刊数据库; Ch'en, "Tianxin chashang," 401. Two related terms—*jingzhuang* 京莊 versus *guangzhuang* 广莊—existed in the 1830s. Likely a synonym of the *tuzhuang*, the *jingzhuang* satisfied domestic consumption. Distinctive from it was the *guangzhuang* for the overseas markets, which resembled the *yangzhuang*. Also see Wu, *Wanzhe xin'anjiangliuyu*, 16–17, 30; Zhang, Wang, and Sun, *Huishang yanjiu*, 227–29.

107. Yu Xie, "Zhenxing zhongguo chaye qianshuo," 5; "Our Tea-Table," 542; Macgregor, *Commercial Statistics*, 5:64; Heard, "Old China and New," 17–18.

108. Yu, "Zhenxing zhongguo chaye qianshuo," 5; He, "Huishu chawu tiaochen."

109. "Qi. Cha" 七. 茶 [Chapter 7. Tea economy], in Shaoxingshi renmin zhengfu, *Shaoxingshi difangzhi*, vol. 11.
110. "Zhongwai ribao chawu shuaifei shuo."
111. "Qi. Cha."
112. Jianshe weiyuanhui jingji diaochasuo, *Zhejiang zhi pingshui cha*, 18; Yu Xie, "Nigailiang huizhou chaye yijianshu," 1–2.
113. "Qi. Cha." For reports on small chops, see "Hangao chashi chutan" 漢皋茶市初譚 [Preliminary discussion of the Hankou tea market], *Shenbao*, May 13, 1895, 1; Yu Xie, "Nigailiang huizhou chaye yijianshu," 2.
114. Edward Cunningham to Francis Blackwell Forbes, June 21, 1876, P-55, reel 25, no. 3, folder 2, FFP.
115. "烏龍號." Yu Xie, "Nigailiang huizhou chaye yijianshu," 2; "Nigailiang huizhou chaye yijianshu (xu)," 3:11–13; and "Nigailiang huizhou chaye yijianshu (xu)," 4:19–20.
116. "Trade Reports, 1882, Kiukiang, 106," in Yao, *Zhongguo jindai duiwaimaoyishi ziliao*, 3:1537.
117. Moorhead, "Hankow," in IGCMC, *Decennial Reports*, 177–78.
118. Yu, "Nigailiang huizhou chaye yijianshu (xu)," 11.
119. "Yi xibao lun zhongguo chaye jiyizhengdun" 譯西報論中國茶業亟宜整頓 [On the urgency to reform China's tea economy: Translated from Western newspapers], *Shenbao*, October 22, 1890, 1.
120. Jianshe weiyuanhui jingji diaochasuo, *Zhejiang zhi pingshui cha*, 19–20; Shaoxingshi renmin zhengfu, *Shaoxingshi difangzhi*; "Zhongwai ribao chawu shuaifei shuo."
121. "Zhengdun chawu shi," *Shenbao*, February 15, 1895; Washington Letter to the Philadelphia Ledger, "Better and Cheaper Tea"; "Taiwan baohu chaye" 臺灣保護茶業 [Taiwan protects its tea economy], *Shiwu bao* 時務報, no. 40 (1897): 14–15, Hytung Chinese Periodicals Database 瀚唐近代报刊数据库; Henry J. Fisher, "Tamsui Trade Report, for the Year 1882" and T. F. Hughes, "Amoy Trade Report, for the Year 1889," in ZGJHGSLBJWYH, *Zhongguo jiuhaiguan shiliao*, 9:751, 15:389; "Dancha dao xia" 淡茶到厦 [Danshui tea arrived in Xiamen] and "Chashi chuyan" 茶事芻言 [Preliminary observation on the tea trade], *Shenbao*, May 20, May 23, 1889.
122. F. Hirth, "Tamsui Trade Report for the Year 1890," in ZGJHGSLBJWYH, *Zhongguo jiuhaiguan shiliao*, 16:361.
123. For *yinguang* 陰光, see "Huguangduxian Zhang chijinlüchaweizhi zha" 湖廣督憲張飭禁綠茶僞制札 [Huguang Governor-General Zhang's memorial on prohibiting green tea adulteration, January 27, 1898], *Hubei shangwubao* 湖北商务报, no. 3 (1899): 52–57, Chinese Periodical Full-text Database 全国报刊索引. Descriptions of coloring tea abound in historical documents

and scholars' research. For some examples, see Ball, *Account of the Cultivation and Manufacture of Tea*, 239; "Facts for the Consideration of Tea Drinkers," *Graham Journal of Health and Longevity* 2, no. 6 (August 4, 1838): 247; "Coloring Green Tea," *American Agriculturist*, January 1, 1851, 35; Ch'en, "Tianxin chashang," 406–7; Hellyer, "Quality as a Moving Target," 97–98.

124. "Health Department of the City of New York," 6–7.
125. "Huguangduxian Zhang chijinlüchaweizhi zha."
126. The green teas on American market were two categories: Pingsueys (gunpowder tea) and Fychows (hyson and young hyson). See Yu, "Youmei diaocha chaye zhi baogaoshu," 3, 8. For the qualities and prices of Fychows versus Pingseuys, see "Zonglun yiyounian benbu shimian" 綜論乙酉年本埠市面 [A comprehensive review of the Shanghai market in the year of yiyou], *Shenbao*, February 1, 1886.
127. R. E. Bredon, "Shanghai Trade Report, for the Year 1892," in ZGJHGSLBJWYH, *Zhongguo jiuhaiguan shiliao*, 18:248.
128. "Good Tea to be Scarce."
129. Besky, *Tasting Qualities*, 77; Walcott, "Tea Production," 63; "Java's 'Million Pound' Plantation," *St. Louis Republic*, October 20, 1901, Chronicling America; Liu, *Tea War*, 90–97.
130. Remarks & Statistics about Tea, November 5, 1864, 1863–65 Tea Statistics, reel 86-4543 R-139, HFBR.
131. Hellyer, "Quality as a Moving Target," 95.
132. Francis Blackwell Forbes to King, July 9, 1872, series N, vol. N-5, FFBR.
133. Francis Blackwell Forbes to E. F. Hale, December 7, 1866, series N, vol. N-1a, FFBR. For the quantities of Japanese green tea versus Chinese green, see Hippisley, "Part I. Report on the Trade of China," 37.
134. Gardella, *Harvesting Mountains*, 131–32, 135–36; Hellyer, "Quality as a Moving Target," 98–104, and *Green with Milk and Sugar*, 124–33, 137–40; Rappaport, *Thirst for Empire*, 164–66; Yurman, "Assessing State Food Safety Performance," 16.
135. "For Drinkers of Tea," *New York Times*, December 11, 1870, ProQuest Historical Newspapers. The scholars' publications cited above have detailed negative advertisements targeting Chinese tea.
136. "Tea Importers Here Tell of Favoritism," *New York Times*, January 8, 1912, ProQuest Historical Newspapers.
137. "欺誑狡獪詆毀華茶之讏言矣." Yu Xie, "Yu Huizhou zhujun shangque gailiangshu," 8.
138. Yu, "Yu Huizhou zhujun shangque gailiangshu," 4–8; Yu Xie 俞燮, "Yi tuiguang chazhan yu guowai shuo" 宜推廣茶棧于國外說 [On the need to expand tea warehouses overseas], *Anhui shiye zazhi* 安徽實業雜誌, continued issue, no. 6 (1917): 8–13, Chinese Periodical Full-text Database 全国报刊索引.

139. Thomas J. Van Buren, "Tea Adulteration in Japan," in U.S. Department of State, *Commercial Relations of the United States, 1882*, 435–36.
140. Yu, "Youmei diaocha chaye zhi baogaoshu (xu)," 16. The 2024 value shows the worth of "real wealth," indicating the purchasing power of the value. See Williamson, "Seven Ways."
141. "China Losing Tea Trade," 22.
142. Yu, "Youmei diaocha chaye zhi baogaoshu (xu)," 16. For the Chinese presence at World's Fairs, see Chun Quan Kee & Co., Tea, box 1, WCBA; "A Remarkable Document. Memorial for International Arbitration. Distinguished Signers," *State* (Columbia SC), December 25, 1893, America's Historical Newspaper; Yu Xie, "Youmei diaocha chaye zhi baogaoshu," 5.
143. "To Supplant China Teas," *New York Times*, June 23, 1895, ProQuest Historical Newspapers.
144. Young, "New Life in China," 421–22. Also see Norwood, *Trading Freedom*, 177–78.
145. Washington Letter to the Philadelphia Ledger, "Better and Cheaper Tea," 3.
146. Heard, "Old China and New," 42, 43.
147. Heard, "Old China and New," 2, 42.
148. Heard, "Old China and New," 15. For the tea season in Fuzhou, see Lockwood, *Augustine Heard and Company*, 45. For the tea season in Shanghai, see W. H. Medhurst, "Shanghae," in *CRHMCC, 1875–76*, 32.
149. Heard, "Old China and New," 43.
150. Norwood, *Trading Freedom*, 157–80.
151. "The Situation in China," *Current History and Modern Culture* 11, no. 12 (February 1, 1902): 715, ProQuest American Periodicals; Zhongguo renmin yinhang jinrong yanjiusuo, *Meiguo huaqiyinhang zaihua shiliao*, 13–14; Bergère, *Golden Age*, 67.
152. For the transition, see Zheng, "Shangwu san" 商務三 [Commerce], *Shengshi weiyan*, 3:16a. On tea trade's significance to national revenue, see "Tongzhi shiernian siyue ershibari minzhe zongdu Li Henian dengpian" 同治十二年四月二十八日閩浙總督李鶴年等片 [Memorial by Li Henian, general-governor of Fujian and Zhejiang, et al., submitted on lunar April 28 in the twelfth year of the Tongzhi reign (May 24, 1873)] and "Guangxu sannian eryue ershisiri zongli yamen Yi Xin deng zou" 光緒三年二月二十四日總理衙門奕䜣等奏 [Memorial by Yixin and others from the Zongli Yamen on lunar February 24 in the third year of the Guangxu reign (March 28, 1877)], 1877, both in *WQYWYDSLHB*; "Sinong zoudu" 司農奏牘 [Memorial from the minister of revenue], *Shenbao*, March 20, 1896.

153. E. Ohlmer, "Foochow Trade Report for the Year 1890," in ZGJHGSLBJWYH, *Zhongguo jiuhaiguan shiliao*, 16:340.

154. U.S. Department of Agriculture, *Food and Drug Manual*, 85–87.

155. "方今軍需奇绌, 時事艱難. 茶葉為華稅所關, 不敢不切實維持." "Huguang-duxian Zhang chijinlüchaweizhi zha." For the 1897 act, see U.S. Department of Agriculture, *Food and Drug Manual*, 85–87.

156. "故近十年以來, 中國銷花旗的大帮, 已無希望了." Yu, "Zhenxing zhongguo chaye qianshuo," 5. Also see F. E. Taylor, "Report on the Foreign Trade of China for the Year 1898," in ZGJHGSLBJWYH, *Zhongguo jiuhaiguan shiliao*, 27:9.

157. Sheng, "Qing jianqing chashui zhe" and "Zunzhi michou jiashui mianli shiyi zhe"; Robert Hart, "Report on Tea Addressed to the Tsungli Yamen by the Inspector General of Customs," in IGCMC, *II-Special Series*, 2; "Yi xibao lun zhongguo chaye jiyi zhengdun" 譯西報論中國茶業亟宜整頓 [A translation of a Western press discussion on the urgent need for reforming China's tea economy] and "Zhongguo chayehui" 中國茶業會 [Chinese tea association], *Shenbao*, October 22, 1890, May 8, 1907.

158. "Lun zhongguo jiekuan" 論中國借款 [On China's debts], *Shiwu bao* 時務報, no. 46 (1897); "Fuzhou sheli zhicha gongsi zhangcheng shuolue" 福州設立製茶公司章程說畧 [Summary of the company charter for the Tea Manufacture Company in Fuzhou], *Nongxue bao* 農學報, no. 18 (1934), Dacheng Old Periodical Full-text Database 大成老旧刊全文数据库; Edkins, *Banking and Prices*, 37; Hamashita, *Zhongguo jindai jingjishi yanjiu*, 1:121.

159. "Dai E'du tiaochen liguoziqiang shu" 代鄂督条陈立国自强疏 [A discourse on nation building and self-strengthening, written for Hubei governor], July 10, 1895, in Zhang, *Zhang Jian quanji*, 1:15.

CONCLUSION

1. Lipton Tea Company, "Tea Is an American Drink," circa early or mid-twentieth century, Tea, box 4, WCBA.
2. Fichter, *So Great a Proffit*, 33–34; Perkins, *Financing Anglo-American Trade*, 5.
3. For an example of the research on promissory notes in the early U.S. economy, see Wright, *Origins of Commercial Banking*, 27.
4. For the emergence of the exchange markets in the Atlantic ports, see Perkins, *Financing Anglo-American Trade*, 4–11, 29.
5. Fitcher, *So Great a Proffit*, 33–35.
6. For specie scarcity and credit in antebellum America, see Hammond, *Banks and Politics in America*, esp. 11–14, 52, 80–86, 95–102; Freyer, "Negotiable Instruments"; Fitcher, *So Great a Proffit*, 33–35.

7. Perkins, *Financing Anglo-American Trade*, 115.
8. For example, Woodman examines how the transatlantic cotton trade generated international and internal credit relations through advance payments and bills of exchange. Woodman, *King Cotton*, 119.
9. Perkins, *Financing Anglo-American Trade*, 28; Woodman, *King Cotton*, 121n19, 167–68.

Bibliography

ARCHIVES AND MANUSCRIPT MATERIALS

Archives Center, National Museum of American History, Washington DC.

WCBA. Warshaw Collection of Business Americana, NMAH.AC.0060.

Baker Library, Harvard Business School, Boston.

FFBR. Forbes Family Business Records, MSS:766 1803–1942.

HFBR. Heard Family Business Records, MSS:766 1754–1898.

RCR. Russell & Co. Records, MSS:766 1820–1891.

Collection of the Historical Society of Pennsylvania, Philadelphia.

JAL. Joseph Archer Letterbooks, Am.9057.

WFP. Waln Family Papers, Collection 1651.

WFR. Willings and Francis Records, Collection 1874.

WSP. William Shaler Papers, Collection 1172.

Joseph Downs Collection of Manuscripts and Printed Ephemera, Winterthur Museum, Garden, and Library, Winterthur DE.

LFP (W). Latimer Family Papers, Collection 235.

Kislak Center for Special Collections, Rare Books, and Manuscripts, University of Pennsylvania, Philadelphia.

JGR. John Green, Receipts, Canton in China, 1784–86, MS Collection 499.

Manuscript Division, Library of Congress, Washington DC.

JRLP. John Richardson Latimore Papers, MSS29520.

RWSP. Robert Wilson Schufeldt Papers, MSS52688.

Manuscripts Collection, G. W. Blunt White Library, Mystic Seaport Museum, Mystic CT.

BCL. D. G. & W. B. Bacon & Co. Letters, MSS-Coll-107.

Massachusetts Historical Society, Boston.

FFP. Forbes Family Papers, Ms. N-49.

FGDP. Franklin Gordon Dexter Papers, Ms. N-1117.

LH. Letterbook of Houqua, Ms. N-49.32.

THPP. Thomas Handasyd Perkins Papers, Ms. N-648.

Phillips Library, Peabody Essex Museum, Rowley MA.

HHCTL. Henry Hollingsworth China Trade Letters, MSS 374.

LFP (P). Low Family Papers, MSS 193.

NKP. Nathaniel Kinsman Papers, MSS 43.

Rare Books and Manuscripts Division, New York Public Library.

IWSL. Ira W. Steward Letters, MssCol 17892.

WLP. William Law Papers, MssCol 1698.

Rhode Island Historical Society, Providence.

ECP. Edward Carrington Papers, MSS 333.

JBP. John Brown Papers. MSS 312.

SDP. Sullivan Dorr Papers, MSS 390.

PUBLISHED WORKS

Abridged Work of Admiralty Proceedings before the Judicial Committee of Her Majesty's Most Honorable Privy Council. Hartford: Press of Case, Lockwood & Company, 1860.

Accounts and Papers: Thirty-Seven Volumes. China. Session January 19–July 23, 1847. Vol. XK. London: T. R. Harrison, 1847.

Anderson, B. L. "Money and the Structure of Credit in the Eighteenth Century." *Business History* 12, no. 2 (1970): 85–101.

Anderson, Heather Arndt. *Breakfast: A History.* Lanham MD: AltaMira Press, 2013.

Archer, Samuel. *Memorial of the Merchants of the City of Philadelphia, Engaged in the China Trade, on the Subject of a Regulation of the Duty of Tea, January 31, 1828, Referred to the Committee on Finance.* 20th Cong., 1st sess., serial vol. 165, sess. vol. 3, S.Doc. 77, at 1–6 (January 31, 1828). U.S. Congressional Serial Set.

Bailey, David H. "Banking Facilities between the United States and China." In U.S. Secretary of State, *A Communication from the Consul at Hong-Kong, China, in relation to the Manner of Transacting Business between Citizens of the United States and the East, with a Letter from the Secretary of the Treasury on the Same Subject.* 42nd Cong., 3rd sess., serial vol. 1567, H.Exdoc. 159, at 1–4 (January 25, 1873). ProQuest Congressional.

Ball, Samuel. *An Account of the Cultivation and Manufacture of Tea in China.* Longman, Brown, Green, and Longmans, 1848.

Baster, A. S. J. "The Origins of the British Exchange Banks in China." *Economic Journal* 44, issue supplement 1 (January 1, 1934): 140–51.

Baughman, James P. "Early American Checks: Forms and Functions." *Business History Review* 41, no. 4 (1967): 421–35.

Benton, Thomas H. "Chinese Mission." In *Masterpieces of American Eloquence,* edited by Alexander Johnston, 120–23. New York: Christian Herald, 1900.

Berdichevsky, Norman. "Coffee or Tea? The Cultural Geography of Consumption." *New English Review*, May 2008. https://www.newenglishreview.org/articles/coffee-or-tea/.

Bergère, Marie-Claire. *The Golden Age of the Chinese Bourgeoisie, 1911–1937*. Cambridge, UK: Cambridge University Press, 1989.

Besky, Sarah. *Tasting Qualities: The Past and Future of Tea*. Oakland: University of California Press, 2020.

Birla, Ritu. "Speculation Illicit and Complicit: Contract, Uncertainty, and Governmentality." *Comparative Studies of South Asia, Africa, and the Middle East* 35, no. 3 (2015): 392–407.

Blankaart, Steven. *The Physical Dictionary*. London: Printed for Sam. Crouch and John Sprint, 1708.

Bowen, H. V. "British Exports of Raw Cotton from India to China during the Late Eighteenth and Early Nineteenth Centuries." In *How India Clothed the World: The World of South Asian Textiles, 1500–1850*, edited by Giorgio Riello and Tirthankar Roy, 115–37. Leiden: Brill, 2009.

Bruun, Ole. "The Fengshui Resurgence in China: Conflicting Cosmologies between State and Peasantry." *China Journal*, no. 36 (July 1996): 47–65.

Burns, Arthur Robert. *Money and Monetary Policy in Early Times*. New York: A. A. Knopf, 1927.

Carp, Benjamin L. "7 Myths about the Boston Tea Party." *Journal of the American Revolution*, November 12, 2013. https://allthingsliberty.com/2013/11/7-myths-boston-tea-party/#_edn8.

Carroll, Abigail. *Three Squares: The Invention of the American Meal*. New York: Basic Books, 2013.

Carter, Susan Boslego. "Oong (Charles) Ar Showe: Navigating Chinese Stereotypes and Making a Fortune in Mid-Nineteenth-Century New England." *Chinese America: History & Perspectives*, January 2019, 1–28.

Carter, Susan Boslego, Scott Sigmund Gartner, Michael R. Haines, Alan L. Olmstead, Richard Sutch, and Gavin Wright. *Historical Statistics of the United States: Earliest Times to the Present*. Millennial ed. New York: Cambridge University Press, 2006.

Chan, Wellington K. K. *Merchants, Mandarins, and Modern Enterprise in Late Ch'ing China*. Cambridge MA: East Asian Research Center, Harvard University, 1976.

Chang, Hsin-pao. *Commissioner Lin and the Opium War*. Cambridge MA: Harvard University Press, 1964.

Chen, Ciyu 陈慈玉. *Jindai Zhongguo chaye de fazhan yu shijieshichang* 近代中國茶業的發展與世界市場 [The development of modern Chinese tea economy and the world market]. Taipei: Institute of Economics, Academia Sinica, 1982.

Ch'en, Kuo-Tung Anthony. *The Insolvency of the Chinese Hong Merchants, 1760–1843*. Nankang, Taipei: Institute of Economics, Academia Sinica, 1990.

———. "1760–1833 nianjian Zhongguo chaye chukou de xiguan zuofa 1760–1833" 年间中国茶叶出口的习惯做法 [The customary practices of Chinese tea exports during 1760–1833]. In *Dongya haiyu yiqiannian* 東亞海域一千年 [One thousand years of maritime East Asia], 312–41. Taipei: Yuanliu chubanshe, 2013.

———. "Tianxin chashang de zhouzhuan kunju: Qianjianianjian guangzhoumaoyi yu Wuyuan lüchashang" 馫馨茶商的周转困局—乾嘉年间广州贸易与婺源绿茶商 [Insolvency of the "Tianxin" tea-dealer: On the Canton export trade and the green-tea merchants of Wuyuan during the turn of the nineteenth century]. *Haiyangshi Yanjiu* 海洋史研究 [Maritime history studies], no. 10 (June 15, 2017): 393–434.

———. "Transaction Practices in China's Export Tea Trade, 1760–1833." In *The Second Conference on Modern Chinese Economic History*, 745–70. Taipei: Institute of Economics, Academia Sinica, 1989.

Chen, Song-Chuan. *Merchants of War and Peace: British Knowledge of China in the Making of the Opium War*. Hong Kong: Hong Kong University Press, 2017.

Chen, Tao 陈涛. "Cong 'yichazhiyi' dao 'chaye gailiang': Qingji shishen huacha waixiao guannian de shanbian" 从"以茶制夷"到"茶业改良": 清季士绅华茶外销观念的嬗变 [From "rein in foreigners with tea" to "reform the tea economy": The changing perceptions of the foreign tea trade among Qing scholars and gentry]. *Nongye kaogu* 农业考古 [Agricultural archaeology] 2 (2018): 110–17.

Chen, Zongmao 陈宗懋. *Zhongguo chajing* 中国茶经 [Chinese classics of tea]. 3 vols. Shanghai: Shanghai wenhua chubanshe, 1992.

———. *Zhongguo chaye dacidian* 中国茶叶大辞典 [Dictionary of Chinese tea]. Beijing: Zhongguo qinggongye chubanshe, 2019.

Chen, Zugui 陳祖槼, and Zizhen Zhu 朱自振. *Zhongguo chaye lishiziliao xuanji* 中國茶葉歷史資料選輯 [Selected historical documents on China's tea economy]. Beijing: Nongye chubanshe, 1981.

Cheng, Linsun. *Banking in Modern China: Entrepreneurs, Professional Managers, and the Development of Chinese Banks, 1897–1937*. Cambridge University Press, 2003.

Cheong, W. E. "The Beginnings of Credit Finance on the China Coast: The Canton Financial Crisis of 1812–1815." *Business History* 13, no. 2 (1971): 87–103.

———. "China Houses and the Bank of England Crisis of 1825." *Business History* 15, no. 1 (1973): 56–73.

———. *The Hong Merchants of Canton: Chinese Merchants in Sino-Western Trade.* Richmond: Curzon Press, 1997.

———. *Mandarins and Merchants: Jardine, Matheson, & Co., a China Agency of the Early Nineteenth Century.* London: Curzon Press, 1979.

———. "Trade and Finance in China: 1784–1834: A Reappraisal." *Business History* 7, no. 1 (1965): 34–56.

Chitty, Joseph. *A Practical Treatise on Bills of Exchange, Checks on Bankers, Promissory Notes, Bankers' Cash Notes, and Bank Notes.* G & C. Merriam, 1849.

Commercial Reports from Her Majesty's Consuls in China. ProQuest UK. Parliamentary Papers.

Commercial Reports from Her Majesty's Consuls in China, Japan, and Siam. ProQuest UK. Parliamentary Papers.

Consequa. "To James Madison from Consequa." February 10, 1814. Founders Online, National Archives. Accessed February 22, 2016. http://founders.archives.gov/documents/Madison/03-07-02-0242.

Corning, Howard. "Sullivan Dorr, an Early China Merchant. Extracts from a Notebook Kept by Him in Canton, 1801." *Essex Institute Historical Collections* 78 (January 1942): 158–75.

Currency in the East, Hearing before the Subcommittee of the Committee on the Philippines, Friday, March 27, 1902, Statement of Mr. George H. Macy. Washington DC: Government Printing Office, 1902.

Dai, Xuewen 戴学文. "Qingdai huipiao xilun" 清代会票析论 [An analysis of *Huipiao* during the Qing dynasty]. *Zhongguo qianbi* 中国钱币 [Chinese money], no. 4 (1994): 9–13.

Davidson, James Wheeler. *The Island of Formosa, Past and Present. History, People, Resources, and Commercial Prospects. Tea, Camphor, Sugar, Gold, Coal, Sulphur, Economical Plants, and Other Productions.* London: Macmillan & Co.; Yokohama: Kelly & Walsh, 1903.

De Lano, M. M. "China—Treaty Ports." In *Letter from the Secretary of State, Transmitting a Report on the Commercial Relations of the United States and Foreign Nations, for the Year Ending September 30, 1870.* 41st Cong., 3rd sess., H.Exdoc. 93, at 71–83 (1871). U.S. Congressional Serial Set.

Deng, Kent G. "Miracle or Mirage? Foreign Silver, China's Economy, and Globalization from the Sixteenth to the Nineteenth Centuries." *Pacific Economic Review* 13, no. 3 (2008): 320–57.

Dennett, Tyler. *Americans in Eastern Asia: A Critical Study of United States' Policy in the Far East in the Nineteenth Century.* New York: Macmillan Company, 1922.

Derks, Hans. *History of the Opium Problem: The Assault on the East, ca. 1600–1950.* Leiden: Brill, 2012.

Douglass, Elisha P. *The Coming of Age of American Business: Three Centuries of Enterprise, 1600–1900*. Chapel Hill: University of North Carolina Press, 2011.

Downs, Jacques M. *The Golden Ghetto: The American Commercial Community at Canton and the Shaping of American China Policy, 1784–1844*. Hong Kong: Hong Kong University Press, 2014.

Du, Dan. "'Flying Cash': Credit Instruments on the Silk Roads." In *The Silk Roads: From Local Realities to Global Narratives*, edited by Jefferey Lerner and Yaohua Shi, 237–64. Oxford, UK: Oxbow Books, 2020.

———. "Green Gold and Paper Gold: Seeking Independence through the Chinese-American Tea Trade, 1784–1815." *Early American Studies* 16, no. 1 (2018): 151–91.

Dudden, Arthur Power. *The American Pacific: From the Old China Trade to the Present*. New York: Oxford University Press, 1992.

Edkins, Joseph. *Banking and Prices in China*. Shanghai: Presbyterian Mission Press, 1905.

Effros, Robert C. "The Problem of Postdated Checks in the Republic of China." *Staff Papers (International Monetary Fund)* 18, no. 1 (1971): 113–35.

Ellis, Markman, Richard Coulton, and Matthew Mauger. *Empire of Tea: The Asian Leaf That Conquered the World*. London: Reaktion Books, 2015.

Ellison, Thomas. *The Cotton Trade of Great Britain, including A History of the Liverpool Cotton Market and of the Liverpool Cotton Brokers' Association*. London: Effingham Wilson, Royal Exchange, 1886.

Elwell, Craig Kent. *Brief History of the Gold Standard in the United States*. June 23, 2011. Congressional Research Service. DIANE Publishing, 2011.

Engerman, Stanley L. "A Note on the Economic Consequences of the Second Bank of the United States." *Journal of Political Economy* 78, no. 4 (1970): 725–28.

Esteves, Rui Pedro, and Pilar Nogues-Marco. "Monetary Systems and the Global Balance-of-Payments Adjustment in the Pre-Gold Standard Period, 1700–1870." In *The Cambridge Economic History of the Modern World*, 1:438–67. Cambridge, UK: Cambridge University Press, 2021.

Etherington, Dan M. *Green Gold: The Political Economy of China's Post-1949 Tea Industry*. Hong Kong; New York: Oxford University Press, 1993.

Etherington, N. "Natal's First Black Capitalists." *Theoria: A Journal of Social and Political Theory*, no. 45 (1975): 29–40.

Fairbank, John K. "The Creation of the Treaty System." In *The Cambridge History of China*, edited by John K. Fairbank, 10:213–63. Cambridge, UK: Cambridge University Press, 1978.

Faure, David. *The Rural Economy of Pre-Liberation China: Trade Expansion and Peasant Livelihood in Jiangsu and Guangdong, 1870 to 1937*. Hong Kong: Oxford University Press, 1989.

Fetter, Frank Whitson, and Herbert M. Bratter. "China and the Flow of Silver." *Geographical Review* 26, no. 1 (January 1936): 32–47.

Feuerwerker, Albert. "The Foreign Presence in China." In *The Cambridge History of China*, edited by John K. Fairbank, 12:128–207. Cambridge, UK: Cambridge University Press, 1983.

Fichter, James R. *So Great a Proffit: How the East Indies Trade Transformed Anglo-American Capitalism*. Cambridge MA: Harvard University Press, 2010.

———. *Tea: Consumption, Politics, and Revolution, 1773–1776*. Ithaca NY: Cornell University Press, 2023.

Flagg, Edmund. "China." In *Report on the Commercial Relations of the United States with All Foreign Nations*. 34th Cong., 1st sess., serial vol. 854, sess. vol. 10, vol. I Commercial Digests, H.Exec.Doc. 47 pt. 1, at 3 (1856). U.S. Congressional Serial Set.

Forbes, Robert Bennet. *Personal Reminiscences*. Boston: Little, Brown, and Company, 1882.

———. *Remarks on China and the China Trade*. Boston: Samuel N. Dickinson, 1844.

Frank, Andre Gunder. *ReOrient: Global Economy in the Asian Age*. Berkeley: University of California Press, 1998.

Frank, Caroline. *Objectifying China, Imagining America: Chinese Commodities in Early America*. Chicago: University of Chicago Press, 2011.

Freyer, Tony A. "Negotiable Instruments and the Federal Courts in Antebellum American Business." *Business History Review* 50, no. 4 (1976): 435–55.

Fu, Weiqun 傅为群. "Shanghai qianzhuang yu zhuangpiao (xia)" 上海钱庄与钱庄票 (下) [Shanghai qianzhuang and zhuangpiao II]. *Zhongguo qianbi* 中国钱币 [Chinese money] 1 (2001): 69–72.

Furniss, Edgar Stephenson. *Foreign Exchange, the Financing Mechanism of International Commerce*. New York: Houghton Mifflin Company, 1922.

Gardella, Robert. *Harvesting Mountains: Fujian and the China Tea Trade, 1757–1937*. Berkeley: University of California Press, 1994.

———. "The Min-Pei Tea Trade during the Late Ch'ien Lung and Chia-Ch'ing Eras: Foreign Commerce and the Mid-Ch'ing Fu-Chien Highlands." In *Development and Decline of Fukien Province in the 17th and 18th Centuries*, edited by Eduard B. Vermeer, 317–47. Leiden: E. J. Brill, 1990.

———. "Squaring Accounts: Commercial Bookkeeping Methods and Capitalist Rationalism in Late Qing and Republican China." *Journal of Asian Studies* 51, no. 2 (1992): 317–39.

Ge, Yuanxu 葛元煦. *Huyou Zaji* 滬遊雜记. 1887. 4 vols. Google Books.

Gelderblom, Oscar, and Joost Jonker. "Enter the Ghost: Cashless Payments in the Early Modern Low Countries, 1500–1800." SSRN, May 8, 2015. https://papers.ssrn.com/sol3/papers.cfm?abstract_id=2604089.

Geva, Benjamin. *The Payment Order of Antiquity and the Middle Ages: A Legal History*. Bloomsbury Publishing, 2011.

Giffen, Robert. "On the Fall of Prices of Commodities in Recent Years." *Journal of the Statistical Society of London* 42, no. 1 (1879): 36–78.

Goetzmann, William N., and Elizabeth Koll. "Paying in Paper." In Goetzmann and Rouwenhorst, *Origins of Value*, 91–103.

Goetzmann, William N., and K. Geert Rouwenhorst. "Introduction: Financial Innovations in History." In Goetzmann and Rouwenhorst, *Origins of Value*, 3–16.

———, eds. *The Origins of Value: The Financial Innovations That Created Modern Capital Markets*. Oxford, UK: Oxford University Press, 2005.

Goldstein, Jonathan. *Philadelphia and the China Trade, 1682–1846: Commercial, Cultural, and Attitudinal Effects*. University Park: Pennsylvania State University Press, 1978.

———. *Stephen Girard's Trade with China, 1787–1824: The Norms Versus the Profits of Trade*. Portland ME: MerwinAsia, 2011.

Gottesman, Aron A. *Derivatives Essentials: An Introduction to Forwards, Futures, Options and Swaps*. Wiley Finance Series. Hoboken NJ: Wiley, 2016.

Grant, Frederic D., Jr. "The April 1820 Debt Settlement between Conseequa and Benjamin Chew Wilcocks." In Van Dyke, *Americans and Macao*, 73–94.

———. *The Chinese Cornerstone of Modern Banking: The Canton Guaranty System and the Origins of Bank Deposit Insurance, 1780–1933*. Leiden: Koninklijke Brill, 2014.

———. "The Failure of the Li-ch'uan Hong: Litigation as a Hazard of Nineteenth Century Foreign Trade." *American Neptune* 48, no. 4 (1988): 243–60.

———. "Hong Merchant Litigation in the American Courts." *Proceedings of the Massachusetts Historical Society* 99 (1987): 44–62.

Greenberg, Michael. *British Trade and the Opening of China, 1800–1842*. Cambridge, UK: Cambridge University Press, 1951.

Greenbie, Sydney, and Marjorie Barstow Greenbie. *Gold of Ophir; or, The Lure That Made America*. New York: Doubleday, Page & Company, 1925.

Grigg, David. "The Worlds of Tea and Coffee: Patterns of Consumption." *GeoJournal* 57, no. 4 (2002): 283–94.

Habib, Irfan. "Merchant Communities in Precolonial India." In *The Rise of Merchant Empires: Long-Distance Trade in the Early Modern World, 1350–1750*, edited by James D. Tracy, 371–99. Cambridge, UK: Cambridge University Press, 1990.

Haddad, John Rogers. *America's First Adventure in China: Trade, Treaties, Opium, and Salvation*. Philadelphia: Temple University Press, 2013.

———. *The Romance of China: Excursions to China in U.S. Culture, 1776 to 1876*. New York: Columbia University Press, 2008.

Hall, Elton Wayland. *Carter, Macy & Company, George H. Macy & Company: Importers of Tea*. Dartmouth: Brookside Press, 2016.

Hall, Henry, ed. *America's Successful Men of Affairs: The City of New York*. New York Tribune, 1895.

Hamashita, Takeshi 滨下武志. *China, East Asia, and the Global Economy: Regional and Historical Perspectives*. New York: Routledge, 2008.

———. *Jindai Zhongguo de guoji qiji: Chaogong maoyitixi yu jindai yazhou jingjiquan* 近代中国的国际契机: 朝贡贸易体系与近代亚洲经济圈 [*The International Opportunity for Modern China: The Tributary System and Modern Asian Economic Zones*]. Translated by Zhu Yingui 朱荫贵 and Ouyang Fei 欧阳菲. Beijing: Zhongguo shehui kexue chubanshe, 1999.

———. *Zhongguo jindai jingjishi yanjiu: Qingmo haiguan caizheng yu tongshang kouan shichangquan* 中国近代经济史研究: 清末海关财政与通商口岸市场圈 [A study of modern Chinese economic history: Imperial Maritime Customs' revenue and the trading zones of the treaty ports during the late Qing dynasty]. 2 vols. Nanjing: Jiangsu renmin chubanshe, 2008.

Hammond, Bray. *Banks and Politics in America, from the Revolution to the Civil War*. Princeton: Princeton University Press, 1957.

Hanser, Jessica. *Mr. Smith Goes to China: Three Scots in the Making of Britain's Global Empire*. New Haven CT: Yale University Press, 2019.

Hao, Yen-p'ing. "Chinese Teas to America—a Synopsis." In *America's China Trade in Historical Perspective: The Chinese and American Performance*, edited by Ernest R. May and John King Fairbank, 11–31. Cambridge MA: Harvard University Press, 1986.

———. *The Comprador in Nineteenth Century China: Bridge between East and West*. Cambridge MA: Harvard University Press, 2013.

He, Xiaoxin, and Jun Luo. "Fengshui and the Environment of Southeast China." *Worldviews* 4, no. 3 (2000): 213–32.

"The Health Department of the City of New York and the Board of Health of the Health Department of the City of New York against James Purdon, Augustus Wiggin, John H. Draper, and George T. Kellock." In *Superior Court of the City of New York*. New York: Martin B. Brown, Printer and Stationer, 49 and 51 Park Place, 1884.

Hellyer, Robert. "1874: Tea and Japan's New Trading Regime." In *Asia Inside Out: Changing Times*, edited by Eric Tagliacozzo, Helen F. Siu, and Peter C. Perdue, 186–206. Cambridge MA: Harvard University Press, 2015.

———. *Green with Milk and Sugar: When Japan Filled America's Tea Cups*. New York: Columbia University Press, 2021.

———. "Quality as a Moving Target: Japanese Tea, Consumer Preference, and Federal Regulation on the US Market." In *Imitation, Counterfeiting, and the Quality of Goods in Modern Asian History*, edited by Kazuko Furuta and Linda Grove, 93–106. Singapore: Springer, 2017.

Hidy, Ralph W. *The House of Baring in American Trade and Finance: English Merchant Bankers at Work, 1763–1861*. Cambridge MA: Harvard University Press, 1949.

Ho, Ping-Ti. "The Salt Merchants of Yang-Chou: A Study of Commercial Capitalism in Eighteenth-Century China." *Harvard Journal of Asiatic Studies* 17, nos. 1/2 (1954): 130–68.

Holden, J. Milnes. *The History of Negotiable Instruments in English Law*. London: Athlone Press, 1955.

Homans, J. Smith, Jr. *An Historical and Statistical Account of the Foreign Commerce of the United States*. New York: G. P. Putnam and Sons, 1857.

Homer, Sidney, and Richard Eugene Sylla. *A History of Interest Rates*. New Brunswick NJ: Rutgers University Press, 1996.

Horesh, Niv. *Chinese Money in Global Context: Historic Junctures between 600 BCE and 2012*. Stanford CA: Stanford University Press, 2013.

———. *Shanghai's Bund and beyond British Banks, Banknote Issuance, and Monetary Policy in China, 1842–1937*. New Haven CT: Yale University Press, 2009.

House of Commons. *Returns of the Trade of the Various Ports of China, for the Year 1847 and 1848*. London: Printed by Harrison and Sons, 1849. Command Papers. ProQuest UK. Parliamentary Papers.

———. *Tea. Returns Showing the Number of Pounds Weight of Tea Sold by the East India Company, for Home Consumption, in Each Year from 1740 down to the Termination of the Company's Sales*. Vol. 46, April 28, 1845. House of Commons Papers. ProQuest UK. Parliamentary Papers.

Hoyt, Edwin Palmer. *That Wonderful A & P!* New York: Hawthorn Books, 1969.

Huang, Shijian 黄时鉴. "Cha chuanru Ouzhou jiqi ouwen chengwei" 茶传入欧洲及其欧文称谓 [The introduction of tea into Europe and the European Terminology]. In *Huang Shijian Wenji* 黄时鉴文集 [The works of Huang Shijian]. Shanghai: Zhongxi shuju, 2011.

Huang, T. H. "Tea Processing and Utilisation." In *Science and Civilisation in China*, vol. 6, *Fermentations and Food Science*, 503–70. Cambridge, UK: Cambridge University Press, 2000.

Huang, Yanpei 黄炎培, and Pang Song 龐淞. *Zhongguo shangzhan shibaishi: Zhongguo sishinian haiguanshangwu tongjitubiao* 中國商戰失敗史: 中國四十年海關商務統計圖表 [The history of China's failures in the commercial war: Forty-year statistics from China's Imperial Maritime Customs]. Shanghai: Shangwu yinshuguan, 1917.

Huangchao jingshiwen tongbian 皇朝经世文统编 [A collection of economic essays during the Qing dynasty]. 107 vols. Chinese Text Project.

Hung, Ho-fung. "Imperial China and Capitalist Europe in the Eighteenth-Century Global Economy." *Review—Fernand Braudel Center for the Study of Economies, Historical Systems, and Civilizations* 24, no. 4 (2001): 473–513.

Hunt, Freeman. *Lives of American Merchants*. 2 vols. New York: Derby & Jackson, 1858.

Hunt, Michael H. "Americans in the China Market: Economic Opportunities and Economic Nationalism, 1890s–1931." *Business History Review* 51, no. 3 (1977): 277–307.

Hunter, William C. *The "Fan Kwae" at Canton before Treaty Days, 1825–1844*. London: Kegan Paul, Trench, & Co., 1882.

The Indian Stamp Act, 1899 (II of 1899) as Modified up to the 1st August, 1921. Calcutta: Superintendent of Government Printing, India, 1921.

Ingersoll, Charles Jared. *A View of the Rights and Wrongs, Power and Policy, of the United States of America*. Philadelphia: C. & A. Conrad & Co., 1808.

Inglis, Robert Harry. *The Chinese Security Merchants in Canton and Their Debts: Canton, 1838*. Canton: Canton Press Office, 1838.

Inspector General of Chinese Maritime Customs. *At the Treaty Ports in China, for the Year 1876*. Shanghai: Statistical Department of the Inspectorate General of Customs, 1877. Hathitrust.

———. *Decennial Reports on the Trade, Navigation, Industries etc. of the Ports Open to Foreign Commerce in China and Corea and on the Condition and Development of the Treaty Port Provinces, 1882–1891*. Shanghai: Statistical Department of the Inspectorate General of Customs, 1893. China: Trade, Politics and Culture.

———. *Decennial Reports of the Trade, Navigation, Industries, etc. of the Ports Open to Foreign Commerce in China, and on the Condition and Development of the Treaty Port Provinces, 1892–1901*. Second Issue. 2 vols. Shanghai: Statistical Department of the Inspectorate General of Customs, 1906. Internet Archive.

———. *Reports on Trade at the Ports of Shanghai, Canton, Swatow, Amoy, Ningpo, Hankow, Kiukiang, Chefoo, and Newchwang for the Year 1864*. Shanghai: The Imperial Maritime Customs' Press, 1865. Hathitrust.

———. *Reports on Trade at the Treaty Ports in China, for the Year 1867*. Shanghai: The Customs' Press, 1868. Hathitrust.

———. *Reports on Trade at the Treaty Ports in China, for the Year 1868*. Shanghai: The Customs' Press, 1869. Hathitrust.

———. *Reports on Trade at the Treaty Ports in China, for the Year 1869*. Shanghai: The Customs' Press, 1870. Hathitrust.

———. *Reports on Trade at the Treaty Ports in China, for the Year 1870*. Shanghai: The Customs' Press, 1871. Hathitrust.

———. *Reports on Trade at the Treaty Ports in China, for the Years 1871–1872*. Shanghai: Imperial Maritime Customs Statistical Department, 1874. Hathitrust.

———. *Reports on Trade at the Treaty Ports in China, for the Year 1873*. Shanghai: Imperial Maritime Customs Statistical Department, 1874. Hathitrust.

———. *Reports on Trade at the Treaty Ports in China, for the Year 1874*. Shanghai: Imperial Maritime Customs Statistical Department, 1875. Hathitrust.

———. *Reports on Trade at the Treaty Ports in China, for the Year 1875*. Shanghai: Statistical Department of the Inspectorate General of Customs, 1877. Hathitrust.

———. *Reports on Trade at the Treaty Ports, for the Year 1881*. Shanghai: Statistical Department of the Inspectorate General of Customs, 1882. Hathitrust.

———. *II-Special Series, No. 11-Tea, 1888*. Shanghai: Statistical Department of the Inspectorate General of Customs, 1889. Hathitrust.

———. *Trade Statistics of the Treaty Ports for the Period 1863–1872*. Shanghai: Printed at the Imperial Maritime Customs Press, 1873. Hathitrust.

Irigoin, Alejandra. "The End of a Silver Era: The Consequences of the Breakdown of the Spanish Peso Standard in China and the United States, 1780s–1850s." *Journal of World History* 20, no. 2 (2009): 207–44.

———. "A 'Trojan Horse' in Daoguang China? Explaining the Flows of Silver (and Opium) in and out of China." PLSE Economic History Department Working Papers, vol. 2013, no. 173 (January 25, 2013): 1–34.

Irigoin, Alejandra, Atsushi Kobayashi, and David Chilosi. "China Inside Out: Explaining Silver Flows in the Triangular Trade, c.1820s–1870s." LSE Economic History Working Papers, no. 357 (July 2023): 1–45.

Irving, William, and Daniel Irving Larkin. *Dear Will: Letters from the China Trade, 1833–1836*. Amherst NY: D. I. Larkin, 1987.

James, Harold. "International Capital Movements and the Global Order." In *The Cambridge History of Capitalism*, edited by Larry Neal and Jeffrey G. Williamson, 2:264–300. Cambridge, UK: Cambridge University Press, 2014.

Janin, Hunt. *The India-China Opium Trade in the Nineteenth Century*. Jefferson NC: McFarland & Company, 1999.

Jefferson, Thomas. *Notes on the State of Virginia by Thomas Jefferson*. Richmond: J. W. Randolph, 1853. Google Books.

Ji, Zhaojin. *A History of Modern Shanghai Banking: The Rise and Decline of China's Finance Capitalism*. Armonk NY: M. E. Sharpe, 2003.

Jianshe weiyuanhui jingji diaochasuo 建設委員會經濟調查所, ed. *Zhejiang zhi pingshui cha* 浙江之平水茶 [Pingsuey tea of Zhejiang province]. Jianshe weiyuanhui jingji diaochasuo, 1937.

Johannessen, Jon-Arild. "The Long Depression: 1873–1893." In *Innovations Lead to Economic Crises: Explaining the Bubble Economy*, edited by Jon-Arild Johannessen, 89–109. Cham, Switzerland: Springer International Publishing, 2017.

John Matthews Apparatus Company. *Book of Directions for Carbonated Beverages.* New York: John Matthews Apparatus Company, 1832.

Johnson, J. W. *Promissory Notes, Bills of Exchange, Cheques, and Other Negotiable Instruments: A Reference Book for Business Men and a Text Book for Commercial Students.* Belleville ON: Ontario Business College, 1911.

Johnson, Kendall, ed. *Narratives of Free Trade: The Commercial Cultures of Early US-China Relations.* Hong Kong: Hong Kong University Press, 2012.

Johnson, William. *Reports of Cases Adjudged in the Court of Chancery of New York.* Vol. 3. New York: E. F. Backus, State Street, C. S. Van Winkle, Printer, 1819.

Jones, Susan Mann. "Finance in Ningpo: The 'Ch'ien Chuang,' 1750–1880." In *Economic Organization in Chinese Society*, edited by W. E. Willmott, 47–77. Stanford CA: Stanford University Press, 1972.

King, Frank H. H. *The History of the Hongkong and Shanghai Banking Corporation.* 4 vols. Cambridge, UK: Cambridge University Press, 1987.

Klose, Nelson. *America's Crop Heritage: The History of Foreign Plant Introduction by the Federal Government.* Ames: Iowa State College Press, 1950.

———. "Experiments in Tea Production in the United States." *Agricultural History* 24, no. 3 (1950): 156–61.

Knodell, Jane. "Rethinking the Jacksonian Economy: The Impact of the 1832 Bank Veto on Commercial Banking." *Journal of Economic History* 66, no. 3 (2006): 541–74.

Kuhn, Philip A. "The Taiping Rebellion." In *The Cambridge History of China*, edited by John K. Fairbank, 10:264–317. Cambridge, UK: Cambridge University Press, 1978.

Lai, Chi-Kong. "Li Hung-Chang and Modern Enterprise: The China Merchants' Company, 1872–1885." In *Liu Hung-Chang and China's Early Modernization*, edited by Samuel C. Chu and Kwang-Ching Liu, 276–313. London: Routledge, 2015.

Lapavitsas, Costas. *Marxist Monetary Theory: Collected Papers.* Leiden: Brill, 2016.

Latourette, Kenneth Scott. *The History of Early Relations between the United States and China, 1784–1844.* New Haven CT: Yale University Press, 1917.

Latter, Tony. *Hong Kong's Money: The History, Logic and Operation of the Currency Peg.* Hong Kong: Hong Kong University Press, 2007.

Le Gendre, C. W. "Amoy." In *A Report on the Commercial Relations of the United States and Foreign Nations, for the Year Ending September 30, 1869.* 41st Cong., 3rd sess., H.Exdoc. 18, at 49–71 (1870). U.S. Congressional Serial Set.

Lepler, Jessica M. *The Many Panics of 1837: People, Politics, and the Creation of a Transatlantic Financial Crisis*. Cambridge, UK: Cambridge University Press, 2013.

Letter from the Secretary of State, Transmitting a Report on the Commercial Relations of the United States and Foreign Nations. ProQuest Congressional.

Levinson, Marc. *The Great A&P and the Struggle for Small Business in America*. New York: Hill & Wang, 2012.

Li, Guorong 李国荣, Tan Bo 覃波, and Li Bing 李炳, eds. *Qingchao yangshang midang* 清朝洋商秘档 [The archival documents of merchants engaged in the foreign trade of Qing China]. Beijing: Jiuzhou chubanshe 九州出版社, 2017.

Li, Hongling 李宏齡. "Shangxi piaoshang chengbai ji" 山西票商成敗記 [A chronicle of Shanxi Piaohao's accomplishments and failures]. 1917. Chinese Text Project.

Li, Lillian M. *China's Silk Trade: Traditional Industry in the Modern World, 1842–1937*. Cambridge MA: Council on East Asian Studies, Harvard University, 1981.

Li, Mengting 李梦婷, and Ding Yishou 丁以寿. "Qingmo zhongmei chaye maoyi de shuailuo jiqi yuanyin" 清末中美茶业贸易的衰落及其原因 [The decline of the China-U.S. tea trade during the late Qing period and its causes]. *Chaye tongbao* 茶业通报 [Journal of tea business] 42, no. 2 (2020): 92–96.

Li, Yaohua 李耀华. "Shanghai jindai zhuangpiao de xingzhi, shuliang yu gongneng" 上海近代庄票的性质, 数量与功能 [Property, quantity, and function of Shanghai native order in Shanghai history]. *Caijing yanjiu* 财经研究 [Journal of finance and economics] 31, no. 2 (February 2005): 98–109.

Liang, Tingnan 梁廷枏. *Yifeng wenji* 夷氛闻记 [Messages from abroad]. 5 vols. Chinese Text Project.

———. *Yue haiguan zhi* 粵海關志 [Gazetteer of the Canton Custom]. 25 vols. Chinese Text Project.

Lien, Heng. *Taiwan tongshi* 臺灣通史. 37 vols. Chinese Text Project.

Lin, Man-houng. *Cha, tang, zhangnao yu taiwan zhi shehui jingji bianqian, 1860–1895* 茶, 糖, 樟腦業與臺灣之社會經濟變遷, 1860–1895 [Tea, sugar, camphor, and socioeconomic changes in Taiwan]. Taipei: Lianjing chuban shiye gongsi, 1997.

———. *China Upside Down: Currency, Society, and Ideologies, 1808–1856*. Cambridge MA: Harvard University Asia Center, 2006.

Lin Qingyuan 林庆元, ed. *Fujian jindai jingjishi* 福建近代经济史 [Modern economic history of Fujian]. Fuzhou: Fujian jiaoyu chubanshe, 2001.

Liu, Andrew. *Tea War: A History of Capitalism in China and India*. New Haven CT: Yale University Press, 2020.

Liu, Kwang-Ching. *Anglo-American Steamship Rivalry in China 1862–1874*. Cambridge MA: Harvard University Press, 1962.

Liu, Qiugen 刘秋根, and Han, Ruijun 韩瑞军. "Qingdai qianqi Guangzhou zhongxi shangyexinyong bijiao yanjiu" 清代前期广州中西商业信用比较研究 [A comparative study of Chinese and Western commercial credit in Canton during the early Qing dynasty]. *Jiangsu shanglun* 江苏商论 12 (2007): 174–76.

Liu, Qiugen 刘秋根, and Xie Xiuli 谢秀丽. "Mingqing minjian shangyexinyong piaojuhua de chubu fazhan—yi huipiao, huidui wei zhongxin" 明清民间商业信用票据化的初步发展—以汇票, 汇兑为中心 [The early development of private commercial credit instruments in Ming-Qing China: Focusing on exchange and bill of exchange]. *Zhongguo huobi* 中国货币 1, no. 92 (2006): 3–11.

Liu, Yong. *The Dutch East India Company's Tea Trade with China, 1757–1781*. Leiden: Brill, 2007.

Lockwood, Stephen Chapman. *Augustine Heard and Company, 1858–1862: American Merchants in China*. Cambridge MA: Harvard University Press, 1971.

Lou Min 娄敏. "Jindai Zhongguo changjiangshangyoudiqu de shangyexinyong-piaoju: Yi Baxian yu Jiangjin weili" 近代中国长江上游地区的商业信用票据: 以巴县与江津为例 [Commercial credit instruments in the Upper Yangtse River area of modern China: A case study of Baxian and Jiangjin]. *Zhongguo jingjishi yanjiu* 中国经济史研究 [Chinese economic historical review], no. 6 (2020): 118–32.

Lovell, Julia. *The Opium War: Drugs, Dreams, and the Making of Modern China*. New York: Overlook Press, 2014.

Lowenstein, Matthew, and Shuji Cao. "Business Accounting at Fengshengtai in Late Imperial China: Is There New Evidence of Double-Entry Bookkeeping?" *Business History Review* 97, no. 1 (March 2023): 33–65.

Macfarlane, Alan, and Iris Macfarlane. *The Empire of Tea: The Remarkable History of the Plant That Took Over the World*. Woodstock NY: Overlook Press, 2009.

Macgregor, John. *Commercial Statistics: A Digest of the Productive Resources, Commercial Legislation, Customs Tariffs, Navigation, Port, and Quarantine Laws, and Charges, Shipping, Imports and Exports, and the Monies, Weights, and Measures of All Nations*. Vol. 5. London: Whittaker and Co., 1850.

Marriner, Sheila. *Rathbones of Liverpool, 1845–73*. Liverpool: Liverpool University Press, 1961.

Matson, Cathy D. *Merchants & Empire: Trading in Colonial New York*. Baltimore: Johns Hopkins University Press, 1998.

Mauger, Matthew. "Charting the East India Company's Tea Trade." Tea in Eighteenth-Century Britain. History of Tea Project at Queen Mary University of London. October 17, 2013. https://qmhistoryoftea.wordpress.com/2013/10/17/charting-the-east-india-companys-tea-trade/.

Mazumdar, Sucheta. *Sugar and Society in China: Peasants, Technology, and the World Market*. Cambridge MA: Harvard University Asia Center, 1998.

McCants, Anne E. C. "Poor Consumers as Global Consumers: The Diffusion of Tea and Coffee Drinking in the Eighteenth Century." *Economic History Review* 61, no. S1 (2008): 172–200.

McElderry, Andrea Lee. *Shanghai Old-Style Banks (Ch'ien-Chuang), 1800–1935: A Traditional Institution in a Changing Society*. Ann Arbor: Center for Chinese Studies, University of Michigan, 1976.

McFaul, John M. *The Politics of Jacksonian Finance*. Ithaca NY: Cornell University Press, 1972.

McMahon, Sarah F. "A Comfortable Subsistence: The Changing Composition of Diet in Rural New England, 1620–1840." *William and Mary Quarterly* 42, no. 1 (January 1985): 26–65.

Melitz, Jacques. "Some Doubts about the Economic Analysis of the Flow of Silver to China in 1550–1820." *Open Economies Review* 30, no. 1 (February 1, 2019): 105–31.

Merritt, Jane T. *The Trouble with Tea: The Politics of Consumption in the Eighteenth-Century Global Economy*. Baltimore: Johns Hopkins University Press, 2017.

Miao, Kunhe 缪坤和. *Songdai xinyong piaoju yanjiu* 宋代信用票据研究 [Credit instruments during the Song dynasty]. Kunming: Yunnandaxue chubanshe, 2002.

Michie, Ranald. "Financial Capitalism." In *The Cambridge History of Capitalism*, edited by Larry Neal and Jeffrey G. Williamson, 2:230–63. Cambridge, UK: Cambridge University Press, 2014.

Moazzin, Ghassan. *Foreign Banks and Global Finance in Modern China: Banking on the Chinese Frontier, 1870–1919*. Cambridge, UK: Cambridge University Press, 2022.

Morrison, Dane A. *True Yankees: The South Seas and the Discovery of American Identity*. Baltimore: Johns Hopkins University Press, 2014.

Morse, Hosea Ballou. *The Chronicles of the East India Company: Trading to China, 1635–1834*. 5 vols. Oxford, UK: Clarendon Press, 1926.

———. *The International Relations of the Chinese Empire*. London: Longmans, Green, and Company, 1910.

Moulton, Harold Glenn. *Principles of Money and Banking; a Series of Selected Materials, with Explanatory Introductions*. Chicago: University of Chicago Press, 1926.

Mui, Hoh-Cheung, and Lorna H. Mui. "William Pitt and the Enforcement of the Commutation Act, 1784–1788." *English Historical Review* 76, no. 300 (1961): 447–65.

Musson, A. E. "The Great Depression in Britain, 1873–1896: A Reappraisal." *Journal of Economic History* 19, no. 2 (1959): 199–228.

Nash, R. C. "The Organization of Trade and Finance in the British Atlantic Economy, 1600–1830." In *The Atlantic Economy during the Seventeenth and*

Eighteenth Centuries: Organization, Operation, Practice, and Personnel, edited by Peter A. Coclanis, 121–33. Columbia: University of South Carolina Press, 2005.

"Native Banks in Foochow." *Chinese Economic Journal* 10 (May 1932): 440–47.

Neal, Larry. "Introduction." In *The Cambridge History of Capitalism*, edited by Larry Neal and Jeffrey G. Williamson, 1:1–23. Cambridge, UK: Cambridge University Press, 2014.

Nie, Baozhang 聂宝璋. *Zhongguo maiban zichanjieji de fasheng* 中国买办资产阶级的发生 [The making of Chinese comprador capitalists]. Beijing: Zhongguo shehuikexue chubanshe, 1979. https://www.sklib.cn/booklib/databasedetail?SiteID=122&Type=literature&ID=5710160.

Nierstrasz, Chris. *Rivalry for Trade in Tea and Textiles: The English and Dutch East India Companies (1700–1800)*. London: Palgrave Macmillan, 2015.

Nishimura, Shizuya. "The Foreign and Native Banks in China: Chop Loans in Shanghai and Hankow before 1914." *Modern Asian Studies* 39, no. 1 (2005): 109–32.

Nogues-Marco, Pilar. "Trade Imbalances or Silver Arbitrage? Anglo-Asian Bullion Flows in the Early Modern Period, 1664–1811." Financial History Network Lecture Series. December 5, 2022.

Norwood, Dael A. *Trading Freedom: How Trade with China Defined Early America*. Chicago: University of Chicago Press, 2022.

Nye, Gideon. *Tea: And the Tea Trade*. New York: G. W. Wood, 1850.

Officer, Lawrence H. *Between the Dollar-Sterling Gold Points: Exchange Rates, Parity, and Market Behavior*. Cambridge, UK: Cambridge University Press, 2007.

Ogden, James Matlock. *The Law of Negotiable Instruments, Including Promissory Notes, Bills of Exchange, Bank Checks, and Other Commercial Paper, with the Negotiable Instruments Law Annotated and Forms of Pleading, Trial Evidence, and Comparative Tables Arranged Alphabetically by States*. Chicago: Callaghan & Company, 1909.

Orrell, David, and Roman Chlupatý. "Virtual Money." In *The Evolution of Money*, edited by David Orrell and Roman Chlupatý, 55–73. New York: Columbia University Press, 2016.

Pamuk, Şevket. *A Monetary History of the Ottoman Empire*. Cambridge, UK: Cambridge University Press, 2000.

Pan, Shü-lun. *The Trade of the United States with China*. New York: China Trade Bureau, 1924.

Peng, Xinwei 彭信威. *Zhongguo huobi shi* 中國貨幣史 [Monetary history of China]. Shanghai: Shanghai renmin chubanshe, 2015.

Peng Zeyi 彭泽益, ed. *Zhongguo gongshang hanghui shiliao ji* 中国工商行会史料集 [Collected historical documents on Chinese commercial and industrial guilds]. 2 vols. Beijing: Zhonghua shuju, 1995.

Perkins, Edwin J. *Financing Anglo-American Trade: The House of Brown, 1800–1880*. Cambridge MA: Harvard University Press, 1975.

"Perkins and Company, Canton 1803–1827." *Bulletin of the Business Historical Society* 6, no. 2 (1932): 1–5.

"Perry Expedition to Japan (Correspondence to and within)." Baxley Stamps. Accessed April 17, 2022. http://www.baxleystamps.com/litho/perry_correspond/ten_letters.shtml.

Peters, John R., Jr. *Guide to, or Descriptive Catalogue of the Chinese Museum: In the Marlboro Chapel, Boston, with Miscellaneous Remarks upon the Government, History, Religions, Literature, Agriculture, Arts, Trade, Manners, and Customs of the Chinese*. Boston: Eastburn's Press, 1845.

Peters, Richard. *Reports of Cases Argued and Determined in the Circuit Court of the United States for the Third Circuit, etc., 1803–1818*. Vol. 1. Philadelphia: Courts of Justice, Circuit Courts, 1819.

Pettigrew, Jane. *The Tea Companion*. London: Apple Press, 1997.

Philanthropus. *The Lady & Gentleman's Tea-Table and Useful Companion, in the Knowledge and Choice of Teas*. London: By J. C. Kelly, for J. Mann, and for Bysh and Button & Son, et al., 1818.

Phipps, John. *A Practical Treatise on the China and Eastern Trade: Comprising the Commerce of Great Britain and India; Particularly Bengal and Singapore, with China and the Eastern Islands*. London: W. H. Allen and Company, 1836.

Pitkin, Timothy. *A Statistical View of the Commerce of the United States of America: Including Also an Account of Banks, Manufactures, and Internal Trade and Improvements*. New Haven: Durrie & Peck, 1835.

Platt, Stephen R. *Imperial Twilight: The Opium War and the End of China's Last Golden Age*. New York: Alfred A. Knopf, 2018.

Polachek, James M. *The Inner Opium War*. Cambridge MA: Council on East Asian Studies, Harvard University, 1992.

Pomeranz, Kenneth. *The Great Divergence: China, Europe, and the Making of the Modern World Economy*. Princeton: Princeton University Press, 2000.

———. "'Traditional' Chinese Business Forms Revisited: Family, Firm, and Financing in the History of the Yutang Company of Jining." *Late Imperial China* 18, no. 1 (June 1, 1997): 1–38.

Price, Jacob M. *Capital and Credit in British Overseas Trade: The View from Chesapeake, 1700–1776*. Cambridge MA: Harvard University Press, 1980.

———. "Joshua Johnson in London, 1771–1775: Credit and Commercial Organization in the British Chesapeake Trade." In *Tobacco in the Atlantic: The Chesapeake, London, and Glasgow, 1675–1775*, 153–80. Brookfield VT: Variorum, 1995.

Purtle, Jennifer. "Money Making Nation: Picturing Political Economy in Banknotes of the Qing-Republican Transition." In *Looking Modern: East*

Asian Visual Culture from Treaty Ports to World War II, edited by Jennifer Purtle and Hans Bjarne Thomsen. 106–39. Chicago: Center for the Art of East Asia, University of Chicago, 2009.

Qian, Chengxu 錢承緒. *Huacha zhi yanjiu* 華茶之研究 [Research on Chinese tea]. Nanjing: Zhongguo jingji yanjiuhui, 1940.

Qiao, Zhijian. "The Rise of Shanxi Merchants: Empire, Institutions, and Social Change in Qing China, 1688–1850." PhD diss., Stanford University, 2017.

Quinn, Stephen, and William Roberds. "The Evolution of the Check as a Means of Payment: A Historical Survey." *Economic Review—Federal Reserve Bank of Atlanta* 93, no. 4 (2008): I, 1–28.

Rabel, Ernst. *The Conflict of Laws: A Comparative Study*. Vol. 4. Ann Arbor: University of Michigan Law School, 1958.

Rappaport, Erika Diane. *A Thirst for Empire: How Tea Shaped the Modern World.* Princeton: Princeton University Press, 2017.

Rawski, Evelyn S., and Susan Naquin. "A New Look at the Canton Trade, 1700–1845." *Harvard Journal of Asiatic Studies* 78, no. 2 (December 2018): 491–514.

Ray, Nicholas Dylan. "The Medieval Islamic System of Credit and Banking: Legal and Historical Considerations." *Arab Law Quarterly* 12, no. 1 (1997): 43–90.

Ray, Rajat Kanta. "Asian Capital in the Age of European Domination: The Rise of the Bazaar, 1800–1914." *Modern Asian Studies* 29, no. 3 (1995): 449–554.

Redlich, Fritz, and Webster M. Christman. "Early American Checks and an Example of Their Use." *Business History Review (Pre-1986)* 41, no. 3 (Autumn 1967): 285–302.

Regelski, Christina. "The Revolution of American Drinking." U.S. History Scene. Accessed October 12, 2017. http://ushistoryscene.com/article/american-drinking/.

Reilly, Thomas H. *The Taiping Heavenly Kingdom: Rebellion and the Blasphemy of Empire*. Seattle: University of Washington Press, 2004.

Remer, C. F. "International Trade Between Gold and Silver Countries: China, 1885–1913." *Quarterly Journal of Economics* 40, no. 4 (1926): 597–643.

A Retrospect of Political and Commercial Affairs in China, 1868–1872. Shanghai: "North-China Herald" Office, 1873.

Roberts, Alasdair. *America's First Great Depression: Economic Crisis and Political Disorder after the Panic of 1837*. Ithaca NY: Cornell University Press, 2012.

Roberts, Michael. *The Long Depression: Marxism and the Global Crisis of Capitalism*. Chicago: Haymarket Books, 2016.

Rogers, James Steven. *The Early History of the Law of Bills and Notes: A Study of the Origins of Anglo-American Commercial Law*. Cambridge, UK: Cambridge University Press, 2004.

Rong, Xiaofeng 荣晓峰. "Jindai Tianjin boma zhidu yanjiu" 近代天津拨码制度研究 [Research on Boma Institution in modern Tientsin]. *Zhongguo jingjishi yanjiu* 中国经济史研究 [Chinese economic historical review] 2 (2023): 67–85.

Rosenthal, Jean-Laurent, and Roy Bin Wong. *Before and beyond Divergence: The Politics of Economic Change in China and Europe*. Cambridge MA: Harvard University Press, 2011.

Roth, Rodris. "Tea Drinking in 18th-Century America: Its Etiquette and Equipage." *United States National Museum Bulletin* 225 (1961): 61–91.

Rousseau, Peter L. "Jacksonian Monetary Policy, Specie Flows, and the Panic of 1837." *Journal of Economic History* 62, no. 2 (2002): 457–88.

Rowe, William. *Hankow: Commerce and Society in a Chinese City, 1796–1889*. Stanford: Stanford University Press, 1984.

Royal Society of Chemistry. "How to Make a Perfect Cup of Tea." ZME Science. Accessed August 11, 2014. https://cdn.zmescience.com/wp-content/uploads/2017/11/RSC-tea-guidelines.pdf.

"Salmagundi." In *The Concise Oxford Companion to American Literature*, edited by James D. Hart. Oxford, UK: Oxford University Press, 1986.

Schaede, Ulrike. "Forwards and Futures in Tokugawa-Period Japan: A New Perspective on the Dōjima Rice Market." *Journal of Banking & Finance* 13, no. 4 (1989): 487–513.

Seaburg, Carl, and Stanley Paterson. *Merchant Prince of Boston: Colonel T. H. Perkins, 1764–1854*. Cambridge MA: Harvard University Press, 1971.

Shanghai Branch of the People's Bank of China 中国人民银行上海市分行, ed. *Shanghai qianzhuang shiliao* 上海钱庄史料 [Collected historical documents on native banks in Shanghai]. Shanghai: Shanghai remin chubanshe, 1960.

Shaoxingshi renmin zhengfu. *Shaoxingshi difangzhi* 绍兴市地方志 [Shaoxing municipal gazetteer]. Accessed January 10, 2021. http://www.sx.gov.cn/col/col1462659/index.html (site discontinued).

Shaw, Samuel, and Josiah Quincy. *The Journals of Major Samuel Shaw: The First American Consul at Canton; With a Life of the Author*. Boston: Crosby and Nichols, 1847.

Shi, Tao 石涛. *Jinshi yilai shijie chayeshichang yu Zhongguo chaye* 近世以来世界茶叶市场与中国茶业 [Research on the world tea market and Chinese tea industry since modern times]. Beijing: Shehui kexue wenxian chubanshe, 2020.

Shi, Tao 石涛, Dong Xiaofen 董晓汾, and Wei Yu 卫宇. "Shijiu shiji shangbanye zhongmei chaye maoyi zhong jiacha wenti yanjiu 19" 世纪上半叶中美茶叶贸易中假茶问题研究 [Fake teas in the China-U.S. tea trade during the first half of the nineteenth century]. *Shanxi daxue xuebao* 山西大学学报 [Shanxi University journal] 41, no. 6 (2018): 46–56.

Six Essays on the Trade of Shanghai; Reprinted from "The Celestial Empire." Shanghai: Gazette Office, 1874.

Smith, Philip Chadwick Foster. *The Empress of China*. Philadelphia: Philadelphia Maritime Museum, 1984.

Smith, Samuel, and Isaac Ilsley. *Trade with China*. Senate Committee on Finance, 19th Cong., 1st sess., no. 736, at 266–82 (February 6, 1826). ProQuest Congressional.

Sommers, Amy L., and Kara L. Phillips. "The P.R.C.'s Negotiable Instruments Law: An Instrument for Facilitating Private Economic Activity or Monetary Control?" *Houston Journal of International Law* 20, no. 2 (1998): 317–51.

Spahr, Walter Earl. *The Clearing and Collection of Checks*. New York: Bankers Publishing Co., 1926.

Spalding, William Frederick. *Eastern Exchange Currency and Finance*. I. Pitman, 1924.

Stanton, Elizabeth Cady, et al. *History of Woman Suffrage*. New York, London, and Paris: Charles Mann and G. Fischbacher, 1887.

Stelle, Charles C. *Americans and the China Opium Trade in the Nineteenth Century*. New York: Arno Press, 1981.

———. "American Trade in Opium to China, Prior to 1820." *Pacific Historical Review* 9, no. 4 (1940): 425–44.

———. "American Trade in Opium to China, 1821–1839." *Pacific Historical Review* 10 (1941): 57–74.

Stevens, Robert White. *On the Stowage of Ships and Their Cargoes, with Information regarding Freights, Charter-Parties, & c., &c.* Longmans, Green, Reader, & Dyer, 1878.

Taiwan Tea Exporters' Association. *The Historical Brevities of Taiwan Tea Export, 1865–1965*. Taipei: Taiwanqu cha shuchuye tongyegonghui, 1965.

Tao, Dechen 陶德臣. "Zhongmei chaye maoyi de fazhan jieduan ji tedian" 中美茶叶贸易的发展阶段及特点 [Phases and features of the China-U.S. tea trade]. *Gujin nongye* 古今农业 [Ancient and modern agriculture], no. 3 (2015): 56–66.

———. "Zhongmei chaye maoyi de xingqi jiqi tedian" 中美茶叶贸易的兴起及其特点 [The emergence and features of the China-U.S. tea trade]. *Guizhou chaye* 贵州茶叶 [Guizhou tea] 43, no. 3 (2015): 44–46.

Temin, Peter. "The Economic Consequences of the Bank War." *Journal of Political Economy* 76, no. 2 (1968): 257–74.

———. *The Jacksonian Economy*. New York: Norton and Co., 1969.

Thurber, Francis B. *Coffee: From Plantation to Cup: A Brief History of Coffee Production and Consumption*. New York: American Grocer Publishing Association, 1884.

Topik, Steven. "How Mrs. Olson Got Her Full-Bodied Coffee: The Industrialization of the Coffee Service Sector in the United States, 1760–1950." American Studies Group, University of California at Irvine, April 2004.

Tsaing, T. F. "Notes and Suggestions." *Chinese Social and Political Science Review* 15, no. 4 (1931): 597–607.

Tsin, Michael Tsang-Woon. *Nation, Governance, and Modernity in China: Canton, 1900–1927*. Stanford: Stanford University Press, 1999.

Ukers, William H. *All about Tea*. 2 vols. New York: Tea and Coffee Trade Journal Company, 1935.

United Nations. "United Nations Convention on International Bills of Exchange and International Promissory Notes." December 9, 1988. https://uncitral.un.org/en/texts/payments/conventions/bills_of_exchange.

University of California, Los Angeles Center for Medieval and Renaissance Studies. *The Dawn of Modern Banking*. New Haven CT: Yale University Press, 1979.

U.S. Bureau of the Census. *Historical Statistics of the United States: Colonial Times to 1957*. Washington DC, 1960.

U.S. Department of Agriculture, Bureau of Chemistry. *The Food and Drug Manual, Instructions to Officials, Analysts, and Inspectors of the Bureau of Chemistry Relating to the Procedure for the Enforcement of the Food and Drugs Act of June 30, 1906*. Washington DC: Government Printing Office, 1920. Google Books.

U.S. Department of Commerce and Labor. *The Foreign Commerce and Navigation of the United States for the Year Ending June 30, 1907*. Washington DC: Government Printing Office, 1908. Google Books.

———. *The Foreign Commerce and Navigation of the United States for the Year Ending June 30, 1912*. Washington DC: Government Printing Office, 1913. Hathitrust.

———. "The World's Production and Consumption of Coffee, Tea, and Cacao in 1905." In *Monthly Summary of Commerce and Finance of the United States for the Fiscal Year 1906*. 59th Cong., 1st sess., serial vol. 4975, sess. vol. 35, H.Doc. 15 pt. 1, 2, and 3, at 11–163 (1906). U.S. Congressional Serial Set.

U.S. Department of Commerce and Labor, Bureau of Manufactures. *Monthly Consular and Trade Reports*. 58th Cong., 3rd sess., H.Doc. 335 (August 1905). ProQuest Congressional.

U.S. Department of State. *Commercial Relations of the United States. Reports from the Consuls of the United States on the Commerce, Manufactures, etc., of their Consular Districts. For the Months of September and October, 1882*. 47th Cong., 1st sess., serial vol. 2061, sess. vol. 25, H.Misc.Doc. 65 (1882). U.S. Congressional Series.

———. *Report of the Secretary of State, Transmitting a Statement from the Superintendent of Statistics of the Commercial Relations of the United States with Foreign Nations, for the Year ending September 30, 1856*. 34th Cong., 3rd sess., serial vol. 901, sess. vol. 7 (1857), H.Exec.Doc. 60. U.S. Congressional Serial Set.

U.S. Patent Office. *Report of the Commissioner of Patents for the Year*. Washington DC: Government Printing Office, 1870.

U.S. Treasury Department. *Statements of Imports of Tea and Coffee into the United States Each Year from 1789 to 1882, Also Showing Production and Consumption of Tea and Coffee and Customs Duties Imposed Thereon in the United States, Being Part of* Quarterly Report, *no. 3, series 1882–'83, of the Chief of the Bureau of Statistics, Treasury Department.* Washington DC: Government Printing Office, 1883.

Van De Mieroop, Marc. "The Invention of Interest: Sumerian Loans." In Goetzmann and Rouwenhorst, *Origins of Value*, 17–30.

Van Driem, George L. *The Tale of Tea: A Comprehensive History of Tea from Prehistoric Times to the Present Day*. Leiden: Brill, 2019.

Van Dyke, Paul A., ed. *Americans and Macao: Trade, Smuggling and Diplomacy on the South China Coast*. Hong Kong: Hong Kong University Press, 2012.

———. "Bookkeeping as a Window into Efficiencies of Early Modern Trade: Europeans, Americans, and Others in China Compared, 1700–1842." In Johnson, *Narratives of Free Trade*, 17–31.

———. *The Canton Trade: Life and Enterprise on the China Coast, 1700–1845*. Hong Kong: Hong Kong University Press, 2007.

———. *Merchants of Canton and Macao: Politics and Strategies in Eighteenth-Century Chinese Trade*. Hong Kong: Hong Kong University Press; Kyoto: Kyoto University Press, 2011.

———. *Merchants of Canton and Macao: Success and Failure in Eighteenth-Century Chinese Trade*. Hong Kong: Hong Kong University Press, 2016.

———. "Smuggling Networks of the Pearl River Delta before 1842: Implications for Macao and the American China Trade." In Van Dyke, *Americans and Macao*, 49–72.

Van Dyke, Paul Arthur, and Susan E. Schopp. *The Private Side of the Canton Trade, 1700–1840: Beyond the Companies*. Hong Kong: Hong Kong University Press, 2018.

Van Winter, Pieter J. *American Finance and Dutch Investment, 1780–1805: With an Epilogue to 1840*. Vol. 1. New York: Arno Press, 1977.

Von Glahn, Richard. "The Changing Significance of Latin American Silver in the Chinese Economy, 16th–19th Centuries." *Revista de Historia Económica / Journal of Iberian and Latin American Economic History* 38, no. 3 (2020): 553–85.

———. "Cycles of Silver in Chinese Monetary History." In *The Economy of Lower Yangzi Delta in Late Imperial China: Connecting Money, Markets, and Institutions*, edited by Billy K. L. So, 35–97. London: Taylor & Francis Group, 2012.

———. "Economic Depression and the Silver Question in Nineteenth-Century China." In *Global History and New Polycentric Approaches: Europe, Asia, and the Americas in a World Network System*, edited by Lucio De Sousa and Manuel Pérez García, 81–118. Springer, 2017.

———. *Fountain of Fortune: Money and Monetary Policy in China, 1000–1700*. Berkeley: University of California Press, 1996.

———. "The Origins of Paper Money in China." In Goetzmann and Rouwenhorst, *Origins of Value*, 65–89.

Wagel, Srinivas Ram. *Finance in China*. Shanghai: North-China Daily News & Herald, 1914.

Wakeman, Frederic E. *Strangers at the Gate: Social Disorder in South China, 1839–1861*. Berkeley: University of California Press, 1966.

Walcott, Susan M. "Tea Production in South Carolina." *Southeastern Geographer* 39, no. 1 (January 1, 1999): 61–74.

Walsh, Joseph M., and William Saunders. *"A Cup of Tea," Containing a History of the Tea Plant from Its Discovery to the Present Time, Including Its Botanical Characteristics . . . and Embracing Mr. William Saunders' Pamphlet on "Tea-Culture—a Probable American Industry."* Philadelphia: Published by the Author, 1884.

Walsh, William I. *The Rise and Decline of the Great Atlantic & Pacific Tea Company*. Secaucus NJ: L. Stuart, 1986.

Wang, Luman. *Chinese Hinterland Capitalism and Shanxi Piaohao: Banking, State, and Family, 1720–1910*. London: Routledge, 2021.

Wang, Qingcheng 王庆成. *Xijian qingshi shiliao bing kaoshi* 稀见清世史料并考释 [A collection and interpretation of rare historical documents from the Qing dynasty]. Wuhan: Wuhan chubanshe, 1998.

Wangqing yangwu yundong shiliaohuibian 晚清洋務運動史料彙編 [Collected historical documents on the self-strengthening movement in the late Qing dynasty]. Shutongwen guji shujuku 书同文古籍数据库.

Ward, Barbara E. "Cash or Credit Crops? An Examination of Some Implications of Peasant Commercial Production with Special Reference to the Multiplicity of Traders and Middlemen." *Economic Development and Cultural Change* 8, no. 2 (1960): 148–63.

White, Charles A. "The Archaic Monetary Terms of the United States." *Smithsonian Miscellaneous Collections* 50, no. 11 (1908): 93–104.

White, Harold. "The Convention on the Uniform Law of International Bills of Exchange and International Promissory Notes: A Comparison to the Uniform Commercial Code." *Georgia Journal of International & Comparative Law* 5, no. 1 (1975): 216–47.

"Why Most Americans Drink Coffee Not Tea." *Marcus's Tea Blog*. Accessed October 12, 2017. https://www.goldenmoontea.com/blogs/tea/106692871-why-most-americans-drink-coffee-not-tea (site discontinued).

Williams, S. Wells. *A Chinese Commercial Guide, Consisting of a Collection of Details and Regulations Respecting Foreign Trade with China, Sailing Directions, Tables, &c.* Canton: Printed at the Office of the Chinese Repository, 1856.

Williamson, Samuel H. "Seven Ways to Compute the Relative Value of a U.S. Dollar Amount, 1790 to Present." Measuring Worth, 2026. https://www.measuringworth.com/calculators/uscompare/.

Wong, John D. *Global Trade in the Nineteenth Century: The House of Houqua and the Canton System*. Cambridge, UK: Cambridge University Press, 2016.

Wong, R. B. "China before Capitalism." In *The Cambridge History of Capitalism*, edited by Larry Neal and Jeffrey G. Williamson, 1:125–64. Cambridge, UK: Cambridge University Press, 2014.

Woodman, Harold D. *King Cotton and His Retainers: Financing and Marketing the Cotton Crop of the South, 1800–1925*. 3rd ed. Washington DC: Beard Books, 2000.

Wright, Robert E. *Origins of Commercial Banking in America, 1750–1800*. Lanham MD: Rowman & Littlefield, 2001.

Wu, Juenong 吳覺農. *Wanzhe xin'anjiangliuyu zhi chaye* 皖浙新安江流域之茶業 [Tea economy in Anhui, Zhejiang, and the Xin'an river valley]. Anhui: Anhui shengli chaye gailiang chang, 1934.

———. *Zhengli wuyichaqu jihuashu* 整理武夷茶區計劃書 [A plan to reorganize the Wuyi tea district]. Fujian, Chongan, Chishi, 1943.

———. *Zhongguo difangzhi chaye lishiziliao xuanji* 中国地方志茶叶历史资料选辑 [Selected historical documents on tea from Chinese local gazetteers]. Beijing: Nongye chubanshe, 1990.

Wu, Juenong 吳覺農, and Hu Haochuan 胡浩川. *Zhongguo chaye fuxing jihua* 中國茶業復興計劃 [A plan to revive China's tea economy]. Shanghai: Shangwu yinshu guan, 1935.

Xu, Run 徐润. *Xu yuzhai zixu nianpu* 徐愚斋自叙年谱 [Autobiographical chronicle of Xu Yuzhai]. 1910.

Yan, Zhongping 严中平, ed. *Zhongguo jindaijingjishi tongjiziliao xuanji* 中国近代经济史统计资料选辑 [Selected statistics on modern Chinese economic history]. Beijing: Kexue chubanshe, 1955.

Yang, Duanliu 楊端六. *Qingdai huobi jinrong shigao* 清代貨幣金融史稿 [A draft history of money and finance in the Qing period]. Wuhan: Wuhan daxue chubanshe, 2007.

Yang, Liansheng. *Money and Credit in China, a Short History*. Cambridge MA: Harvard University Press, 1952.

Yao, Xianhao 姚賢鎬, ed. *Zhongguo jindai duiwaimaoyishi ziliao* 中国近代对外贸易史资料: 1840–1895 [Collected historical documents of China's modern foreign trade]. 3 vols. Beijing: Kexue chubanshe, 2016.

Young, John Russell. "New Life in China." *North American Review* 153, no. 419 (1891): 420–31.

Yu, Simin 余姒珉. "Lun Wang Tao *yiru zazhi zhi* quanli xiangzheng yu shidaixing" 論王韜《瀛壖雜誌》之權利象征與時代性 [On the symbolism of rights and contemporaneousness in Wang Tao's *Travels to Shanghai*]. *Renwen xuebao* 人文學報 [Humanities] 12, no. 30 (1995): 239–62.

Yuan, Weipeng, Richard Macve, and Debin Ma. "The Development of Chinese Accounting and Bookkeeping before 1850: Insights from the Tŏng Tài Shēng Business Account Books (1798–1850)." *Accounting and Business Research* 47, no. 4 (June 7, 2017): 401–30.

Yu Hongchang 俞鸿昌. "Guangxu huipiao" 光绪会票 [The *Huipiao* of the Guangxu period]. *Zhongguo qianbi* 中国钱币 [Chinese money], no. 4 (1994): 38–39.

———. "Qingdai huipiao de hanzimiya" 清代会票的汉字密押 [The use of Chinese characters as the insignia on the *Huipiao* of the Qing dynasty]. *Zhongguo qianbi* 中国钱币 [Chinese money], no. 99 (2007): 10–11, 9.

———. "Qingdai huipiao gailun" 清代会票概论 [An introduction to the *Huipiao* of the Qing dynasty]. *Zhongguo qianbi* 中国钱币 [Chinese money], no. 4 (1995): 14–17.

Yurman, Rebecca L. "Assessing State Food Safety Performance and FDA Contrast: The Public Health Implications of State Variations in a New Regulatory Regime." PhD diss., American University, Washington DC, 2016.

Zadok, R., and T. Zadok. "A Promissory Note from the Atkuppu Archive." *Nouvelles Assyriologiques Brèves et Utilitaires*, 2004, entry 44. http://www.achemenet.com/pdf/nabu/Nabu2004-044.pdf.

Zhang, Dengde 张登德, ed. *Zhongguo jindai sixiangjia wenku—Chen Chi Juan* 中国近代思想家文库. 陈炽卷 [Compendium of modern Chinese thinkers—Chen Chi's writings]. Beijing: Zhongguo renmin daxue chubanshe, 2015.

Zhang, Haipeng 张海鹏, and Sun Shulin 孙树霖, eds. *Huishang yanjiu* 徽商研究 [A study of Huizhou merchants]. Hefei: Anhui renmin chubanshe, 1995.

Zhang, Haipeng 张海鹏, and Wang Tingyuan 王廷元, eds. *Mingqing huishang ziliao xuanbian* 明清徽商资料选编 [Selected historical documents of Anhui merchants during the Ming and Qing dynasties]. Hefei: Huangshan shushe, 1985.

Zhang, Jian 张謇. *Zhang Jian quanji* 张謇全集 [Complete works of Zhang Jian]. 5 vols. Shanghai: Shanghai cishu chubanshe, 2012.

Zhao, Erxun 趙爾巽. *Qing shigao* 清史稿 [The draft history of the Qing]. 1928. Scripta Sinica 漢籍電子文獻資料庫.

Zheng, Beijun 郑备军, and Chen Quanya 陈铨亚. "Ningbo qianzhuang de zhiduchuangxin yu ningbobang de jueqi" 宁波钱庄的制度创新与宁波帮的崛起

[Innovations in Ningbo Qianzhuang Banking System and the rise of Ningbo Group]. *Zhejiang xuekan* 浙江学刊 [Zhejiang academic journal] 5 (2011): 89–94.

Zheng, Guanying 鄭觀應. *Shengshi weiyan* 盛世危言 [Words of warning to a prosperous age]. 1893. 6 vols. Shanghai: Shanghai shuju, 1898. Chinese Text Project.

———. *Shengshi weiyan houbian* 盛世危言後編 [Words of warning to a prosperous age: Sequel]. 1911. 8 vols. Google Books.

Zheng, Yifang 鄭亦芳. *Shanghai qianzhuang, 1843–1937: Zhongguo Chuantong Jinrongye de Tuibian* 上海錢莊, 1843–1937: 中國傳統金融業的蛻變 [Shanghai qianzhuang, 1843–1937: The transformation of China's native finance]. Taipei: Academia Sinica, 1981.

Zhong, Weimin 仲伟民. *Chaye yu yapian: Shijiushiji jingjiquanqiuhua zhong de Zhongguo* 茶叶与鸦片: 十九世纪经济全球化中的中国 [Tea and opium: China in the process of economic globalization in the nineteenth century]. Beijing: Shenghuo, dushu, xinzhi sanlian shudian, 2010.

Zhongguo renmin yinhang jinrong yanjiusuo 中国人民银行金融研究所. *Meiguo huaqiyinhang zaihua shiliao* 美国花旗银行在华史料 [Historical documents of U.S. Citibank in China]. Beijing: Zhongguo jinrong chubanshe, 1990.

Zhonguo jiuhaiguan shiliao bianji wenyuanhui, ed. *Zhongguo jiuhaiguan shiliao, 1859–1948* 中國舊海關史料 (1859–1948) [Historical documents of the China Imperial Maritime Customs]. 170 vols. Beijing: Jinghua chubanshe, 2001.

Zhu, Zizhen 朱自振, and Chen Zugui 陳祖槼. *Zhongguo chaye lishiziliao xuanji* 中國茶葉歷史資料選輯 [Selected historical documents on the history of Chinese tea]. Beijing: Nong ye chu ban she, 1981.

Zhuang, Guotu. *Tea, Silver, Opium and War: The International Tea Trade and Western Commercial Expansion into China in 1740–1840*. Xiamen: Xiamen University Press, 1993.

Zhuang, Weimin 庄维民. *Zhongjianshang yu Zhongguo jindai jiaoyizhidu de bianqian: Jindai hangzhan yu hangzhanzhidu yanjiu* 中间商与中国近代交易制度的变迁: 近代行栈与行栈制度研究 [Brokers and the evolution of the trading system in modern China: A study of modern Hangzhan and the Hangzhan system]. Beijing: Zhonghua shuju, 2012.

Index

Page numbers in italics refer to illustrations.

IN THE STUDIES IN PACIFIC WORLDS SERIES

This World in a Teacup: Credit, Taste, and Power in the U.S.-China Tea Trade, 1784–1911
Dan Du

Dreams of a Young Republic: The American Vincentians in China
John J. Harney

Imperial Zions: Religion, Race, and Family in the American West and the Pacific
Amanda Hendrix-Komoto

Raising the Redwood Curtain: Labor Landscapes and Community Violence in a Pacific Littoral
Michael T. Karp

Ties That Bind: People and Perception in U.S. and Korean Transnational Relations, 1905–1965
Hannah Kim

California and Hawaiʻi Bound: U.S. Settler Colonialism and the Pacific West, 1848–1959
Henry Knight Lozano

How to Reach Japan by Subway: America's Fascination with Japanese Culture, 1945–1965
Meghan Warner Mettler

Sea Otters: A History
Richard Ravalli

Hawaiian by Birth: Missionary Children, Bicultural Identity, and U.S. Colonialism in the Pacific
Joy Schulz

When Women Ruled the Pacific: Power and Politics in Nineteenth-Century Tahiti and Hawaiʻi
Joy Schulz

Forward without Fear: Native Hawaiians and American Education in Territorial Hawaiʻi, 1900–1941
Derek Taira

Of Love and War: Pacific Brides of World War II
Angela Wanhalla

To order or obtain more information on these or other University of Nebraska Press titles, visit nebraskapress.unl.edu.